ON GERMANS
AND
OTHER GREEKS

Dennis J. Schmidt

ON
GERMANS

&

OTHER
GREEKS

Tragedy and Ethical Life

INDIANA
UNIVERSITY
PRESS

BLOOMINGTON & INDIANAPOLIS

This book is a publication of

Indiana University Press

601 North Morton Street
Bloomington, IN 47404-3797 USA

http://iupress.indiana.edu

Telephone orders 800-842-6796
Fax orders 812-855-7931
Orders by e-mail iuporder@indiana.edu

Schmidt, Dennis J.
    On Germans and other Greeks : tragedy and ethical life / Dennis J. Schmidt.
        p.   cm. — (Studies in Continental thought)
    Includes bibliographical references (p.   ) and index.
    ISBN 0-253-33868-9 (alk. paper) — ISBN 0-253-21443-2 (pbk. : alk. paper)
    1. Greek drama (Tragedy)—History and criticism—Theory, etc. 2. Greek drama (Tragedy)—Appreciation—Germany. 3. Kant, Immanuel, 1724–1804—Views on tragedy. 4. Kant, Immanuel, 1724–1804—Influence. 5. Kant, Immanuel, 1724–1804—Ethics. 6. Criticism—Germany—History. 7. Ethics—Germany—History. 8. Tragedy.   I. Title.   II. Series.

    PA3131 .S366 2001
    882'.0109—dc21
                                                            00-050642
    1 2 3 4 5   06 05 04 03 02 01

To my parents

Art is the greatest enigma of all. The human being is but one answer to it.

—Joseph Bueys

CONTENTS

IN LIEU OF A PREFACE

Let me speak personally . . .

One of my favorite passages in the works I will address here is from Hölderlin; it is a passage that begins with the words "Let me speak humanly." I wish I possessed the insight, courage, and conviction that would permit me to begin with those same words. But I do not, and so I will begin this book with the much less modest and far less significant words that ask you to let me speak personally.

This book has been a long time in the making, and so saying something of its genesis, the place it wants to arrogate to itself, and speaking of the tentacles which might reach between its concerns and wider concerns —all so that it might open itself to you—is a very complicated matter. And since in the end it remains for me a deeply personal matter, I will tell it briefly in that self-indulgent form.

The seeds of this project go back almost a decade. Whatever series of chances were working then, I found myself fascinated by a sentence from Hegel in which he says that "the wounds of spirit heal and leave no scars behind." I was wooed by its promise. And yet, I could not wed that promise to another ongoing fascination of mine which manifested itself in the yearly project of reading Homer during my summers. I would read Homer (and I confess that I still have not outgrown this practice) every summer on the southern coast of Italy, where I would look out over the sea toward the islands that local legend claimed were the home of the Scylla and Charybdis found elsewhere in Homer's imagination. I also had the practice of making one trip each summer to the ruins of the Greek temple at Paestum, where I would spend the day reviewing my work on translating Hölderlin. That setting, those texts, even, I must confess, the loneliness that could be my companion on those stays, coupled to cultivate in me a mood and sensibility which seemingly could not come to terms with Hegel's promise. And for that reason above all perhaps, the way it wooed me was all the more puzzling. Completing this bewilderment on my part, I found myself often thinking of Shakespeare's famous invocation of wounds that remain as a badge of honor: "Then he will strip his sleeve and show his scars / And say, 'These wounds I had on Crispin's day'." Simply put, the power of the wound seemed so great that I did not understand how Hegel could write such a sentence, but I knew as well that Hegel considered it a hard-won insight, and I have learned that overlooking such claims from Hegel is a great mistake. That is how this project was born for me: I simply started to counterpose the claims of impossible conflict and ineradicable wounds that one finds in tragedy with the claim of reconciliation and union one finds in Hegel. It was not simply a matter of weighing out the claims of a philosopher and a tragedian; rather, it began by asking how it was that Hegel could write such a sentence *after*—even *because*—he had taken up the claims of tragedy. From this point it was not long until my efforts to answer this competing set of views of life came to involve the roster of philosophers who are considered here. I found that Hegel had come to dominate a project and tradition that far exceeded the context of Hegel's own claim. In the end, though, I do not believe that I have strayed far from my curiosity about Hegel's sentence and the wish for the wonderful sense of affirmation that he expresses there and elsewhere.

What I soon discovered was that the history of this tension between tragedy and philosophy was much richer in the tradition of German philosophy than I had anticipated—which is to say that it is quite powerful indeed, since I was not unaware of the prominence of the role that the idea of tragedy had played in the post-Kantian tradition of German philosophy. As I began to think through this tradition I also learned that it is much more diverse in its contents that I might have anticipated. The word "tragedy" is a strong presence in the works of German philosophy after Kant, but just what this word means, and even what should be understood as the real works of tragic art, is very much in dispute. I hope to have unfolded something of the wealth of the debates which emerge in this tradition.

One final impulse to take up this topic should be noted. Early in my relation to philosophy, already as a very young student, I was of the view that philosophy needed—by virtue of its own nature—to be committed to progress and emancipatory political practices. I will not try to defend that view, but only assert it as one I somehow, despite everything, still hold true. I was also, and still remain, of the view that Heidegger's work represented one of the ways in which avenues toward this progressive politics could be opened up. I hope it goes without saying that Heidegger's own overtly political remarks are not what I mean by progressive and emancipatory. So for a long time, confronting the question of politics in his thought has been a central concern for me. What unites this with the question of the formation of my interest in the topic of this book is the simple fact that Heidegger's own interest in the question of tragedy is almost entirely contained in his work from the years 1933–46. Somehow it was clearly the case that the topic of tragedy played into the question of politics in a rather direct manner for Heidegger, and to understand that was one of my earliest motivations in the outline of this project. This concern with the progressive political and ethical possibilities of the idea of the tragic, and with the effort to enlist tragedy as a model for coming to terms with the present age, has remained one of the central concerns of this book.

*   *   *

Four remarks about this book:

Among my intentions is the attempt to stitch together something of a narrative about one thread of concerns and questions in one aspect of the history of philosophy. That becomes evident only by reading the chapters seriatim. The chapters have been written with this in mind, not as discrete studies in individual philosophers. I would also like to believe that a systematic point is made in this book, one which is to be found in no single chapter taken in isolation. Nonetheless, this book does not need to be read in any order, and so a reader could, without too much loss, simply read only selected chapters.

This book makes no claims to completeness; the lacunae are too obvious to even pretend otherwise. The list of what is missing here—either specific texts or philosophers—is too long to try to remedy with the quick nod such a list could make. Nonetheless, two glaring absences should be conceded. First, Benjamin should be counted in here. My only defense is the limitation of my competence and the fact that this book is already too long. I hope that someone will remedy my failings in this case. Second, comedy should have been an issue. Far too much would have to be said about this, but the reader is right to ask how it can be absent. My only defense in this case is simply to say that it strangely, but clearly, is in fact absent as a question in the history of philosophy. I apologize for continuing in the tradition of this fundamental mistake.

You will notice that every chapter, except the chapter that is entitled "Questions," which functions as an introduction of sorts, begins with a citation from Roberto Calasso's *The Marriage of Cadmus and Harmony*. When that book first appeared all I could say was that it, more than anything else I had ever read, was the book I had dreamed of writing. Setting up this book with that one as a quiet counterpoint to my own concerns is only one of the ways I would like to think I have learned from that wonderful book.

Finally, you will notice that there is no conclusion here, but that I end with the acknowledgment of some "Convictions and Suspicions." I make this distinction simply as a way of saying that I have come away from this project with some convictions that I am not sure merit being called "conclusions" since they have simply taken hold of me, often without any single or clear basis. So I hesitate to suggest that such matters are conclusions we should all reach. Likewise with what I take to be some suspicions that have grown up with this book. What has happened to me as I have written this book is a noticeable shift in the perspective and assumptions from which I find myself addressing issues. Curiously, something about this point of view that has emerged seems to resist any sort of meta-effort to thematize it as a series of conclusions. Perhaps what might simply be said of this final chapter and the resistance there to announce any firm conclusions is that it is the one chapter that is written from the point of view that I believe has formed itself in me very much as a result of having worked through the various questions in this book.

At the end of three of the chapters there are appendices in which I provide translations of texts by Schelling, Hegel, Hölderlin, and Heidegger. I have chosen to translate these various works because they play such a pivotal role in my own argument. In addition, many of these works have not yet been translated or are simply inaccessible. Finally, some were in need of a new translation. My hope is that by making these texts available, I will win a new hearing for some of the most powerful expressions of the philosophic effort to take up the themes of tragedy and ethical life.

*   *   *

This book was written in several places, and while the effect of those places might not be evident to anyone but me, it is worth noting something about how this is the case. I have already indicated that the seascape and ruins of southern Italy belonged to the moment in which this project first took its shape. So too did a semester in Tübingen, the place which provided inspiration to Hegel, Hölderlin, and Schelling and continues to be just such a place. It was there that I was able to look at what I take to be the church tower to which Hölderlin refers in "In lovely blueness . . . ," and it was in looking at this structure, which operates as a metaphor for Hölderlin's understanding of language, that I first had an inkling of how it was that he thought the emergence of language. There too I had the good fortune to hear Bruno Ganz do a reading of Hölderlin's works and came at that moment, in part from the strange capacity of the voice to animate an idea, to realize how deeply Hölderlin had addressed the question of tragedy in texts where I had not initially recognized it. Finally, Philadelphia: Near where I live in Philadelphia there is a small statue which was given to "the people of Philadelphia" from "the people of Athens." The kinship between it and Athens, a bond formed around the axis of attempts to forge genuine democracies, has become a fascination for me, and so it is that the questions of political life, of revolution, and of democracy—

though largely unspoken here—have shadowed so many of the questions I have tried to address.

But people, far more than places, belong to the hidden fabric of this book. Secluded in the Alps, off in a small cabin and quite alone, Mahler wrote a letter to his wife in which he said that "no sound reaches me except now and again the sound of the bells which reminds me that people belong together." It was a line that returned to me frequently over the years of working on this project, for several reasons, not the least of which is that even when I was isolated friends were such a constant presence in the words I read, wrote, and thought about. I am very lucky to have had the support and friendship of so many good people over these years, and I hope they will see how much I have learned from them. More people than I could begin to acknowledge here have had an impact upon how I have come to think about these texts and issues: some have come to help me understand my own views, others have reminded me of differing views; however it happened, I have come to have many and deep debts working through this book. And now it is a pleasure to acknowledge some of them.

I must say that I cannot imagine having written this book without the conversations I have been privileged to have at the Collegium Phaeno-menologicum over the years. One year in particular was decisive for my understanding of this matter: it was a year devoted to the topic of the tragic, structured around week-long courses by Rodolph Gasché, John Sallis, Dominique Janicaud, and Françoise Dastur. Likewise, I owe a large debt to my students at both Binghamton University and Villanova University. They have helped me come to understand my own mind better and have been wonderful dialogue partners. Among these, two have made special efforts: Theodore George read and commented extensively upon several of the chapters, and Maggie Ziemianek prepared the bibliography.

I discovered as well how close I remain to my years as a student since my teachers Hans-Georg Gadamer, Joseph Fell, and Jacques Taminiaux somehow kept resurfacing throughout so much of this book. Professor Gadamer's presence and friendship for almost a quarter of a century now has been at the heart of so much more than I could ever acknowledge, and I doubt I will ever finish saying that. Some of the debts I have incurred in connection with the writing of this book must be singled out, and while I wish that I could take the time to tell the story behind the contribution of each of these friendships, that will remain a private matter which is no less heartfelt for being simply private. So I am honored to thank Robert Bernasconi, Walter Brogan, Günter Figal, Hans-Georg Gadamer, Brendali Reis, James Risser, John Sallis, and Charles Scott. Dee Mortensen and Janet Rabinowitch waited patiently over the years for this book to come to an end, and their persistence and help made a real difference. There are so many lovely stories to be told in connection with their help, but let me simply say that each of them has, in a special way, directly helped this book come to see the light of day. It is a wonder that this book is not much better than it is given what these people have done to help it, and me, along.

All of them have, each in his or her own way, been like the sound of bells to me.

PHILADELPHIA, OCTOBER 1999

KEY TO FREQUENTLY CITED WORKS

In my work I used the Loeb editions of Greek texts. None of the passages cited seemed to diverge in any significant respect from the Oxford Classical Text editions which I would also consult. Occasionally I have retranslated passages from the Greek, but the translations typically cited have been noted below. When citing a citation of a Greek text in a German text, I have translated the German translation if it was given; otherwise I have consulted the English translation. Citations for all Greek texts refer to the line number for the Greek text in the Loeb edition.

All of the translations from German texts here are my own. Occasionally I will consult other translations, and this has typically been noted in the body of footnotes. Page references to standard English translations of works are usually listed for the convenience of the reader who would like to compare translations. Footnotes which list both the German and the English reference will always indicate the German reference first.

Translations of works of Aristotle cited:
Poetics. Janko translation. Indianapolis: Hackett Press, 1987.
Works of Hegel cited:
Phänomenologie des Geistes. Hamburg: Meiner Verlag, 1952. (Cited as *PG* followed by paragraph number.)
Philosophie des Rechts. Frankfurt am Main: Suhrkamp Verlag, 1970.
Vorlesung über die Aesthetik. Frankfurt am Main: Suhrkamp Verlag, 1986.
Works of Heidegger cited:
Einführung in die Metaphysik. Tübingen: Niemeyer Verlag, 1966. (Cited as *EM*.)
Gesamtausgabe. Frankfurt am Main: Klostermann, 1976. (Cited as *GA* followed by volume number and page number.)
Holzwege. Frankfurt am Main: Klostermann, 1972.
Introduction to Metaphysics. Mannheim translation. New Haven: Yale University Press, 1959. (Cited as *IM*.)
Martin Heidegger, Elisabeth Blochmann: Briefwechsel, 1918–1969. Marbach am Neckar: Deutsche Schillergesellschaft, 1989.

Works of Hölderlin cited:

Sämtliche Werke. Munich: Hanser Verlag, 1992. (Cited as *SW* followed by volume number and page number.)

Translations of works of Homer cited:

The Iliad. Fagles translation. New York: Viking Penguin, 1990.

The Odyssey. Fagles translation. New York: Viking Penguin, 1996.

Works of Nietzsche cited:

Also Sprach Zarathustra. Berlin: W. de Gruyter, 1988.

The Birth of Tragedy. Kaufmann translation. New York: Viking, 1967. (Cited as *BT*.)

Die Geburt der Tragödie, et al. Berlin: W. de Gruyter, 1988. (Cited as *GT*.)

Introduction aux leçons sur l'Oedipe-Roi de Sophocle. Versanne: Encre Marine Fougères, 1994.

Nachgelassene Fragmente: Juli 1882 bis Winter 1883–4. Berlin: W. de Gruyter, 1977.

Translations of works of Plato cited:

The Republic. Bloom translation. New York: Basic Books, 1968.

Works of Schelling cited:

Ausgewählte Werke. Darmstadt: Wissenschaftliche Buchgesellschaft, 1967. (Cited as *ScW*.)

Translations of works of Sophocles cited:

Three Theban Plays. Fagles translation. New York: Penguin Books, 1984.

ON GERMANS
AND
OTHER GREEKS

Questions

On the morning of my departure, I had seen
thirty-eight Blood Moons, an age that carries its
own madness and futility. With a nearly
desperate sense of isolation and a growing
suspicion that I lived in an alien land, I took to
the open road in search of places where change
did not mean ruin and where time and people
and deeds connected.
      —William Least-Heat Moon, *Blue Highways*

Twenty-four centuries ago Aristotle posed the question "Why do human
beings make art?" The threefold answer he gives is clear: it is *thrilling*—it
gives us a unique pleasure—it is *natural*—it is a native impulse to play with
the imagination as we learn most clearly from the behavior of children—
and it is *educational*—this play and pleasure enable and enlarge us and
our world. Most of all, we learn about ourselves since in art a certain self-
presentation of our nature is brought to light. Aristotle continues this
analysis of the place of art in human affairs by suggesting that tragic art is
among the final achievements of the possibilities of art—indeed, it might
mark the singular destination of art. So as the possibilities of this play and
pleasure that belong to our natures are set free and elaborated, art takes
more clearly the form of tragic poetry. Art, as a form, cannot go beyond
the form it takes in the tragedy. Tragedy can then be said to be the perfected form of art, so what can be learned from art will receive its most
precise, its most pristine expression in tragic art. So, according to a rather
loose interpretation of the *Poetics,* says Aristotle.

    The claim that tragedy is the perfection of the possibilities of art—of
the alchemy of play and pleasure that circumscribe a peculiar region of

1

experiences—is not unique to Aristotle. It will be repeated frequently over the centuries, finding its most compressed and committed expression in Hölderlin's struggles to press our experience of tragic art to new extremes. But despite the frequency of this argument, it is certainly not lacking in provocation. The more extreme and persuasive it becomes, the more it is in need of scrutiny, since it represents an important decision about the possibilities of art, of an entire region of human making, and about ourselves as beings somehow needing to make art.

This question—whether or not tragedy is the final achievement of art in general—is among the most basic concerns of this book. But it will remain nonetheless secondary to another question, namely, how are we to understand the way in which we are "educated" by the work of art, specifically tragic art (whether or not it is the supreme form of art). Like Aristotle, Hegel will argue quite clearly that tragic art is especially well suited for educating us as citizens of a world that is larger than the world we define. In other words, tragic art has a special capacity for presenting ethical and political "truths," and, for this reason above all, it merits our attention. But, again like Aristotle, Hegel will ultimately argue that the insights about human nature and the enigmas of our shared life in time that art can present are limited by the very form of art itself. In the end, according to this argument, the kind of work that can bear the name of art, that belongs to the specific making that governs poetic practices, and the knowledge that the experience belonging to art can yield are not the greatest work or the highest knowledge that we can achieve. Consequently, Hegel grants a great dignity to the work of art, taking its possibilities very much to heart, especially in his efforts to develop an ethics and a politics; however, in the end, Hegel argues that the dignity of art, even its highest dignity as it is found in tragic art, is surpassed by the conceptual possibilities of philosophy. That is why art, as Hegel remarks in a celebrated passage in his lectures on aesthetics, is passé from the standpoint of philosophy.

Despite such a remark, it is clear that Hegel places an enormous weight upon what he believes can be learned from art in his efforts to come to terms with ethical and political questions. Spirit is educated early and repeatedly in the school of the tragedians. What is important to note at this point is that Hegel's reliance upon art, especially tragedy, for the formulation of an ethics, coupled with Kant's *Critique of Judgment,* where the dignity of art and its unique place in human experience are affirmed almost without qualification, helps renew the question "Why do human beings make art?" and to focus the import of that question upon the relation of art to ethical life.

The turn to the work of art by philosophers since Kant and Hegel, and the central role granted to an image of the tragic in philosophy since then are rather easy to see. In some measure it is best understood as a return to Aristotle's claim that the impulse to make art, which Schelling and Hölderlin will call the *Bildungstrieb,* is native to human beings. This move to reaffirm the integrity of the work of art for the project of self-understanding is clearly evident in contemporary works such as one finds by Derrida, Gadamer, Deleuze, Foucault, and others. Although decisive for contemporary philosophizing, this turn to the work of art might have found its most extreme expression long ago in Nietzsche, who argues that when the mind is free and unfettered, in the dreams of sleep, we make images of light, and in doing this we demonstrate just how deep the impulse to art is in us. But it is Nietzsche who also argues that the enemy of this impulse is the drive to philosophy, saying that "we have art lest we perish of the truth."[1] The turn to the achievements of the work of art in contemporary philosophizing gives a new spin to the question of truth.

Somewhat less evident than this generalized "aesthetic turn" but—as I want to argue in what follows—perhaps even more potent in the shaping of contemporary philosophical discourse is the quiet recuperation of the dual assumptions which were so basic to both Plato and Aristotle, namely, that tragedy represents the high point of the possibilities of the work of art, and that tragic art nourishes an ethical sensibility that is crucial for the formulation of an ethics and politics responsive to contemporary life. This is the hypothesis that is to be tested here: that examining the appropriation of the tragic art, typically only Greek tragic art, in the philosophers considered in this book provides unique insights into the possibilities for the ethical and political assumptions working in those philosophers. While I refer to a number of post-Hegelian thinkers, four figures dominate my concerns and receive far more detailed treatments than the others: Hegel, Hölderlin, Nietzsche, and Heidegger. At least for the cases of Nietzsche and Heidegger the contention that the contours of an ethics is to be found here, in their respective turns to tragic art, is clearly controversial. But the motive that has guided me most surely is precisely this contention. Because it is so basic to my interpretation, that claim—namely, that an ethical impulse drives the fascination with Greek tragic art found in a certain post-Hegelian tradition of philosophizing—will be the argument put to the test throughout this book.

*   *   *

So the questions that animate this book arise out of a curiously German effort to rejuvenate and reappropriate the possibilities of tragedy—specifically Greek tragedy—for thinking today. The claim is simple and clear: that Greek tragedy, a literature so decisive for the formulation of Western culture (some reference to it has been pivotal in our notions of art and theater, death and grief, madness and self, law and family, fate and freedom), has a special significance for the wider cultural questions of the present age. The claim is not that such a literature needs to be repeated, to be written, today. Quite the contrary: among the most haunting questions that are posed, and posed repeatedly thanks above all to Hölderlin and Benjamin, is whether tragedy is a viable form, or even a possibility, for art today. Rather, the claim that is found (if only covertly) in the thinkers to be addressed here and that forms the most elemental provocation for this book is that thinking today, especially insofar as it is a matter of the critique of cultural forms today, is enriched and enlivened by taking to heart questions that emerge out of a philosophical appropriation of the idea of tragedy—even if it is the case that the realization of such an idea is foreclosed today—as well as out of an understanding of the still unthought possibilities of the literature of ancient Greece. Furthermore, the claim is that, properly understood, the decision to take up such questions—to struggle to ask again or anew the questions put in tragedies—is not an arbitrary one, nor is it the expression of a nostalgia for another time; rather, this decision is best understood as the response to a certain assignment of history. Without exception, the German figures who are treated in this book regard the question of the tragic as somehow a "fated" question for this historical juncture. But, of course, such a view turns the question of tragedy back upon itself, squaring its significance, since the very notion of a fated question, of a destiny unfolding, is itself drawn from the idea of tragedy. In the end it will be necessary to ask whether or not the turn to the question of tragedy is indeed an imperative of history at this historical juncture, and whether or not this imperative permits itself to be explained and justified with reference to a notion of destiny.

These questions find their first formulations in Hegel, and they seem only to continue to gain an increasing prominence in German thought up through Nietzsche, Benjamin, and Heidegger. The specificity of the timing and the place of the arrival of these questions is crucial: for the most part, these are questions posed in German philosophy about Greek literary texts (though in what follows it will be necessary to remember that "Germany," like "Greece," is not, in the first instance, a geographical designation, but is itself a thoroughly problematic political and historical notion; likewise, these texts uniformly breach the contemporary disciplinary boundaries that separate philosophy and literature today). The most readily visible common denominator of those for whom the question of tragedy is central is that they are all concerned with the question of the end of philosophy. In other words, other differences notwithstanding, they share the view that the tradition and style of thinking that begins with Plato and that eventually comes to be governed by the ideal of an infinite and omnipresent, a deathless, mind is no longer tenable. Fundamental assumptions that have saturated Western cultures for centuries, assumptions found powerfully present in metaphysics, Christianity, sciences, technology, as well as the influence of these upon the real formations of cultural and political life, now reveal themselves as presumptions

4

which we can no longer share. So it seems that today the only shared assumption is that the present age is a time in need of radical transformation. This is an age calling for essential alterations in the ways we speak and think about ourselves and our world. However the transformation needed is diagnosed, whatever specifics or generalities are mobilized to illuminate the nature of the epochal fault lines on which we find ourselves, the general claim uniting those to be considered in this book is that the assumptions of the past have revealed themselves as no longer serviceable for understanding the questions that we face as the future. So it is that those who argue most powerfully for a revitalization of the question of tragedy are united by the assumption that the present era is a time of crisis, of exhaustion, of historical limits reached. Of course, the argument here is not that philosophy comes to an end because philosophers have become feebleminded. Rather, the argument is that it ends because it reaches the limits of its possibilities.

From this point of view the question of the end of philosophy, the question of its scope and limits, has always accompanied philosophy, and that is one reason that the question of tragedy nags the history of philosophy so persistently (even if the tradition of that nagging is a discontinuous one). But after Kant exposed the ineluctibility of the question of limits for thinking by demonstrating how it is that those limits belong to the enabling conditions of any human experience, the question of the end of philosophy became the decisive question for thinking. The question of limits belongs to the question of human self-understanding in general. But, while Kant is the one who drives home the tragedy of reason without relent, beginning with the opening sentence of the First Critique where he refers us to the "peculiar fate of reason," it is left to those after Kant to expand the scope of this peculiar fate and to demonstrate that the fate of philosophy, namely, to suffer what is indispensable as what is impossible, becomes the fate of human experience and of all history. This sensitivity to the contradiction, or conflict, at the heart of the human situation becomes finely tuned in post-Kantian thought. Compounding this sense of profound contradiction, this human (one is tempted to say "existential") situation is typically described as itself situated in a time of catastrophe, of the real and even violent overturning of life by the forces of history. Heidegger frequently despairs that this is the case—that we must recognize not only that we are conflicted beings but also that we also live in deeply conflicted times—and when he does, it seems to take on a deeply personal tone: "I believe that an era of loneliness must come over the world, if it is ever again to take a fresh breath and turn to a creativity that returns to things their essential power."[2] In other cases this situation of contradiction at the heart of experience is taken as the signal of a new beginning about to emerge—new times and possibilities are being prepared to surpass the past. Hegel does not mince words about this possibility: "It is not difficult to see that our time is a time of birth and of transition to a new period. Spirit has broken with the existence and the representation of its world up to this time, now it can let those forms sink into the past and set itself to the work of its transformation."[3] But whether this is taken as the time of either catastrophe or birth, those who take tragedy as a central axis for thinking are united in the claim that this time of crisis is a time in which destiny is exposed and we are confronted by our truth: the truth of a past that has rendered us possible but that is impossible for the needs before us.

It is no accident then that at the very moment the question of the end of philosophy came to prominence the topic of tragedy—not taken as a specialized literary genre but as a way of asking about ends, destiny, and history—comes forward as a sort of model for asking and answering the questions of such times. What becomes most visible in this coincidence is the link that is drawn between the notions of tragedy and history: an image and conception of tragedy is forged—inevitably with reference to Greek tragedy—in order to illuminate and render intelligible a uniquely contemporary historical situation. Reciprocally, some analysis of the present age, as bereft of possibilities, as the time of endings and genuine crisis, is employed to explain the dynamics of tragedy. It is this affiliation between the idea of tragedy and history that most defines contemporary appropriations of the notion of tragedy, and it is this kinship that is perhaps most remote from the conception of tragedy active in antiquity itself. In antiquity tragedies raised questions about how human beings carry destiny concealed within themselves. In the present age the question is rather how history conceals human beings within its own distinctive tragic logic.

*　　*　　*

The first of three rather specific sets of questions that govern the concerns of this book becomes visible at this point: How are we to understand this project of interpreting history as the unfolding of a tragic destiny? What about this choice of tragedy as a model for interpreting the present age? What conceptions of history and of ethico-political life collaborate in such a choice? What directives emerge out of such a model? The claim is not that tragedy is one among competing models for thinking the "logic" of history, but that it is privileged, even mandated, by history itself. This, in part, is what Heidegger means when he proposes that "In the history of what is essential, it is the prerogative, but equally the responsibility, of every descendent to become the murderer of their predecessors, and that they themselves submit to the fate of a necessary murder!"[4] We are, in other words, assigned, indexed, fated to the question of tragedy, and our place in this question is a complicated one. The force of the question put to us is redoubled: it is our destiny to pose the question of destiny precisely at the historical juncture in which destiny seems lacking and the continuity of history appears to be broken since in this discontinuity it has finally exposed the finitude of its own law. The time of crisis is then the crisis of time itself.

But is the crisis of the present best interpreted in the light shed by the literature of crisis that belongs to the beginnings of the tradition now in question? This is the question that Lacoue-Labarthe raises when he suggests that "Auschwitz belongs to a sphere beyond tragedy."[5] In other words, his claim is that no justice is done to the specific crisis of our times if an effort is made to house such crisis, to interpret it, in the form of tragedy that emerges in ancient Greece. But again it is Heidegger who most explicitly locates the crisis of the present in the situation of the birth of Western values (of course, the secret of a tragedy belongs to the time of birth, not the death which results) and most explicitly finds that crisis to be the very tragedy of tragedy itself that is exposed in the present: "We must understand that Greek life is found in the figure of Oedipus in whom we find the basic passion of [the West] most extensively and most unrestrainedly, the passion for the disclosure of being."[6] And so, just as Oedipus suffers his "flaw" must we, according to Heidegger, suffer the "errancy" of history. And likewise, just as Aristotle reminds us and Plato cautions, what we witness in the tragedy is ethically instructive, so too do those who take up tragedy as a model for interpreting history argue that some ethical and political imperative is at work. In the end, then, it will be necessary to understand that this turn to tragedy as a model for thinking the historical present is at the same time a search for an ethics and politics responsive to these times and the crises specific to them. The retrieval of the question of tragedy belongs to the search for an ethics responsive to these destitute times. This means that the choice of one's tragedy, the conception of tragedy driving the interpretation of history, is all important for the ethical results of that interpretation.

This fascination with tragedy as a genre of possibilities preeminently suited to understanding the present is not an idea simply plucked out of some bin of interpretive options available to those struggling to understand the turbulence of these days and the riddles of history. It is important to acknowledge how many factors collaborated to bring tragedy to the forefront of contemporary concerns. Perhaps most of all one needs to recognize how well suited the literature of incommensurability and irreconcilable conflict is to an age attuned to the complexity, the messiness of human affairs, to what Heidegger referred to under the auspices of the phrase "the hermeneutics of factical life." Tragedy is not only the literature of crisis; it is equally the literature of impossibles and incommensurables, the literature of our vulnerability and fragility. In tragedies we are reminded that we live in a world larger than that of our own making or control, and yet a world to which we are answerable. Nussbaum makes this element of tragedy the axis of her interpretation of its ethical sensibility, declaring at the outset

> I begin from [the] position that . . . I am an agent, but also a plant; that much that I did not make goes toward making me whatever I shall be praised or blamed for being; that I must constantly choose among competing and apparently incommensurable goods and that circumstances may force me to a position in which I cannot help being false to something or doing some wrong; that an event that simply happens to me may, without my consent, alter my life; that it is equally problematic to entrust one's good to friends, lovers or country and to try to have a good life without them.[7]

Such a view of the finitude of human life, of the porosity of "the self" which is exposed to the world, belongs not just to the presentation of human life in ancient Greek tragedies, but also in an equal measure to the view of life prevalent among those who are engaged in the contemporary philosophical project of centering thinking today upon the question of tragedy. Even Hegel, who thanks to the power of his speculative drive doubtless has the tidiest conception of human life among those considered here, never fails to call attention to the entanglements and contradictions that lie at the heart of such a life. But again it is Heidegger who presses this point most vigorously. His discussion of "guilt" in *Being and Time* needs to be understood in the light of this exposure which we suffer. It is so pervasive a sense for Heidegger that at one point he even speaks of "the tragedy of appearance" as such.[8] Consequently (but this will most certainly need to be put to a test in what follows) tragedy is not merely an option for the self-interpretation of beings defined by being-in-the-world and its equiprimordial involvement in desire, language, and others, rather than by an "I think" that resolves itself into the glassy essence of an ego. Confronting tragedy is rather, somehow, an obligation for reflection. But to say this is no more a value judgment about human life than is Aristotle's notion of *hamartia;* it does not mean that human life is full of suffering that ends in grief. It is, however, an expression of the indebtedness of human life to a world larger than that which we can either make or define.

Shorn of enlightenment conceptions of the autonomy of the subject, philosophy was once again able to take to heart this element of tragedy that refers to our vulnerability and to the quite different sense of responsibility—a sense of care and the need for caution—that results. In tragedies we are summoned to an experience of that which is greater than us and yet to which we belong. In this summons we are brought before our finitude not by being brought before an infinite, a god, before whom we pale, but by being reminded of a different sort of infinity, namely, the infinity and inexhaustibility of our limits. But in tragedies we are also reminded that as such finite beings we might find in this infinity an experience of the monstrous or of the divine (or—as is the case with Oedipus who kills the one who, as a parent, must be like a god to him—the divine in the form of the monstrous). There is here a powerful sense of what today we refer to as an experience of "alterity" expressed. In the end, what we find in tragedy is the presentation of the experience of limits, of what is beyond measure and capture by any calculus. This experience, as tragedy reminds us, is finally the experience of death—the preeminent force of the limit in mortal life—and so it is this experience out of which each of us must think and understand ourselves. It is the knowledge won from this experience that, as one commentator puts it, "is sad to have to know."[9] The knowledge of tragedy is coupled then with its own special mood: it is a knowledge distinguished by being "sad." It is, Aristotle argues, a knowledge communicated through its own distinctive wedding of the moods of fear and pity. Heidegger, on the other hand, will think this knowledge with reference to the mood of "sacred mourning." But, however the mood solicited by the experience of tragedy is precisely defined, the basic point remains the same: namely, that we suffer rather than cognize our relation to what is exposed in tragedy as the alterity to which we belong. This point is all important and will lead to the second of the three questions that overarch the concerns of this book.

Nietzsche makes the point explicit when he contends that "what is not intelligible might not be unintelligent."[10] In other words, that which is not cognizable in the form of the concept, that which might remain that which we can "only" ever suffer, might still bear a knowledge for us. However, this insight which opens the door for the recovery of the philosophic concern with tragedy does not begin with Nietzsche but with Kant, who never thematizes the question of tragedy, but who nevertheless makes it an unavoidable question for those following in his wake. Having exposed our constitutional inability to cognize our relation to universal, but having equally exposed the moral need for understanding that we are nonetheless bound to universals, Kant finally argues—significantly he does this in a work dedicated to aesthetic experience—that "faith (as habitus not actus) is reason's moral form of thinking and affirming as real that which is inaccessible to theoretical cognition."[11] Here faith refers not to any religious conviction, but to suffered knowledge that resists cognition by concepts. In contrast to Kant, Hegel begins his philosophical career in *Faith and Knowledge* by taking issue with this claim, arguing instead that, in the end, even the knowledge that we suffer is able to be, indeed must be, cognized. Among those who are considered in this book, Hegel stands alone in suggesting that the knowledge that is to be won in tragedy can be cognized. The later Schelling and Kierkegaard both react forcefully against this Hegelian claim and in so doing accelerate the move to grant an integrity and worth to what cannot be grasped in the form of the concept. Freud, who was captivated by Greek culture and appropriately chose to name so many of the dynamics of psychic life after figures in Greek tragedies, belongs to this movement as well.

But to suggest that knowledge is not only communicated in the language of the concept, to argue that the limits of cognition are not identical with limits of what can be known, is to suggest that the conceptuality, the mother tongue of philosophy, does not define the limits of knowledge. Coupled with this insight into the limits of philosophic discourse one finds the effort to speak another language than the language of philosophy which operates according to the law of conceptuality. One finds then the turn to literature, to language in the poem, language wed not to the idiom of the universal which can be cognized, but to the idiom of the idiom itself that refuses to be translated or sublated into a concept. Such an idiom of the idiom, the language of literature, is, or so the argument goes, the bearer of that knowledge which can be told and suffered, but not cognized. The turn to literature—and eventually the turn to art that operates outside of the language of words and in tone, color, and movement—by those who are considered here needs to be understood as a response to this conviction that there is a knowledge that is suffered but not cognizable.

*   *   *

This is the point at which the second guiding question of this book can be formulated: How is the experience of tragedy to be spoken and written? Can the knowledge found in tragedy be taken up into the language of the concept and the law of generalization, the law finally of law itself, governing such a language? Hegel, who most clearly persists in arguing for the rule and language of the concept for the understanding of human affairs, grants that art and literature were once the forms in which truth happened, but in the end he argues that they have become passé with respect to truth, that is, they can teach us nothing that cannot be communicated more appropriately in the concept. But Heidegger, who turns increasingly to poetic texts in order to find a language more agile, more adept, at disclosing this knowledge that we suffer but cannot grasp, takes direct issue with Hegel and contends that this question of the relation of art and truth is among the most critical questions at issue today.[12] Is it the case that language and its possibility of conceptualization is able to translate every basic experience into itself? If not, then how is it that such mute experience is to be thought and understood? How might such an experience be acknowledged in its significance if not in words? What is at stake in this set of questions is a quite basic point, the point which becomes the focus of Plato's quarrel with poets: namely, how are we to speak and write—even if

10

we can speak or write at all—about the most elemental truths which we can know about ourselves? The decisions made about these questions at the outset of the philosophic tradition have had an enduring impact, and assumptions about the character of ethico-political discourse made long ago still powerfully govern Western culture. For the most part those assumptions tend toward the view that all that is ethically significant submits itself to the language of conceptuality, to the law of the law of universalization.[13] Human experience does not escape the law of generalization, the law of conceptuality. Kant's conception of the categorical imperative stands as the summit of such assumptions. But even apart from the refinements of Kant's explicit formulation of ethical thought in the Second Critique, it is clear that laws and the debates about the nature of ethical life and action are defined by the parameters of the language of generalities and abstraction. This is defended because in such language the messiness of particulars is avoided. But it is precisely such a move that is called into question by the turn to the literature of knowledge suffered, to tragedy and the limits of language to which it refers us. And so the question that is now raised, and raised with increasing urgency since Kierkegaard, who was among the first to take this question upon himself as a praxis, is how one needs to speak if one is not to betray the deepest insights that we must suffer without conceiving.

This question, of course, is not new—for instance, it is this sensitivity to the need to avoid the possible ossification of language in the concept that lies behind Plato's insistence on writing dialogues—but it is raised today with a renewed vigor and self-reflexive energy. As the limits of conceptuality, as the agility of language itself is probed, the question of art and the variety of its forms becomes increasingly urgent. New forms of art —or at least forms that announce themselves as new—appear ever more frequently, especially with the rapid growth of technology, and the claim of such forms to open alternative horizons of experience needs to be taken seriously. Doing that means, in part at least, asking whether there are indeed genuinely different possibilities for art being exposed or simply alterations in the shape of the general possibilities which Aristotle long ago outlined. But, as the reach of language is called into question and as this move to asking about the uniqueness of the knowledge found in the work of art is advanced, it becomes increasingly clear that philosophy must learn to speak differently as well. Consequently, those philosophers considered in this book are united by the effort to find a new voice. Nietzsche goes far in this direction but, nonetheless, laments his own failures to recognize the distance that must be traveled in this regard, writing in retrospect of his own work that "it should have sung this 'new soul'—and not spoken! How sad that I did not attempt to say what I had to say as a poet."[14] Kierkegaard, Heidegger, Derrida are clearly self-conscious about the question of voice and have brought it forward as a question no longer able to be evaded. But it will be Hölderlin who moves language the far-thest toward this new voice, bringing it finally to the point at which, as Benjamin suggests, "the gates of language threaten to slam shut."[15]

These questions—of language and of the relation of art to truth—will prove to be the dominant concerns of this book. These questions also appear as a sort of Trojan horse within which a host of questions—about body, desire, and affective life—are smuggled. The decision that, as Hei-degger claims, "pain is an essential form of knowledge according to which spirit knows itself"[16] is equally a decision to grant to the body a knowing unique to it. Not by accident do the limits of the speakable begin to be felt here. We speak of unspeakable pain, and by this we refer to the truth that pain robs us of language.[17] This is only one of the reasons that philoso-phers have a tendency to regard bodiliness with suspicion, but the suspi-cion that results is unmitigated. Descartes's reflections on pain—espe-cially the moves that he makes with reference to those reflections in the first and sixth of his *Meditations*—mark the high point of the refusal of suffered knowledge that is interpreted as a phantom of knowledge, and not as an exceptional form of knowing which is somehow different than conceptual reasoning.[18] The more the question of suffered knowledge is taken seriously the more the question of the body returns for thinking.

But the most general form of the question regarding suffered knowl-edge here refers to the work of art, and only in this mediated sense does the question of the body arise. So it is important to bear in mind that the question of knowledge won in suffering is not identical with the question of suffered knowledge that has achieved the form of art. There is in the work of art an alchemy at work, one which relies on what Kant, in his discussion of the sublime, referred to as a "safe place."[19] A distance, a re-move, belongs to the work of art, and it is in this distance that the presen-tation of suffered knowledge can happen. That is why Aristotle's analysis of tragic theater will center itself on the place of the spectator. Focusing upon this space for the presentation of the work of art, philosophers who take up the question of tragedy, at least until Nietzsche, tend to focus on the transformation that happens in that space of presentation: suffered knowledge, pain, death become beautiful.

*   *   *

This is the point at which the third of the three governing concerns of this book arrives. This question is perhaps the "most Greek" that needs to be asked: Why is tragedy, "a calamity . . . such as death . . . acute suffering and wounding,"[20] beautiful? What magic governs the work of art permitting it to present as beautiful what would be, according to the rules of a different presentation, simply gruesome? Of course, the beauty of a tragedy, like the aria of an opera sung from the moment before death, is not pacifying.

It is not comforting. Quite the contrary, such beauty is captivating and disquieting at once; it is an experience of strangeness, of something foreign. To say then that a work of art is beautiful is not to say that it is "easy on the eyes" or that it is "pleasing" or "entertaining." The notion of beauty as it will be discussed here, especially in Greek texts, is not to be confused with bourgeois conceptions of what relaxes and calms. It is a stimulant more than a sedative, though neither word does justice to its "effect."[21] It is rather the designation of the peculiar pleasure that bears knowledge to which Aristotle referred in his *Poetics*. To ask then about the wedding of beauty and tragedy is to ask how it is that the presentation of "a knowledge which is sad to have to know" could, at the same time, be the seat of a strange pleasure.

Hegel, who Heidegger calls "the last Greek," is especially smitten by this question of the relation of tragedy and beauty, and as an answer suggests that this transformation worked in the work of art, this rendering of suffering beautiful, is an indication that beauty is the glimmer, still unconceived, of the infinite in the finite. Schelling, Schiller, and German Romanticism as a whole also need to be aligned with this tradition: the question of beauty that dominates there, though immediately inspired by Kant's Third Critique, at bottom has to be seen as giving expression to a very Greek sensibility. The intervention of Kant is all important here. Coupled with Kant's analysis of beauty as the nonconceptual presentation of a *sensus communis,* a sense of community that lies outside of the orbit of schematic presentations, the post-Kantian work on the relevance of the beautiful for the question of tragedy distinguishes itself from the general Greek sensibility by virtue of Kant's effort to render the question of beauty explicitly as an ethical question. After Kant, the claim of beauty is that it is a communiqué of an ethical law that does not abide by the law of conceptuality, and so after Kant beauty is taken into the problematic of judgment, specifically the critique of judgment.[22] The argument is an imposing one and, in part, behind the claim one finds in Hegel, Schelling, and Schlegel that the critique of beautiful works is of an even higher order than their production.

But it is this decision that tragedy is indeed beautiful, the very assumption inspiring so many Greek conceptions of tragedy as well as those found in German Idealism and Romanticism, that will be called into question by Nietzsche and Heidegger, among others. Here contemporary treatments of tragedy part ways with what one might call a more Greek sensibility about the question. So when Nietzsche writes that art, especially tragedy, "should not be measured according to the category of the beautiful,"[23] he begins the move that will end with the withdrawal of the beautiful from the consideration of art.[24] With the important exceptions of Adorno, Bloch, Arendt, and Gadamer, the very topic of beauty is most conspicuous by its absence from contemporary philosophical discourse

13

that self-consciously defines itself as working in the wake of Hegel, Nietzsche, and Heidegger. Severed from what had long been considered an essential connection with beauty, art today no longer defines itself with respect to the claims of beauty. Or, from an equally just and maybe more open perspective, one might say that today art awaits a new conception of beauty.

But art and reflections upon it have not renounced the link to the sense of strangeness, of alterity, felt so powerfully in Greek conceptions of art. What might be different today is the sense of danger that seems to belong to that experience of the foreign today. Rilke takes this as the opening for his *Duino Elegies:* "For beauty is nothing but the beginning of the terror that threatens to destroy us."[25] The darker side of the knowledge that is won in suffering loses its illuminating power, and with that, or so it seems, the strange pleasure that was called beauty becomes something different. Art, which once was thought as belonging to "the idiom of the ideal,"[26] that is, as somehow lifted above its own dark suffering, now has to be interpreted as compressed in the idiom of the idiom. Accompanying that move we now find the tendency to interpret the knowledge won through suffering in psychological terms.

This tendency to psychologize, to subjectivize, the work of art is nowhere more evident than in contemporary tragedies. Both Kierkegaard and Hegel make a special point of this, suggesting that the great insight into the psychodynamics of characters which one finds so sharply delineated in Shakespeare and which is so obviously thin in Sophocles is precisely the difference between the modern and ancient senses of tragedy. The staging of the conflicts of the inner life of the characters, such as one finds so powerfully in *Hamlet* or *Othello,* for instance, increasingly becomes the axis along which tragic drama comes to operate. One sees this contrast between the ancient and modern presentations of the tragic quite clearly when one compares, for example, the renditions of *Antigone* by Sophocles, Brecht, and Anouilh. For Sophocles Antigone belongs too much to the peculiar idiom of the ideal to permit the idiosyncracies of her specific subjectivity to come forward. Yet it is precisely this that renders her a character of beauty and of destiny. What one sees in Anouilh's Antigone on the other hand is a figure tormented by her own place in a fate that has swept her away. The result is a drama that presents a much clearer picture of the threat that inhabits the world that is larger than that of our own making and definition.

Much will need to be said about how the difference between ancient and modern forms of tragic drama are to be conceived (note that the specification of "drama" is significant here; painting, music, and perhaps film might operate differently in this difference). Hölderlin will propose the most nuanced analysis of this difference and will even suggest that this difference is the definitive feature of the present age. But it is important to bear in mind that the focus upon the possibilities opened by tragic art in the present age remains centered on ancient Greek tragic art. Despite the significance of the difference in the forms of tragic art, and despite the puzzle that is posed by the qualification that it is "ancient Greek" tragic art that is of special significance today, there remains something common to all forms of tragedy. The common element is not, as a commonplace interpretation might have it, that someone dies. It is rather that someone is *born*. One arrives in a world already made, it is a world prepared in advance of one's appearance in it, and it is a world larger than one will ever be able to know or define. And yet, one is open and exposed to this expanse that one cannot know and cannot determine; one is responsible beyond the limits of what the conditions of the possibility of experience enable one to know. The vulnerability, the fragility and exposure of human life to what is strange and foreign, to what today is referred as "alterity," is, in part, what seems common to the tragic arts. It is, according to Greek tragedy, the source of human greatness and ruin at once. In the celebrated choral ode in Sophocles' *Antigone* this is characterized as *to deinon*. That word, according to Heidegger, will name the secret that belongs to tragedy and the knowledge that cannot be grasped, only suffered. It is a difficult word to translate; perhaps, as Heidegger argues, it is the lack of this word that remains the obstacle for any understanding of the ancient world.[27] Translations of this word (in English they range from "wondrous" to "strange" to "enormous" to "monstrous") do in fact serve as a kind of a litmus test for the reception of tragedy. Hölderlin will set the tenor for the understanding of the word in German thought when he translates the word as *ungeheuer,* as what we must call "monstrous." This, according to the line of argumentation that grants a separate integrity to the knowledge presented in tragic art, is the name of what comes to presentation in tragic art and that we suffer without fully grasping. It is perhaps this presentation of human life as *to deinon,* this presentation of what is ultimately unpresentable, that defines tragic art. The claim of such art, or so it must be assumed at the outset here, is that it remains opaque to the full clarity of the concept; and yet, it is this knowledge that captivates us, that is strangely pleasurable, that is beautiful. Furthermore, it is this knowledge of what is *to deinon* about human life that is so crucial for understanding the full force of what is at work in the horizons of our responsibility. In tragedy one learns that the sway of the ethical is not commensurate with the horizon of the human.[28]

*   *   *

Posing such a range of questions raises thorny hermeneutic problems. The literature on the question of tragedy is staggering in sheer quantity, and so there is inevitably some quirkiness in whatever selection one makes among such literatures. The strategy of this book is simple: to watch the life of one set of texts at work in a very different set of texts composed in very different times and worlds.[29] In other words, the conducting wire of the interpretations here follows the route of ancient Greek literary texts as those select texts inform recent German philosophic arguments in decisive ways. Of special interest is the way in which this turn to Greek art helps shape and give life to the ethical and political sensibilities of the philosophers considered. As will become evident, there is a clear preference (typically unthematized as such) for Sophoclean tragedy, in particular his *Oedipus Rex* and *Antigone*. Occasionally Homer comes into play, but references to Aeschylus and Euripides (and even to other Sophoclean tragedies) are curiously few and far between. This conspicuous specificity of tragic art is revealing and will need to be addressed.

Some figures are obvious choices for consideration here: Hegel, Nietzsche and Heidegger are such choices not only because of their own prominence, but also thanks to the fundamentality of the question of tragedy for their work as a whole. But Hölderlin, Kierkegaard, Benjamin, Adorno, and Lacan also have a pivotal role to play in the elaboration of the questions at hand. But the complexity of such a list and the complications of the choice of texts to consider begins to be felt once one recognizes how much exchange, how much layering, there is here. One cannot, for instance, take up Heidegger on the question of tragedy without granting that his contributions to that question are mediated by Hegel and Nietzsche, but by Hölderlin most of all. At times the strata of mediation become so thick that one seems to lose sight of the Greek tragedies themselves. But that only seems to be the case: as one lets the discussions of the question of tragedy mount up, one sees as well that there is a remarkable compression of the question at work. This continual process of distillation is most clearly felt in Heidegger, for whom the question of tragedy is of fundamental import, but who refers only rarely to specific works.

Of course, everything is also mediated through Plato and Aristotle. In a very real sense, the language and frames of reference that shape the discourse about art and especially tragic art come from Plato and Aristotle—even more so than Homer and Sophocles, since, justly or not, it is through Plato and Aristotle that Western culture has learned to interpret and evaluate such art. They were speaking very much to their own times, and they were speaking from the very new—and ultimately quite revolutionary—vantage point of philosophy. As they sought to come to grips with the experiences found in tragic art and to locate the new styles of thinking found in philosophizing with reference to such experiences, they did so independently of calcified categories and rigid assumptions about the nature of art. Although Plato remarks that the "quarrel" be-

tween philosophers and poets is already "old" by his time,[30] it is evident
that the terms according to which this so-called quarrel was to be debated
had not yet been fixed. Nonetheless, the place of art, especially tragedy, in
Greek cultural life and its role in the ethical education of its citizens were
firmly established, and so such works were something of an irritant in
Plato's own efforts to legitimate the ethical views which a different way of
speaking and thinking made evident.[31] Consequently, one finds a remarkable persistence in his efforts to shed light upon the horizons of art as
they are disclosed through the optic of the ideas. It is precisely this effort
that Nietzsche suggests forecloses the truth of the experience conveyed in
tragic art, and so, against Plato, he will propose scrutinizing philosophy
under the lens of art.[32] But apart from this conversion of Plato that will
need to be addressed in Nietzsche, it must be acknowledged that so many
of the elemental notions according to which we carry on any discussion
about the achievements of art remain Plato's own. And, perhaps even
more so, Aristotle's.

In light of this enduring effective history of Plato's and Aristotle's
analysis of tragic art, it is necessary that this book, which is focused principally on the interpretations of such art in German thought, begin with
Plato and Aristotle. The title of this book—"On Germans and Other
Greeks"—makes its reference to Plato and Aristotle as the "other Greeks"
and in doing so proposes that the word "other" here be read in several
registers. But most importantly, as Plato and Aristotle are read along the
axis of their respective concerns with tragedy, it will be important that the
context of their engagement with tragic art be borne in mind: they wrote
at a time when great authority belonged to tragedies, and such works belonged to an oral tradition and to the spectacle of performance, not to an
archive. When they wrote metaphysical rationality, the vantage point of
reflection which they pioneered and helped secure, had not yet reached
the time of its closure (though it will be a question just how much the
seeds of that closure belong to its beginnings with Plato and Aristotle). In
other words, when reading them it is necessary to remember that both
tragedy and philosophy were significantly different from how they are
found in the forms to which we have become accustomed. So, besides the
obvious difference conveyed in such a switch between ancient Greece and
post-Kantian Germany, there is a somewhat concealed, but quite significant, double difference at work when making the move from Aristotle to
Hegel: by the time of Hegel, tragedy had become a literary genre and had
begun to lose its defining relation to performance, and at the same time
philosophy had become a discipline which was entering the time of its
closure. No symmetry, then, can be assumed between the question tragedy puts to Plato and Aristotle and the question it poses for Hegel and
those who follow him. For the Greeks, the question concerns the analysis

and critique of a discourse that has already achieved ethical legitimacy; for the Germans, it concerns the production, the creation of an ethical idea responsive to the crises of the present age.

From the outset, it should be clear that the German relation to ancient Greek art is not driven by an urge to restore the works or views of a bygone era. There are, of course, instances and elements of such nostalgia present to some degree in the thinkers considered here. But it should quickly become clear that the turn to Greece is propelled by a desire to arrive at an ethical idea that is far-reaching enough to serve as a reply to times of crisis in the present age. Given the sense that our present crisis is sufficiently severe and profound to be called a crisis of the fundaments of Western culture, such an idea must clearly be revolutionary and radical in its reach. The coincidence of such an effort on Heidegger's part with what might be the supreme crisis of the West, namely, the Holocaust, may not be accidental and does need to be addressed. But the argument that I want to make is that this does not imply that the ethical intentions here need to be discarded, rather, that they have been insufficiently thought.[33]

It should go without saying that my argument is that in this tradition, especially in this turn to Greece and to the promises of art, there is the prospect of a progressive ethical and political sense—that what is at stake is the opening of a future, one different in a very real sense from that which we can conceive on the grounds and frameworks of the present. At this point, all that can be said is that it would be the opening upon a future that inscribes the gesture of openness as such in its every reinscription. Such a time would be perpetually revolutionary, because it would not defer the differences that time itself produces. When difference is simply deferred rather than set free, it ceases to belong to the natural order of time and is turned instead merely into a matter of conflict. In that regard, it would be a time otherwise than our present one. The question is whether the crises of the present can be thought in such a way that the seeds of such an open future can be found. The specific question of this book is whether or not the turn to the disclosures of tragic art might, in some way, contribute to such an advance.

*   *   *

Philosophy at its best has always provided an "analytic of ultimates."[34] In some of its instantiations it has also argued on behalf of an assumed purity of thought in which there is a harmony among the ultimates that govern us.[35] Tragedy, on the other hand, is an art of the conflict of ultimates, of discord that cannot be effaced or overcome but that opens upon catastrophe and ruin. Both are discourses fundamentally addressed to the questions of ethical and political life, to the enigmas of shared life in time.

What one finds in the dialogue between them is the struggle to speak about the ultimates to which we belong—birth, death, and the freedom that lies between them.

This book has the limitation that it is written from one side of that dialogue. With the single exception of the treatment of Hölderlin, there is no protracted effort here to provide a reading of tragic art apart from the reception of such works in philosophic texts (it should be said from the start that Hölderlin will repeatedly prove to be an exception and so needs to be singled out as offering something unique). This lacuna will need to explain and justify itself over time, but it is not an oversight. Rather, there is a curious lack of exchange in this debate which seems to be carried on chiefly from the side of philosophy. With the exception of Hölderlin and the failed attempts of Nietzsche, both of whom struggled to write a tragedy with the philosopher Empedocles as the "hero," there has been little effort to take up the dialogue between tragedy and philosophy from within tragedy. When art has taken up philosophy it is done so much more frequently in the form of comedy.[36] In the end, the full treatment of the relation of tragedy and philosophy (which involves a host of questions and concerns far larger than those which govern the present study) needs to address the place of comedy in that relation. Both Hegel and Nietzsche will acknowledge this—if only marginally—while in Heidegger and Hölderlin one finds only a remarkable absence even of the word.

For the present only one further preliminary remark remains. It is really something of a caveat for the reader: namely, that the question of the voice of this text which is itself so immersed in the question of voice should be of concern. It will be suggested that tragedy, this literature of suffered knowledge, is a sort of cri de coeur in which what is to be said migrates to a point beneath, or maybe beyond, language to the point of silence. If what is said here has been said with a sense of the propriety, then it will need to have been said reticently. Were I a poet, perhaps I might have done so better.[37]

1 Plato

The most discreet and delicate way of having the gods understand the irreversible, scourge of mortals, was the libation: you poured a noble liquid on the ground and lost it forever. It was an act of homage, of course: the recognition of the presence and rights of an invisible power. But it was something else as well: an attempt to make conversation. As if men were saying to the gods, Whatever we do, we are this liquid poured away.

—Roberto Calasso,
The Marriage of Cadmus and Harmony, p. 293

Death frames the *Republic,* and it does so with such force that every topic taken up in it needs to be read as sandwiched between two potent, and very different, discussions of "what awaits the dead" (614a). Precious little is said of birth. But one should not understate the riddle that birth introduces into the concerns of the *Republic.* Indeed, the decline of the city is linked explicitly to birth since that decline begins precisely at the point where the proper time for begetting is miscalculated with the result that children are born out of season.[1] However, the bulk of the conversation is not about either birth or death proper, but is preoccupied with questions about the education of children, with the cultivation of those who are still too young to cultivate themselves. According to Plato, the chief, perhaps sole, concern of such education is to foster in children, in the citizens of a future community, a knowledge of justice. But, as will become readily apparent, what is to be known of justice is deeply indebted to how the appearance of death in the community comes to be thought. The ability to understand the proper relation of death and the logic of community, namely, law, might be the preeminent measure of the knowledge of justice.[2] And so death will remain a central concern in this project of founding a community in words.

The questions posed by the relation of law and death are certainly not unique to Plato and clearly remain among the most pressing, and puzzling, questions for contemporary jurisprudence in the form of abortion, assisted suicide, and capital punishment. It is also a topic that has long formed the central axis for the action of some of the most celebrated tragedies. In the ancient world one sees the question of the relation of law and death played out most vividly and thematically in *Antigone,* where the enigma that death poses for the living is evident and compressed from the outset. There the drama begins with the question raised by a corpse: Antigone argues that in death we leave the empire of the law, we move beyond its reach into a different, more elemental set of relations. She contends that the law of the community must, in the end, yield to a different law, and that law, if it is to bear any relation to justice, must recognize its own limits before the limitlessness of death. Against Antigone, Creon argues that the rule of law is not limited by death. The community contains death within its own dominion, and, if the law of the community is to retain its force, it must reserve the power of death for itself. The dispute between Creon and Antigone over the relation of death and the polis itself precipitates even more deaths, ruining those who do not know the answer to its riddle.[3] But *Antigone* is far from being the only tragedy to play itself out in the dynamics of the question of this relation of death and the community.[4] Indeed, as Plato will argue, it seems rather to belong to the very nature of tragic art that it center itself upon this question. One of the defining characteristics of a tragedy for Plato is precisely that it takes up this question of the relation of death and shared life. Tragedy poses the riddle of death as a question which the living must learn to answer. Since it is dedicated to this question, Plato understands that tragic art always stands in close proximity to what is requisite for a knowledge of justice.

However, it is the conception of the relation of death and the polis proper to tragedy that will drive Plato's critique of art in the *Republic.* This concern with the tragic conception of death's relation to justice is so great in Plato that it will regularly form the counterpoint to the arguments about the nature of the healthy community in the *Republic.* But it is important to note that when Plato addresses these questions it is Homer, not Sophocles, who serves as the paradigm case. The critique of tragedy here will center itself chiefly on Homer and most of all upon the understanding of death that is conveyed by Homer. No sustained effort is made to articulate differences among the tragedians, nor even among the arts. In the end, Plato's critique of poetic practices singularizes itself as a critique of Homer. Or, better, the critique of Homer in Plato generalizes itself into a critique of all art.[5]

Of course, the *Republic* is not the only dialogue in which these topics are addressed. One thinks, for instance, of the *Phaedrus, Ion, Symposium,*

22

Apology, Phaedo, and *Crito* among others. There are a body of texts, not always obviously coordinated with one another, in which questions concerning art, writing, language, death, law, and ethical life are central. Nonetheless, in the *Republic,* where we find the argument that the life of the philosopher represents the best choice of a life for a human being who would know something of justice, we find the sharpest delineation of the contrast of such a life with the view of life that is presented in tragic art.

*　　*　　*

In the *Republic* death seems somehow less virulent, less menacing, than it does in either Homer or Sophocles, for instance. Here it is never enacted and so it possesses an almost abstract quality. Nonetheless, as the opening and ending of the dialogue make abundantly evident, the question put to us by death fundamentally shapes the course of the entire dialogue. The first word of the *Republic, kateben,* echoes what Odysseus says to Penelope when he describes how he went down to the realm of the dead.[6] The appearance of death at both ends of the *Republic* is simultaneously thematic and dramatic; that is, it is addressed as a topic for conversation, and it is portrayed in the form of dramatic figures. The first figure bearing this question of death, the aged Cephalus, who appears at the very outset of the dialogue, quickly and quietly totters off and is forgotten. Its final figure, Er, who will see the choices of souls before their birth into bodies, will himself never have been really dead. In the opening scene Cephalus speaks of how his past looks to him from this time when death seems near, and he suggests that this past has led him to know more clearly the importance of a knowledge of justice. In the last scene of the *Republic,* a scene that will both confirm and problematize all that precedes it, Er will have the chance to witness the actions of the dead, and in witnessing this he comes to understand how a knowledge of justice bears upon those choices we each must make and that will seal our fates. Cephalus and Er become the twin bookends of the *Republic.* Clearly very different figures—Cephalus is elderly, wealthy; Er, seemingly dead upon a battlefield, is "not strong of mind, but strong"[7]—they nonetheless function together to highlight the centrality of the riddle of death for the question of the community. Neither dies, but both are defined by their relation to death—as, to a large measure, is Socrates who does not die in the *Republic* but who will have already died for every reader of it. The dialogue takes place at the Piraeus, the limits of the city of Athens, but it is immediately clear that here it is death that will form the limit of the city to be formed in words.

Cephalus's arrival early in the action of the *Republic* is itself preceded by a curious mime of a death to come; namely, Socrates' own death.[8] We learn all this from Socrates, who is narrating in the first person and recounting a lengthy conversation that has just taken place the previous day.[9] Socrates tells his unnamed listener that after watching a religious festival he encountered Polemarchus, who, along with some friends, first threatened then enticed Socrates to visit Polemarchus's house. There he pays his respects to Cephalus (whose name is a tag-name that refers to the "head"), the head of the household, who is described as sitting on a chair with a headrest and wearing a wreath on his head. Cephalus greets Socrates by bemoaning the frailty of his body, which keeps him from visiting the city where he might find good conversation. Presenting himself as lacking any real physical stamina, Cephalus says that as his physical appetites wither, his pleasure in words grows. Socrates in turn replies that he is delighted to converse with the very old. Citing Homer (but without attribution), he then says somewhat tactlessly that he especially enjoys talking with those on the verge of death. Cephalus responds then by citing Sophocles (this time by name), saying that the advantage of such a time of life is that one is no longer a slave to erotic desires. As the capacity for intercourse ebbs, the desire for discourse grows. Logos, in the eyes of Cephalus, seems to be a sort of substitute for eros.

Before this brief, but decisive, exchange between Socrates and Cephalus comes to an end two more references to poets are made. Both references seem to be only of passing significance, but both quietly foreshadow themes of great importance that appear later in the dialogue. Both references come in answer to Socrates' second, and again seemingly tactless, question to Cephalus. Commenting upon Cephalus's great wealth, Socrates asks whether he earned his money or inherited it. Socrates' explanation of his rather strange curiosity about this matter is that he has observed that Cephalus does not seem overly fond of money, which Socrates typically finds to be a trait of those who have not earned money on their own. To clarify his observation Socrates says, "Those who do make it are twice as attached to it as the others. For just as poets are fond of their poems and fathers of their children, so money-makers too are serious about their money" (330c). Three varieties of making are set up parallel to one another: making poems, making children, and making money.[10] Socrates seems to suggest that they resemble one another, but this resemblance will come under more serious scrutiny later in the conversation when the effort is to make a city in words and the nature of such making, especially the making of poems, is problematized. But for the present the question of the similarity of these forms of making passes unnoticed as Socrates puts one final question to Cephalus, a question that crystallizes the brief discussion up to this point: what good has this wealth brought Cephalus at this stage of life? Cephalus answers this time by citing yet another poet, namely, Pindar, and here at last the question of justice is broached. Cephalus says simply that the leisure and absence of passion have bred in him a new concern with what awaits the dead and how the life one has led might influence what will follow death. The question which occupies his final days is the question of justice.

Socrates tries to pursue this question with Cephalus, but the latter's lack of energy overtakes him, and he who presented himself as so enamored of conversation walks away just as the conversation takes hold. Much of the dialogue that ensues is concerned with the regulation of the passions and with the problems posed by those with excessive passion. The only word said about those who lack passion is found enacted here in the way that Cephalus quietly drops out of language.[11]

But his withdrawal does manage to sharpen the question of justice for those who remain. When younger figures take over the conversation it also seems to shift away from Cephalus's concern with how death bears upon justice. Now that the place of the head of the household is vacated, there is the question of who will inherit it. This is the second time the topic of inheritance is raised, but now it will be explored in detail. Now the conversation will open itself to ask the broader question about cultural inheritances: how does one hand down values? It is clear how one passes along money, but how is one to pass along what one has learned? This is the question that sets the project of the *Republic* in motion and that ultimately leads to the effort to found a city in speech.[12] The topic of inheritance, of the transmission of values, calls attention to the need for moral education if such a city is ever to sustain itself. The city must be able to preserve what it founds by forming those who form its future. Here then the question of *paideia* begins. Soon the question will be able to be: how is the just soul nourished?

When Socrates tries to make this question of *paideia* more precise he does so by dividing it and establishing a sort of parallel between the education of the body and the education of the soul (376e). The body is handed over to gymnastics, while the soul, which is to be cultivated first, is assigned to the arts (*mousike*). Both the body and the soul are nourished, and so the growth of each is promoted by the appropriate "diet" and by the exercise of a set of practices. The route by which one fosters the health of the body is not in dispute: Plato concedes its maintenance to the authority of medicine and the established practices of gymnastics.[13] The health of the soul, on the other hand, is precisely the point of controversy here. Athenian culture had granted tragic poets, especially Homer, great authority in the clarification of what is requisite for the health of the soul. Plato's intention here is to claim for philosophy that same authority. In doing this the parallel between the care of the body and of the soul which is established at the outset of this project is invoked frequently so that Plato will, from time to time, bounce his analysis of art and his conception of the healthy soul off of the principles that maintain bodily health. Later this parallel will grow in significance when Aristotle, a doctor who was the son of a doctor, draws the principles of medicine into the heart of the analysis of art and into the terms of ethical life. Now, though, the question is clear: the question of *paideia* is a question about the healthy diet and practices for the soul.

*   *   *

An unexpressed assumption in the discussion that follows is that nothing touches the soul more than language. There is a conviction that language and the soul, *logos* and *psyche,* have an essential kinship such that each is able to care for the other—and in the process of this care, problematize one another. If the soul has a "diet" proper to its own nature, then words must be counted among the "foods" of the soul.[14] While the question of the relation of language and the soul will be raised by Socrates in the larger horizon of *mousike,*[15] the arts of painting and language will dominate the analysis that follows and will be developed as counterpoints to one another.[16] It will be important to note just how much Plato's analysis of tragic poetry is informed by his conception of painting. He presents the analysis of painting as somehow less problematic than the question of language: the mimetic character of painted images is never fully problematized by Plato. Nonetheless, his critique of tragic art which he finds worthy of close analysis will, in part, rest upon a critique of such mimetic practices as they are exhibited by painting.[17] But the chief concern of Plato's investigation of the role of the arts in the cultivation of the soul is to determine how words touch and form the soul—more precisely, to ask if there is a certain relation to language that is better suited to the cultivation of a healthy soul. Such a soul, for Plato, is a soul at one with itself.

Plato knew well that words change people. He also argued that the souls of the young are most malleable and so most readily affected by the words and the images that they take in.[18] But while the impact of language and the stories we tell is most visible in the souls of children, it is not confined to them. Plato knew that even seemingly subtle alterations in our relation to language touch us profoundly. He was, for instance, extraordinarily sensitive to the different effect that words can have once they have been transformed into script, that is, once the iconographic potential of language, its relation to images, is realized in language that is written. In the end, if one wants to address Plato's conception of language, one must take up the question of this potential of language to transform itself into script (which he describes as "the corpse of a thought").[19] That means, of course, that the full elaboration of the question of tragic poetry is shadowed by this question of the difference between writing and speaking, and—as Nietzsche will point out—by the question of the role of the image in the presentation of tragic art. But the manner in which the question of such art is raised in the *Republic* is not, in the end, fundamentally disrupted by this distinction since here the question of the ethical force of tragic art always assumes simply that such art is performed. The tragic poem here is never taken as a text for solitary or silent reading (as is the text by Lysias that Phaedrus smuggles under his cloak); rather, even if it is first a written text, it is understood to be a text that is enacted and said aloud. Largely untroubled by the question of writing here, the critique of tragic poetry in the *Republic* is focused instead upon two interrelated concerns: the content of such works and the style of such works. It is thus a two-pronged critique that will be presented at two rather distinct stages of the dialogue: first in Books 2–3, then again in Book 10. By opening and closing this dialogue on the nature of the just community with discussions of tragic art, Plato acknowledges the importance of the question put to the polis by such art.

Thus it is that the question of tragic art is by nature political, just as the question of the polis is by nature engaged in a critique of such art.[20] The reason for this is clear: the question of justice is, as has already been established in the discussion with Cephalus, essentially related to the enigma of death, and tragic art, as Socrates will soon demonstrate, bears a conception of death within itself simply by virtue of the language and practices upon which it rests. The claim will be that the style and the substance of tragic art cannot help but be the presentation of a conception of death that is unhealthy for the souls of the citizens of the just community.

*   *   *

Book 2 of the *Republic* ends with a brief discussion of the poetic presentation of the gods and heroes who are the models for human conduct. The discussion is in response to Socrates' own expression of concern about the sort of words and stories that will be used to educate children, who are not themselves duplicitous enough to see through an act of duplicity. Rather quickly, Socrates contends that he can conclude that there is a lie that seems to belong to the very nature of poetic speech and that this deceptive element of such speech will need to be regulated if the just community is to preserve itself. The reason such lies need to be regulated is that a lie debilitates the soul insofar as it cultivates contradictory images in the soul, images that cannot be maintained in a soul which seeks a harmony with itself. Here Plato refers to images such as those which we find in Homer that present the gods as warring. In short, the lie in the poem breeds an ignorance in the soul of those who take it to heart insofar as it gives birth to a phantom of truth (382b). Socrates never quite explains why he believes that the poetic presentations of the models for human beings are lies. He only suggests that we should reject the work of those who make "bad representations in speech" (*eikaze tis kakos to logoi*), just as we would reject the work of a painter whose work does not resemble the things painted (377e). The first liability of language is visible now: language can unfold freely, that is, it can speak both the true and the false, and it is not bound in itself to one or the other.[21] Before any real analysis of the arts is undertaken, Socrates has already proposed that they will be in need of regulation, and at this stage such regulation seems to legitimate itself by reference to some sort of authority of the gods.[22] This first exchange about the nature of tragic poetry—where it is established that language has no intrinsic relation to truth—is rather problematic in the way in which the decision about the nature of its "lie" is made, and yet the issues left in suspense here are never clearly taken up in the fuller analysis that follows.

The discussion deepens in Book 3, which opens with Socrates announcing his concern about the content (*logos*) of tragic poetry (386a–392c). The discussion of the question of style follows immediately on the heels of this renewed concern with the content of poetry. Not surprisingly, the examples of the content of tragic poetry that Socrates singles out as most troubling are found in passages which have to do with death. Suggesting that proper moral education should cultivate courage rather than fear, Socrates argues that a certain species of remarks ought to be expunged from the works of "Homer and other poets" (387a). Leaning upon his self-authorized right of censorship, Socrates rapidly catalogs a variety of improprieties of tragic poetry. The specific passages selected, which with one exception refer to Achilles, are not as significant as the more general assumptions which support Socrates' critique of those passages.[23] Two assumptions about such poetry underpin his criticisms: first, once again, that poets lie "by nature," and, second, that the poetic presentation of death bears an essential relation to lamentation, to grief, which in turn warps the just soul. Both of these claims need to be expanded, but neither is unpacked in the exchange at this stage, which is focused on the "content" of tragic poetry. What remains to be explained is why the "content" of such poetry—instances of which Socrates presents—emerges out of the inner nature and general style of such works. Why, according to Plato, "must" a poet speak falsely simply by virtue of being a poet? And why "must" a poet lament or mourn simply by virtue of being a poet? In other words, what must be shown is how the specific examples of the representation of death singled out in Homer and Hesiod here are best understood as illustrations of a general criticism of art. As always, this criticism is leveled against art with reference to what Plato understands to be its pedagogical and ethical significances.

In the course of the dialogue it becomes clear that the first claim, namely, that poets must lie, cannot be explained by referring to the content, the substance, of such works. It is, however, decided that such lies are unhealthy for the soul, and that such falsehoods are not rooted in the malice of poets. In other words, according to Socrates, such lies as are found in the content of tragic poetry need to be censored, and for that to be accomplished the roots of such poetic lies must be clarified. Since it is clear that those lies are not rooted in the malice of individual poets, but rather that the impulse to lie belongs to the very nature of poetry itself, Socrates suggests that the "style" (*lexis*) of poetry must next be considered. By saying this, Socrates is implying that one is not a poet on the basis of "what" one speaks about, but on the basis of "how" one speaks. There is no poetic "topic" as such (a poem may equally well speak of plums, flowers, love, death, or the noise of a car passing in the street); however, there is a poetic relation to language, and it is this relation to language, this experience of language, that is now to be addressed under the rubric of poetic "diction" (*lexis*). Likewise, it is by speaking about the poetic relation to language that the second claim, namely, that poetry cultivates an unhealthy relation to death in its natural kinship with lamentation, will be unpacked. Again the claim is not that poets are by chance individuals with mournful temperament, but rather that a relation to mourning belongs to the nature of poetry itself. But although this criticism of tragic poetry will be touched upon in the discussion of style in Book 3, it will not receive its full explanation until Book 10, where the discussion centers upon what happens to a soul that is nourished on the language of grief (606a). In other words, both of the criticisms leveled against the contents of tragic poetry await their legitimation in the discussions that follow in which the nature of art, and in particular of tragic poetry, is analyzed.

Given the weight that it must bear in this discussion, it is not surprising that the inquiry into the nature of poetic "style" is complex and rather dense. It is also tacitly a comment upon itself, since here, in this written text, Plato has Socrates commenting upon the varieties of literary form. That is especially the case when the discussion is punctuated by the claim that "there is a style and narrative in which the person of good birth and breeding narrates whatever must be said . . . he will imitate the good man most when he is acting steadily and prudently; less, and less willingly, when he's unsteadied by diseases, loves, drink or some other misfortune" (396b–c). In other words, in the middle of this discussion—a discussion which begins with Socrates' second disavowal of any relation to the poetic—"I'll speak without meter; I'm not poetic" (393e)—the literary form of the *Republic* itself seems to find its self-authorization. Here the reader is addressed (differently than Socrates' interlocutor, Adeimantus) *as* a reader who knows that what is imitated here is the practice of a "good man."

While the presentation of the specific forms and combinations of poetic "diction" here seems to offer a grid for classifying literary works, the lasting and most decisive claim of this exchange in Book 3 is the decision made about the "grounds" of poetic practices that render such practices problematic for the task of *paideia*. This claim, namely, that we must consider tragedy and comedy as thoroughly mimetic (394c), will provide the basis for the most severe critiques of tragic poetry. Those critiques, and the more precise determination of the nature of *mimesis*,[24] are deferred until Book 10, where the knowledge that can be had on mimetic grounds will be set against the measure of truth established by *mathesis*. At this phase in the conversation, the introduction of the notion that tragic poetry is mimetic simply serves as the impulse for Socrates to ask "whether or not tragedy and comedy should be admitted into the city" (394d). Clearly the suspicion with which mimetic praxis is regarded seems almost self-evident to Socrates, so the association of tragedy with *mimesis* is sufficient reason to render tragedy itself suspect. The reason he finds *mimesis* so clearly problematic is twofold: first, it is a potent force in development of the soul, and, second, it is completely unreliable. The recognition of the power of mimetic practices (which Aristotle will take as the opening observation for his *Poetics*) is put bluntly: "Imitations, if they are practiced continually from youth onwards, become established as habits and nature, in body and sounds and thought" (395d). The second reason for the condemnation of *mimesis*, namely, that it is an unreliable practice, has been established repeatedly in several Platonic dialogues and so has taken on the traits of a commonplace. One thinks, for instance, of the lampooning of mimetic practices in the *Ion*, where Socrates is relentless in illustrating the fraudulence of the knowledge that is represented in Homer's mime of a variety of activities. Thus Socrates asks Ion whether Homer or a general would be the one who has the knowledge of how to lead troops, etc. Despite his gushing admiration for Homer, Ion repeatedly concedes that Homer's knowledge of such matters is, in the end, merely the mime of such knowledge. Homer, Socrates concludes, is not a reliable authority in such matters and precisely because his work is mimetic in nature. On the basis of these exchanges Socrates comes to the conclusion that, since art is fundamentally mimetic, all that is disclosed in art is founded upon such unreliable grounds. Stripped of any claim to knowledge of the real practices of life, Socrates argues that Homer's poetry, and poetry generally, is ultimately nothing more than an appeal to the irrational element of the soul.

According to Socrates, then, the trouble with mimetic practices is twofold. First, works that are governed by mimetic principles have no allegiance to truth. We see this, for instance, when we think about actors who, even though they are not able to do all things equally well, nonetheless can play a variety of different roles in which they represent themselves as having such abilities. There is a sort of incommensurability between word (*logon*) and deed (*ergon*) at work here: what one says (e.g., that one is a doctor or that one is in love) and what one does (acting) are not one with one another. Just as actors do not hesitate to pretend to be a variety of characters, so too with the mimetic the artist does not hesitate to represent a variety of forms of knowledge. In short, mimetic practices thrive on the protean quality of *mimesis,* and there is nothing in their nature that leads them to regulate themselves.[25] Second, since there is a lack of any real knowledge in works grounded in imitation, we must recognize that the true appeal of such works is not to the rational faculties of the soul where knowledge thrives, but to the irrational part of the soul. The second trouble with works that rest upon the mimetic power of language is that, since they do not have any stable relation to what can be known, they do not "speak" to the rational part of the soul where knowledge thrives; rather, such works appeal to the irrational elements of the soul. Since mimetic works reach powerfully into the soul (*psyche*), while opening it to its own irrational elements, it is clear that the mind (*phrenes*) is no longer "safe" (*sophron*) in the presence of such works.[26]

Thus, according to Socrates, the danger of the work of art is that it seduces us by means of an appeal to desires, and, of course, the most powerful desires, namely, those that have to do with eros and death, are those which are most able to affect us. The more deeply works of art insinuate themselves into the souls of those who take them to heart, the more directly they operate with passion and with the question of death. There is thus a natural gravitation of the work of art to concerns with both love and death.

Here the path is cleared for a renewal of the questions that were posed in Socrates' brief exchange with Cephalus, who presented himself as lacking all passion for sex and as disquieted by death. Death and desire now return as concerns for the investigation into the impact of art in the education of young citizens. With the return of these topics the focus of the conversation shifts twice and finally shifts away from a special concern with tragic poetry, leaving the question of such poetry in abeyance until the final book, Book 10, of the *Republic,* where the consequences of death and desire for the knowledge of justice is dramatized in the "Myth of Er." But, in order for those topics to be shelved properly so that they might reappear later at the appropriate moment, two more moves are required at this point. The first shift here is to the topic of music, and then, quite rapidly, the conversation shifts again to a concern with gymnastics, at which point the problem of understanding our desire is removed from the inquiry into art and given over to the question of the education of the body.

The discussion of music is not so much a departure from the question of tragic art as a step that deepens the inquiry into such works. From the outset it is made clear that music is not to be regarded as a distinct mode of expression governed by principles other than those mimetic principles of poetry; rather, music is presented as a vital element of poetry generally. There is even some measure in which music needs to be understood as a more elemental form of tragic art than poetry: "The rearing in music is most sovereign . . . because rhythm and harmony most of all insinuate themselves into the inmost part of the soul and most vigorously lay hold of it in bringing grace with them" (401d). Of course, it is Nietzsche who will write of the birth of tragedy from out of the spirit of music, and when he does so he will reserve some of his most stinging remarks for Socrates' relation to tragedy. Nonetheless, there is a very real sense in which what Socrates is saying here is that tragedy is founded, if not in music, then in the privileged relation of words and music. But it should be clear that the conceptions of music operative in Nietzsche and Plato remain quite distinct so that, in the end, the differences between them about the question of tragedy are simply clarified, not lifted.

The presentation of music that one finds in the *Republic* is rather clipped and does not press upon many of the points which one might expect to emerge from such an analysis in this context. The strong Pythagorean strain in Plato shows itself here, but not quite in the manner, nor quite as prominently, as one would anticipate. What one finds lacking, against expectation, is any clear or extended discussion of the relation of music to mathematics.[27] There is, however, a clear concern with the question of the various "rhythms of life," especially with those that resonate with and reinforce "an orderly and courageous life" (399d). Clearly, music properly understood is dedicated to the cultivation of a sense of proportion and harmony, and rhythms that harmonize aid in tuning the soul to the just proportion and in setting it in harmony with itself. But what is of special concern is the relation of words to music and the effort to clarify the musical element of language. Claiming that "the music and the rhythm must follow the speech" (398d), Socrates reminds Adeimantus that although music is more primitive in its appeal to the soul, and so in some sense more original, it is necessary that language, especially the proper language of the rational soul, be acknowledged as the most potent entry into the soul: "And when we see the [rhythms of an orderly and courageous life] we'll compel the foot and the tune to follow the speech of such [a life], rather than the speech following the foot and the tune" (399e). Here, then, Plato recognizes that when words are put to music, the music itself needs to accommodate itself to the rhythms, syntax, and rhymes of the language.[28] That is why music has developed so differently in different countries: insofar as words have been put to music, the beat and shape of music have, of necessity, molded themselves to the elements of the language it must bear. In this way the cadence of a language comes to shape the rhythms of music.[29] After taking note of this bond between language and music the conversation about the rhythms of music turns us back to the task of finding a language appropriate for the task of educating the young about justice. And we are turned back to the criticism of the appeal that mimetic language makes to the irrational, the speechless, passions of the soul. In particular, Socrates comes again to remind us that "there is no further need of wailing and lamentation [*threnon te kai odyrmon*] in language" (398d), and consequently we must guard against reinscribing them in language via music, just as we must guard against letting our language subtly import such dispositions into music. But the crucial point here is that the speechless contact of music and the soul is channeled into the passions, to the point at which the soul itself is speechless, the point of pleasures and pains. Abruptly, Socrates brings this exchange about music to a close by introducing a concern about the relation of music and love (*eros*); in particular, note is made of the relation of the "right kind of love . . . [namely, love] in a moderate and musical way" (403a). It is a remark introduced without further explanation or ado, and it brings this stage of the conversation to a close, ending "where it ought to end . . . for the consummation of musical concerns should concern beautiful [*kalon*] things" (403c). It is a conclusion that is never fully explained here. But with this remark the conversation moves to the next phase in which the topic is education of the young in gymnastics. That shift occurs, in part, because the persistence of the question of human desires makes the question of the care of the body, where desire is exhibited, even more urgent.

This exchange about how we are to conceive the role of the arts in the ethical education of the young has left a number of important questions unanswered. Many of these matters are simply tabled until Book 10, which opens with a renewal of the question of the role of tragic poetry in the community. But some decisions and important insights have been achieved at this stage in the examination of that question. Four points in particular stand out. First, the mimetic principle upon which poetic practices rest has been established, and some of the consequences of that principle (e.g., its unreliability and its "lie") have been clarified. Second, the native tendency of poetic practices to lamentation and to appeal to our passions has been asserted (along with the damage that such passions can inflict upon the soul). Third, on this basis of these first two points, the privileged relation of the soul to language has been suggested. Finally, there is also an implicit understanding working throughout these exchanges that the soul is vulnerable to both desire and language, that it is by nature touched by language and what remains speechless, and that it must be vigilant about the manner in which such forces are present for it. It is in view of this final point that the decision to purge the community of tragic poetry made at the conclusion of Book 2 is legitimated. But what has been demonstrated above all in this set of exchanges is that in these criticisms of tragedy Plato has shown himself to be acutely self-conscious about the relationship between language and the soul, as well as between the choice of a style and the content of an argument.[30] From this point forward, the *Republic* needs to be read as a book that has problematized its own status as a book, and we, as readers, need to recognize that much of what is to be said in it is made clear by *how* it is said. That might be nowhere more significant, yet nowhere more puzzling, than in the final portion of the *Republic,* namely, the "Myth of Er."

* * *

The set of topics and thread of the issues raised but not fully answered in Book 3 reappear in Book 10, which opens with Socrates' self-congratulatory remark that "I recognize that we were entirely right in not admitting into the city any part of poetry that is mimetic" (595a). It is a comment that will be qualified in the discussion that ensues, and it will be the final clarification of these matters concerning mimetic art that permits the larger concerns of the *Republic* to at last be brought to some closure. In what follows we quickly discover that it is not the tyrant, who is confronted in Book 9, who poses the most serious challenge to the preservation of the just community; rather, it is the poet.[31] Here, then, it is not only poetry and the figures of poetry (especially Achilles) which, as in Book 3, form the focus of the conversation; rather, it is equally the poet, especially Homer himself, who comes in for criticism. In Book 10 the criticism of poetry and poets is at its sharpest, and yet it is here that the terms of a possible reconciliation of the community and poets are spelled out.

The judgment under which tragic poetry now stands, after the intervention of so many new concerns between Books 3 and 10, is a harsh one: "All such things seem to maim the thought of those who hear them and do not as a remedy [*pharmakon*] have the knowledge of how they really are" (595b). In order to unpack the grounds of this judgment Socrates once again raises his concerns about the mimetic character of such works. But this time, after the presentation of the divided line and the allegory of the cave, after the *mathexis* of ideas has been disclosed, Socrates says, "I myself scarcely comprehend what *mimesis* is" (595c). That, of course, is an invitation to deepen the understanding of *mimesis* and of the way in which mimetic principles repeat themselves in the soul of those who partake of mimetic works.

This new analysis begins by drawing upon the assumed resemblance of painting and poetry, words and images, and so representational images in painting become the model for the further analysis of the mimetic dimension of tragic poetry. Although a great deal rests upon this assumed kinship of poetry and painting, it has not yet, nor will it ever be, discussed and defended. Nonetheless, the assumption here is that both words and images copy and repeat a world that has already been constituted beforehand. Consequently, works that rely upon mimetic operations, such as painting and poetry, do not have an original relation to the world; that is, they are not disclosive of the world in its truth, but are derivative by nature. In the celebrated example that follows, Socrates seeks to make more precise the distance of *mimetic* disclosure to the truth as it now can be said

34

to be disclosed in the *idea:* the poet or the painter not only does not copy the original of truth, but rather copies the copy that can be seen. Thus "the maker of tragedy, if he is an imitator . . . is naturally third from . . . the truth, as are all other imitators" (597e), and so poetic representation is by nature misrepresentation of the truth of a matter. But, according to Socrates, Homer and the other imitative artists have not removed themselves from the truth out of any malicious desire to mislead, but simply because they do not know better (since no one who knew the truth of a matter would rest content with a mere imitation of it). The conclusion is clear, and not far from the conclusions that were reached in Book 3: "The imitator knows nothing worth mentioning about what he imitates; imitation is a kind of play and not serious; and those who take up tragic poetry in iambics and in epics are all imitators in the highest possible degree" (602b). What makes such works so pernicious is that, because of their nature, they have power of that part of the soul "that is far from prudence [*phroneseos*], and is not a companion and friend for any healthy or true purpose" (603b). In other words, because mimetic works are "ordinary things that have intercourse with what is ordinary" (603b), they do not relate to and nourish that part of the soul that "trusts in measure [*metro*] and calculation [*logismoi*] and which is the best part of the soul" (603a).

The decision here is to abrogate mimetic works to the "lower regions" of the soul, to the faculties of a human being that are neither stable nor reliable; such regions of the soul are rather protean, porous, and hence vulnerable to contradictions. In other words, mimetic works nourish that part of the soul which can never take the lead in turning the soul toward justice, if we understand justice to refer to the harmony of the soul with itself and the fidelity of the soul to truth. This assessment of mimetic works rests, in large measure, upon an unproblematized conception of language that is founded upon an image of painting in which painting is understood as the representation of the surface of matters. Fastened only upon surfaces, making only copies of such surfaces found in life, mimetic works are never able to illuminate the unity, the harmony, that belongs to life. That means that mimetic works are never able to bring the soul into harmony with itself and its world; rather, such works, thriving on their protean nature, leave the soul "teeming with the countless oppositions [*gignomenon*]" found on the surface of things. Operating in a region of conflict and struggle, targeted at the passions, mimetic art gravitates of itself to tragedy which is the art of passion and conflict.

Plato's deepest convictions about the importance of the harmony of the soul with itself begin to emerge at this point. Such a just soul is able to resist the changes of fortune to which it might find itself subject. In other words, the just soul is blessed not because it does not suffer misfortune, but because such a person "will bear it more easily than others" (603e). But being unconflicted in itself, being at home with itself and so self-contained, is possible only if the soul is not formed and affected by unreliable practices. It is not good fortune that brings happiness, not even simply the absence of misfortune; rather, it is the solidity of the soul resting within itself, invulnerable to fortune, that lets one say that one is blessed and happy: "One must always habituate the soul to turn as quickly as possible to curing and setting aright what has fallen and is sick, doing away with lament by medicine" (604d–e). Of course, Socrates' argument here is not simply that we should be optimists, or simply oblivious to the course of life. Quite the contrary: one is urged to be profoundly sensitive to the events of one's life and to the life of the community in which one lives; Socrates is, however, arguing that in order to be responsive and responsible justly, one must cultivate a measured soul, one that harmonizes with both itself and the law of the common. The argument is similar to the arguments one finds in the *Symposium* and *Phaedrus,* where one is cautioned against attaching oneself to individuals because in so doing one risks ruining one's soul. The image of the proper distance and detachment is dramatized in the figure of Socrates, and it is illustrated especially well in the speech of the tragic poet Alcibiades about *eros,* a speech which is, in the end, a speech about the unique object of his desire, namely, Socrates. That speech is the story of Socrates' erotic charm and of his insurmountable distance. It is the story of the way in which that charm is found precisely in such distance such that the more one draws near to Socrates the more one understands that he is infinitely unknowable. Infinitely unattainable, Socrates is for Alcibiades the object of a deathless desire. When Alcibiades concludes his story of *eros,* he does so with reference to the tragic dictum "one learns through suffering" (*pathonta gnonai*). When one attaches oneself to another, to an individual, one cannot conceive of that experience, one cannot translate it into what is common; rather, one can only narrate it, as Alcibiades does in the *Symposium;* one can only mime and represent it for others and suffer it for oneself.

In the *Republic* Socrates argues that when one permits the soul to attach itself to another soul (which the soul, as porous and protean, is capable of doing), one renders the soul vulnerable to the loss of that to which it has wedded itself. Such a loss ruins the soul, disrupts its balance, disfigures it for itself, and so leaves the soul chronically unstable, and thus unable to be a just member of the community of others. Since others die, the loss of the other always shadows the love of an individual. This means, of course, that the companion of such a love is, in the end, a knowledge that can only be suffered. This coupling of love and death, this insight into the damage that ultimately belongs to the passion for another, is what drives tragic poetry. But it is precisely this risk of damage that Socrates wants to purge in the *Republic,* suggesting that to permit such attachments to thrive in the community, and to nourish the souls of the young upon the images and language which represent attachments that can only lead to sorrow, is to undermine the elemental logic which governs the just community, namely, the law of the common. Thus, "the law presumably says that it is finest to keep as quiet as possible in misfortunes and not be irritated. . . . [B]eing in pain is an impediment to the coming of that thing the support of which we need as quickly as possible in such cases" (604c–d). The law of the idiom, which is the element in which art operates, is never able to illuminate the law of the common as Socrates presents it.[32] This drive to cultivate the common and to dilute the force of any attachments to particulars is what led Socrates to propose the rather radical distribution of both property and families in Book 5. There even the bonds of family and sexual differences, bonds and differences which, as Freud persistently reminds us, clearly belong to those which become the seat of tragic action, are loosened.[33] Children are distributed among the citizens, and the different roles of women and men are effaced. In the *Laws* this drive to eradicate the force of the idiosyncratic leads to the suggestion that "the notion of the private [*idion*] will be, by every possible stratagem, completely uprooted from every sphere of life. Everything possible will have been devised to make even what is by nature private, such as eyes and hands, common in some way, in the sense that the young will learn to see and hear and act in common" (739c–d). The claim is that what is best in each of us emerges out of that which is common to all of us. Socrates clarifies this argument by saying that "after feeding fat the emotion of pity, it is not easy to restrain the soul in one's own suffering" (606b); in other words, what we share in common cannot be found in what we discover through pity and the compassion peculiar to it. But, insofar as art dedicates itself to the *mimesis* of individuals, insofar as tragic poetry operates according to the order of the idiom, it is at odds with what is our best. Thus it is, says Socrates, ever more evident that the gravitation of such mimetic works to mourning, to the lament over the loss of the individual, feeds what "ought to be dried up, and sets . . . up as rulers in us what ought to be ruled" (606d).

While such a view provides the confirmation that Socrates needs for the earlier decision to purge the city of tragic poetry, it also seems to open the door for a rapprochement between the poet and the philosopher. Expressing confidence in the judgments about such works that were reached in Book 3, Socrates now says, "Let it be our apology that it was fitting for us to send it away from the city on account of its character" (607b). Immediately following this self-affirmation of the philosophic judgment about mimetic poetry, Socrates proposes a highly qualified reversal of that judgment by saying that poetry will be permitted back into the community governed by the rule of the law of the common "when it has made a defense in lyric or some other meter" (607d). It is important to note that such a qualification does not fundamentally change the criticisms raised about tragic poetry thus far: "We are . . . aware that such poetry mustn't be taken seriously . . . but that one who hears it must be careful, fearing for the regime in oneself and one must hold to what we have said about poetry" (608a). What is suggested here is that perhaps poetry can be enlisted to the same ends as those which govern philosophy. In other words, perhaps we might begin to speak of a poetry that was not governed by mimetic, but by eidetic, laws. What is not said, but is quite clear, is that such a philosophical poetry might very well take the form of something like the Platonic dialogues themselves.[34]

But such a possibility is not explored here immediately. It will, however, come in the final section of the *Republic,* where Socrates concludes with a very different sort of literary form in the "Myth of Er." Only one more remark about the place of poetry in human affairs remains to be made. It is seemingly causal, but revealing nonetheless. By way of bringing this final discussion of tragic poetry to a close, Socrates says that we can understand our relation to it by likening it to a "love that is not beneficial" (607e). Here the danger of poetry is compared with the danger of *eros.* Not by accident does Socrates speak of poetry and love in the same breath (as he does, for instance, in the *Symposium* and *Phaedrus*). He knows that in its truth poetry is a loving act, just as he has also argued that it is, by nature, an act of mourning. Here, though, the final words about tragic poetry refer to it as to a dangerous love.[35] Words, like the other whom one loves, enter the deepest regions of the soul where one is most vulnerable to ruin. According to Socrates, words that are born of mimetic practices, words that belong to the idiom of the idiom—to that which, in the end, we can only mourn—are, like the lover, dangerous and ruinous to the harmony of the soul with itself. Just as desire changes the lover, so do such words which touch upon desires change those who take them seriously. But, Socrates argues, it is a risky change since our desires are contradictory. Taking such words to heart, admitting into the soul the sort of language and rhythms of desires that the poet cultivates, leaves the soul wedded to contradictions. It is no accident, then, that the art of passion and contradiction, namely, tragedy, is, according to Socrates, the destination of all mimetic practice. The soul nourished upon such practices exposes itself to what will finally bring it to ruin. The final judgment of poetry in the *Republic,* while seeming to mitigate the earlier harshness of Books 2 and 3, never retreats from the view that in tragic poetry the soul risks something not worth the risk: it risks the capacity to be one with itself and so just in the larger community of which it is a member. There is, however, a very real sense in which the entire critique of mimetic practices is problematized by the irony of the very form of this discussion: the riddle of mimesis is itself enacted and performed in the very texts that set forth its critique. One could say that "by placing the Socratic criticism of writing inside his own writing, Plato invites us to ask . . . to what extent his own literary innovations have managed to circumnavigate the criticism."[36]

But one might also need to recognize that here the enigma of mimetic practice is folded back upon itself in the performance of its own self-critique. In other words, this critique of tragic poetry might very well hold within itself a sort of comedy.[37]

But at this point the discussion of the tragic poem comes to a close. As a sort of contrast with the corruptibility of the soul brought into contact with such works, the discussion now turns to the topic of the immortality of the soul, to the incorruptible element of it that needs to be tended. Here we find the counterpoint to the sufferings that the soul is able to suffer when it feeds upon tragic works, and so here, as the successor to the final words concerning tragedy, we find a brief presentation of the "prizes, wages, and gifts coming to the just person while alive" (614a). With this set of remarks the drama of ideas that is the *Republic* concludes its first stage and takes a dramatic turn as Socrates suggests that only one more topic remains. Here the full measure of what has been said of justice and injustice is laid out. For the full measure of justice to be taken we must understand "what awaits the dead" (614a). The *Republic* reaches its summit here, and when it does a transformation in its own style is evident. It almost seems as if the *Republic* rewrites itself from this point.

*   *   *

The beautiful story that follows is stunning in light of all that has been said about how tales are to be told. Likewise, the mere fact that this conversation about the nature of the just soul should reach its conclusion in a narrative, rather than a summary argument, is surprising. Read closely, as it must be, the "Myth of Er" does not "merely reiterate [the] message [of the arguments of the *Republic*]";[38] rather, it contributes something new by virtue of the style in which its "message" is presented. Here the meaning of the foregoing discussions for the individual is depicted in the idiom par excellence, namely, the proper name. The point is made that justice is never a generality, never "merely" an idea, but always something that makes the difference of a life. In the question of the justice of the soul we are confronted with the question of the destiny that we bear as our own.

The basic elements of the story here are simple, and yet the details that belong to its telling are quite complicated and heavy with references to other texts. It also serves to bring the *Republic* full circle since it unites the end of the *Republic* with its opening. This happens insofar as the story recovers the sort of concerns that Cephalus said haunted him as he thought more about death, namely, how is it that death confronts each of us with a question about the justice of one's soul? There is a very real sense in which this story is Socrates' reply to Cephalus, but the shift from the confusions of that conversation to what can be said now is dramatic. To understand this shift, one need only imagine how the "Myth of Er" would read, how it would sound, if it had been spoken by Socrates immediately upon Cephalus's remark which first raised this question of what awaits the dead. If this story had been told at the outset of the *Republic,* then one might have been tempted to understand it as a sort of theological or religious presentation of an afterlife. But, in light of all that has been said, one knows now that nothing could be farther from the intentions of this passage. As seemingly evident as such an interpretation might be in light of the habits to which we have long since been acclimated, the "Myth of Er" should not be read according to some sort of Christian model of a story of heaven and hell. Dante and Blake might well have had Plato in mind when they wrote of such matters after the arrival of Christian theology, but Plato had different intentions than those animating them, and he had a different poetic conception of those concerns in mind: Homer. As this passage is read it needs to be viewed as an answer to Homer, specifically to the *Odyssey* Books 9–12, where Odysseus tells King Alcinous of his adventures.[39] The text which Plato is obviously reimagining here is the eleventh book of the *Odyssey,* traditionally titled "A Gathering of Shades," in which the story is told of Odysseus's descent "to the cold homes of death . . . to hear Teiresias tell of time to come."[40] It is a text that Plato has already singled out as presenting objectional images which are typical of the misrepresentations to which tragic poetry is prone: the opening of Book 3 of the *Republic* cites, in order to criticize, the words which Achilles speaks to Odysseus. The words which Socrates finds so disturbing there come in reply to Odysseus's remark that Achilles "need not be so pained by death." In reply to that diminution of the force of death, Achilles says that it would be better "to break sod as a farm hand for some poor country man . . . than to lord over all the exhausted dead" (575). But that, according to Socrates, is the sort of remark which breeds an unhealthy relation to death since it arouses our pity and fosters a fear of death. Here, however, in the "Myth of Er," Achilles, who is frequently a target of Socrates' covert criticisms, is conspicuous by his absence from the roster of the dead who appear before Er.

Plato's concerns in the "Myth of Er" certainly extend far beyond some sort of reworking of a portion of the *Odyssey;* nonetheless, contrasting the tone of these two texts helps highlight what one might call the anti-tragic element of Plato's text. One notices most of all that Homer's text is full of poignancy. Odysseus has gone to the realm of the dead to speak with the prophet Teiresias, who retains his wisdom in the afterworld and who, precisely because he is blind, is able to see in the darkness of that world.[41] Odysseus learns that there is a ritual that must be observed for the living and the dead to converse, but if it is followed the dead will speak only the truth. After learning what he must know from Teiresias about the route home and about his own fate, Odysseus comes to speak to the shade of his mother. Having been gone for many years he had not known of her death and so grieves what he now knows of her fate. He says that he longs to embrace her one more time, to "touch with love, and taste salt tears' relief, the twinge of welling tears." But since she is dead that can no longer happen, and so her answer to his heartbroken entreaty is to remind him that the finality of death is "the *dike* of mortal life" (225). In other words, Odysseus learns that the justice (*dike*) that mortals can give one another comes ultimately in the form of mourning. What we witness here is the manner in which death becomes the memento of our apartness and the preserve of that which we can only suffer. Socrates is aware that such a lesson undermines the project of the *Republic* to institute and preserve the law of the common.

Plato is much more elaborate in the presentation of the realm of the dead than Homer is. Er's story begins at "a certain demonic place," and from there he moves to the extreme of the cosmos where strict procedures and a sort of calculus of sufferings and punishments are enforced upon the souls who arrive there. The trip that is recounted here is long, measured in days, and seems to take Er as far as the point from which time itself is meted out according to an intricate series of whorls. Like Odysseus, Er enters the company of the dead while still alive. Unlike Odysseus, he does not make this journey by design, nor as part of some larger journey, and he never quite knows "in what way and how he came into his body" (621b). Er does not engage the dead in conversation, as does Odysseus, but has the role only of a spectator. Odysseus went specifically to speak with the shade of the prophet Teiresias, but there encountered and addressed others whom he had known in life. Er sees many souls about whom he knew stories, but only because of their own fame from the life they led. Such specific comparisons aside, what is most noteworthy about the differences between Homer and Plato in their respective reports about the fate of the dead is the moral tone that each has. The "Myth of Er," the pinnacle of this drama of ideas that are dedicated to illuminating the law of the common, is issued, in part, as a warning. There we witness how the soul we cultivate in life determines the fate of that soul. Most of all we learn something of the fate that a soul suffers when it has failed to nourish itself on the idea of justice belonging to the law of the common. All this is seen by Er as the souls of the dead prepare for a new life and choose such a life on the basis of what was learned from the life now past. This scene, this preparation for the spectacular birth of souls "shooting like stars" (621b), is the final scene of the *Republic*.

It is the scene in which Er watches as lots are cast and each soul is required to choose its future fate. There is an abundance of possible lives displayed so that "even for the one who comes forward last . . . a life of content is available" (619a). Er describes the event of these choices as "worth seeing . . . it was pitiable, laughable, and wonderful" (620a). Several such choices are presented in detail, some the choices of well-known poets and figures of tragedies (Orpheus, Thamyras, Ajax, Agamemnon, Epeius are among those who choose a life to come). The two most significant, and most divergent, are the first and the final choices which we, along with Er, witness. The first choice is given to an unnamed man who did not heed the warning of the dispenser of lots to choose with care, but instead chose imprudently (*aphrosynes*) and with greed. The life that he chose out of such impulses was the life of a tyrant. But he soon discovers that, thanks to such thoughtlessness, not only would such a life not give him the power to serve his desires, but that it included the fate of eating his own children and other horrors. The fate presented here, murdering one's own child, is an image found frequently in myths and tragedies and is perhaps the preeminent image of horror for the Greek literary imagination.[42] Such an act is simultaneously a self-mutilation and a way of consuming one's future even in advance of its own full arrival. Such destruction and ruin, such injustice, is presented in this case by Plato simply as the result of a careless choice by one who "lived in an orderly regime and participated in virtue by habit but without philosophy" (619d). In other words, it is the disaster that befalls one unpracticed in the cultivation of the higher order of the soul that is nourished by philosophy, and thus unable to know how to "flee excesses" (619a).

A series of choices follow this ruinous one. What is most interesting about the choices that follow is that we see the line between the human and the animal crossed here in both directions. Orpheus, Thamyris, Ajax, Agamemnon, Thersites all chose lives of various animals, while Er sees a swan changing to the choice of a human life and other animals, like the nightingale, doing the same thing. Likewise, "from other beasts . . . some went into human lives and into one another—the unjust changing into savage ones, the just into tame ones, and there were all kinds of mixtures" (620d). All manner of crossings and rebellions against fates suffered are evident here. But it is the final choice that is most revealing. It was, says Socrates, simply "by chance [*kata tuche*] that Odysseus's soul had drawn the last lot of all . . . and from memory of its former labors it had recovered from love of honor [*philostimias*]; it went around for a long time looking for the life of a private man who minds his own business [*bion andros idiotou apragmonos*]" (620c).[43] He happily finds such a soul, appropriately lying off by itself, neglected by the others. It is a curious and significant choice: the supreme Homeric hero chooses a reconciled life, a life removed from the turmoil, a life that is measured only against itself. It is a choice made on the basis of what was learned from his life as it was presented by Homer; in other words, here the hero of the Homeric tragedy shows that he has learned, on the basis of a tragic life, not to choose such a life once again. It is, one should also note, a life which the community described in the *Republic* might render difficult since that community, which relentlessly politicizes everything (and so always has the shape of a totalitarian regime), does not leave much room for a life apart from others.[44] It is also, quite obviously, the life that Socrates expressed as his wish for himself at the very outset of the *Republic* when he suggested that he simply wanted to return home after having witnessed the religious celebrations. Of course, the life that Socrates led, the life of a gadfly who could never completely "mind his own business," was itself far removed from such a choice.

*   *   *

At the outset of the *Republic* Cephalus confessed that the thought of death brought with it a heightened concern for the health of his soul and the justice of his life. At the conclusion of the *Republic* Socrates presents us with an uncommon image of the experiences of the dead and how such concerns about the justice of the soul matter for such experiences. In between those twin references to death a host of questions have been taken up, some of which reflect upon the presentations of death found in works of art. Some of the most nagging questions which issue out of those reflections are those that concern the language, rhythms, and images which cultivate and nourish the just soul. While the thematization of those questions is localized in Books 2, 3, and 10, it is important to recognize that the entire *Republic* has, in view of its own style, been a massive and extended performance of the language, images, and rhythms that it wants to cultivate. The dialogue form that we find here is itself a new kind of writing in which the established literary genres, especially those belonging to tragic poetry, are criticized as detrimental to the health of the soul.[45] While the dialogue form here owes a clear debt to the dramatic works that it criticizes, it is also clear that when Plato tries to illuminate his own ethical insights he does so most of all by situating those views against those emerging out of the tradition of tragic poetry.

There are two kinds of objections that Plato expresses to the impact of tragic poetry upon the soul. The first has to do with the image of political life that belongs to such works; the second has to do with the ramifications of such works for the harmony of the soul with itself. The first set of troubles is clearly stated: tragic art fosters a sense of the apartness of people thereby weakening, if not destroying, the sense of the common that is needed for a community to thrive. Whereas the *Republic* presents protracted arguments on behalf of the abolition of separateness, tragic poetry must, simply by virtue of the language, images, and rhythms which define it, present images of death that remind us of our apartness. The second set of objections that Plato raises against such works of art is that they threaten the soul of one who takes them to heart because they appeal to the speechless desires and fears of the soul. Against this Plato argues that the soul is at its best when it is governed by a language that

43

speaks to the so-called higher regions of the soul, since such aspects of the soul are capable of setting the soul at peace with itself and are able to grasp the law of the common that sustains the just community. Taken together these objections to the force of works that grow out of mimetic practices make clear that Plato's chief reason for wanting to subject such works to a sort of censorship is that they are ethically suspect. There is, according to Plato, something like a poetic imperative at work in tragic art. Borne by the language, images, and rhythms that lead us to deem a work a work of art, this imperative is not an option for the poet. It is, according to Plato's analysis of the poetic work, an imperative to present and even celebrate what remains ultimately private and a riddle that we cannot grasp. Furthermore, this imperative, simply by virtue of what it presents, must disturb both what is common between us and what the soul must grasp about itself if it is to be one with itself. In other words, the poetic imperative is at odds with the ethical imperative as Plato understands it. Because it is the extreme form of such an imperative, because it is defined as the art of the crisis that the individual can only suffer, tragic poetry needs to be recognized as exhibiting the most pronounced form of such a poetic imperative. That is why the sweep of Plato's argument against the tragic poets brooks no exceptions: it belongs to the nature of such works to destabilize the principles of community.[46] There is an admiration for the tragic poets evident in Plato's works—his own literary innovations are defined and refined in his struggle with the poets about the language, images, and rhythms of the just soul—but it is, in the end, an admiration that he persistently resists as he would resist a love that was not beneficial (607e). It simply is not good for the health of the soul.

Plato has argued that our ethical sensibility achieves its most perfected form when it is informed by our capacity for ideation. It is a capacity that is most "visible" in the manner in which language (*logoi*) reflects the truth of things (*ton onton ten aletheian*).[47] But, as his discussion of mimetic practices (for instance, in the *Ion*) makes clear, language also has the capacity to unfold not into the ideal but into nothing, bringing in its wake unspeakable desires and fears.[48] This anarchic potential of language troubles Plato.[49] Such is the threat of the work of art. But it should not be overlooked that the magnitude, and even vehemence, of his critique of such works, however, is a sort of homage to the force of such works as they work upon the soul. In the end, they pose a threat to the health of the soul precisely because they are so powerful in it. The critique of the work of art in Plato is not, by any means, to be taken as anything less that a full recognition of the significance of such works in human affairs. But, for Plato, the threat they contain is clear and must itself be contained. It is a threat which receives its most extreme formulation in the work of tragedy where, as one sees so clearly in *Antigone,* the idiom of death, the enigma of our apartness, confronts and undermines the rule of the common. Clearly then, the tragic work, which is the summit of the potentials of the work of art, is not criticized on aesthetic grounds, but strictly on ethical grounds.

The claim that tragic poetry is governed by an imperative that departs from the ethical requirements of the community has something extreme about it.[50] Moreover, it is a revolutionary claim in light of the ethical authority that was held by tragic art in Athens. When Plato's arguments about art are properly understood this revolutionary flavor is preserved. But, in light of the effective history of Plato's arguments, that is, in light of the force with which art has been stripped of its ethical efficacy over two millennia of ethical discourse shaped by an image of philosophy drawn from Plato's texts, such a clear sense of the radical and revolutionary quality of the *Republic* is difficult to retain. In order to preserve that quality it is necessary to recognize that Plato, perhaps more than any other philosopher, united philosophy and a literary genre drawn from poetic practices. By acknowledging the extent to which Plato has moved the language and style of his own texts outside of the orthodox form which philosophy subsequent to Plato adopted and legitimated, one is able to discover in the dialogues a sort of "theater of truth"[51] which has yet to be matched with respect to the challenge it poses to any ethical discourse. As crucial as such an insight is for an understanding of Plato, it was largely a neglected point until Schleiermacher—until, that is, the precise moment that Greece, and especially Greek art, formed itself into such a special question for German philosophy in its efforts to address the crises of the present historical juncture.

From the moment that German philosophizing develops its fascination with Greek thought, it too will exhibit an acute sensitivity to the sort of questions that provided Plato with a creative impulse. Like Plato, Hegel and his successors in this tradition will have an acute sensitivity to the riddle of the relation of death and ethical life. And, like Plato, the question of the mode of presentation—as well as the questions of art, writing, and the limits of philosophy itself—will prove to be of central importance. Plato paid art the tribute of granting that it is a form of thinking to be taken seriously. But, thanks to Plato's conception of justice as governed by the law of the common, of the idea, he found it necessary to argue that art is a dangerous form of thinking when it is seen through the optic of ethical concerns. When the question of art reappears in renewed form—that is, liberated from the ghetto of aesthetic theories themselves governed by a metaphysics that has never taken art seriously—it will return bearing a promise for the renewal of thinking for the task of ethical life, and that promise will be manifest in the very same features of art that Plato held to be so pernicious. Something of the radical and revolutionary force of Plato's analysis of art will be recovered against the tradition of metaphysics that took shape in large measure thanks to Plato.

2 Aristotle

Victims who are too perfect scare people,
because they illuminate an unbearable truth.
—Roberto Calasso,
The Marriage of Cadmus and Harmony, p. 165

A common sensibility hides itself beneath the glare of the differences between the analyses one finds in Plato and in Aristotle regarding the achievements of art. It is a common bond that is obviously hidden quite well: Aristotle's rather congenial relation to poetic practices, and his clear admiration for the achievements of tragedy, seems to contrast sharply with Plato's more pronounced animosity. A list of obvious differences between them is easy to compile: for instance, while Plato finds pity to be the signal of a corrupted and debilitated soul, Aristotle argues that it is precisely in the production of the experience of pity that tragic poetry performs its highest contribution to ethical life. While both take *mimesis* to be the key to understanding poetic practices and works, they define the most concentrated expressions of *mimesis* according to quite different examples: Plato directs his remarks about mimetic practices mostly to Homer and to what Aristotle will define as "epic," whereas Aristotle mostly focuses upon Sophocles and the theatrical performance of tragedies.[1] Even the literary shape of their respective treatments of art seems evidence of a divergence: in Plato we find a dialogical performance of the question of art which culminates in a sort of philosophical poetry that imagines a time in which the enigma of fate is revealed; in Aristotle we have frequently sketchy and rather terse lecture notes that often read like a handbook for either a playwright or an art critic. Nothing sings in Aristotle's praise for the capacity of poetry to sing, whereas Plato's suspicions of poetry are couched in a form and language that is itself distinctively poetic. But beneath all these contrasts what unites Plato and Aristotle is the intractable need which drives each to take up the question of the relation of thinking and poetizing. Nothing more clearly manifests the common bond between Plato and Aristotle, and nothing more defines "Greece" for the Germans who seek to recover its philosophical experience, than this *necessity* to take up the question of poetic practice. Art, and its most concentrated achievements, not only had an established authority in the culture of the time, but was acknowledged by both Plato and Aristotle—even if only by the tribute of a powerful critique—as one of the elemental forms in which we make sense of our world and our shared life in time. Other differences aside, both Plato and Aristotle consider the ability to poetize illustrative of something distinctively human and a native impulse, and consequently not as an option for reflection.[2]

In holding this view they set themselves apart from the tendencies of the tradition that is their combined legacy, and thereby they define something distinctively "Greek." Not until Kant's turn to aesthetic experience as the third of three irreducible domains of experience will the relation between thinking and poetic practice be accorded such a fundamental place in philosophic reflection again. There is a double import—retrodictive upon the texts of Plato and Aristotle—in the way Kant recovers the experience of art from the ghetto to which it had been assigned by the tradition of metaphysics. First, he does so as part of a critique of metaphysics; in other words, the rehabilitation of the experience of the work of art goes hand and glove with the demarcation of the limits of conceptual reason, the limits, namely, of the tradition of philosophizing that Plato and Aristotle inaugurate. Second, his analysis of the relation of thinking and poetic experience is contextualized in the larger problematic of judgment, specifically ethical judgment. This second point will prove to be especially decisive for Hegel and all those who eventually take up the question of Greek art. The reason is clear: both Plato and Aristotle demonstrated that the task of thinking this experience could not be understood except as a task that belonged to the ethical life of human beings, but for each of them this fundamental truth of the experience of the work of art had a certain self-evidence about it, and so it was never quite thematized as such. Without reference to either Plato or Aristotle, Kant's great service to each of them is to render visible the ethical import of the experience of art, and to do so with such force that those, like Hegel, who follow him cannot take up the question of art in Greece except as a question of ethical life.

Here, then, is the subtle, but significant, common ground of the otherwise divergent presentations of poetic practices in Plato and Aristotle: for each, something specifically human and something about the possibility of the ethical life of such beings is in play and at risk in such practices. The common ground they share is the simple fact of having taken as a serious matter for reflection a set of questions that is seldom acknowledged as such by their successors. Even if they judge its value differently, they share a sense of the force of art—of style, performance, writing, images, rhythm—in human affairs. Neither regards art as a specialized topic, neither relegates it to what today goes under the heading of aesthetics. Both regard the question of the experience of both making and witnessing works of art as an ineluctable question for the most basic concerns of philosophy. Every difference between them regarding their respective estimations of art must be understood as emerging out of that common ground.[3]

* * *

The *Poetics* presents itself as a specialized text inquiring into the specific character of poetic practice; more precisely, since the word is taken to be the highest form in which such practice is set to work, it presents itself as an inquiry into the nature of literary practices and genres.[4] Despite its self-presentation, in the end, it will be clear that the *Poetics* needs to be read in the context of other Aristotelian texts—most notably the *Physics, Ethics,* and *Politics*—and when it is thus situated it quickly becomes clear that the *Poetics* poses questions that reach far beyond the resources which it uncovers. The connection of the *Poetics* with the *Ethics* and *Politics* is most evident in the concern of each text with the various dimensions of human praxis. The link to the *Physics,* where *physis* is presented as the perfected form of *mimesis,*[5] is less evident but no less significant. Aristotle, like Kant and Heidegger, regards the question of art as inextricably wedded to the enigma of *physis,* and in holding to this view Aristotle is perhaps most remote from his teacher Plato. When one reads Aristotle it is important that one take seriously the remarks which suggest that our impulse toward mimetic praxis is "according to nature" (*kata physin*) (1448b7) and that the language, the proper diction (*lexeous*), of tragedy, namely, the iambic meter, is "from nature itself" (*auto he physis*) (1449a18). From the outset it is clear: for Aristotle the urge to make poetry needs to be understood as a "natural" impulse: "Speaking generally, poetry seems to owe its origin to two particular causes, both natural" (1448b2). The naturalness of the impulse to make works of art is such that Aristotle suggests that poetry is produced "out of improvisations" (1448b8). The word he uses here, *auto-schediasymaton*—"off-handed" or "impromptu"—carries with it a sense of the casualness and ease, the naturalness, with which we make art. Poetry, then, needs to be understood simply as the most refined and reflected form of that impulse. It is the natural result of human nature. In the end, the riddle of mimetic practices belongs to the even larger enigma of nature itself and to the question of how we ourselves are of nature.

Nonetheless, his introduction into the investigation of our love of making art is much more narrowly focused: art is to be thought initially according to the guidelines opened by *mimesis* itself. Aristotle makes it clear that a work is a work of art first of all by virtue of its mimetic element. Criticizing those who would define a work by virtue of its meter alone, Aristotle points out that "Homer and Empedocles have nothing in common except the meter, so it is proper to call one a poet and the other not a poet but a scientist" (1448a11). One is not a poet simply because one plays with the metric possibilities of language. In other words, the musical element of language alone cannot convert an experience into a work of art; some element other than meter provides the passage to the poem. Aristotle is blunt here: the distinctive element of the work of art lies in its mimetic potential, and so it is this potential which forms the axis of Aristotle's interpretation of art in general. If we are to understand the work of art and its fascination for us, then we must understand the secret of *mimesis* itself, but in order to do that we need to know something about our own nature since, as Aristotle introduces it, *mimesis* is to be understood with reference to human instincts and pleasures. We need to know that "from childhood human beings have an instinct [*symphuton*] for representations [*memeisthai*], and in this respect they differ from other animals in . . . learning first lessons by representing things" (1448b2).[6] We must also know that *mimesis* is something "pleasurable" (*to chairein*) for us (1448b3). The pleasure and the education imparted by mimetic works collaborate with one another, and understanding their special symbiosis is the first stage in understanding the nature of art.

In order to understand Aristotle's conception of this natural delight we take in *mimesis* it is helpful to refine its sense by contrasting it with the way in which Plato links the notion of *mimesis* with desire. Plato argued that desire characterized the operations of a "lower" region of the soul and consequently that the cultivation of desires which one finds in mimetic works is never able to educate the soul to its full capacity. Furthermore, he argued that such desires leave one vulnerable to the foibles of the world; in our emotions we are invaded by the world, and thus vulnerable to its variability, we lose our independence, we even lose our reason. This is especially evident in children, in whom the rational powers of the soul are not fully developed, and who are consequently most vulnerable to the force of desire. On the other hand, the rational part of the soul is reliant upon nothing but itself, and this rational power of the soul, which is independent, opens avenues for thinking how it is that we belong together. The economy of the soul is a closed one, and so the pleasures of desire are cultivated at the expense of the well-being of reason; consequently, the more desires are cultivated the less we are able to be free. In short, for Plato, the undeniable pleasure that one can find in mimetic works hinders, if not outright damages, the human capacity to answer ethical questions. Aristotle's sense of our delight in mimetic works is quite different. Although the child who plays and toys with imitative life seems to take a natural delight in *mimesis,* that is not a signal that such delight is a lower form of the soul. Quite the contrary, such delight in "imitation" is native to human nature, and so it needs to be understood as the delight we take in the free expression of our own nature. The play space of imitation is a realm in which possibilities are explored (just as a child might play at being a doctor or a philosopher), and it is a realm in which our instinct to enlarge our world is unfolded. Later (1451a36), Aristotle argues that this kinship of mimetic works to possibility is what distinguishes such works from history (where a story is also told). It also accounts for the bond (and so strains) between art and philosophy: both refer themselves to generalities that escape the confines of the particularities that have happened. Art is thus not simply the expression of feelings, but is rather an exploration of what can be otherwise. Far from disfiguring or weakening the soul, mimetic practices for Aristotle number among the most basic forms in which human nature exercises itself and grows beyond the orbit of the given.

Aristotle is aware that pleasure is elemental and so has no "reason" which can be inspected according to a certain form of analysis. But there is a dynamic in pleasure, and he is especially intent upon unpacking that dynamic in order to understand better just where the delight that we take in imitations might lead us. To that end Aristotle notes that this delight is so strong that it is capable of transforming the character of our experience: "We enjoy looking at likenesses of things which are themselves painful to see, obscene beasts, for instance, and corpses" (1448b3). Kant too will call attention to this power of art to convert experiences into something that holds and attracts us—even those experiences that might otherwise repel us. But, unlike Aristotle, Kant sets limits on this power of art to illuminate experience anew: art, he says, cannot render beautiful what would otherwise disgust us. When Kant unpacks the pleasure we take in this transformation effected by the work of art he does so by arguing that it is a pleasure rooted in a sense of the common. It is, he argues, the pleasure we take in being alerted to that to which we belong but do not define alone. It is, for Kant, the pleasure of belonging, a pleasure which we cannot conceive but can only know symbolically. Aristotle has a different account of the roots of this pleasure, but, insofar as it eventually leads to the pleasure we find in metaphor and riddles, it bears significant affinities with Kant's account.

The specific character of this pleasure is described by Aristotle rather abruptly when he says simply that "the reason we enjoy seeing likenesses is that, as we look, we learn and infer what each is, for instance, 'that is so and so'"(1448b5–6). The point is clear but not terribly illuminating: we find pleasure in such works because they instruct us. What is not said here is precisely how we are instructed by such works. The "logic" of this instruction, at least insofar as it happens in words, will not be explained until Aristotle takes up the nature of "resemblances" in words—that is, metaphor and riddle—and seeks to show just how it is that these move the mind beyond the given. There we learn more clearly that the mimetic operation involves an otherwise impossible collaboration of sameness and difference. Aristotle is aware that a perfect imitation is a contradiction that would destroy itself, since it would cease being an imitation by being perfect, and that every "imitation" is a repetition which involves the recognition of samenesses in differences. This means that there is an ambiguity in the law of resemblances operative in *mimesis*. Aristotle, like Heraclitus, knows that resemblances are never simple matters, and that as such, genuine *mimesis,* the play of resemblances, is by its very nature inventive.

The specific nature of the ambiguity that inhabits the likeness, the resemblance, characterizing mimetic works needs a more precise determination. Aristotle will not help much to fill this need at this stage of the *Poetics,* although later, in the treatment of riddle, pun, and metaphor, we do find some further clues about how the projection of sameness upon difference active in mimetic works is to be thought. But there are other texts in which we find a fascinating and revealing structure parallel to that found in *mimesis,* namely, in some of Aristotle's remarks about friends. Aristotle defines the relationship of friends as a sort of resemblance, and one can clearly see that it is, like *mimesis,* a sort of re-presentation which is disclosive. One see this clearly in a passage from the *Magna Moralia:*

> Now supposing a person looks upon his friend and marks what he is and what is his character and quality; the friend—if we figure a friend of the most intimate sort—will seem to him to be a kind of second self, as in the common saying "This is my second Hercules." Now to know oneself is a very difficult thing—as even philosophers have told us—and a very pleasant thing. . . . Direct contemplation of ourselves is moreover impossible. . . . And so just as when wishing to behold our own faces we have seen them by looking upon a mirror, whenever we wish to know our own characters and personalities, we can recognize them by looking upon a friend; since the friend is, as we say, our second self. (1213a12–23)[7]

Again, we are referred to a resembling, a repetition. This time it is not actors who are mirroring something about life, but it is the soul that is being reflected for itself. What we are told is that a more revealing likeness of the soul than the likeness of one's image in a mirror is the likeness found in the eyes of the friend. In the repetition, the re-presentation, of

51

myself in the eyes of those I love I find the clearest insight into the nature of my own soul. We can recognize the structure of representation working in *mimesis* in this structure of the event of revelation communicated in the eyes of the friend. Something is exposed which can be exposed only in a representation which is not a simple copy.

Mimetic re-presentation thus escapes the logic of identity governing the operations of reflection. It is more like the self-discovery one finds in the eyes of a friend than it is like the self-identification one achieves by looking in a mirror. In mimetic re-presentation the resemblance, the "imitation," which is produced is simultaneously the communication of differences. As such, the knowledge it imparts is what one might call stereoscopic: in it the mind holds together two notions which otherwise could not be brought together. In its best forms, for example, in metaphor, riddle and witticism—ultimately in tragic poetry—this stereoscopic mimetic operation enables something to be recognized which is otherwise impossible; it enables the mind to combine what is otherwise simply distinct. The logic of the concept prohibits us from holding certain thoughts together such as the position of a thing and its velocity, or, as Hegel will repeatedly remind us, the thought of the beginning. But in metaphor, which Aristotle will argue belongs naturally to mimetic works, we break the bonds of the logic of identities governing ordinary reflection and stereoscopically hold otherwise impossible combinations together as when we say, with Sappho, that *eros* is "sweetbitter" (*glukupikron*).[8] As Empedocles, cited by Aristotle, will say, "From the two comes one seeing" (*mia ginetai amphorteron ops*) (1458a19). The most developed forms of *mimesis* thus enable the mind to recognize something and to surpass it at the same time: "And the soul seems to say—'how true, but I missed it.'"[9] This liberation, this creative stereoscopy, that belongs to *mimesis* is the delight specific to the learning that belongs to the human instinct for mimetic practices. This pleasure cannot give an account of itself as a pleasure, but we can say that it is the pleasure that belongs to synthesis, the pleasure simply of knowing. Furthermore, as will be seen, once this pleasure achieves its fullest formulation in tragic poetry we learn that it is instructive for ethical life and one of the ways we affirm the risks of such a life.

But it needs to be noted that while the mimetic dimension of the art work is privileged in the explanation of tragic poetry, especially insofar as it accounts for the delight we take in art, *mimesis* is not the only human instinct that lies at the roots of poetic practices. Harmony and rhythm—instincts that belong to what Plato analyzed as music (instincts as well that are temporal and mathematizable)—also number among the instincts that gradually develop into poetry. So it is that Aristotle traces the varieties of poetic forms (tragedy, comedy, epic) according to the various permutations by which these instincts work and develop together. Saying that such art forms evolve out of the improvisations of our natures means, of course, that these forms are, in some manner, exteriorizations of human nature as such. It is to say, with Hölderlin, that "man is born for art"[10] or, with Schelling, that there is a *Bildungstrieb,* an impulse to art, which belongs to our nature. That does not mean that art is a form of "self-expression" in the rather private and trivial sense of that phrase as it is spoken today where it refers to a sort of self-display. Rather, saying that art emerges from our instincts means that it is the presentation—Kant will call it the "free play"—of our very nature. By giving an account of poetic practice that grounds such practices in our natures, Aristotle provides an explanation for the power of art in human life. It is not, as with Plato, a power we need to master because it might otherwise disrupt the harmony of the soul with itself; rather, it is a power to be cultivated because it is revelatory in a unique manner.

*   *   *

Suggesting that epic poetry and comedy will be dealt with later, Aristotle turns his attentions specifically to tragic poetry. The promised analysis of epic will form the concluding section of the *Poetics;* the section on comedy, like Aristotle's three-book dialogue entitled *On Poets,* is lost among the casualties of history. When the treatment of comedy was lost for posterity, the significance of the analysis of tragedy was shifted since it lost an essential counterpoint, not a mere pendant. One can only wonder what might have been said about comedy in light of what is said of tragedy; one wonders what must be said of comedy would mean for what might be said of tragedy.[11]

Finally, then, Aristotle wagers a definition of tragedy. As Aristotle himself notes much of what is said here has been prepared for by the earlier discussion, but there is unquestionably a new key to interpreting tragic poetry introduced here in the form of the notion of *katharsis.* It is a notion that is introduced after a slight preparation. Aristotle begins by saying that "tragedy is a *mimesis* of an action [*praxis*] that is heroic and complete and of a certain magnitude—by means of language enriched with all kinds of ornament [*hedysmnoi logoi*]" (1449b24–25). Here, even before the new elements to be introduced are mentioned, Aristotle refines, and thereby advances, his earlier discussion of *mimesis.* Now it is made clear that tragedy is the *mimesis* of a *praxis* as such; it is not the *mimesis* of the people engaged in actions. The qualification is significant. Since Aristotle holds that all praxis is purposive, this means that tragedy is a reflection or repetition, a *mimesis,* of the aims of human life, not of individual human beings. What is at issue is not the character or the psychological complexes of those who are acting; rather, what is crucial, what makes tragedy ethically instructive and gives us delight to see, is the illumination into the nature and possibilities of *praxis,* of purposive action. Aristotle will reinforce this claim later, saying that "while character makes people what they are, it is their actions and experiences that make them happy or the opposite. . . . [Y]ou could not have a tragedy without action, but you can have one without character-study" (1450a12–15).[12] In tragedy we see into the nature of human *praxis* and into the ends of such actions; ultimately, we see into the possibilities of happiness (*eudaimonia*), and there we find the insight of the *Nicomachean Ethics* confirmed by tragic poetry: "Happiness is not a thing that we possess all the time, like a piece of property" (1169b33).[13] Tragedy, then, is the representation of action in such a way that we win a glimpse into the possibilities of action as such. More precisely, it is an insight that is directed by "embellished language" and that is imparted by pity, fear, and the *katharsis* which these emotions are able to effect. The comments on language here seem to be made as if in passing. The more sustained analysis of the language of tragedy comes later. But the reference to *katharsis,* which is the only use of the word in the *Poetics,* marks one of the most original contributions of Aristotle's presentation of tragedy.[14]

By and large, Aristotle regards the "embellishments" of language as an extraneous matter. The word he uses here, *hedysmnoi,* refers to something added to food to give it a heightened flavor. It is the same word that Plato uses as a sign of his contempt for poetry in the *Republic* (607a).[15] Aristotle seems to be saying simply that the language of tragedy, like a spice, is best when it heightens the effect of the *mimesis* of a *praxis*—here *katharsis*—but that embellished language alone not does accomplish that effect. To amplify this point Aristotle remarks that the language of tragedy is not narrative, but rather dialogue, since dialogue is the supreme form of language in action. Narrative will be reserved for epic where the compression of action is not an issue, since epic can be presented over long periods of time. Here, though, the point is that the language of the tragedy is in the service of the *mimesis* of a *praxis* that, by means of an alchemy of pity and fear, solicits a *katharsis.*

When Aristotle introduces his definition of tragedy here he says that it has been prepared for by the foregoing discussions. But there is one apparent exception to this claim: the notion of *katharsis* seems to have no antecedents to its appearance here. *Katharsis* is a medical word and typically is interpreted according to the ideal of a purgation; in other words, it effects a moral purge of the soul; in it the emotions which are toxic for the healthy ethical life of the soul are removed. It is also able to be understood in the less specialized, but still related, sense of a "clarification" of the soul.[16] Much as tears remove toxins from the body when one cries, the experience of the *katharsis* in tragedy leaves one feeling cleansed. The idea of *katharsis* here clearly signals a sort of return or restoration of a balance in the soul. It is a clarified state; just as sometimes the air is un-

commonly clear after a storm, so too does the soul achieve a sort of clarification after fear and pity have moved through it.

Aristotle will unpack this claim when he says that "two of the most
important elements in the emotional effect of tragedy [are] 'reversals'
[*peripeteiai*] and 'discoveries' [*anagnorisis*]" (1450a18). But before the relation of those elements to *katharsis* is taken up it is first necessary to be
clear about an assumption underpinning Aristotle's conception of fear
and pity, namely, that they are indicative of a solidarity, not, as in Plato, of
a weakness. We feel such emotions for those whom we resemble, those in
whom we see ourselves. There is a healthy fellow feeling, a mimetic identification, that lies at the basis of *katharsis*. The reason for this is clear: if I
do not identify with those who arouse my fear and pity, *katharsis* is not possible.[17] The effect of the *mimesis* of a *praxis* itself rests on a *mimesis* that operates between the witness and the tragic drama. The identification and
difference which operates in the tragedy is also operative between the
audience and the performance of the tragedy. In other words, *katharsis*
itself rests upon a sort of mimetic identification that involves those it effects in the *praxis* itself. By virtue of this mimetic identification, *katharsis*
belongs to the witness as well as to those who suffer a *praxis*. It is a form of
praxis suffered but diluted greatly. Much like the homeopathic conception of medicine, such a diluted form of suffering should, according to
Aristotle, have a very significant effect. It is an emotional event in which a
knowledge about the aims of life is imparted through a double mimetic
act: it is the *mimesis* of an action with which the witness mimetically identifies. In it a certain clarity, an insight, is obtained about the aims of life.
One learns to see without, like Oedipus, needing to go blind. The supreme kathartic moment comes when one sees oneself in the empty sockets where once Oedipus had eyes. When that void becomes the mirror
wherein one sees one's own soul reflected, one experiences what Aristotle
calls *katharsis*.

Such an experience is difficult to bring about, and so from this point
forward Aristotle is interested in asking how one can achieve it in the
drama. Aristotle, who was an avid theater-goer, thus tries to sort out the
components of the successful tragedy before he asks about the specific
knowledge of this kathartic experience, namely, the knowledge of our
"error" (*hamartia*). The remarks about the six components of a successful
tragedy (1450a9) both build and expand upon the definition of tragedy
up to this point. Collectively these components reaffirm the centrality of
praxis in tragedy. Aristotle even warns against letting any of these elements
overwhelm the representation of *praxis* in the drama. So, for instance, he
expresses the concern that the visual component of the play, the spectacle
(*opsis*) of its staging, should not "kidnap the soul" (*psychagogikon*) by being
too dazzling (1450a18). In other words, the playwright should not turn to

gimmicks in order to startle the audience: if, for example, the staging of *Oedipus Rex* overly exploits the sight of his appearance on stage with bloody eye sockets, if there the visual effect overwhelms the emotional effect, then the drama has failed.[18]

But the most important of the components of the tragedy is, according to Aristotle, its "plot" (*mythos*) (1450a12), which he describes as "the synthesis of events" (*synthesis ton pragmaton*) (1450a12). The sense of Aristotle's use of this notion needs some clarification. Aristotle, unlike Plato, is not interested in the adaptation of traditional legends for tragic poetry. He knows that tragic poets typically dramatized traditional stories (1451b8), but he also suggests that tragic poetry need not be bound to such stories since poetry, like philosophy, belongs to the realm of the possible, to general truths, and not, like history, to particular events. The work of the tragic poet is not to tell the story of an individual, but to compose the course of events in such a way that we might all recognize ourselves in the way such a plot illuminates human *praxis* as such. For Plato, on the other hand, the poet fiddles with a sort of cultural icon or memory in taking up its legend (*mythoi*); for Aristotle, the appropriation of such legends is merely to lend a sort of added dimension of force to the whole drama. But, for Aristotle, a tragedy can quite well have both plots and characters that are completely invented "as is shown in Agathon's *Antheus*" (1451b8). So the discussion of plot in Aristotle does not refer to content of the stories which might provide a sort of fund from which tragic poets draw; rather, it refers simply to the ordering of the events as the drama unfolds them.

As Aristotle elaborates upon the nature of the successful plot he remarks that what is most crucial is that it have both "reversals" and "discoveries" (1450a18). In a moment he will add it has a third part, perhaps the most fatal element, the root of what we fear and pity, namely, suffering (*pathos*) (1452b9). But in order for the specific character of the suffering that belongs to tragedy to be fully appreciated, the dynamics of the plot that pivot around "reversals" and "discoveries" need to be made more precise. In the reversal and discovery that animate the plot the sufferings of the tragic figure are compressed and sharpened; by means of them suffering is not protracted but is compacted and thereby powerfully delineated. What is most important, and yet most difficult, is the need to understand how it is that in these elements of the plot the ambiguity that inhabits the law of resemblances at the heart of mimetic practices, the stereoscopic riddle that drives the tragic drama, finds its manifestation. Just as this ambiguity in the law of resemblance belonging to mimetic practices rendered metaphor the preeminent form of language for the tragic poem (thus, according to Aristotle, we find a natural impulse to metaphor in poetic language), so too does this ambiguity find expression in the reversals and discoveries which propel the plot of the tragic poem.

The definitions of these elements are unproblematic: "A 'reversal' is a change [*metabole*] in what is being practiced [*ton pragmattomenon*] into its opposite" (1452a22). Furthermore, it is a change that is probable or even necessary; that is, it belongs naturally to the evolution of events. Part of the surprise that belongs to this reversal is precisely that it is so unsurprising from another point of view: "A 'discovery' . . . is a change [*metabole*] from ignorance to knowledge" (1452a31). The key to the plot, then, is found in these two transformations in the situation of *praxis,* both changes being metabolic, that is, sudden. In them the tragic vision of human life is first performed: they disclose a situation that is rent by contradictions and ambiguities that easily—and without warning—convert into their opposite. They thus expose the fragility, the vulnerability, of human affairs. Aristotle indicates that while such changes can operate independently, they are most effective, most potent in their capacity to solicit fear and pity, when they happen simultaneously as they do in *Oedipus Rex:* the instant in which Oedipus learns the truth he sought is the same instant that his happiness is gone forever. Everything changes in a flash; there is no reversal that subsequently takes time to unfold its meaning. What is most important is to see that a reversal of fortune such as Oedipus's—from savior to pariah—is not merely a trick that the dramatist introduces to win our attentions; rather, it must be understood as reflecting the divided possibilities which human beings confront in acting. Likewise, the recognition of this reversal, the discovery that what one believed to be true has turned out to be otherwise, is not a comment upon the stupidity of those involved, but upon the opacity which belongs to human life generally. In reversal and recognition, in these elements of plot, the tragic poem imparts a sense of the conflict and the opacity belonging to human *praxis* as such. In this way tragedies illuminate the ultimates, the extreme possibilities, of human life. More precisely, what is illuminated is how hidden such possibilities remain from us for the most part. Not by accident does Oedipus first encounter his fate at a crossroads where he proves that he is blind to the choices that he makes.

What is crucial, then, is to see that here the poetic work is not about characters, but about the possibilities that inhabit the very nature of human *praxis.* The kathartic effect is indexed not to the characters and our feelings about them, but to the action and the reflection of the possibilities of human life that such action offers us. Thus Aristotle argues that the work of art is, like philosophy, indexed to the realm of possibility: "A poet's object is not to tell what actually happened but what could and would happen. . . . The difference between a historian and a poet is not that one writes in prose and the other in verse—indeed the writings of Herodotus could be put into verse and yet would still be a kind of history. . . . The real difference is that one tells what happened and the other what might happen. For this reason poetry is something more philosophic and of graver import than history, since its statements are of the nature of universals, whereas those of history are singulars" (1451b2–4). The relation of history to *praxis* is different than that found in poetry, where the elements of plot illuminate its hidden possibilities, as possibilities to which we, the audience, belong as well. What is more problematic, but not addressed by Aristotle at this point, is the question of the respective relations of poetry and philosophy—the relation that is of suffered knowledge presented mimetically to reasoned knowledge presented conceptually.

At this point Aristotle's concern is rather to complete his analysis of plot by introducing its third, and final, constituent—suffering (*pathos*). But before he does that we find a passing, and puzzling, reference to beauty (*kalon*)—a word that, for Aristotle, refers to something that is good to look at. Speaking of the well-constructed plot he remarks that "in everything that is beautiful . . . [its] parts must not only exhibit a certain order in its arrangement of parts, but also be of a definite magnitude" (1450b36).[19] The reference to beauty is surprising: one might have expected that a text on poetics, on the achievement of art in human life, would have made the beauty of art a central concern. But here we find a remark made almost en passant and not in order to introduce the topic of beauty, but in order to clarify the orderliness of the plot. The marginal role that beauty plays in the question put to us by art serves only to reinforce the point that Aristotle made at the outset of the *Poetics:* mimetic practices are, at bottom, an exploration of the possibilities of *praxis,* and the pleasure that accompanies the experience of such works is best explained as an example of the delight we take in all learning and self-disclosure.

When Aristotle finally introduces the third element of tragic art—namely, suffering, misery, calamity—he does so abruptly, without a clear preparation and without much by way of subsequent discussion. All that is said—but, of course, this brief passage says a great deal here—is that "suffering is a *praxis* of a destructive or painful nature, such as the presentation of death, torture, woundings and the like" (1452b12). After noting that the other two elements of plot have been explained, he drops the topic of plot and the question of how to conceive this suffering. Or so it seems.

The question posed by the operations of *pathos* is one of the central questions of the *Poetics*. It is however not immediately clear how we are to think this third element of the plot in light of the brief remarks Aristotle makes about it. In the end, the full sense of the *pathos* of tragic art, and of the knowledge that it communicates, becomes clear only after we have understood why it is that death is preeminent among the ways in which *pathos* is experienced. Here the discussion refers both backward—to the sudden change that characterized the other two elements of plot—and forward—to the "error" belonging to the human condition.

From the reversals and discoveries in the plot of the tragic poem we learn something about the mutability of human *praxis*. We learn that things may well, without warning, convert into their opposite. We learn that what was once divine might, in a flash, become monstrous. We learn, as Oedipus does, that at any moment we might approach a crossroads and meet another who could become for us either a god or a monster (or, as in the case of Oedipus, both: his father, who in belonging to his own creation is a god, becomes, unwittingly, a monster). In these elements of plot, then, one learns that one is ultimately "enigmatic, without consistency . . . with no defined essence, [one realizes that one] oscillates between being the equal of the gods and the equal of nothing at all."[20] What becomes visible here is the expanse of the human condition—the possibilities belonging to *praxis*—an expanse so great that it is capable, at any given moment, of converting its situation into its other. In the end, all life belongs to the possibility of this conversion insofar as life, at any given moment, is convertible into death. This inevitable conversion of the whole of life which every life suffers is the reason that death plays a preeminent role in the conception of tragedy.[21] What is opened up in the exposure of this change is a space of strangeness, a space that is abyssal. It is enough, as Plato repeatedly reminds us, to drive one mad. *Mania* is one of the real possibilities of how reversals and discoveries are experienced: "Quem deus vult perdere, demantant prius."[22] When Aristotle refers to the *pathos,* the suffered experience, of tragic art he calls attention to a knowledge that we cannot resolve, but can only endure. It is the knowledge that *praxis* is riddled with ambiguities and contradictions that are opaque, and yet motile and so powerfully disruptive. It is also the knowledge that one cannot lift oneself out of this torn condition. Tragic *pathos* is the signal of the "gap between our goodness and our good living, between what we are . . . and how humanly well we manage to live."[23] It is a reminder that being of good character is not sufficient for human happiness, which depends in part upon good fortune (*tuche*).

When Aristotle discusses the possible trajectories of such disruptions, when he examines the representation of such upheavals in tragic art, he asks which sort of change of fortune best arouses our pity and fear. Is it the change from good to bad fortune, from bad to good; is it the change in the situation of a cruel person or a good person? In response to his own question he introduces the notion of *hamartia:* we feel "pity for undeserved misfortune [and] fear for the person like ourselves" (1453a4). This is made more precise when he says, "This is the sort of person who is not preeminently virtuous and just, and yet it is through no badness or villainy of his own that he falls into misfortune, but rather through some error of judgment [*hamartia*]" (1453a9). The reversal of fortune that is most pitiable and fearful, and which we do well to understand as the greatest form of suffering, is one that is owing to *hamartia,* to some sort of mistake in *praxis* that is intelligible—that is not, in other words, simply sheer "bad luck"—and yet that is not simply a matter of bad character.[24] Aristotle makes this explicit: "It must not be due to villainy but to some great error [*hamartian megalen*] in such a person as we have described" (1453a15). Fear and pity are not the response summoned for the villain who suffers; they are rather reserved for those who call suffering upon themselves through an act of ignorance, an act of bad judgment, that is not to be explained by reference to the malice or ill will traceable to a bad character.

Something unwelcome, dangerous, and disruptive makes its appearance in the possibility described by the notion of *hamartia*. In the literature of suffering, in tragic poetry, *hamartia* functions as the word that best explains why people suffer. We experience the *katharsis* when a light is shined upon the operations of *hamartia,* and we learn something about how we need to understand beings capable of such profound suffering. A chronic possibility of human life and an "error" which even a person of good *hexis,* of good *ethos,* can suffer, *hamartia* names the axis along which tragic reversals are formed. Since we live and act in a world that is larger than our knowledge of the world, we are persistently confronted with questions that are matters of judgment rather than clear knowledge. As finite beings we are, as Socrates never ceases to remind us, defined by our relation to our ignorance. Acting in the dark we are thus exposed to reversals of fate since the orders in which we live and act are clearly far larger and more powerful than the human capacity to know them. Plato is clearly trying to harness such orders and to steel the soul against desires which might admit powers into soul which the soul can neither know nor master (powers such as *eros*); Aristotle, on the other hand, is willing to grant that human life is risky and that the elements of the plot of tragic poetry—reversal, discovery, and suffering—cooperate to call attention to this risk insofar as it is a matter of *hamartia,* of errancy. The differing assessments that Plato and Aristotle accord to tragedy for human understanding are thus traceable to the differences in their respective conceptions of human life. In both the *Politics* and *Ethics* Aristotle affirms the importance of the risk that belongs to human life, the risk that is a matter of judgment but never control: the risk of loving another or of having a friend. There he argues that, besides being a futile gesture—one can never, in the end, close off the world which possesses the power of invading a life, no matter how well armored, at any moment—the desire to eradicate such risks would be the desire to erase what enriches life. It would be the desire for a life closed to human goods which are greater than those which one defines alone. It would be the desire for an arid life. But it is also the desire for a life without the possibility of suffering.

But insofar as we, like Aristotle, affirm the risks of finite human *praxis,* insofar as we acknowledge that the reach of human knowledge and the realm of human affairs are not commensurate, then we open ourselves to the sort of suffering disclosed by tragic art. The incommensurability between the spheres of knowing and acting that tragic art illuminates is the space in which *hamartia,* errancy, is possible. It is this abyssal space, this impossible gap we must continually traverse, that we see mirrored in, for example, the vacant eyes of Oedipus. According to Aristotle, the healthy response to it is to know how deeply it must be suffered to be understood and to have the twin feelings of fear—for ourselves—and pity—for others—as we experience its mimetic contagion. The high esteem in which Aristotle holds tragic art emerges out of his fundamental agreement with the view of human life it presents. It is a view of life that cultivates a deep sensibility to the enigma of finite life and to the proximity of monstrosity and divinity, of suffering and happiness, in such a life. Such a sensibility is profoundly ethical in nature: it is a sense of life, of its strangeness and largeness, born out of the solidarity belonging to fear and pity. But, more so, it is a view of life and of oneself that emerges out of the law of resemblances in which we see ourselves mirrored in the eyes of the other.

*   *   *

With the presentation of the notion of the errancy exposed by the *mimesis* of *praxis,* the analysis of the plot, the composition, of the work of art is completed. But, according to Aristotle, there are five additional elements that belong to such works, and so the *Poetics* continues with an analysis of these as they function in the tragedy before turning to the concluding remarks about epic art. Of those five other elements, two (spectacle and song) have been dismissed as largely marginal, possibly even distracting; they are matters of concern more to the theatrical production of the work than to the insights proper to tragedy. A third element (character) has been limited in its importance for our understanding of tragedy, so it is simply that "most important is that the character [*ethos*] be good" (1454a22). The remaining two elements (diction and thought) dominate the second half of the *Poetics.* The reason for this dominance is clear, even though Aristotle himself never makes it explicit: both of these elements concern language, and the effort here is to demonstrate how it is that language itself, the medium of human *praxis,* is destined to the presentation of action as tragic. In other words, the attempt is to illuminate the tragic possibilities borne by language itself. This demonstration of the kinship between language and tragedy runs even into the capillaries of language, even into the alphabet.[25] Here the stereoscopy of the law of resemblances governing mimetic practices is made clearer.

Aristotle's concern here is chiefly with the question of diction or style (*lexis*), since thought (*dianoia*), which he defines as "all the effects produced by words" (1456a34), is more proper to the inquiry of the *Rhetoric.*

One notices immediately that Aristotle's approach to the question of style is conspicuously different from that found in the *Republic,* where Plato both mimetically performs the question in his own distinctive philosophical style and translates the question into the topic of music and harmony. Here, in Aristotle, the discussion is mostly concerned with metaphor, riddle, and pun as well as with the analytic of the components of language in general. But what is most notable given the discussion is that here one can no longer avoid the question of Aristotle's own relation to style in the *Poetics.*

Of course, there are several reasons why such a question, though important to pose, cannot be properly addressed. The status of the text of the *Poetics* is simply too unclear for any judgment to be made about its own style. It is, it seems, a compilation of notes, for lectures perhaps, likely never intended for publication, and so it is simply illegitimate to assume that anything could be gleaned from the nature of the writing here. Nonetheless, a general question, one that reaches beyond Aristotle, needs to be posed about the language of criticism, the language of theory, the language in which art—with its deliberative and reflected relation to style—is most properly addressed. It is also a question which recoils upon these very words. The issue is simple: if style is so significant to what is communicated in the work of art, can that which comes to be known thanks to the experience of such a work be said again, but in a different style? Is the knowledge that emerges, in part at least, out of a sensitivity to matters of style betrayed once it is taken up again in a language that is governed by the logic of the concept? More generally: can philosophy appropriate the insights of art without distorting, or even simply missing, those insights insofar as they are indebted to elements of language absent from the language of philosophy? Can a knowledge that is performed simply be said? Such questions can be taken up as referring to the problematic of translation, but that might already be a theorization of a question and so a privileging of the language of theory. In antiquity Plato is clearly most alert to this problematic (though it is said that Aristotle's own dialogues were delightful, flowing and like a "golden river"),[26] but otherwise it is not often taken up as a question. However, when the reappropriation of the question of art from antiquity sets to work in German philosophy, this question of the propriety of philosophic style to its insights becomes one of the most pressing of all questions. That is why we find such stylistic acrobatics and innovations in writers such as Hegel, Kierkegaard, Nietzsche, and Heidegger. With them we are confronted forcefully with the question of philosophic writing. But Aristotle is mute on such matters. What we do find in Aristotle is an extended analysis of language that illustrates how it is able to represent the ambiguity at work in the law of resemblances governing *mimesis.* We learn, in short, how it is that language can lend itself to the special insights of tragic art.

That analysis begins with a microscopic look at the radical elements of language, namely, the vowel, consonant, and syllable. In an attempt to clarify the distinctive features of human language Aristotle notes that "animals utter indivisible sounds but none I should call a letter" (1456b20). He continues by saying that for an intelligible sound to be made, a vowel or semi-vowel is requisite. Pure consonants, which Plato said had "no voice"[27] (such as d, j, s), are unpronounceable without the addition of the breath provided by a vowel. The innovation of the Greek alphabet, to which both Plato and Aristotle were very alert, was the representation of a system of writing in which the separate elements of the act of speech are noted (the Phoenician sign, by contrast, represented the consonant plus any vowel determined by the context).[28] Aristotle begins his discussion of poetic language by drawing upon the possibilities of abstraction provided by the alphabet and so stripping language in general down to its most radical element. He then reassembles language, as it were, discussing the possibility of words, phrases, and parts of speech, always emphasizing the complex character of language involved in the unique process of symbolization that belongs to words that can be written according to such an alphabet.[29] Suddenly Aristotle, saying that "metaphor consists in giving the thing a name that belongs to something else" (1457b9), introduces the notion of metaphor. Later, while commenting upon the various possibilities of language that have been enumerated in this discussion, he will underscore the fundamentality of metaphor for the task of tragic poetry: "It is a great thing, indeed, to make a proper use of these poetical forms, as also of compounds and strange words. But the greatest thing by far is to be a master of metaphor. It is the one thing that cannot be learned from others; and it is a sign of genius, since the right use of metaphor implies an eye for resemblances" (1459a4–5). Metaphor, then, is the most fitting possibility of language for the *mimesis* of *praxis*.

Thus in metaphor we give a name to otherwise nameless things: "For instance, to scatter seed is to sow, but there is no word for the action of the sun in scattering its fire. Yet this has to the sunshine the same relation as sowing has to the seed, and so you have the phrase 'sowing the god-created fire'" (1457b25). The specific dynamic of such naming is, according to Aristotle, helpful in illuminating something of the nature of tragic poetry. Metaphor is "an intuitive perception of the similarity in dissimilars" (1459a5), and in this one can easily see how it is that the delight we take in metaphors is like the delight we find in the eyes of the friend: it is the experience of the mind moving beyond the dichotomous taxonomy of either/or. In some regard there is a fundamental metaphoricity of all thinking insofar as to think is more than to merely calculate and is instead the creative movement of the mind beyond the terms which it is given. We project sameness upon difference, and by means of this act of impertinence we are able to stereoscopically expand the horizon of what we know and can understand. A Chinese proverb has it that "no brush can write two words at the same time";[30] yet in metaphor language is able to do just that. A name unknown is brought forward by virtue of its intuited resemblance with a name known. Two things are known at once, both the same, both different. The gap which defines their differences becomes the space in which language and knowing play. It is a sort of stereoscopic knowing that violates the law of identity governing conceptual reason.[31] The line that Aristotle cites from Empedocles at this point—it is cited simply as an example of how a word can be compressed—is perfectly revealing: "From the two comes one seeing" (*mia ginetai amphoteron ops*) (1458a4).

But here one must ask what metaphor has to do specifically with the inquiry into tragic art in the *Poetics*. What does language accomplish in metaphor that advances, or at least augments, the insights proper to tragic art? Why is metaphor a privileged mode of "diction" in mimetic practices? By overcoming, or by not being contained by, the dichotomies of either/or, metaphor becomes the manner in which language compresses contradictories in itself and is thereby the way in which unresolved differences are able to be expressed in their belonging together. Metaphor thus has a dual advantage for tragedy: first, it is able to speak what is otherwise unspeakable; second, it is able to present a double truth without thereby extinguishing the ambiguity proper to it. Both of these features need to be unpacked with reference to the general nature of tragic art.

To say that metaphor is able to name the otherwise nameless is to affirm that it is a way in which language gropes into the realm of our ignorance. Language then becomes a sort of compensation for our blindness. What is important here is to understand that it is when metaphor is necessary, and not simply a poetic device to spice the poem, that it first reveals its imaginative reach and the significance of that reach for knowing. Metaphor is necessary when what must be said presents itself simply as unknown, as lacking a word, as even unnameable and yet still summoning speech. The truth of the metaphor belongs thus to the finitude of our knowing. Metaphor is the imaginative countermovement of language before the limitations of my knowledge; by means of it I can struggle to say something about what I do not fully grasp. With respect to the task of tragic poetry it is clear that metaphor is more than what Aristotle earlier characterized as an "embellishment" of language; rather, it is an essential manner in which language in the tragic poem contributes to naming what we know most of all through *pathos*, through suffering. I cannot, for instance, know my death—that necessary ultimate that perfects human *praxis*—but in metaphor I can, in a paradoxical manner, know something of it. Likewise with the error of judgments to which I am blind (which is why the image of blindness belongs so natively to Greek tragedy). Likewise with the ability to know myself. Insofar as tragic art is dedicated to marking the *hamartia,* the ineluctable errancy of *praxis,* which we cannot, in the end, fully know, it needs to rely upon this gift of metaphor to speak, without betraying, what cannot be named.

By means of the metaphor we accede to the importance of what we cannot fully know. In metaphor, then, we elliptically disclose what is hidden and otherwise inscrutable. It accomplishes this stereoscopic disclosure thanks to the ambiguity that belongs to the law of resemblance: as in a translation, there is a double disclosure, a doubled naming, that belongs to metaphor. Like paternal twins, the operations of metaphor are twinned—the same but not identical. This means, though, that there is also a natural kinship of the metaphor with the riddle as well as to the expression of an *agon,* a conflict. The ambiguity, the difference, belonging to the two things named gives rise to a semantic friction which jars us. One example that Aristotle provides moves rather clearly in this direction: "For instance a cup is to Dionysus what a shield is to Ares; so one can speak of the . . . shield as 'Ares's cup.' . . . Having given the thing a strange name, one may by a negative addition deny it some attribute of that new name [as when] one calls the shield not 'Ares's cup' but a 'wineless cup'" (1457b33). By violating our expectations, language in the metaphor arrests us and fixes our attentions upon the friction, the disparities, between what is hidden (Dionysus's shield), its name (wineless cup), and the indirect manner in which it is named (metaphor). In the semantic friction of the metaphor, language in the tragic poem repeats the logics of both the reversal and the discovery belonging to the plot. It thereby adds to the liveliness and the force of the new idea: "Because the hearer expected something different, his acquisition of the new idea impresses him all the more. His mind seems to say 'Yes, to be sure, but I never thought of that.' . . . The thought is startling because, as Theodorus puts it, it does not fit in with the ideas you already have."[32] In this way, the experience of naming in the metaphor mimes the experience of the plot; both are mimetic of an *agon* that is characteristic of *praxis* and of our capacity to speak about our experience. Speaking as it does in a double register, metaphor operates on the axis of a paradox; so does the plot of the tragedy: "The dramatist plays on this to transmit his tragic vision of a world divided against itself and rent with contradictions."[33] In both cases the mind of those who hear and witness the tragic poem is brought into a conversation with itself because of the contradiction.

But Aristotle finds more still to be said about the propriety of metaphor for the tragic poem, namely, that its relation to riddle, and to jokes as well, renders it especially well suited to impart the insights of tragic art:[34] "The essence of the riddle consists in describing a fact by an impossible combination of words. By merely combining the ordinary names of things it cannot be done, but it is made possible by combining metaphors" (1458a28). By bringing together impossible combinations of words, by the play of ambiguities animating it, the metaphor opens the enigmatic space of the riddle in which the nature of the impossible is presented as such. Delineating a special form of unknowability, the riddle belongs natively to the logics of reversal and discovery, and, by extension, to the dynamic of human *praxis* itself. That is why the riddle plays such an important role in tragedy. The force of the riddle is nowhere more evident than in the tragedy that serves as the model tragedy for Aristotle, *Oedipus Rex*: "*Oedipus Rex* is not only centered on the theme of the riddle but . . . in its presentation, development, and resolution the play is itself constructed as a riddle. The ambiguity, recognition, and *peripeteia* all parallel one another and are all equally integral to the enigmatic structure of the work."[35] In thinking about the nature of the riddle we learn just how much the tragic art is about what is irreconcilable and impossible, about what is indispensable for us to know yet impossible at the same time. We learn that human *praxis* cannot, in the end, be substantivized, it cannot be defined or essentialized, it cannot even be described; it is rather a riddle, full of double meanings and ambiguities that exceed our abilities to give answer in a simple or final fashion. Tragedy turns to the riddle precisely because it presents such an enigma: "The Greeks were drawn to enigmas. But what is an enigma? A mysterious formulation you could say. Yet that would not be enough to define an enigma. The other thing you have to say is that the answer to an enigma is likewise mysterious."[36] Therein lies the difference between the enigma and the problem: the problem admits of a solution; the enigma does not but, rather, demands that we shift our perspective in order to grasp what is disclosed by the riddle. Such a shift is, in part, aided by the metaphor. Like Oedipus without eyes, we learn to see differently once we learn to grasp the nature of the riddle.

Of course, it is precisely Oedipus who is an enigma to himself, the paradigmatic enigma perhaps. At the outset of his story he appears as the solver of a riddle and so comes to be greeted as the savior of the city of Thebes. In the course of governing the city he is confronted with a new riddle: namely, who killed Laius? As that question moves toward its resolution, Oedipus becomes a riddle to himself. He no longer knows who he is, and he who was once a king and savior becomes an outcast. The solver of the riddle about everyone becomes the very embodiment of the riddle of human identity. At the moment he discovers this, the chorus speaks of Oedipus as "strange, monstrous and mad" with one of the most compact expressions of the enigma of human *praxis* found in tragedy: *"ho deinon idein pathos anthropois, o deinotaton panton hos ego prosekurs' ede"* (Terrible sight! None more terrible have these sad eyes looked upon).[37] The reversal that belongs to *praxis*, the errancy of our knowing, is not always benign. In these possibilities of human *praxis*, which are illuminated in tragic art, we are exposed to what can leave us strange to ourselves and those we love, to discovering that one who was once a god can become, in a flash, a monster; we are exposed finally to madness. We learn that such are the possibilities belonging to every life, and that even the well-conducted life cannot immunize itself against such risks which belong to the "flaw" to which we expose ourselves and by which we are able to call disaster down upon ourselves and those we love. The greatness of the work of art is precisely its capacity to present this impossible truth without infecting us with such madness. Nonetheless it presents us with the kathartic event that lets us understand something of what makes such madness possible. Risk belongs to the realm of *praxis*. *Hamartia*, calling the damage of such risk down upon oneself, does not come about through some irresponsibility—the notion of responsibility does not belong to what art teaches us of ethics—but through a simple defect of the mind, a lapse in judgment. Art, the *mimesis* of *praxis*, gives us the peculiar pleasure of knowing something of that risk and of being able to see into our own defect. Aristotle is of the conviction that such a truth, which complements the insights of ethical inquiry, should make a difference in how one lives. That, and simple good fortune, can make all the difference in the question of one's happiness.

*   *   *

But Aristotle does not end the *Poetics* on such a note. Rather, he continues by reminding us that tragedy—with its dialogue form and specific elements—is not the sole mimetic practice that illuminates something of the possibilities of human *praxis*. Epic, which has a somewhat different structure than tragedy, also qualifies for treatment in a text such as the *Poetics* which is devoted to investigating the nature of art's capacity to educate us about ethical life. Comedy too, according to Aristotle's promises at the outset of the *Poetics*, belongs to such an investigation, but that section of the text—whether never written or lost—does not exist.[38] So it is that the analysis of epic brings the *Poetics* to a close. It does not, however, bring it to full closure with respect to the question the text lays out for itself.

What is striking from the outset is the disproportion between the quantities of the text devoted to tragedy and to epic: tragedy occupies Aristotle for the bulk of twenty-two chapters; epic, on the other hand, is dealt with in three chapters (two of which seem rather out of touch with the remainder of the *Poetics*). The chapters on tragedy contain few references to epic; those on epic are primarily concerned with comparing it with tragedy. But this disproportion in the respective sizes of the analyses is not alone in making clear that Aristotle regards tragedy as the highest and most far-reaching form in which art is able to shed light upon human affairs. Aristotle is unhesitating about passing judgment here: "Since it attains the poetic effect better than epic, tragedy is clearly the higher form of art" (1462b13). Tragedy sets the standard for literature, and the formal differences between epic and tragedy (they differ chiefly in length and meter) do not challenge that standard, but confirm it with only one significant exception. The exception is that epic is better portraying the marvelous (*thaumaston*) since the illogical (*alogon*) is more readily achieved in the epic where we do not actually see the persons in the story (1460a12–14). It is an exception about which Aristotle makes no further comment. What one finds instead is a catalog of the ways in which tragedy achieves the form of art with greater force than epic does. Thus, for example, Aristotle points out that tragedy is a more concentrated form than epic: "Suppose Sophocles' *Oedipus* were to be turned into as many lines as there are in the *Iliad*. . . . It would seem thin and diluted" (1462b15). But then one must ask why, if everything epic does tragedy does better, does Aristotle devote any time to epic at all? Why discuss a diluted form of art after the more concentrated form has already been presented? The answer to this question comes in the form of a proper name: Homer. Homer, who is the only poet Aristotle ever calls "divine" (*thespesios*) (1459a29), is not regarded as a typical epic poet even though it is the case that Aristotle formulates the definition of epic largely with reference to him. What makes Homer such an exemplary poet is precisely that, as Aristotle reads him, he is basically a dramatist and not a narrator. In the final analysis, Homer's literary gifts, while best exemplifying the genre of epic, are themselves not contained by the form of that genre. Nonetheless, one must say that, despite his gifts and innovativeness, Homer does not represent the final form of poetic art: *Amicus Homer magis amica veritas.*

But to follow Aristotle as he tries to sort out the lines between epic and tragedy, and tries as well to find the place of Homer in those lines, risks leaving one entangled in subtleties that might obscure an important point about the definition of tragedy already achieved. In that definition Aristotle not only created the new genre of literary criticism, but he set in motion a shift in Greek thought about art. That shift is twofold. On the one hand, it is simply the solidification of the claim already tacit in Plato, namely, that tragic art marks the summit of the possibilities of art in general. On the other hand, it signals the recentering of the accomplishment of tragic art from Homer to Sophocles. Despite all of the praise for Homer found in the *Poetics* and the unqualified admiration expressed for his achievements, it is evident that the most perfected form of the possibilities of tragedy are found in Sophocles. This shift—from the heroic Achilles to the pathetic Oedipus—is fundamental. It marks a displacement of the Homeric vision of *praxis* by a Sophoclean one, a move from one temperament to another. It is a decisive shift and one that will remain in force, and largely unquestioned, for centuries to come. Plato sought to replace Achilles with Socrates as the image of the hero, but it was Aristotle who removed Achilles from the premier place in tragic art and in that place inserted Oedipus. Both Socrates and Oedipus are figures defined by their incessant questioning. Both "suffered" in order to persist in that need to interrogate the world. But they remain indisputably distinct as models for how we might best probe the regions of our ignorance as well as for illustrating the ethical significance of that ignorance which so profoundly defines human being. In the figure of Socrates Plato sets up a new model for a life with questions, a *bios theoretikos,* one that is not, like the *bios politikos* which he finds presented in tragedy, attached to *praxis* and to the ambiguities which belong to it.[39] By being dispassionate and disengaged Socratic questioning armors itself against the divisions and reversals which are the ever-present possibilities of human *praxis.* Socrates recognized the necessity of removing himself from mimetic practices precisely because such practices are, by their very nature, wedded to the tragic possibilities of *praxis.* Aristotle's reply, his acknowledgment of the worth of the work of art for the understanding of human life, is to call attention to a very different kind of questioning as it unfolds in the figure of Oedipus.

*   *   *

Both Plato and Aristotle argue that mimetic works, representations or imitations of *praxis,* expose the soul to ambiguities, conflicts, enigmas, and other destabilizing forces that can present themselves in a human life. Although the differences in their respective presentations of tragedy are significant—differences that crystallize in the differences between epic and tragic drama, Homer and Sophocles—they are in accord in suggesting that the experience of tragic art cultivates an openness to the multiple forces which can divide the soul against itself and its world. Both suggest that in tragedy one is alerted to the gap between the respective horizons of our knowledge and our actions, as well as to the conflicts and risks inherent in our desires. Both grant that the experience of the work of art as it presents such gaps touches us profoundly, and so both take this experience to be a serious matter worthy of sustained reflection. But whereas Aristotle finds that art sheds a light on human affairs that adds a certain texture to what is disclosed in the theoretical analysis of *praxis,* Plato argues that when it is properly understood art issues a warning about the danger which art itself poses to the soul. In other words, for Plato, the dangers which art illuminates—all of which can be explained as the danger of a soul not one with itself—are precisely what the experience of art cultivates. That is why art, for Plato, poses a threat which needs to be controlled. For Aristotle, the matter is different: such a danger is native to human *praxis,* and to wish to eliminate it would be to drain *praxis* of its nature. Art poses not a threat, but a delight, since in it we come to learn something of that danger, something of ourselves, that we cannot control but we can respect. We witness a dangerous truth about ourselves that—reflected in a language, re-presented in the structure of the drama, and mediated by the distance of the theater—we stereoscopically come to understand without ourselves being destroyed. The real hero of the work of art, the one to whom we are beholden for its pleasure and its knowledge, is the artist (for example, Sophocles), thanks to whom the sufferings of Oedipus can be instructive. The merit of the work of art is that it introduces an element of what is dangerous, without itself being dangerous; as such, it homeopathically serves the health of the just soul.

This disagreement between Plato and Aristotle about the significance of art reflects their obviously differing view on the nature of human *praxis,* as well as the nature of the vantage point from which the truth of *praxis* is best made visible. The theater of the truth of ideas and the theater of the tragedian offer competing insights about human affairs. But what is perhaps less obvious, but no less significant, are the different conceptions of language at work here. Plato's dialogues are like palimpsests—full of puns and rhetorical transitions—expressing a concern about language that is not self-consciously enlisted in the task of moving the soul beyond the reach of time. For Plato, it is the eidetic possibility of language that needs to be summoned by our speaking. When we participate fully in the dialogue we are drawn forward by the draft of that possibility: everything that begins in a now exposes itself as belonging to an always.[40] We are, as it were, translated into the idea by the dialogue. Aristotle, on the other hand, whose own texts have a spare and even skeletal quality, celebrates the ability of language to expose the ambiguities and conflict of those who live and die in time. The agonistic possibilities of language as they are expressed in metaphor and riddles amplify and drive home the deep conflicts and enigmas that belong to all human *praxis.* Governed by different languages (the eidetic and the mimetic), different relations to *praxis* (detached and displayed), these different theaters (of the truth of ideas and of the tragedy of life in time) are, in the end, different ways of thinking the lives of those who die in time.

*　　*　　*

Aristotle begins his *Poetics* by asking why human beings make art. He moves to answer that question by posing a question about the pleasure we take in works of art, in re-presentations of human *praxis* (given the tone of the *Poetics* one must imagine that this was a pleasure that Aristotle himself knew quite well). The art that he interrogates to this end is quite specific: it is the art focused upon human *praxis*—it is not, for instance, about nature—and it is the art that culminates in the art of the word, ultimately in the work of tragedy. Consequently, what one finds in the *Poetics* is not a full theory of art. The few references to painting, music, and other forms of art are all made in order to call attention to the role they play in the tragic work, or as a sort of mirror which clarifies some element of the tragedy. Even epic is presented in the shadow of tragedy. This does not signal a myopia before other possibilities of art, nor is it simply the expression of a specialized concern with one genre of literature. Aristotle's ambitions in this text extend far beyond those of a literary critic. His concern is rather to drive to the roots of the peculiar pleasure that belongs to mimetic practices.

What is latent in this decision to follow the question about making art in general with the inquiry into the specifics of tragedy is the presumption that tragedy represents the summit of the work of art. It is an assumption that Plato and Aristotle both share and that is rooted in the notion of *mimesis* which each identifies as the trademark of the work of art. In the mimetic element of art each finds that re-presentation—whether it be in words, stone, pigment, tone, or movement—is destined to the expression of what is wedded to desires and ignorance, and consequently to what is conflicted, divided, ambiguous, enigmatic—in short, tragic. Representation in language, the *mimesis* of *praxis* that is governed by meter and rhythm, plot and song is simply the most articulated form of the possibilities of art. One might say, then, that, for Aristotle, all art strives to be tragic. If we were to develop a theory of painting or architecture or music, then it would not be far removed from the analysis of what finds expression in literature. Furthermore, because it belongs to the realm of intelligibility found in language, tragedy exhibits the greatest kinship to philosophy and so is most worthy of its attention.

Aristotle inquires into the nature of tragedy with genuine sympathy and curiosity with respect to its power in our lives. His attempt is to understand how it is that language can move us and be made to solicit potent emotions which themselves "speak" powerfully to us about ourselves and our relations with others. The kathartic event which is possible when language and the arrangement of the telling live up to their potential opens us to insights that confirm what theoretical contemplation discloses. The experience of *katharsis* becomes a sort of shortcut to the same insights disclosed with only more clarity by the conceptual analysis of ethical life. In sum, the philosophical analysis of the experience of tragic art reinforces the insights into human affairs found in philosophical experience itself. Perhaps the lost book on comedy would offer a different perspective of the relation of philosophy and the arts, since from what little is said of comedy it seems that it might have come in for some rather strong criticism regarding the view of human life which it promotes.

It is difficult to say whether anything "new" with respect to human *praxis* is introduced in art that is not found in philosophy proper as each is defined by Aristotle. Tragedy clearly sits at the top of the hierarchy of the arts, but it remains subordinated to philosophy in the larger hierarchy of human achievements. It is reasonable to suggest that he would accept the notion that art might lend a sort of precision in certain aspects of our understanding of *praxis* (for instance, in the way the logic of reversal is elaborated). Furthermore, in its appeal to our emotions art lends an immediacy and texture to the enigmas of ethical life. But it is also clear that Aristotle is not troubled by the simple fact that his analysis of mimetic practices is carried on in a thoroughly conceptual language. In other words, he is not troubled by his own translation of the language of art into the language of philosophy, and there is no discussion of what might be lost in that translation. He remains unswervingly guided by the conceptual possibilities belonging to language even in the moments of his highest praise for the achievements of its mimetic possibilities.

Unlike Plato, Aristotle does not find it necessary to exile the poets. Quite the contrary, it is, he suggests, both delightful and instructive to participate in their works. But it must also be said that Plato's sharp criticisms of the achievements of art are indicative of his acknowledgment that in art something different appears, something that is apart from, other than, what one learns from philosophic questioning. Philosophy cannot fully appropriate the insights of artists because art proposes a different view of human affairs. For Plato, the insights of the work of art challenge, threaten, the knowledge won by the concept. The separate integrity of art is preserved, but only at the price of its separation from the *polis*. On the other hand, Aristotle's genuine appreciation for theater, to which all art is in some respect subsumed, led to some keen insights into the nature of poetic practices. That same appreciation risks obscuring what is distinct in such practices, what is not to be found in the practice of philosophy. Such a subordination of art to philosophy will be the effective history of Aristotle's text even, for the most part, among those who grant real dignity to the work of art. The debate about the work of art that is opened up between Plato and Aristotle is not only about the achievements of such works for human understanding; it is also, equally, about the commensurability of those achievements with the understanding that emerges out of conceptual reason.

Nonetheless, there is perhaps the seed of something new, something possibly untranslatable into the language of the concept which is contributed to our understanding of ethical life by art as Aristotle unpacks it. It is to be found in the singularity of its presentations; in other words, the *mimesis* of *praxis* operates in the realm of the unique, in the idiom of the proper name, while still being an exploration of the possibilities which belong to *praxis* as such. That is what is proper to the fear and pity of the work of art, to its summons to the common grounds of our singularity, which is exposed by our fear, and of our solidarity, which is exposed in our pity. It is an insight about the unique contribution of art to human understanding that will need to wait until Kant before it begins to receive its full due.

Interlude:
Kant and Schelling

Imitation is the most dangerous of activities for
world order, because it tends to break down
boundaries.
　　—Roberto Calasso,
　　　The Marriage of Cadmus and Harmony, p. 358

The moment that the topic of tragedy (and again it will be Greek tragedy
that is meant here) reappears as a central question for philosophizing is
easy to date: after Aristotle it must wait until 1795 to resurface with a
prominence similar to that found in Plato and Aristotle.[1] Twenty-one centuries after Aristotle's *Poetics,* Schelling's *Letters on Dogmatism and Criticism*
(in particular the Tenth Letter) heralds the return of tragic art as an ineluctable question for philosophy, and it does so by issuing something
of a challenge to the history of philosophy that is inaugurated by Plato
and Aristotle. The challenge is for philosophizing—and for Schelling that
means thinking speculatively, thinking under the sign of a differentiated
unity—to take to heart both the phenomenon that is presented by tragedy and the form of its presentation as the highest possibility of the work
that is proper to art. Rather than exile the claims of tragedy, as Plato does,
and rather than subordinate its claims to principles of thinking, as in
Aristotle, Schelling asks if philosophizing can let itself be changed by a
different sort of engagement with tragic art. He will, however, pose this
challenge only after having given a clearly philosophical determination of
the nature of the tragic.

Schelling does this first in a text which is presented as a series of ten letters addressed to an unnamed "friend."[2] This choice of the format of a letter, coupled with the conversational tone of the letters in which transitions are made rhetorically as well as conceptually, signals a self-conscious departure from traditional philosophical formats and styles and so is designed to reinforce the move of the language of the text beyond the limits of philosophy as it is defined at the time. The law defined by the genre of philosophy is quietly broken by the form of the letter. More precisely, what is being performed in these letters is something that philosophic concepts cannot fully articulate, namely, the claim that the insights of art overreach those found in philosophy: "You are right, one point remains— to know that there is an objective power which threatens to annihilate our freedom—to fight against this power, to offer against it one's entire freedom, and thus to collapse. You are right again, my friend, because even when it becomes invisible to the light of reason, this possibility must be preserved for art—for the highest in art."[3] In the course of this letter it becomes clear that tragedy is "the highest in art" and that when the powers of reason fail, when the philosophy gives out, the disclosive powers of this highest possibility in art still preserve what is most in need of being understood. Art, specifically tragic art, takes over when philosophy comes to an end. A few years later, in the *System of Transcendental Idealism* (1801), Schelling will put the point even more bluntly: philosophy becomes an organon of art, and, in the end, the highest accomplishment of philosophy is to know that it must empty itself into "the universal ocean of poesie."[4] This is the point at which the Platonic decision about art is overturned; here the deep insight of philosophy is that the accomplishments of art which peak in tragic art outstrip the achievements of reason. Here, *avant la lettre*, we find Nietzsche's claim that "we have art, lest we perish of the truth."[5]

But while Schelling makes the rejuvenation of the question of tragedy an explicit matter, it is Kant who makes its return inevitable, and so it is no surprise that when Schelling highlights the achievements of tragic art he does so against the backdrop of Kantian concerns. So it must be said that the predominance, if not the complete domination, of the question posed by the idea of the tragic in the past two centuries is owing to the work of Kant, who made precious few remarks about tragedy (as a literary genre) or about the tragic (as a philosophical idea).[6] One cannot understand the full force of the return of the question of tragedy without first coming to see it as a response to the challenge Kant poses to thinking. This is the case at least in the first phase of the renewal of the question of tragedy, namely, its elaboration in German Idealism and Romanticism. In the second phase of its development—in Nietzsche—new elements will be introduced. But at first, it is against this backdrop formed by the Kantian concern with the limits of speculative thought, above all, that the relation of the modern concern with tragedy differs from that relation as it is defined in antiquity.

This Kantian background can be defined in three essential aspects. First, the tragic conflict is now presented as mirroring the antinomy of reason as it is unfolded in the *Critique of Pure Reason* (here it is the third antinomy between freedom and nature that plays a special role). Second, the recuperation of the work of art for the task of comprehending ethical life is owing to the dignity granted to aesthetic experience in the *Critique of Judgment*. And, third, by reinvigorating the notion of the sublime Kant created a place for the philosophical discussion of the presentations of the monstrous and sacrifice which are so central to Greek tragedy. In short, the opening gesture as well as the basic framework for the recovery of art, in particular tragic art, for the question of ethical life are both clearly indebted to Kant. However, it is also clear that Kant himself does not engage the question of the relation of art and ethical life as it is formulated by Schelling. There are two reasons why this is the case. First, aesthetic experience for Kant is ultimately to be understood as an experience of nature, not art, and furthermore even when he does speak of art there is nothing he says that privileges Greek art among the cultural forms that art has taken.[7] Second, Kant himself does not identify the antinomy of reason (its "peculiar fate") with tragic conflict. Kant fundamentally shifts the paradigm for questions and in this regard does inaugurate a revolution in the frameworks for self-understanding defining Western culture. However, though this paradigm shift is perhaps the most radical and far-reaching transformation in the history of Western thought (one Goethe signaled by writing of Kant that "von hier und heute geht eine neue Epoche der Geschichte an"), its measure has yet to be taken.

Kant himself frequently retreats from the full force and radicality of the insights he unleashes in the Third Critique. One sees this effort to tame this transformation in a number of telling passages, two of which are especially central for my concerns. The first passage refers to the significance of the sublime, the second to the relation between taste and genius. When introducing the notion of sublimity, of the experience of the excessive and uncanny, Kant concludes his general comments with the remark that "the concept of the sublime in nature is not nearly as important and rich in implications as that of the beautiful in nature. . . . The theory of the sublime [is] a mere appendix to our aesthetic judging."[8] Later, after having introduced the notion of genius as a revolutionary and disruptive force, Kant concludes the discussion of the reach of this force by saying that "Taste, like the power of judgment in general, consists in disciplining genius. It severely clips the wings of genius, and makes it civilized, or polished. . . . Therefore, if there is a conflict between these two properties

. . . , and something has to be sacrificed, then it should rather be on the side of genius."[9] In short, the very points at which Kant most radically unleashes the revolutionary elements of his analysis of aesthetic experience become the points which he most severely restrains by other means. But if it is the case that Kant takes away the truly subversive dimensions of his analysis in his interpretation of that analysis, that he immediately tames the forces that he has disclosed, it is also the case that those forces he has disclosed will be the sites of reflection that take off in Kant's wake. In order to see how his successors continue his revolution by deepening and intensifying its revolutionary force, one needs to see how the decisions Kant makes regarding sublimity and genius—decisions motivated by his attempt to subdue the anarchic force of what he had opened up—are overturned by those who take up the promises of the Third Critique.[10] It is not by chance that the notions of genius and sublimity move very much to the center of philosophic reflections in the wake of Kant. This is a tendency that will only accelerate until it reaches its high point in Nietzsche, who will celebrate both forces above all other experiences proper to the realm of art.

Schelling is the one who gathers together Kant's achievements and still undeveloped promises, and, because Schelling is so profoundly faithful to Kant's achievements, he attempts to answer Kant's limitations from within the perspective opened up by his accomplishments. His concern is to ask how the insights of criticism—Schelling's term for Kant's achievement in philosophy—can live up to the speculative task of thinking and yet evade the seductions that might induce it to become a new dogmatism. For Schelling the greatest insight of criticism is found in the testimony it gives on behalf of human freedom, and it is this above all which needs safeguarding. Schelling develops this point by focusing his attentions upon the insights of Greek tragedy. Greek tragedy shows how it is that thinking can endure rather than shirk the most extreme contradiction, namely, the contradiction between freedom and necessity, and in this way it comes to stand as the true homage to human freedom. Schelling makes this point in the opening passage of the Tenth Letter:

> It has often been asked how Greek reason was able to bear the contradictions of its tragedy. A mortal fated by destiny to become a criminal fights *against* this destiny, and in spite of this he is horribly punished for a crime that is the work of fate! The *reason* for this contradiction, that which made it bearable, lay deeper than the level at which it has been sought: it lay in the conflict of human freedom with the power of the objective world, a conflict in which the mortal necessarily had to succumb when that power was a superior power—a *fatum;* and yet, since he did not succumb *without* a struggle, he had to be *punished* for this very defeat. The fact that the criminal succumbed only to the superior force

of fate and yet was *punished* all the same—this was the recognition of human freedom, an *honor* owed to freedom. It was by *allowing* tragedy to *struggle* against the superior power of fate that Greek tragedy honored freedom. In order not to transgress the bounds of art, tragedy was obliged to have the mortal *succumb;* yet, in order to compensate for this humiliation of human freedom imposed by art, it also had to allow him to undergo punishment—even for a crime committed on account of *fate.* . . . It was a *great* idea to have man willingly accept punishment even for an *inevitable* crime; in this way he was able to demonstrate his freedom precisely through the loss of this freedom.[11]

Schelling frames the new philosophical form of the most extreme contradiction as played out in the differences between dogmatism (Fichte) and criticism (Kant), and he indicates that it is Kant's great merit to have set himself into this contradiction, thereby exposing it as such, and also to have opened the way to its overcoming by disclosing the ability of aesthetic experience to exceed the powers of conceptual reason in thinking such contradictions. But it is Schelling's own innovation to have insisted that Greek tragedy offers a site in which this overcoming is performed. This innovation, announced in the *Letters on Dogmatism and Criticism,* would leave its mark upon philosophizing until the present age. With Kant we encounter the revolution in thinking, but Schelling is the first to propose a path to a new future for thinking in the wake of this revolution.

It is important to see clearly what this location of the contemporary struggles of thinking in the operations of Greek tragedy signals. Szondi is quite right when he writes that "after Aristotle there is a poetics of tragedy, only after Schelling is there a philosophy of the tragic."[12] That is the essential shift effected by the modern form of the question derived from the philosophical encounter with Greek tragedy. But one could argue that this way of characterizing the shift does not exhaust its significance; even more, it might be necessary to think the shift that Schelling's work introduces at this point as even more profound in its reach. In order to see this it is important to bear in mind both that there is a peculiar necessity driving this move—that is, Schelling's decision to single out Greek tragic art is not an arbitrary one, but very much a response to the needs of history at that moment—and it is equally important that one acknowledge that *this renewal of the questions of Greek tragedy is equally its reinvention.* The philosophical question of tragedy that reappears at the very end of the eighteenth century is marked by such a profound shift away from the terms and concerns that characterized Plato's and Aristotle's treatment of it that its reappearance coincides, not by chance, with the claim that the very same tradition inaugurated by Plato and Aristotle had reached the point of its own closure. *The reappearance of the topic of tragedy—now posed as a matter of the tragic—is contemporaneous with the arrival of the end of metaphysics as a possibility.* In this regard the arrival of the topic of the tragic in philosophy must be understood as marking a double event: the reinvention of the question of tragedy and the closure of the possibility of metaphysics. The recovery of the experience of Greek tragedy in post-Kantian thought needs to be addressed in conjunction with the end of the ontotheological tradition which the return to the topic of tragedy seeks to overcome.

The question as to what is signaled by the central role assigned to the theme of the tragic after Kant does not permit an uncomplicated answer. Indeed, it is this very question, in part the relation of the ancient and modern world, which, perhaps more than any other question, defines and distinguishes contemporary reflections on the tragic.[13] Beginning with Hölderlin the effort to formulate the relation of ancient and modern forms of tragedy will frame and dominate the treatments of tragedy in the modern world. Why this is the case can be clarified only in the more detailed remarks of the following chapters; however, some preliminary indications and general features of this trademark of contemporary philosophical reflections on the tragic can be made at this point. What is most important in this regard is understanding just what is at stake in this matter. Why, in other words, should one worry about the question of this sudden fascination with Greek tragedy in post-Kantian thought? How is it then that this Hellenotropism that seems to define post-Kantian German philosophy is precisely the means by which such philosophizing sets itself apart from the ancient world?

The turn to ancient Greek art, though powerfully defined by the specifically Greek character of what serves as a sort of inspiration for German philosophizing, is not driven by any simple nostalgia for the Greek world. It is driven more by the effort to release as yet undeveloped promises which, once unfolded, will carry modern Western culture beyond itself. The return to Greek art will signal a recovery, but the strange recovery of what has not yet appeared. The reappearance of Greek tragedy as a theme for reflection takes a shape that is different from the shape it found in antiquity. What will be important in what follows is to understand how the question posed by Greek tragedy for Schelling and those who follow his lead in this matter is a radically new question, one not yet posed even in the ancient world which produced the great works of tragedy.

Some preliminary clarity about what constitutes this newness and difference is achieved by asking why it is that modern tragedies do not gather together the same themes as Greek tragedies. What sets modern and Greek tragedies apart? It is, for instance, striking that Shakespeare's tragedies seldom, if ever, are even noted when efforts are made to formulate the notion of the tragic. Kierkegaard, the great psychologist of philosophy, will give the crispest explanation of this significant fact when he suggests that

What specifically characterizes ancient tragedy is that the action does not proceed only from character, that the action is not subjectively reflected enough, but that the action itself has a relative admixture of suffering. Ancient tragedy, therefore, did not develop dialogue to the point of exhaustive reflection with everything merged in it; the distinct components of dialogue are actually present in the monologue and chorus. . . . This, of course, is because the ancient world did not have subjectivity reflected in itself.[14]

He will then elaborate upon this further by saying, "Our age has lost all the substantial categories of family, state, kindred; it must turn the single individual over to himself completely in such a way that, strictly speaking, he becomes his own creator. Consequently his guilt is sin, his pain repentance, but thereby the tragic is canceled."[15] In other words, modern tragic literature differs from Greek tragedy because it is saturated by the problem of subjectivity, and this means that the reach and locus of the struggles it exposes, the sweep of what was once referred to as destiny, is different from what is outlined in Greek tragic literature. One sees this difference when one looks at Shakespearean tragic figures—Lear and Hamlet are excellent examples in this instance—especially the interiority of the turmoil they present on stage, and how this contrasts with figures such as Antigone and Oedipus whose interior life remains almost completely hidden from us. Modern retellings of ancient dramas—for example, a case such as Jean Anouilh's 1944 version of *Antigone*—often highlight this difference in an extreme fashion. It is not only the case that a new social reality has appeared and with it the possibilities for tragedy have been altered. Rather, a new understanding of the characters of the tragic drama, in particular a new understanding of the relation of the individual to the larger world, shapes the possibilities of the tragedy. Hegel put the point clearly when he wrote, "When Napoleon spoke with Goethe about the nature of tragedy he said that contemporary tragedy was to be essentially differentiated from ancient tragedy in that we no longer have a destiny which supports human beings, and that in the place of this ancient fatum politics has entered."[16] But the point which most clearly explains the basis of this difference is the force of the notion of subjectivity. One sees then that the contemporaneity of Descartes and Shakespeare is telling in this matter.

The ultimate outcome of this modern emphasis on the issue of subjectivity in connection with the dynamics of tragedy is most clearly expressed in Freud's theory of psychological complexes. It is not by accident that when Freud chooses to name the complexes which forge and shape the development of the self, he names these forces after figures in ancient Greek tragic drama. Freud could not use figures from Shakespearean tragedy as models to exemplify such dynamics because those characters are already too clearly defined as psychological types and by forces too obviously directed at the specific subjectivity of the characters. Since the hiddenness of the complex belongs to its basic nature, those characters, so profoundly alert to their own subjective life, cannot serves as models for such unconscious complexes. In the final analysis, Freud's theory of complexes needs to be seen as the final consolidation of this modern shift in the presentation of tragedy. It is the ultimate destination of the specifically modern experience of tragedy. It is also the point at which the specifically ancient Greek character of the experience of tragedy is most obscured.[17]

But in the philosophical reappropriation and reinvention of the issue of tragic drama that begins with Schelling the effort is to recover something of what initially is deemed the specifically *Greek* character of tragic drama. This effort is guided by the desire to recover, or to discover, that which *evades* this contemporary coalescence of the notions of tragedy and subjectivity. That is why the question of the "Greekness" of tragedy as it is taken up by German philosophizing after Kant is so decisive: it is precisely this that is seen as offering a way of thinking freedom that does not frame the question of freedom within the field of human subjectivity. Even more: Greek tragedy is seen as offering a point of view that is not already captured by the tradition of metaphysics, nor is it able to be co-opted by the Christian tradition and its claims of salvation. And yet at the same time—at least this is why the theme of tragedy reappears for Schelling—Greek tragedy offers the possibility of exposing a speculative unity, a fully differentiated conception of the unity of life. This is what it means to characterize the shift between Aristotle and Schelling as being a shift from the ancient philosophical concern with tragedy to the modern philosophical concern with the idea of the tragic.

After Schelling, then, the ante gets upped and the stakes are higher and more extensive in the matter of how tragic art is understood. This happens because several hitherto largely disparate concerns, drawn mostly from Kant's Third Critique, coalesce in the topic of tragedy and the manner in which it unites the most extreme forms of contradiction in a form of presentation that is not captured by the logic of the concept. Curiously, though Schelling will announce the paramount significance of the topic of the tragic in 1795, and though in later years he will take it as a theme for extended reflection, tragedy will not saturate his work systematically to the same extent that it will come to define Hegel's thought. While Schelling will give a name to the theme which will become the center for the speculative answer to the challenge of Kant's insights regarding the limits of philosophy, it will be Hegel who first lets this center thoroughly define his own philosophizing. And so the struggle to take to heart, and to provide a reply to, the complexity of the tragic will determine the direction, and even the specifics, of Hegel's work as will no other topic. But the seeds of this force of the idea of the tragic for Hegel belong to the time of his early friendship and collaborative efforts with both Schelling and Hölderlin. The shared intellectual passions of their youth will set the tone—in part at least—for the lifetime of each.

The text that is especially decisive for each of them is one with a quite unusual provenance: its authorship is uncertain (at least if we operate with the unwarranted assumption that every text must have a single author), and so it appears in the collected works of Hegel, Schelling, and Hölderlin alike. It is a text composed in 1796, only one year after Schelling's *Letters on Dogmatism and Criticism,* and though we have only a fragment of a complete text, the programmatic force of its assertions is so clear that the work almost has the quality of a manifesto: here the program of idealism is announced. The text, entitled "Earliest System-Program of German Idealism," wears its debt to Kant's *Critique of Judgment* on its sleeve: we find the coupling of aesthetic experience and ethicality along with the conviction that the role of reason is to preserve the life of freedom. The opening sentence of the essay makes this clear: "Since the whole of metaphysics falls for the future within *moral theory*—something which Kant . . . has given us only an *example,* not *exhausted,*—this ethics will be nothing other than a comprehensive system of all Ideas or, and this is really the same, of all practical postulates. Naturally, the first idea is the representation *of my self* as an absolutely free nature."[18] Three paragraphs later the essay sets out the summit of this system of Ideas, saying, "Finally, the idea that unites all the rest, the idea of beauty, taking the word in its higher Platonic sense. . . . The highest act of reason, the one through which it encompasses all ideas, is an aesthetic act, and . . . *truth and goodness only become sisters in beauty.* The philosopher must possess just as much aesthetic power as the poet. . . . The philosophy of the spirit is an aesthetic philosophy."[19] Finally, after having announced that "there is no philosophy, no history, left; the poetic art alone will survive,"[20] the text concludes with an elaboration of the speculative conception of the *hen kai pan*[21] where it is said that "Monotheism of reason and heart, polytheism of the imagination and of art—this is what we need."[22] In short, the text makes clear that the task of thinking, to foster and preserve human freedom, which is ultimately an ethical task, will find its answer in the work of art, not in conceptual reason. The debt to Kant's Third Critique is clear, and the endurance of the impulse laid out here is evident in the evolution of German Idealism that will follow in only a few years. For an understanding of the role assigned to the work of art at this point this is a crucial text; all that it lacks is a clear indication that the true destination of the work of art, the final signature of the beautiful, is found in tragic art. But such an indication almost goes without saying at this point in time since for Hegel, Schelling, and Hölderlin that move is the most natural, the most direct, next step in this program. It is also the most decisive step, one which will fundamentally shape the very notion of the dialectic which will trace the operations of spirit in its every appearance.

In the *Tenth Letter on Dogmatism and Criticism* and the *Earliest System-Program of German Idealism* we find the first moment in the rebirth, the reinvention, of the question of tragedy as it will come to shape philosophizing even into our present. Both texts have the flavor of manifestos, of calls for a project to come; both texts point to, but neither poses, the question of tragedy with any specificity whatsoever; neither text takes up the questions they indicate are ineluctable. Nonetheless, one sees clearly how Kant's Third Critique sets the stage for the renewal of the thematics of tragedy. One sees as well that the turn to the achievement of the work of art, and the centrality of the topic of tragedy, is borne of ethical concerns. Although this concern with freedom and ethical life will not always be so clearly evident in the work of those who will inherit this topic of tragedy—here one thinks most of all of Nietzsche and Heidegger—the theme of tragedy will never sever its bond with the topic of ethicality. That is the case perhaps most of all for the case of Heidegger. In ancient Greece, tragedy was understood to be the presentation of the enigma of ethical and political life. After Kant, philosophy will recuperate this view, but it will do this for a quite different set of reasons, and with different hopes. Now the question of tragedy is of ethical significance because it is the summit of the possibilities of human invention. But now as well the question of tragedy is understood as somehow remote from the time in which this discovery is made. It belongs to an ancient world, and to another language and culture. In short, when it is reinvented, the topic of tragedy is found to belong to a concern with history.

But all of this will unfold itself in the years to come. At this point what needs to be noted is that the conviction that the work of art owes itself in a fundamental way to freedom and thus provides the most direct route to the task of thinking and preserving freedom defines the origins of German Idealism and will shape its development to come. But even more it needs to be remembered that the distinctive element of German Idealism, the moment at which it comes into its own as a movement beyond Kant, comes precisely in the way that the topic of Greek tragedy enters. It enters as the supreme moment of the possibilities opened up by the work of art, and that means as well that it signals the appearance of the highest speculative moment. It will be Hegel's achievement to see the full possibilities of this moment and to advance the question of tragedy.

With Hegel, then, the second moment in the life of the question of tragedy is fully born for philosophizing. Kant and Schelling, each in his own way, prepare and shape the question as Hegel will take it up. Hölderlin too will give a new force and impulse to the topic of tragedy in the same years—and often even earlier—as Hegel. But Hölderlin's fame as a poet and the romanticization of his private agonies by others will obscure the full force of his contribution to the question of tragedy, and its genuine originality, for a long time. It will take almost the entire century after Hölderlin's death before he will finally find his readers—namely, until there are readers who are able to see the extent to which Hölderlin thinks the question outside of the orbit of the philosophical prejudices that capture even the most innovative of philosophers. So it is Hegel above all who determines the modern appearance of the ancient question put by the tragic work of art. It is Hegel's legacy that one necessarily confronts when taking up the question of the tragic in the present age. This is so much the case that one of the persistent struggles for those who follow in his wake is to keep the topic of tragedy from having a fundamentally Hegelian flavor. We have not yet found a way to speak of the tragic without, in some manner, confronting, if not Hegel himself, then at least Hegel's effective history. This distinction between Hegel's own views and the impact or reception of his work is important to bear in mind since a strange cartoon has replaced Hegel's careful and probing treatment of the idea of the tragic. The subtlety of the dialectical conception of the tragic should not be replaced by the wooden formalism which clunks along to the schematic beat of thesis, antithesis, synthesis.[23] One does not begin to understand Hegel and the movement of the dialectic until one sees how Hegel's thought as a whole emerges out of the reinvention of the question of the tragic. Likewise, one begins to grasp the radicality and sway of the question of tragedy in contemporary philosophy only once one comes to appreciate the far reach and philosophic imagination that characterize Hegel's creative reformulation of the question and the stakes of tragic art for thinking.

APPENDIX A

The Earliest System-Program of German Idealism (1796)

. . . an ethics. Since the whole of metaphysics falls for the future within *moral theory*—something which Kant with both of his practical postulates has given only an *example,* not *exhausted,*—this ethics will be nothing other than a comprehensive system of all Ideas or, and this is really the same, of all practical postulates. Naturally, the first idea is the representation *of my self* as an absolutely free nature. With this free, self-conscious nature there appears at the same time a whole *world*—from out of nothing—the sole true and thinkable *creation out of nothing.* Here I will descend into the fields of physics; the question is this: how must a world be constituted for a moral entity? I would like to give wings once more to our sluggish physics, which advances laboriously by experiments.

Thus—if philosophy supplies the ideas, and experiences the data, we can finally come to have the contours of that physics that I anticipate of later times. It does not appear that a contemporary physics like our own can, or even should, satisfy a creative spirit.

From nature I come to the *work of man.* Starting from the idea of humanity, I will show that it provides no idea of the *State,* because the State is something *mechanical,* any more than it gives us an Idea of a *machine.* Only what is an object of *freedom* is called an *idea.* We must therefore go beyond the state!—For every State must treat free men as cogs in a machine; and this it ought not to do; so it must *cease.* It is self-evident that here all the ideas, of perpetual peace, etc., are only subordinated ideas under a higher idea. At the same time I want here to lay down the principles for a *history of humankind* and strip the whole wretched human work of state, constitution, government, legal system—naked to the skin. Finally there arrive the ideas of a moral world, divinity, immortality—the overturning of all superstition, the persecution of the priesthood which in recent times poses as rational, at the bar of reason itself—absolute freedom of all spirits which bear the intellectual world in themselves, and cannot seek either God or immortality *outside* themselves.

Finally, the idea that unites all the rest, the idea of beauty, taking the word in its higher Platonic sense. I am now convinced that the highest act of reason, the one through which it encompasses all ideas, is an aesthetic act, and that *truth and goodness only become sisters in beauty.* The philosopher must possess just as much aesthetic power as the poet. Men without aesthetic sense are our literal-minded philosophers. The philosophy of the spirit is an aesthetic philosophy. One cannot be rich in spirit, even about history one cannot reason spiritedly—without aesthetic sense. Here it ought to be obvious what it is that men lack who do not understand ideas—and who confess honestly enough that they find everything obscure as soon as it goes beyond the table of contents and the index.

In this way, poetry gains a higher dignity; in the end she becomes again what she was in the beginning—*the teacher of humankind;* for there is no philosophy, no history left; the poetic art alone will survive all the other sciences and arts.

At the same time we so often hear that the great masses must have a *sensuous religion.* Not only the great masses, but the philosopher needs it too. Monotheism of reason and heart, polytheism of the imagination and of art—this is what we need.

First of all I will speak here of an idea which, as far as I know, has never occurred to anyone before—we must have a new mythology, however, this mythology must be in the service of ideas, it must become a mythology of *reason.*

Until we express ideas aesthetically, that is, mythologically, they have no interest for the *people;* and conversely until mythology is rational the philosopher must be ashamed of it. Thus in the end the enlightened and unenlightened must join hands, mythology must become philosophical and the people rational, and philosophy must become mythological in order to make the philosophers sensible. Then eternal unity will rule between us. No more looks of scorn, no more the blind trembling of the people before its wise ones and priests. Only then does the *equal* development of *all* powers await us, of the singular as well as of every individual. No power will be suppressed any longer. Then universal freedom and equality of spirits will reign!—A higher spirit, sent from heaven, must found this new religion among us; it will be the last great work of humankind.

APPENDIX B

Tenth Letter on Dogmatism and Criticism

You are right, one thing remains—to know that there is an objective power which threatens to annihilate our freedom, and, with this firm and certain conviction in our heart, to fight against it putting up against it the whole of one's freedom, and thus to go down. You are doubly right, my friend, because, even after it has vanished from the light of reason, this possibility must be preserved for art—for the highest in art.

It has often been asked how Greek reason was able to bear the contradictions of its tragedy. A mortal fated by destiny to become a criminal fights *against* this destiny, and in spite of this he is horribly punished for a crime that is the work of fate! The *reason* for this contradiction, that which made it bearable, lay deeper than the level at which it has been sought: it lay in the conflict of human freedom with the power of the objective world, a conflict in which the mortal necessarily had to succumb when that power was a superior power—a *fatum;* and yet, since he did not succumb *without* a struggle, he had to be *punished* for this very defeat. The fact that the criminal succumbed only to the superior force of fate and yet was *punished* all the same—this was the recognition of human freedom, an *honor* owed to freedom. It was by *allowing* tragedy to *struggle* against the superior power of fate that Greek tragedy honored freedom. In order not to transgress the bounds of art, tragedy was obliged to have the mortal *succumb;* yet, in order to compensate for this humiliation of human freedom imposed by art, it also had to allow him to undergo punishment— even for a crime committed on account of *fate.* As long as he is still *free,* he holds himself upright against the power of fate. As soon as he yields he ceases to be free. Yielding, he still accuses fate for the loss of his freedom. Even Greek tragedy could not harmonize freedom and failure. Only a being which was *robbed* of freedom could succumb to fate.—It was a *great* idea to have man willingly accept punishment even for an *inevitable* crime; in this way he was able to demonstrate his freedom precisely through the loss of this freedom.

As in all things, Greek art is rule here. No people has been more faithful than the Greeks to this characteristic of humanity.

As long as man dwells in the realm of nature he is *master* of nature, in the authentic sense of the word, just as he can be master of himself. He assigns to the objective world its definite limits beyond which it may not go. To the extent that he *represents* the object to himself, to the extent that he gives it form and consistency, he masters it. He has nothing to fear, for he himself has posited the limits. But to the extent that he sublates these limits, and the object is no longer *able to be represented,* that is, to the extent he has strayed beyond the limit of representation, he finds himself lost. The terrors of the objective world overwhelm him. He has done away with its bounds; how shall he now subdue it? He can no longer give distinct form to the boundless object; it sways before him in its indeterminacy. Where should he chain it, where seize it, where put limits on its excessive power?

So long as Greek art remains within the limits of nature, what people is more naturally at these limits than the Greeks; but as soon as it leaves those limits, what people is more terrible.* The invisible power is too sublime to be subdued by flattery; its heroes are too noble to be saved by cowardice. There is nothing left but—to fight and fail.

But such a struggle is thinkable only on behalf of tragic art; it could not become a system of action because such a system would presuppose a race of titans, and without this presupposition, it would certainly turn out to be an utter disaster to humanity. If our race were to be defined by the terrors of an invisible world, would it not be easier to tremble before the most gentle notion of freedom, to bow to the superior power of that world, instead of going down fighting? In fact, the horrors of the present world would torment us more than the terrors of the future. The same man who would obtain his existence in the supersensuous world by begging will become the tormentor of humanity in this world, who raged against himself and others. Humiliation in that world would find a compensation in power in this world. To the extent that he woke up from the delights of that world, he will return into this one to make it a hell. It would be fortunate were he to be lulled in the arms of that world in order to become a moral *child* in this world.

. . . .

Why do you who believe in reason complain that it is unable to work toward its own destruction, that it is unable to realize an idea the reality of which would destroy everything that you yourself have labored so hard to construct?

. . . .

Let us rejoice in the certainty of having advanced to the last great problem to which any philosophy can advance. Our spirit feels freer now

---

*The Greek gods were still within nature. Their power was not invisible, not beyond the reach of human freedom. Frequently, human cleverness won a victory over the physical power of the gods. Even the bravery of Greek heroes often terrified the Olympians. But the truly *supernatural* realm for the Greeks begins with *fate,* with the invisible power which no natural power could reach, a power which was not even at the disposal of the immortal gods. The more terrifying they are in the realm of the supernatural, the more natural the Greeks are themselves. The more sweetly a people dreams of the supersensible world, the more despicable, the more unnatural it is itself.

to the extent that we return from the situation of speculation to the enjoyment and exploration of nature without the fear of an ever-recurring disquiet of an unsatisfied spirit which might be led back to that unnatural state. The ideas to which our speculation has risen cease to be objects of an idle occupation that exhausts our spirit all too soon; they become the law of our *life,* and, insofar as they themselves change into life and existence, insofar as they themselves become *objects* of experience, they free us forever from the tiresome business of certifying their reality by way of an a priori speculation.

We shall not complain, but be glad finally to have reached the crossroad where a parting is unavoidable, happy that we have investigated the secret of our spirit, by virtue of which the just becomes free *of his own accord,* while the unjust trembles *in himself* before a justice which he did not find in himself and which he had consequently assigned to another world, to the hands of a punishing judge. No longer will the wise person take refuge in mysteries in order to hide his principles from profane eyes. It is a crime against humanity to conceal principles, which are universally communicable. But nature itself has set limits to this communicability: it has—in order to preserve the *dignity* of philosophy which *of itself* becomes esoteric because it cannot be learned and cannot be imitated or recited, nor contained in dead words which secret enemies might pick up—a symbol for the union of free spirits, a symbol by which they all recognize each other, and one that they need not hide, and yet a symbol which is intelligible only to them, whereas for others it will be an eternal riddle.

3 Hegel

Repetition, for a god, is the sign of majesty,
necessity's seal.
          —Roberto Calasso,
          The Marriage of Cadmus and Harmony, p. 33

Hegel's relation to the question of tragedy is doubly distinctive: it is the first thoroughly speculative theory of tragedy, and it is the first theory of speculation to be forged in the crucible of this question. It is a relation to tragedy that suggests, however unspoken, that the only competent spectator of the tragedy, the only one who understands its true nature, is the philosopher who grasps the necessity of regarding the tragedy speculatively. This wedding of the idea of the tragic, which presents a conception of life as torn, conflicted, and agonized, with the idea of speculation, which seeks to grasp all things, in their mutuality and belonging together, that is, as a unity, is the marriage of opposites—or so it would seem. But speculative philosophy does not want to be another metaphysics or philosophy of identity: the unity that is the sign of the speculative is not above or outside or other to the phenomenal world, it is rather the very system of this world itself, and it is as complicated and multiple as the world itself. That is why spirit, which is simply Hegel's name for this unity in its most general form, comes to be known most properly, most as itself, in a phenomenology. Nonetheless, the great danger of speculative thought is

89

always that it might sink into a "night in which all the cows are black," that is, that the thought of the unity of things collapses in upon itself, becoming thereby a simple, undifferentiated identity in which differences are extinguished. There is good evidence that Hegel came to regard Schelling's work as an example of precisely such a danger come to pass. Whether or not such a judgment regarding Schelling is a just one, it is important to always bear in mind when reading Hegel that Hegel's deepest concern is to think the unity of things, to think spirit, as infinitely differentiated, infinitely self-differentiating. This concern is most prominently and powerfully answered in the operations of the tragic which Hegel understands as presenting the highest form of such a conflicted unity. Conflict, contradiction, negation, sacrifice, and death saturate the life of spirit so thoroughly and are so native to it that they define the very truth of spirit, and to hold fast to this truth, to pay tribute to the complexity of life, is the task of thinking. The dynamic of tragedy, the economy of the idea of the tragic, presents a thinking which would answer to this task with the supreme challenge. This, then, is the highest moment for thinking: to grasp the tragedy of spirit speculatively, that is, as a unity which is a unity precisely because it is lodged in the antinomy of its own contradictions. The idea of the tragic stands as a sort of acid test of the capacity of spirit to grasp itself in its radical complexity. And so the question becomes whether or not spirit can take the idea of the tragic into itself without thereby extinguishing the truth of the tragic.

Clearly, then, the idea of the tragic is not merely one idea among others that will appear at various moments in the life of spirit. It will, rather, belong, in some manner, to the life of spirit in general as well as to certain specific moments in which tragedy itself is the form that the life of spirit takes. Consequently, there are always two forms in which the idea of the tragic makes an appearance in Hegel's work. First, and most commonly, it serves as a sort of model for the operations of spirit which repeats itself in infinitely varied sites and forms. In such instances, when tragedy is presented as an exemplary form of the appearance of spirit, Hegel typically hides its presence. In other words, though a specific, virtually always Greek, tragedy (and *Antigone* is overwhelmingly the tragedy of choice) serves as the interpretive framework for a theme to be analyzed, the general framework of tragedy allows Hegel to expose the crisis of spirit at any particular stage and to clarify the ethical overtones of the stakes of that crisis.[1] The other form in which the idea of the tragic makes an appearance in Hegel's work is found on those occasions when Hegel explicitly analyzes a particular tragedy with no clear, overreaching ulterior motivation beyond the effort to understand that particular work as a work of *art*. In such cases, which are predominately found in his *Aesthetics*, Hegel opens his interpretation to the wider significance and concerns of the work. Such are the moments where he does not try to fit the reading of the work into some agenda beyond the work proper; rather, such instances show Hegel to be concerned precisely with what is proper to the work itself. This second form of the appearance of the idea of the tragic is more extensive and detailed in its examination of the sweep of that idea as it is presented in the work of art. Curiously, however, these more detailed analyses of tragic art work, which for the most part are found in works from the final years of Hegel's life, are not necessarily the best places to turn to gain an understanding of how Hegel thinks the nature of the tragic. In the end, those texts which treat tragic works in some detail generally only confirm, rather than revise, the way in which tragedies have provided Hegel with a model for the analysis of the phenomenal life of spirit since his early youthful friendship and collaboration with Schelling and Hölderlin. In short, the idea of the tragic which Hegel formulates rather early in his career sustains his thought in essential ways long before he comes to undertake an extended and detailed analysis of works of tragic art later in his life when he writes the *Aesthetics*.[2]

Despite its centrality and importance for Hegel, despite the fact that one sees its presence in virtually every one of his texts, taking up the question of the tragic work and coming to a clear understanding of its stakes and the nature of its disclosure is not easy in the case of Hegel. There are at least two reasons for this peculiar difficulty that should be noted. First, so many of Hegel's gestures toward tragedy and the idea of the tragic are covert and lack both any reference to a specific work and even any use of the words "tragedy" or "tragic" themselves. But it is precisely at such moments that the power of the image of the tragic, or the force of a particular tragic work, can often be especially powerful.[3] Yet the covert nature of the appearance of the tragedy often makes it difficult to recognize such moments for what they are. Second, Hegel's understanding of tragedy, both as it operates covertly and as it is read overtly in his work, evolves over the years. Precisely because it is such a central notion, precisely because it has the protean quality that permits it to adapt itself to the most disparate forms of the life of spirit, Hegel's understanding of the idea of the tragic is undergoing a constant test and is being constantly challenged to meet ever new and more subtle needs of spirit. Nonetheless, there are some general features of his sense of the tragic that can help navigate the complex terrain of its treatment in Hegel. And there are some texts that can be singled out as providing some of the most innovative and enduring insights regarding the tragic that emerge out of Hegel. In short, despite its difficulties, there is a way of posing the question of how the tragic is thought by Hegel that does not lose itself in the labyrinth of the theme as it unfolds throughout his life.

There are four general features of Hegel's conception of the idea of the tragic that endure throughout his career and so can serve as guidelines in the effort to clarify his contribution to this theme. Each of these points will be repeated, in detail, in the analysis here and so needs only to be noted at this point. Nonetheless, because they are such pervasive traits of Hegel's conception of the tragic, it might help to enumerate them provisionally at the outset.

First, when Hegel enlists a tragic structure as an interpretive model for understanding any particular concept, it invariably appears in the second stage of the development of the concept under consideration. The tragic framework is never appropriate as a way of explaining the origin of any idea. Rather, the tragic moment in any theme is always the moment of its crisis, the moment in which its truth is demanded and summoned. This is one of the indications that the tragic as Hegel understands it always represents an advanced stage in the development of the consciousness of any idea. For the tragic to appear, for the crisis it signals to enter, a past is required. Second, this crisis that the tragic moment signals is inevitably presented as a specific form of crisis, namely, as the crisis of singularity confronting the idea, of the unique confronting the universal. This is perhaps the most pervasive and defining trait of the tragic as Hegel sees it (and it is the trait, more than any other, which is so clearly played out in Hegel's understanding of *Antigone*). In this feature the ethical dimension of the tragic achieves its greatest concretion. It is also the trait that mostly clearly raises the issue of the most radical form of negation as Hegel will call it, namely, death. Hegel understands the tragic as necessarily destined to be a confrontation to the death, and, as a consequence, it stands as the moment in which the unity that is spirit confronts the pure singularity exposed by death. This crisis of the singular also helps clarify the third general trait of Hegel's conception of the tragic, namely, that it always raises the question of law not as an ethical abstraction, not on the plane of metaphysics, but in concretion of singular being. The problem of law as Hegel understands it is clear and is to be understood according to the double imperative at work in the law: on the one hand, it is centered in the universalizability of a rule; on the other hand, it is inscribed in the irreplaceable, the unique life of the singular being in a concrete situation. The law is the form in which the individual takes the claims of the universal upon oneself. As such, it is the law itself which marks the appearance of an extreme contradiction, of a limit, in the phenomenal world. It becomes one of the names for the tragedy of spirit. It is also the constant reminder that the significance of the tragic is not an abstraction, but only to be grasped in the full concretion of ethical life in the phenomenal world. The fourth general feature of Hegel's conception of the tragic follows from this sense of the concretion of the law: the tragic belongs to history and must be thought in conjunction with the full force of history. Here we find something of the ancient sense of the relation of tragedy and destiny. There is a double relation sustaining the kinship of tragedy and history: tragedy becomes the model for thinking the operation of history (and this will be a trademark of philosophizing into the present);[4] in viewing the tragedy we witness the unfolding of the inexorability of history's force, and, in turn, history comes to be seen as the motor of the tragic trajectory.

Such, in crude outline, are the most enduring and decisive features of Hegel's conception of the tragic. They do not by any means exhaust what is remarkable or distinctive about his understanding of the tragic, but they do tend to shape it in most all of its appearances. But such central and enduring themes naturally undergo significant modifications throughout Hegel's lifetime. While these general themes reappear throughout his work, the specifics of how they are unfolded do change over time. Especially since the idea of the tragic forms such a linchpin in Hegel's work, one who would sort out the nature of the tragic as Hegel thinks it faces a serious hermeneutic problem in the sheer volume of works and passages in which the tragic plays either an overt or covert significant role. In some manner, to take up the topic of the tragic in Hegel is to take up the heart of the Hegelian dialectic since it plays itself out in every localized theme. However, a strategy that allows one to focus and manage the issue, without thereby missing all its dimensions in Hegel, is possible. To this end, this chapter will take up two of Hegel's texts almost exclusively, namely, the *Phenomenology of Spirit* (1807) and the *Lectures on Fine Art* (1823–29). The threefold reason for this selection is easily explained: both of these texts represent the culmination of other efforts and so serve to draw together themes from a number of other texts, the texts represent the views of both the early and late years of Hegel's career, and together they approach the question of tragedy in both of the manners which define his relation to the question. This final point is perhaps most significant and so in need of some elaboration. As already noted, Hegel's relation to the topic of tragedy is a doubled one. In general, the *Phenomenology of Spirit* and the *Lectures on Fine Art* each represent one side of this twinned relation. In the *Phenomenology of Spirit* we find the idea of the tragic, and even specific Greek tragic dramas, being enlisted as a sort of model for the presentation and analysis of themes other than the work of art proper. There the saturation of the text with the concerns of tragedy, though almost completely unthematized, is at a maximum, and there the ethical and political stakes of the issue of the tragic are also most clearly highlighted. In the *Lectures on Fine Art*, on the other hand, the approach to the topic of tragic art is taken in terms of its achievement specifically *as* art. In other words, there the issue of tragic art, though extended beyond the special case of tragic drama (and even of Greek tragic drama), is most clearly thematized and considered on its own terms. There the question of tragedy is taken up specifically as a form of art to which the speculative absolute entrusts itself. Here the treatment of Hegel's understanding of the tragic will begin with its appearance in the *Phenomenology of Spirit*, where the largest sweep of the issue is found. The consideration of the *Lectures on Fine Art* will follow. One restriction in both analyses should be noted before beginning: the question of the tragic in Hegel will center primarily on his understanding of *Greek* tragedy. Although the general topic of tragedy and modern forms of tragedy, especially Shakespeare, will be treated, the reason for the preeminent import of the topic of Greek tragedy has already been noted. The stakes of the question of tragedy are at their highest in Greek tragedy since there the overcoming of the metaphysical tradition and the opening of nonmetaphysical forms of speculation are at issue. Greek tragedy marks the highest form of the possibility of tragedy precisely because it is developed prior to the inscription of the language of metaphysics in the heart of culture.

*　　*　　*

One of the concluding remarks of the *Phenomenology of Spirit,* one of the highest insights that spirit has into its own nature, is found in the penultimate paragraph of the text. There Hegel writes that "to know one's limits is to know to sacrifice oneself."[5] By this point we have learned that the life of spirit is animated by repeated sacrifice; indeed, one might justly argue that the optic of sacrifice is the one general point of view that affords the greatest insight into the real movement of the life of spirit.[6] From the outset the movement of spirit coming to itself is driven by self-sacrifice. There is perhaps no pivotal moment in the life of spirit that is not able to be understood as an instance of such sacrifice. The great sacrificial figures, the living images of spirit at its decisive moments— Antigone, Socrates, Christ—all are clearly visible in the text, even when not noted by name. Since Hegel understands tragedy as the illustration of the necessity of this sacrificial moment, it is easy to see how widespread the theme of tragedy is in the text if one considers its special kinship with the notion of sacrifice. And so it does not require much effort to see how frequently tragedy serves as a model at several critical moments in the *Phenomenology of Spirit* (one can even see this to some degree in the dialectic of the master and the slave). Nonetheless, there are two passages where the idea of the tragic is uncommonly powerful in its presence, and these passages can serve as an anchor for treating this topic in this text. The first passage is found in the section on "Spirit," more precisely, in the first two sections devoted to "The *true* Spirit," namely, to "The Ethical Order" (paragraphs 444–77). It is a passage which closely adheres to the themes Hegel will take up in sections 158–69 of the *Philosophy of Right.*[7] The second passage is found in the section entitled "Religion in the Form of Art," especially the section on "The Spiritual Work of Art" (paragraphs 727– 44). Although they are found at quite different moments in the text, and although they are centered upon apparently different themes, these two sections of the text answer to one another and need to be read as a piece. In both texts it is *Antigone,* Hegel's most frequent tragedy of choice, which serves as the conducting wire of the moment at hand. In these passages one sees with clarity the powerful life of one text within another.[8]

The first prominent appearance of *Antigone* is found after consciousness has reached an advanced stage, one that it will only modify and no longer fundamentally alter. It has reached the stage of reason, and so consciousness now knows the ideality of the real (or, from an equally just perspective, the reality of the ideal); in other words, it knows that the life of the idea is just as real as natural life. Consciousness has already learned the meaning of its relation to natural life in its encounters with death. In such encounters it has come to learn the radical singularity of its life. It has also, subsequently, learned that the ideality it brings to experience structures its world and bestows upon it its reality. Having learned the ineluctability of this ideality, this necessary abstraction that is thinking, consciousness has learned as well that it is, by nature, legislative. This means simply, as Kant had shown, that consciousness lays down the law in each and every deed; each of its actions has the weight of a universal action. And consciousness has finally become aware of this truth about itself.

But these two truths which it has learned regarding itself present consciousness with the enigma of how it is to reconcile its understanding of itself as pure singularity, as *this* one, and simultaneously as the entry of universality in the world. Spirit now knows itself to be obliging to a double, and conflicted, imperative in "the duality of a law of individuality and a law of universality."[9] This doublet of the law will be renamed by Hegel as the "human law" and the "divine law," and the polarity which is outlined in these names, a polarity in the relation of spirit to the law, is one that must, by its very nature, produce a conflict. In the end, the origin of each form of the law indexes it to a different destination, and it is this difference which produces the tragic conflict. The dilemma Hegel is analyzing here is not an abstract problem whatsoever. In simple terms (which are not entirely appropriate to Hegel's full intention at this point in the text), it is the question of how one is to reconcile one's own, individual conscience with an awareness of a duty to something that exceeds what such conscience can encompass. After Hegel, we find eloquent reflections on this problem of conscience in Thoreau and King, both of whom not only wrote about, but understood, the relation of this question to action. What we find at this moment in the life of spirit is a crisis in the ethical consciousness of spirit.

Hegel suggests that there is a natural site for the expression of this crisis: it is the site defined simultaneously by natural life—that is, by the singularity of the body and the bonds of blood—and by ethical community—that is, by the bonds of spirit. This conflicted, this doubled, site is the family.[10] It is in and out of the family—defined by natural life, yet with each of its members equally set in an ethical relation not determined by natural life, but by the fact that the family members are also citizens of a state—that this polarity of the law will necessarily become a crisis. Here Hegel poses a remarkably difficult and still timely question. In asking about the passage from natural, blood lines of affinity to larger, ethical forms of relation, Hegel is not simply investigating the complexity of family life; rather, he is asking about ethicality and all forms of "natural" identity, and he is posing the question of how, if at all, such relations can be sublated into a state. This is an ancient question, and our failure to have answered it has left the space for powerful hatreds to emerge. The indication of this failure to find an adequate solution to this question, namely, the residue of tribalism and racism that fix some sense of natural identity outside of the ethical substance of a nation, has led to some of the most bitter conflicts of our age.[11] But Hegel's purpose in this section of the text, which will be the first significant appearance of the tragic model, is to propose at least the general direction of a solution to this issue. It begins with the recognition that the panlogism of the law, at least of the law of reason, cannot give an exhaustive account of the truth of the ethical realm. This, then, is the moment in which all of the divisions in the ethical realm surface in their irreconcilability from the vantage point of law. And the place where this crisis must first develop is the family, the final locus of natural life. Because the issues which emerge as defining this ethical crisis belong to natural life, the development of ethical and political life traced out here is necessarily thought along the lines of kinship, namely, of gender and generation. The first form of politics centers on the questions of sexuality and tradition.

Gender becomes the principal axis along which this ethical crisis will spin, and so it is important to understand why the central figure of this crisis must be a woman.[12] It is also important to bear in mind that the figure of woman will remain for Hegel "the eternal irony of community."[13] In other words, this crisis will never be fully and finally resolved; the locus of its appearance will remain vital in the life of the community. Sexual difference, then, is never fully sublated, never fully resolved as a difference and a source of tension, in the ethical education of spirit. While the origin of sexual difference as Hegel understands it has already been accounted for in the earliest forms of natural life, namely, in the division of the sexes as it emerges in plant life,[14] the significance and endurance of this difference for spirit emerges only in the ethical and political realm. When he analyzes this moment in the formation of the ethical consciousness of spirit by taking the dynamics and deeds displayed in *Antigone* (and the figure of Antigone in particular) as the focal point of this analysis, Hegel's intention is to ask two sets of intersecting questions: first, to ask about the reach of the law and, second, to ask about the reach of natural life. For both sets of questions, death becomes the supreme issue, the point at which such questions enter their crisis. Not by accident, then, is Antigone understood as the figure who represents a sort of solidarity with the dead. But the meaning of death, and of this special form of solidarity, which shapes the experience that educates spirit at the turning point in the formation of its ethical consciousness, becomes clear only by beginning with the force of gender in the situation that unfolds here.

Consequently, to understand this section and the meaning of this special solidarity, and to appreciate the significance of the tragic form defining the development of ethical life, one needs to focus on the specifics which lead Hegel to the choice of Antigone as the center of this development. While it is critical to note that it must be a woman at the center of this development, not any woman would do. Hegel could not, for instance, have taken Jeanne d'Arc as a model here since it is not only *as woman*, but as *sister*, that Antigone serves as the key figure in this moment of spirit's education: "The feminine in the form of the sister has the highest *intuitive* awareness of what is ethical."[15] Moreover, it is only as the sister *of a brother* that Hegel finds Antigone to be the necessary center of this decisive moment. Hegel explains this quite strange contention by suggesting that all the other family relationships of the sister—he names only that of daughter, mother, and wife, not of sister to a sister[16]—are "mixed"; in other words, they are complicated by either inequality or desire, both of which distort the possibility of an unmediated ethical relationship. However, in the relation of the sister to the brother "the recognition of herself in him is pure and unmixed with any natural desire. In this relationship, therefore . . . the moment of the individual self, recognizing and being recognized, can here assert its right, because it is linked to the equilibrium of the blood and is a relation devoid of desire. The loss of the brother is therefore irreparable to the sister and her duty towards him is the highest."[17] But even this strict qualification does not go far enough toward understanding what it is that makes Antigone the key figure in this tragedy of ethical life, since there is no symmetry in the relationship between the sister and brother as Hegel understands it. In other words, the same ethical immediacy is not found in the relationship of the brother to the sister, but is proper only to the sister.[18] Hegel's explanation of this peculiar asymmetry is not very clear, but seems to center on the fact that the man, as a citizen, possesses the "right of desire" and so "preserves a freedom in regard to it,"[19] while the woman is denied this right. It is this freedom of desire that enables the man to choose according to the contingency of his desires, while the "relationships of the woman are based . . . on the universal."[20] The basis on which Hegel makes this distinction is unclear. Initially, it seems that he is making this decision on the grounds of the conventions of heterosexual life and of patriarchy; Hegel is usually careful about not allowing such arbitrary conventions to uncritically seep into what he presents as a necessary movement. And yet, at the outset of his analysis it does seem that Hegel is basing his decision in convention-ally assigned gender roles. However, in the conclusion of this analysis of the different roles found in family life Hegel gives another account of the grounds of this difference when he says that "the divine law has its indi-vidualization . . . in the woman, through whom, as the middle term, the unconscious spirit rises out of its unreality into actual existence, out of a state in which it is unknowing and unconscious into the realm of con-scious spirit. The union of man and woman constitutes the active middle term of the whole and the element which sunders itself into these ex-tremes of divine and human law."[21] Hegel continues this remark by say-ing that the union of man and woman is the union of "opposite move-ments: one from actuality down to unreality . . . to . . . death; and the other, the upward movement of the law of the nether world to the actual-ity of the light of day and to conscious existence [i.e., to birth]. Of these movements, the former falls to man, the latter to woman."[22] In short, the grounds of how Hegel thinks the different ethical positions of the man and the woman are found in the different relations to the singularity of the individual which are granted men and women—better, in the possibil-ity granted to the woman and denied to the man, namely, the possibility of carrying another singularity within herself, the possibility of birth.[23] Because the relation to the brother is shorn of any desire, the loss of the brother is the loss of the only other with whom this possibility is fore-closed. Every other family relation starts as a relation either of inequality (the parents), of desire (spouse), or of a sameness which does not con-front the full extent of natural life and the difference which it introduces (the sister). In other words, the relation of the sister to the brother is "pure." But it still needs to be explained just why there is no symmetry in this relation. Why does the relation of the woman to birth, and of the man to death, render this relationship one-sided with regard to this "purity"?

The answer to this question is found in the role ascribed to death in this struggle of spirit to find a passage from natural lines of kinship, fam-ily, to ethical lines of community, state. It will also explain why Hegel ar-gues that this struggle of ethical life is destined to be one that follows the logic of the tragic.

Death is, according to Hegel, "the absolute master";[24] it is the ulti-mate struggle for consciousness, and as such it defines all of the struggles of consciousness. In the final analysis, it is the struggle animating every other struggle. This struggle for the formation of an independent ethical consciousness is no exception. As noted, it is a struggle that must have its roots in the family since it is in the family that the elemental singularity of the individual, the body, finds its origin: "The positive end peculiar to the family is the individual as such."[25] This is the divine law, the law of singu-larity that the family, ultimately the union of man and woman, represents in the world. It is a law which stands in contrast to the human law, the law of generality and universalizability, which the state must represent, and so one sees already why it is that the family and the state are dedicated to, at least potentially, opposing ends. The point at which this potential for conflict must become real conflict is death, and the reason is simple: death is the "universality which the individual *as such* attains."[26] Death marks the moment which is universal, insofar as it is the end of every individual, and the moment of pure singularity, insofar as it is mine and mine alone. In death, the individual belongs simultaneously to the law of the universal and of the unique; as such, it is the site where the clash of the human and the divine laws must happen. Hegel also makes it clear why the family must precipitate this crisis: "The duty of the family member is . . . that the individual's ultimate being shall not belong solely to nature and remain something irrational, but shall be something *done,* and the right of consciousness asserted in it."[27] Burial and mourning, the final relation of the living to the dead, is thus the way in which the natural phenomenon of death is sublated into a spiritual act. This duty falls to the woman, according to Hegel, because in consigning the dead to the earth one is returning them to the womb, and this, says Hegel, remains the province of woman. And the purest expression of this duty, one "unmixed" by inequality or desire but still defined by difference, is the duty of the sister to the brother. That, of course, is the duty in the name of which Antigone dies.

But the basic elements at play in the story of this ethical crisis have not yet been exposed, and so the logic of the story is not yet ready to unfold. One more element needs to be clarified: it is also necessary to understand the paradox which requires the state to seek to retain for itself, and itself alone, the power of death, "the absolute master."[28] With regard to *Antigone* this means understanding why Creon is committed to executing Antigone for her challenge to his authority. It will also mean understanding why Creon too needs to be understood in the light of his gender.

Hegel's clarification of this point is clear and direct: "The spirit of universal . . . association is the simple and negative essence of those systems which tend to isolate themselves. In order not to let them become rooted and set in this isolation, thereby breaking up the whole and letting the spirit of community evaporate, the government has from time to time to shake them to their core by war. By this means the government . . . violates their right to independence . . . and they are made to feel in the task laid on them their lord and master, death."[29] While the essential task of the family is to preserve the integrity and real singularity of the individual, the essential task of the government is the negative of this, namely, to preserve the equality and sameness of all individuals. The final equalizer, which is at the same time the final singularizer, is death, the moment in which the universal essence of the individual *as such* is achieved. The community therefore possesses the confirmation of its power of assuring equality in preserving for itself the death of its citizens. To use the language of Hegel's analysis at this point, one might say that the human law (of the state) validates itself by retaining the divine right (death) for itself.[30] Furthermore, according to Hegel, the work of securing this validation must be understood as belonging to the man. According to Hegel, the natural work of the man, the only work of the man (since he cannot give birth) with respect to the operations of natural life, is the work of death, the work of killing and of sacrifice. This is why Hegel says that "Nature, not the accident of circumstances or choice, assigns one sex to one law, the other to the other law . . . the two ethical powers . . . actualize themselves in the two sexes."[31] Of course, saying this leads to one of the more interesting paradoxes in Hegel's analysis of this moment, namely, that in her sacrifice Antigone assumes as well the role of the man. This, in part at least, is what Irigaray means when she says of Antigone that "she had digested the masculine."[32]

With this the elements of the ethical tragedy have all been laid out. With this point the fault lines along which the ethical worlds of the family and state will necessarily fracture and fight have been articulated. Now we see the specific issues and the roles in and around which the struggle for recognition will take place. Hegel explains how this dynamic will begin to unfold by saying, "The way in which the antithesis is constituted in this ethical realm is such that self-consciousness has not yet received its due as a particular individuality."[33] In other words, as events unfold they need to be understood as being driven by the need of spirit to recognize itself in its radical individuality and to understand the place of this individuality with respect to the universality which this individuality knows itself to be.[34] Such is the ethical task of spirit. It is the same task that spirit lays out for itself in the dialectic of recognition that animates the struggle of mastery and slavery: it is the task of self-consciousness struggling to reconcile itself with the dual knowledge of itself as free, as radically individuated and so for itself, and as a natural being which is destined to die, and in this to be individuated. This struggle of freedom and death is now being played out on the stage of ethical life. But this means that now this task is fulfilled only to the extent that it is answered by elevating the natural life of the individual to the universal, only insofar as it finds its truth in the wider horizon that spirit has exposed for itself in the form of an ethical community. The task, as Hegel describes it, is for spirit to lift the individuality which is "locked up in the darkness" into the "public meaning open to the light of day."[35] It is, Hegel explains, driven by the deepest desire of spirit, namely, the desire to know itself. But no matter how this task is answered, whether from the side of the human law or the divine law, it will be answered only from one side of its double truth. In short, spirit is destined to a *crime,* and it thereby calls upon itself *punishment.*[36]

This amounts to saying that an errancy, a tragic flaw (here one thinks of Aristotle's notion of *hamartia*), belongs to the very nature of ethical life. Guilt belongs to every deed of the individual since every deed of the individual *as such* is a crime, a rupture of the wholeness of the community. Innocence in the ethical realm is not a possibility: "Innocence, therefore, is merely non-action, like the mere being of a stone, not even that of a child."[37] The reason this conflict is unavoidable, the roots of this necessary crime and of this guilt, is surprising, namely, that the ethical realm has not yet reconciled the force of sexual difference: "The ethical action contains the moment of crime, because it does not do away with the *natural* allocation of the two laws to the two sexes, but rather . . . remains within the sphere of natural immediacy."[38] The two sides of the law are thus linked to one another as are the two sexes.[39] Hegel interprets this by saying that "the two laws being linked in the essence, the fulfillment of the one evokes the other and . . . calls it forth as a violated and now hostile entity demanding revenge."[40] Neither form of the law alone suffices to answer the ethical task of law as such.

The inevitable conflict of laws in the ethical realm—a conflict which emerges in its most pristine form in the question of the place of death in the community and in the relation of the sister to the brother—grips law in such a way as to set it against itself such that it can only bring upon itself destruction: "The movement of the ethical powers against each other and of the individualities calling them into life and action have attained their true end only in so far as both sides suffer the same destruction."[41] What happens, then, is that each side of the ethical consciousness—with roots in the human and divine, the male and the female—summons the other side to the conflict; neither side alone satisfies the desire of consciousness to grasp its truth as both free and as mortal. It is a conflict that is most complete, most ruinous when it is instigated knowingly, as Antigone does, because such a conflict is one in which it is clear that "what is *ethical* must be *actual*."[42] In such a case ethical consciousness "must acknowledge its opposite as its own actuality, must acknowledge its guilt."[43]

This, however, is precisely the moment that must be understood according to the model of tragic consciousness, and so Hegel cites *Antigone* at this point, saying, "Because we suffer we recognize that we have erred."[44] The line Hegel cites here is of one of Antigone's final words as she is being led to the cave that will serve as her tomb. She says simply that she will know whether or not she was wrong by whether or not she suffers. She also says that if her opponents are wrong, that they should learn by suffering. In other words, the knowledge requisite for negotiating this ethical impasse which defines the status of law with respect to the recognition of the individual is a knowledge which, at this stage at least, is given only in suffering. The analysis of ethical life here not only exhibits the form of a tragedy, it also has the result of a tragedy. Thus "only in the downfall of both sides alike is absolute right accomplished, and the ethical substance as the negative power which engulfs both sides, omnipotent and righteous destiny, steps on scene."[45] In the collapse of both sides, in the ruin which the ethical world suffers as a whole, the ethical task of spirit begins to complete itself. In the suffering which the conflict precipitates and the ruin of the individuals who act only one-sidedly, the true end of these ethical powers is reached and "neither power has any advantage over the other that would make it a more essential moment."[46] The very framework according to which the ethical world is articulated renders impossible any other result. Consciousness has not yet advanced to the stage at which it can grasp what is requisite for it to understand itself as destined to die and yet as free, as a singular being and as a citizen of an ethical community. This collapse of the world, this double-sided ruin of the elements of the ethical realm as it is delineated here, is the lesson consciousness must learn if it is to advance itself to the end of its deepest desire for recognition. What must be learned at this point is how the roots of spirit in the ethical realm are doubled and folded into one another. This means that it must learn that the "supreme right is a supreme wrong, that its victory is rather its downfall."[47] There is no possibility of ethical rightness at this point, and so the very assertion of such rightness of a law condemns it to be a supreme wrong. This critique of righteousness is an ongoing concern of Hegel's, and his disdain for those who persist in asserting a rightness that is proper to themselves as individuals is clear: "When anyone says that he is acting according to his *own* law and conscience against others, he is saying, in fact, that he is wronging them."[48] The law itself is a form of crime since it must rob the individual of the singularity proper to it. In the end, this means that the ethical shape of spirit which still thinks itself in terms of the opposition of the individual and the community needs to vanish, it needs to collapse, so that another form of consciousness can take its place.

But before announcing the emergence of the new shape of consciousness (which repeats the movement from the ethical consciousness of Greece to the formal legalism of the Roman world), Hegel makes an important remark that indicates why this paradox of the ethical realm is self-renewing and so inextinguishable. It will also be the reason why the resolution of the conflicts of the ethical realm is not final, but will require another insight if it is to be grasped speculatively. The roots of the continuation of this paradox of ethical life point back to the question of sexual difference. Hegel comments that "Since the community only gets an existence through its interference with the happiness of the family, and by dissolving the individual self-consciousness into the universal, it creates for itself an internal enemy—womankind in general. Woman [is thus] the eternal irony in the life of community."[49] Hegel's explanation of this important remark is not immediately clear. Nonetheless, if one remembers what he has already said regarding the relation of woman to birth, to the introduction of the singular being in the world, then, perhaps, one can begin to make sense of this remark. Woman stands as the irony, the doubled and paradoxical moment, in the life of the community because Hegel identifies woman, more than man, with new life and the singularity that is defined by the body.

The result of this ethical crisis of spirit that thinks itself according to the human and the divine laws is a collapse of both of these sides. The new form that takes its place is "the soulless community,"[50] and so we see that the struggle over the place of death in the community has produced a community which is the very image of death itself. It is a form of community in which the abstract formalism of the law, the equalization of all before the law, is complete. Now consciousness, which struggled to assert itself in the life of the community, "experiences the loss of its reality and its complete inessentially."[51] But Spirit once again shows itself to be protean, to metamorphose into new shapes, and so what results is the formation of a new form of community. With this transformation that follows the ruin of the ethical realm, which is framed by the double relation to law governing the individual and the community—the divine and the human laws—the first stage in which tragedy serves as a model for the interpretation of the formation of consciousness is concluded. The next stage of spirit does not exhibit the same structure.

What is important for the purposes of tracing the meaning and significance of the tragic for Hegel, though, is not this new shape that follows on the heels of this tragic form, but the role that the tragic form played as the ethical realm of spirit unfolded. In order to trace the importance of this form in the education of spirit that is elaborated in the *Phenomenology of Spirit,* and to indicate why a second reference to tragedy is required, it is important to clarify two points. First, Hegel is not offering a reading of *Antigone;* nonetheless, it is abundantly evident that he is interpreting the ethical life of spirit by reading *Antigone* as the preeminent illustration of how this life must unfold. Hegel's modeling of the ethical world and its struggles is so closely wedded to a specific understanding of *Antigone* that one would be hard pressed to comprehend this important section except by reading it along with *Antigone.*[52] In doing this Hegel grants Sophocles an understanding of the complexities of ethical life which he seldom grants any philosopher, and he does this precisely because of the *form* which the tragedy takes. In other words, the great insight of tragedy (and again it is clear that Greek tragedy is the model) concerns ethical life; indeed, one must say that, in the end, ethical life is not intelligible apart from an understanding of the idea of the tragic. Second, Hegel will enlist *Antigone* as a model a second time in the *Phenomenology of Spirit,* and this time he will do so explicitly by taking account of its tragic form, not as an idea. In other words, this first gesture toward the tragedy does not treat the tragedy *as art;* rather, it presents it almost as the case study of a legal struggle.[53] The first turn to the tragedy takes up the tragedy as a presentation of issues and ideas; the second turn to the tragedy takes it up as a form of making proper to language. What is important to understand in moving between these two sections of the text where tragedy serves as a sort of model for thinking is how it is that the first appearance requires the second appearance for its own completion. It is important, then, to recognize that until the form of the tragedy *as a work of art* is grasped, the full insight of the tragedy is not grasped. It is also at this moment that the completion of tragedy in comedy is disclosed.

*　　*　　*

The first moment in the life of tragedy in the *Phenomenology of Spirit* shows up in the context of the explicit formation of ethical life and its structures. In this moment, which takes up the *idea* animating the drama, Antigone is the chief focus of Hegel's concerns. The second moment in the life of tragedy appears in the context of the formation of religious consciousness and the forms in which it is expressed. In this moment, which takes up the *form as art* which is proper to the tragedy, Sophocles is the chief focus of Hegel's concerns. Much has taken place in the education and the life of spirit in the interim between these two moments; most of all spirit now finds itself prepared to enter its "absolute" stage, the stage in which it comes into its own and in possession of itself. The most primitive form in which it enters this stage of its education is that which is proper to "religious" consciousness.

At the outset it should be noted that "religion" for Hegel is not chiefly a matter of faith or of dogma. Religion as Hegel thinks it here is not a matter of theology. Rather, he hears the word "religion" in a double sense: first, experience has led consciousness to a sense of what is sacred, of the divine, and this speculative experience is at the center of religious consciousness; second, Hegel's interest in this form of consciousness is directed largely to the manner in which this consciousness shapes the possibility of community. In other words, here the concern is with the nature of experiences which bind people together.[54] This is the first fully speculative form of experience in the life of spirit, and so it is not surprising to note that this section of the text is sandwiched between two passages which signal reconciliation, and these passages set the tone for the treatment of religion.[55] The passage immediately prior to this section of the text opens the way for this analysis when it speaks of "The reconciling *yes,* in which two 'I's let go their antithetical *existence,* is the *existence* of the 'I' which has expanded into a duality, and therein remains identical with itself, and, in its complete externalization and opposite, possesses the certainty of itself: it is God manifested in the midst of those who know themselves in the form of pure knowledge."[56] In other words, consciousness has reached a new standpoint in its understanding of itself; now it is in a position to grasp its experiences from this standpoint and so see more clearly what those experiences mean for it. The dual purpose of this section on religion is to analyze the character of this new standpoint and to reconsider the experiences which this new standpoint can illuminate anew. Tragedy and the crisis of the ethical realm play a central role in the fulfillment of this purpose. Here the question is again the ethical vocation of spirit, and here again the inevitable crisis which emerges as this vocation develops is to be thought according to the model of the tragedy.

There are three stages in the evolution of this religious consciousness: natural religion, religion in the form of art, and revealed religion. It is in the second stage of this trajectory that tragedy again becomes the focus of Hegel's concerns. This happens when the first form of religion, namely, religion that indexes itself to an experience of nature, shows itself to be shaped and not merely random; in other words, the experience of nature shows it to be full of intelligence, to be the work of an "artificer." With references to Egypt, both covert and explicit, in particular to the role of the geometry of shapes in the Egyptian conception of nature and the gods, Hegel moves to the point at which consciousness comes to understand that such shapes indicate the presence of mind.[57] Once it arrives at this point, spirit comes to appreciate its own power to shape nature; spirit becomes an artist, and with this discovery it moves to another stage in its education and ability to express itself in the world. At this stage, spirit grasps itself as the essence of its world: "This is spirit, inwardly sure of itself, which mourns over the loss of its world, and now out of the purity of self creates its own essence which is raised about the real world."[58] In short, consciousness now enters the stage at which it knows itself to have the power of creation.

What is not so clear, but nonetheless of utmost importance, is that the period in which spirit discovers this power coincides with the period in which spirit undergoes its most profound ethical crisis. The reason for this is simple: both periods are defined by being stages in which spirit struggles to overcome the natural world. When the crisis of the ethical realm fully unfolds, the singular body of the individual will become its focus. When religion takes the form of art, spirit will do so because it has learned how it need not be held captive to the individuality of the body. This means that even though art will initially develop in relation to bodily things—after expressing itself in various rituals[59] and in the cult and the festival, it will relate first to stone and pigment—it will rapidly migrate into increasingly abstract forms until it arrives at the point of its greatest possible truth, namely, the word. This is what Hegel means when he says that "The work of art therefore demands another element for its existence, the god another mode of coming forth than [natural life]. . . . This higher element is language—an outer reality that is immediately self-conscious existence. . . . Language is the soul existing as soul."[60] Spirit presses itself forward to the word, and in this it explores its capacity to create. In coming to the word, spirit comes to its most "natural" element, the element in which it is most at home; it is the medium proper to spirit itself, "the soul existing as soul."[61]

The arrival of spirit in the word will change everything for spirit and the riddle of itself. In the word, consciousness not only finds the element in which it is most itself, but it also learns about itself from the nature of that element, the nature of language. More precisely, it learns about itself most of all in the relation of language to time, and this relation will also be at the heart of the analysis of tragedy which follows. Hegel first indicates that time is the key to understanding the place of language in the work of art when he says that art in the form of language "stands in contrast to the work of art, such as the statue, which possesses the character of the thing. Whereas the statue exists at rest, *speech is a vanishing existence* . . . and like time, [language] is no longer immediately present in the very moment of its being present."[62] In the vanishing of the word, the mortality of individual beings finds itself expressed. In this temporality of language, in rhythm, language will be the vessel of the pathos of spirit (this will also be the reason music, which is nothing but time made loud, so directly appeals to a sense of pathos). It is this kinship of the word and time which so deeply troubled Plato when he turned to an analysis of the nature of poetry, but it is precisely in this kinship that Hegel will find the truth of poetic language.

Up to this point two of the three elements which introduce and structure Hegel's second reference to tragedy in the *Phenomenology of Spirit* have been laid out: that language is the most spiritual element in which consciousness can express itself in the world (it is the "perfect element in which inwardness is just as external as externality is inward"),[63] and that language—here, of course, the reference is to spoken language—is a vanishing, a temporal, existence. The third element is announced when Hegel says that language "unites into a single pantheon, the separate national spirits [the multiplicities of gods]."[64] In other words, language is, by nature, speculative and so unites what is otherwise disparate. Hegel suggests that the multiplicity of gods—all felt within one human heart[65]—find the possibility of their unity first in the word.

So Hegel introduces this final element of the nature of language in the work of art with a cryptic reference to Homer, who gathered all the gods together in his poetic work. The Homeric poems are the "assembly of national spirits [which] constitute a circle of shapes embracing the whole of nature as well as the whole ethical world."[66] In gathering the gods together, in this assembly that is the poem, Homer gives the world of consciousness its first truly speculative shape and in doing this founds the ethical world which will, eventually, unfold itself in the crisis of the dual laws of the human and the divine. Homer does this in the epic; in other words, he does it in the form of a narration that concentrates itself in the individuality of a hero, of one who confronts this assembly of the gods and who, as a mortal, "feels his life is broken and sorrowfully awaits an early death."[67]

But the epic form does not fully permit the elements of language to accomplish their task as art; a "higher language" is called for. The deficit of the epic form from the point of view of this task is clear: its form does not enter into the content; in other words, the epic speaks only *about* this speculative unity, it does not exhibit it in the form itself. Put in yet another way, the language of epic is still bound to representation and so is not sufficiently *performative*. Such an art form in language is the drama. This is what Hegel means when he says that

> This higher language, that of tragedy, gathers closer together the dispersed moments of the inner essential world and the world of action. . . . In regard to form, the language ceases to be narrative because it enters into the content, just as the content ceases to be one that is represented. [In tragedy] the hero is the speaker, and the performance displays to the audience . . . *self-conscious* human beings who *know* their rights and purposes, the power and the will of their specific nature and know how to *assert* them.[68]

In the performance of the drama, which is the form proper to the tragic, all the elements of language come into play, and these elements have a reality in the actual speech of the actors. In this way the tragic drama opens up the highest form that language can take in the formation of the religious consciousness of spirit which expresses itself in art. Tragedy thus shows itself to be the truth, the real destination of art.

But even this point needs one more refinement before we are in a position to understand the significance of the second reference to tragedy in the *Phenomenology of Spirit*. Hegel notes that in the (Greek) tragedy the actors wear masks, and these masks are essential to the nature of the performance since it is only in the mask that the specific individuality of the actor is removed from the play so that the actor can represent individuality in general. In the end, tragedy will reveal its truth—in comedy—only when the mask is dropped. But Hegel argues that until that point, namely, as tragedy in its performance, the most compact expression of the possibilities of language in the tragedy are found in the chorus. Because the chorus lacks any power, because it cannot act, it never "subdues the riches and varied abundance of divine life, and so lets it all go its own way."[69] In short, in the speeches of the chorus the full diversity of the divinity of life finds its truest expression, and in this way the chorus functions as the "general ground" for the movement of the tragedy.

Hegel's comments which follow in the next four lengthy paragraphs are exceedingly difficult. What is clear is that in these passages he is driving at what he takes to be the deepest source of the tragic conflict—no matter what the explicit theme of the tragedy might be. His argument is that the real roots of the tragedy are not ultimately to be explained by any reference to special circumstances (e.g., Antigone's efforts to bury Polynices); rather, the wellspring of the tragic is found in the antithesis between the acting subjects of the drama, who confront the world as a reality to be negated, and the chorus, who confront the action as a truth to be known. What is presented in the tragedy is an antithesis within consciousness itself, the antithesis between knowing and acting: "Consciousness disclosed this antithesis through action; acting in accordance with the knowledge which has been manifested it discovers that this knowledge is deceptive."[70] That remark, which seems, in part at least, to contain some reference to *King Oedipus* when it speaks of "deceptive knowledge" (such as the knowledge Oedipus initially has of his own identity), points to the aporia which the tragic work of art discloses. In the earlier passages on ethical life Hegel had explained this tragic conflict in terms of the human and divine laws; here he explains it as the aporia of individuality and of essence, of acting and knowing, which can never completely coincide.[71] The mask is the effort of the drama to conceal individuality; however, in the end the action of the drama drives every form of individuality to its ruin and shows the higher order which individuality as such cannot grasp. Hinting again at his earlier "interpretation" of *Antigone,* Hegel says here, "The action, in being carried out, demonstrates their unity in the natural downfall of both powers. . . . Individuality that is only superficially attached to essence is unessential."[72] This truth of the tragic drama is visible only to the chorus and to the spectators.

The result of this truth is the dropping of the mask: "The pretensions of universal essentiality are uncovered in the self; it shows itself to be entangled in an actual existence and drops the mask just because it wants to be something genuine."[73] But this moment is the moment of *comedy,* and this is the final truth of tragedy. Whereas the tragic conflict hitherto had centered on the singularity of the individual struggling to find its place in the larger community—even to the point of being centered on the final and most compressed singularity of every individual, that is, the corpse (of Polynices)—and whereas the individual, in wearing the mask, acted according to the pretensions of the universal, now, in comedy, the individual dissolves and "preserves itself in this very nothingness."[74] Now "what this self-consciousness sees is that whatever assumes the form of essentiality in opposition to it, is to be dissolved in itself—in its thinking, its existence and its action—and so is at its mercy. . . . This self-certainty is a state of spiritual well-being and of repose in this well-being which is not to be found anywhere outside of this comedy."[75] Now death, which in tragedy opened up the experience of mourning, is seen as ridiculous. And in this final dissolution of individuality, this exposure of the individual as a nothingness when it is outside of the essential, the riddle of individuality—which originally inaugurated and propelled the tragedy—is solved. The self-certainty of the individual is found in its preservation in this nothingness, which it now knows "to be its sole actuality." In this moment, the individual knows itself to be nothing apart from this knowing.

But why is this comedy? Hegel never clarifies this point; he never takes up the question of the nature of comedy. Nonetheless, the point of view here mirrors the general character of comedy in the ancient world, namely, that comedy, unlike tragedy, centered on individuals and their quirks. In tragedy the hero was very much an ideal, a type, and one never learns much about the particularity of the hero. Comedy, on the other hand, works precisely in its attention to the foibles and particularities of its characters. That is why, as legend has it, Socrates could stand up during a performance of Aristophanes' *The Clouds* and point to his face as a way of saying "that is not me." The claim of tragedy, on the other hand, is that each of us sees ourselves in the face, the mask, that is, the hero. But the truth of the work of art in the form of language belongs to the speculative unity that holds tragedy and comedy together. Neither alone tells the full story of the being of individuality, and so one is reminded here of the haunting conclusion of Plato's *Symposium* where Socrates is speaking with the tragedian, Agathon, and the comedian, Aristophanes, and arguing that the tragedian must be a comedian as well.[76]

Although he makes the question of the speculative unity of tragedy and comedy necessary, he does not take it up in this text. Indeed, what is striking about this second appearance of the idea of the tragic in the *Phenomenology of Spirit* is that much of what it sets up as necessary is not fully unpacked. Perhaps most noticeable in this regard is that the initial approach to the question of tragedy here, the largest context within which it is raised, namely, the aesthetic character of the work, seems to fade from view. Stunning, then, is the fact that there is no discussion here of beauty, which Hegel once (in the "Earliest System-Program") had named the supreme speculative moment. One expects to find some indication of the speculative significance of the beautiful, of the way in which it is the glimmer of the ideal in the real, but such an indication is not forthcoming. But this absence of what one might expect is itself an indication of what serves as the real center of Hegel's concern in the *Phenomenology of Spirit* with the idea posed by the tragic, namely, that this idea serves to expose and resolve the enigma of the individual for speculative thought. From its first appearance in the ethical realm, tragedy serves to highlight the crisis of individuality as the most acute crisis which spirit must confront as it educates itself about itself. Even when tragedy is examined as a work of art, in the section on religion, it is clear that the central concern of this examination is the possibility of community. What the model of the tragedy provides is a way in which Hegel can formulate this question in its widest possible form, that is, in terms of the question of the community of the living and the dead. Such a community opens the deepest ethical crisis for the experience of self-consciousness, a crisis that finds its resolution only in the ruin of the elemental shape of the ethical sense of self-consciousness. The idea of the tragic is not the final word in the education of spirit that Hegel outlines in the *Phenomenology of Spirit*. That education continues and, as it does, the fault lines along which the tragic conflict develops are, according to Hegel, overcome, and those divisions—centered on the riddle of the radical singularity of the individual—are overcome only because they enter the tragic crisis. The final speculative unity that self-consciousness attains is thus shaped fundamentally by this experience of the tragic.

But such is not the full story of the nature of the tragic and its accomplishment for the purposes of speculative thought. There still remains the question of what is achieved once the tragic work is regarded from the point of view of its aesthetic character. That is the question Hegel addresses later in life in his *Aesthetics*.

*   *   *

The problematic shaping Hegel's treatment of the work of art in the *Aesthetics* is, in its largest formulation, the relation of art and truth. But the question of the relation of art and ethical life is never far from Hegel's concerns here (because from the outset he defines the work of art as a product of the freedom of spirit); neither is the question of the relation of spirit and sensuous life. In short, the *Aesthetics* casts the net of its concerns wide and ambitiously. But there are two aspects according to which Hegel takes up these themes which serve to focus and give direction to his investigation: the inquiry into the work of art is undertaken from the point of view of its *speculative* achievement, that is, the manner in which it is the presentation of a unity, and it is undertaken only with respect to the *beautiful* work of art. The consideration of the tragic work of art appears within this context.

Before turning to Hegel's analysis of the tragic work in the *Aesthetics*, two curious assumptions which help shape the *Aesthetics* should be noted. While neither is directly an issue for the topic of tragedy, both drive so deeply to the core of Hegel's sense of art as a whole that some brief mention is called for. First, Hegel's conclusion, announced at the outset, is that "art, considered in its highest vocation, is and remains for us a thing of the past . . . it has lost for us genuine truth and life, and has rather been transferred into our *ideas*."[77] Second, Hegel contends that the beauty of nature is "necessarily imperfect."[78] Both of these points, which are presented as conclusions but are in truth basic assumptions guiding Hegel, need to be thought together. Both are expressions of his conviction that it is spirit that makes the beautiful what it is and gives it its peculiar relation to truth. Both also express the conviction that so long as spirit weds itself to the sensuous world, it does not fully express its greatest promise. Yet art is precisely this "preoccupation of spirit with its opposite [i.e., sensuous life]."[79] In other words, Hegel's deepest criticism of the achievement of the work of art, the reason it is passé from the point of view of truth, is that it remains too bound to sensuous life. This limitation of the work of art will be one reason that the tragic work of art will need to be completed by the philosophical critic; put in other words, it is one reason that the only ideal spectator of the work is the speculative philosopher. Nonetheless, art is born of the need that spirit has to produce itself, to go outside of itself and find itself in its other (in this case, sensuous life). It is, Hegel says, born of the "need to lift the inner and outer world into his spiritual consciousness as an object in which he recognizes again his own self."[80] In art, "man as spirit *duplicates* himself."[81] The task of the philosopher of art is to speculatively recover this presence of spirit in the sensuous world.

This means that in the *Aesthetics* Hegel treats the topic of tragedy not as it is absorbed by other philosophical concerns, but on different terms. Whereas in the *Phenomenology of Spirit* tragedy is enlisted as a model for interpreting ethical life—even when it is treated as a work of art—in the *Aesthetics* Hegel's interest is much wider, much more concerned with tracing the different ways in which spirit expresses itself in the sensuous world. In order to take up the question of the work of art in greatest extent, Hegel divides the *Aesthetics* into three sections, each one repeating, in a certain fashion, the others. Thus the first part lays out a conceptual analysis of the work of art in general, the second part presents the history (and, curiously, the geography) of art as it comes to be seen according to the concepts which govern art in general, and the third part takes up the topic of the different genres, the different forms, of art as they are articulated by the various sensuous forms in which spirit materializes itself.[82] These three parts form something of a palimpsest, and frequently one does well to read across the different parts in order to clarify Hegel's intentions. This is especially the case with Hegel's treatment of tragedy, and so in taking up this topic we will move, typically without comment, between the various contexts within which Hegel addresses tragedy. One final note: in the *Aesthetics* Hegel does not confine his treatment of tragedy to Greek tragedy even if the question of tragedy as he presents it is disproportionately centered on Greek tragedy. Modern tragedy is discussed too; however, the treatment of Shakespeare and Goethe, for instance, is never as extended, nor does it play the pivotal role, as the treatment of Greek tragedians. The reason for this seems relatively simple from Hegel's point of view: modern tragedy appears in the history of spirit only after philosophizing has reached the stage at which it knows itself, however primitively still, to be speculative. Consequently, modern tragedy never plays the role in the education of spirit that tragedy, which flourished before philosophizing had found its footing, was able to achieve. Next, Hegel's interpretation of modern tragic art will be addressed, but to a lesser extent and frequently, as Hegel himself will do, only in order to provide a contrast against which the specific character of Greek tragedy is clarified. This special character of Greek tragic art is, in each of the three approaches that Hegel takes to the work of art, the entry into the question of the tragic work. In other words, in Greece the possibilities of the tragic work reach their summit.

This specificity of Greek tragedy that so captures Hegel's attention is itself also a reflection of the larger cultural differences between the ancient and modern worlds. So, in a passage that sounds astonishingly like a passage Kierkegaard would write three decades later, Hegel says,

> In the plastic totality of antiquity the individual is not isolated in himself; he is a member of his family, his clan. Therefore the character, action, and fate of the family is every member's own affair and, far from repudiating the deeds and fate of his forebears, each member adopts them as his own. . . . [T]he heroic individual [of Greece] is more ideal because he is not content with his inherent formal unity and infinity but remains united in steadfast immediate identity with the whole substantiality of the spiritual relations which he is bringing into living actuality."[83]

This is the kind of passage which calls attention to the fact that even when treating the tragic work as a work of art, even when considering its aesthetic character, Hegel regards the tragedy as fundamentally a work which centers on the questions of ethical life. Furthermore, the reason the Greeks excelled at the production of tragedy is precisely because Greek culture was, by virtue of historical necessity, one in which the question of the individual could never be considered in isolation from the question of community. Tragedy takes up the riddle that each individual is as a singular being, but in Greece it could do this only by asking about the place of the individual in the community. Such a situation, an impossible situation, is ultimately the root of the crisis that animates Greek tragedy.[84] Tragedy thus became the preeminent Greek way of searching for a moral center, an understanding of the singularity of life in the community. Understanding the tragic work aesthetically ultimately requires understanding how it is that the beauty of the work is indexed to this question of ethical life—and why it is that the Greeks excelled at the production of this strange beauty proper to the tragic.

Hegel presents Greek art generally as an instance of the classical form of art. This is the form which follows the symbolic form of art, in which there is a powerful identification of the work of art with nature and the divine. Symbolic works of art, which Hegel locates primarily in the animal and part-animal/part-human images found in India and Egypt, represent a fusion of nature and spirit. It is only the "threshold" of the work of art since it is not yet a work in which spirit has fully distinguished itself from the nature that it fashions; the symbolic work, in being an undifferentiated union of spirit and nature, in which, for instance, animal images symbolize spiritual life (in Egypt the life of the kings and gods), is not a work in which spirit expresses itself *as* spirit. Rather, the "symbol as such is an external existent given to contemplation, which yet is to be understood not simply as it confronts us immediately on its own account, but in a wider and more universal sense . . . the symbol is prima facie a *sign* . . . and by its very nature remains essentially ambiguous."[85]

The move into that form of art, the move into the moment in which spirit expresses itself in and as the freedom that it essentially is, is the move into what Hegel designates the classical form in which "the art allows the [free spirit] to appear in a reality adequate to it . . . [and in which] spirit attains an individuality [which is] inherently independent. . . . [In the classical form of art] humanity therefore constitutes the center and content of true beauty."[86] In the classical form as Hegel understands it there is a unity of the meaning and the shape of the work which permits the outward appearance of the work, its natural shape, to let the inward particularity of spirit appear. Here spirit emerges as itself in the shape of the work; it is no longer submerged in the natural element of the work as it was in the symbolic form. Pressing upon this notion of the individuality of the work of art which is at the heart of the classical form, Hegel concludes that there is a native inclination to works of art centered on the human form, "because the external human form is alone capable of revealing the spiritual in a sensuous way. . . . Through the eye we look into a man's soul . . . we must maintain that art, developed to its maturity, must produce its representations in the form of the external appearance of the human being because only therein does the spirit acquire its adequate existence in sensuous and natural material."[87] This is why sculpture is the first genre in which the classical form will find expression in Greek art. It is also the reason Hegel seeks to understand Greek tragedy by treating it as a continuation of Greek sculpture. This is one of Hegel's most original and provocative elements of the interpretation of tragedy in the *Aesthetics*. Tragedy and sculpture are the chief ways in which spirit concentrates itself in the classical form so that it can become aware of itself. In both cases, what is at stake is the expression of the individuality of spirit in its freedom. Both are expressions of the ideal of spirit as it struggles to know itself in its independence from nature. This is the stage in which spirit first succeeds in making itself, as an independent and free being, into an object for its own contemplation. This, then, is the moment in which it wrestles with the question of its own natural being, and that, of course, means that in the classical form spirit must struggle with the question of its own mortality.

It is important to recognize that in the classical form art, as Hegel understands it, must struggle with the natural life of spirit. It has not yet reached the level on which it is able to center itself on the principle of subjectivity which will govern the third and final form of art, namely, the romantic form, in which lyric poetry is the most appropriate genre.[88] Rather, the special excellence of Greek art is the manner in which spirit turns itself into an object of contemplation by virtue of its relation to natural life. This takes the shape of sculpture because in sculpture the earth itself is given shape. But it takes the shape of tragedy because of the deeper kinship between tragic art and the enigma of natural life, namely, because tragedy necessarily takes up the question of death, of the final meaning of spirit's relation to natural life.

It is important to acknowledge the context within which death becomes a theme for tragedy. It is also important to clarify the nature of the crisis which death brings to an extreme moment; most of all, one needs to understand that this crisis of tragedy brought about by death is ethical in nature, and not existential. All of these points become clearer when one traces the genesis of tragedy as Hegel understands it out of the elements found in epic and lyric poetry. Here tragedy is presented as the conflict of the principles which these represent, and it is presented as answering to their "deficiencies" from the point of view of the speculative task of the work of art.

Not surprisingly Hegel's analysis of both epic and lyric poetry, which here are presented as the antecedents of the tragic work of art, centers on the way in which death is presented in each. The epic (and here Hegel is thinking of Homer) describes "not a single casual deed . . . but an action ramified into the whole of its age and national circumstances so that it can be brought before us only within an outspread world and [so it] demands the portrayal of this world in its entirety."[89] In other words, for an epic to be possible, the ethical life of the individual must still be indistinguishable from wider bonds—of family, of people, of nation. The action of the individual becomes, in a way, the action of a people. Ethical life has not yet codified itself, not yet been articulated into specified obligations or found a home in the form of institutions and laws. The epic, then, is in some sense prior to the law.[90] Achilles' rage is not reserved for Achilles, even though it is this rage that defines him, and his rage has no outlet, no home, in which it can find recourse and an answer apart from his actions. But his actions are not isolated actions, and it is this that makes them an epical event. Achilles' rage is not the expression of the emotion of an isolated, an atomic subject, but is an expression "in substantial unity with the whole."[91] This is why epic action is the action from which the objectification of ethical relations acquires its reality. This is also the reason that the epic poet, the one who brings to language such actions, needs to be understood as the founder of a nation.[92]

What most needs to be clarified here is why the epic is necessarily the story of a violence, and why this violence needs to be understood specifically as a political violence. Hegel will give an indication of this when he suggests that war is the situation most suitable for the epic form.[93] There are two reasons for this: first, in war the whole nation is set in motion, and this is requisite for an action to be epical, to be, in other words, an action that changes the ethical shape of a nation and so the whole of the nation is in play;[94] second, in war the lives of the individuals are presented as transient, the situation is too great to be centered on any one individual and "consequently an air of mourning is wafted over the whole epic, we see excellence pass away early and even Achilles laments over his death during his life."[95] Here we see the elemental nature of epic poetry: the life of the individual is played out, as a mortal life, in the context of larger forces of history, culture, and community. In the epic we see that "with death nature is at an end, but not man, not moral principle."[96] As such, the epic is saturated with the sense of mourning, but also with the sense of the stakes of ethical life.[97] That is why the violence of the epic is a political violence; in the end it is a violence that tears at the very fabric of the polis. That is also why the epic demands heroes who are ready to sacrifice themselves for the community, and so elsewhere in the *Aesthetics* Hegel speaks of the time of epic as the heroic age.

But there is a strange consequence of the epic when it succeeds; namely, it extinguishes the very possibility of epic in general. The reason for this is simple: for epic to be possible, the laws of a nation must still be at a primitive stage and not yet be formalized in institutions and courts. The ethical life of a nation must not yet have transferred itself into an administrative structure which would secure it. Yet, insofar as the epic is the story of a political founding, insofar as its result is the eventual formalization of the ethical life which results from the struggles and violence which it depicts, the epic removes the condition of epical action from the future. The successful epic extinguishes the possibility of future epics. Hegel recognizes this and finds that the residue of the epic sensibility remains only in the degenerated form of romances (he is thinking here chiefly of medieval adventure stories, especially those from France and Spain).

What the epic never succeeded in presenting, though, and so what the poetic imagination gradually came to address, is the *inner* life of those whose lives were presented. There is a curious objectivity, a certain presentation of the depths of a life through a presentation of its surface, in the epic: "Epic is inwardly most akin to the plasticity of sculpture, and of its objectivity, in virtue of both its substantial content and the fact that what it portrays has the form of objective appearance."[98] But the very nature of the poetic medium, the word itself, is so fundamentally spiritual in its nature, so directly emerging out of, and reaching into the inner lives of those who speak and hear, that the poetic work tends, from its own nature, to present the inner life of those of whom it speaks. That is why Hegel writes that "it is the *subjective* side of the poet's spiritual work of creating and forming his material which is clearly the predominant element in his illustrative production, and this is in contrast to the visual arts."[99] But epic is the alienation of this natural inclination of the word, so Hegel finds that the instincts of the poetic imagination drive it to the point at which the subjectivity of the poet is itself brought forward. This is the impulse that produces lyric poetry. If epic poetry is the way in which language grasps the relation of the self to the world and to history, then one can describe lyric poetry as the form in which language grasps the relation of the self to itself and to its freedom: "What leads to epic poetry is the need to listen to something which is unfolded as a . . . totality, objective over and against the subject; whereas in lyric what is satisfied is the opposite need, namely that for self-expression and for the apprehension of the mind in its own self-expression."[100] The genuine lyric poet does not start from external events; indeed, to the extent that such events are addressed, it is as they are taken up into the affective life of the poet: "Here in his subjective inner life the man becomes a work of art himself."[101] As such, lyric stands as the poetic tendency of language which is most directly opposite to that expressed by epic. Not surprisingly, then, the times which are most conducive to epic—times of struggle and even of instability—are least favorable to lyric, which requires periods in which the poet is able to work in a self-concentrated quiet centered on an inner life undisturbed by the external world. In such environments, the lyric is better able to express the content of the human heart.[102] But, of course, when it addresses itself in its deepest forms and most far-reaching concerns, lyric poetry, like epic poetry, finds that it must take up the riddle that death poses for life. In that regard alone lyric and epic poetry are alike.

But in general lyric and epic stand as opposing tendencies of the poetic efforts of spirit, and so neither alone satisfies the deepest artistic impulse of spirit, which is seeking to objectify itself in the world by means of its self-expression in language. According to Hegel, the effort to answer this double-sided dissatisfaction is one of the impulses which leads to the development of tragedy, which takes up into itself these opposing tendencies—toward objectification and the presentation of the whole life of a people and toward the presentation of the inner life of the subject—of epic and lyric poetry. The crisis which defines the tragic action can thus be explained as the crisis which results from the confrontation of these distinct, these opposite poetic impulses. The conflict which is presented in the tragedy, a conflict that Hegel had earlier (in the *Phenomenology of Spirit*) characterized as between the natural life of the individual and the ethical claims of the nation, finds its roots repeated and reinforced in the impulses which drive spirit to form the work of art in language. Now one sees all the more clearly why Hegel can suggest in the *Phenomenology of Spirit* that each of the opposed sides has a justification. Here too, in the *Aesthetics,* he will make the same point and even suggest that "each side can establish the true and positive content of its own aim and character only by denying and infringing upon the equally justified power of the other."[103] Furthermore, like these poetic forms, tragedy will find that it must, in the end, confront the death of its central figures. At this point it should be easy to see why it is that Hegel thinks of the tragic work of art as the final destination of art in general, as the true answer to the task of the poetic project of spirit.

Two more points need to be made before the full significance of the tragic drama is appreciated: the performance character of the tragic work and the role of the chorus in the tragedy. These are the final distinctions of tragic art, and these are the formal elements which it will hand over to the "higher" forms in which spirit will seek to know itself.

The element of performance, the actualization of speech, is all important for the understanding of the final achievement of tragedy, and yet to be understood one needs to acknowledge that for the Greeks words were not merely the expression of thought in the world, language was not a vehicle for the mind; rather, words were deeds—perhaps the most essential and fundamental deed possible. In the Greek world, then, speech was one of the basic ways one was present and acted in the world: *logos* was an *ergon* and is not said to realize its full possibilities until it is understood as itself a deed and not simply an expression of thought.[104] When making this same point Arendt recounts an anecdote which Plutarch reports: when someone told Demosthenes about how terribly he had been beaten, Demosthenes replied, "But you suffered nothing of what you tell me," to which the other person raised his voiced and cried out, "I suffered nothing?" "Now," said Demosthenes, "I hear the voice of somebody who was injured and who suffered."[105] With this identity of word and deed in mind, one can begin to see why the drive to performance, to the actualization and enactment of words on stage, is native to the Greek poetic sensibility. One also sees why the tragic drama must be considered as full of action even though, according to modern sensibilities, "nothing happens."[106] In the performance, then, tragedy begins to perfect its possibilities.[107]

But even the performance does not complete the trajectory of such possibilities. That is reserved for the language of the chorus and the distinctive place from which it is spoken in the performance of the work. Hegel makes this clear when he says that "the chorus confronts us as a higher consciousness, aware of the substantial issues, warning against false conflicts, and weighing the outcome."[108] Hegel is quick to point out that this does not imply that the chorus should be regarded as a moralist or a disengaged spectator, possessing a sort of divine perspective. Quite the contrary: the chorus represents the real stuff, the substance, of the ethical life out of which the conflict grows. In this respect, the chorus marks the speculative site in the tragic work, and in accord with this position the chorus expresses itself lyrically, yet it equally preserves the epic character of the events. The chorus is thus most completely the voice of spirit in the tragedy: "Just as Greek theater itself has its external terrain, its scene, and its surroundings, so the chorus, the people, is as it were the scene of spirit; it may be compared, in architecture, with a temple surrounding the image of the gods, for here it is an environment for the heroes in action."[109] This is the reason that the chorus speaks from the speculative point of view, from the perspective of the reconciliation possible in the tragic work: in the chorus we find the cancellation of the conflicts *as conflicts*. In other words, in the words of the chorus spirit finds the satisfaction of the needs which originally drove it to the work of art, ultimately to the tragic work.

That being said, Hegel is able to draw his analysis of the tragic work of art in the *Aesthetics* to a close. He does this by noting that this reconciliation which is implied by the speech of the chorus provides a *subjective* satisfaction. No final objective resolution of the conflict is presented, but there is harmony, a peace, restored in the subjective relation one has to this conflict. And this new affirmation of the subjective element of the work of art, at this stage in the education that spirit has undergone regarding itself, leads Hegel to make the transition to the sphere of comedy, which, as in the *Phenomenology of Spirit*, complements and so completes the work of tragedy. Thus Hegel says that "comedy has for its basis and starting-point what tragedy may end with, namely an absolutely reconciled and cheerful heart."[110] The one-sidedness which is at the root of the tragic conflict (the one-sidedness of the human and of the divine laws, for instance) is repeated in the form of the tragic drama itself: "it remains one-sided by making the validity of the substance and necessity of ethical life its essential basis and by leaving undeveloped the individuality of the dramatis personae and the depths of their personal life."[111] So tragedy must be seen as summoning the possibility of comedy, in the same way that the human and divine laws summon one another in their differences: "Comedy on its side brings into view a converse mode of plasticity . . . the subjective personality in the free expatiation of its absurdity and its absurdity's dissolution."[112] Together comedy and tragedy tell the story of the truth of the life of spirit in its individuality which spirit desires to know. That is why the development of comedy signals the end of the philosophical investigation of the achievement of spirit in the form of art—comedy marks the dissolution of art in general; in it spirit is satisfied with itself, and by remaining with itself and the nothingness of its own particular subjectivity, spirit no longer finds it necessary to express itself in the sensuous world. In short, it no longer finds art necessary for its education. This is what is meant by Hegel's celebrated claim at the outset of the *Aes-*

thetics that "art, considered in its highest vocation, is and remains for us a thing of the past. Thereby it has lost for us genuine truth and life, and has rather been transferred into our *ideas* instead of maintaining its earlier necessity in reality."[113] This does not mean that art no longer lives as one of the means by which spirit expresses and educates itself about itself, but it does mean that art, the preoccupation of spirit with the possibility of its sensuous expression, is no longer able to nourish the deepest desires of spirit to know itself. Now it knows that it must come to know itself independently of the sensuous world. It must come to know itself in the subjectivity which has been filtered through its experience of making art, that is, of finding itself in sensuous life.

This means that in its dissolution art accomplishes its task, which is the "liberation of the spirit from the content and forms of finitude, with the presence and reconciliation of the Absolute in what is apparent and visible, with an unfolding of truth which is not exhausted in natural history but revealed in world history."[114] The beautiful in art is the single indication that spirit has indeed found itself in the world.[115] Finding this beauty reaches its peak, the point of its greatest difficulty and power, when spirit confronts the price of its natural life in the sensuous world, that is, when spirit confronts its death. But precisely this, and the paradoxes which emerge from the riddle that death poses, is the center of tragic art. Finding beauty in death is thus the final form in which spirit finds beauty in the natural life of spirit: it is the truth of that natural life. This is the greatest achievement of tragedy for Hegel, and in this the Greeks excelled beyond all others.

*   *   *

Hegel understands the work of art as belonging to the realm of reflection; as such, it is a form in which spirit repeats and thereby knows itself (this is the sense of Hegel's otherwise rather puzzling remark that "the beauty of art is beauty *born of the spirit and born again*").[116] Works of art speak to us by leading us to speak with ourselves, by opening the space within which a self-conversation can take place. In the process of this reflection in the other of spirit, in sensuous life, spirit comes to confront the conflict native to this situation; in other words, it belongs to the nature of the work of art to be situated in the conflicted position of finding spirit always in its most radical other. Art is, by nature, a conflicted enterprise.[117] This means that art as such, because it is born of a conflict, is destined to do the work of tragedy. When art expresses its ownmost nature, it expresses this conflict, and tragedy is the highest form of this expression. Thus it is clear that Hegel's interest in tragedy is so great because it represents the summit of the possibilities of the work of art, its genuine end.

So art stands as one of the basic forms in which spirit educates itself, and tragedy marks the fullest development of the possibilities inherent in this form. But Hegel's interest in tragedy is not confined to the manner in which it completes the artistic education of spirit; he is also greatly interested in the logic of the tragic because the tragic work replicates, above all in its performance, the dialectical situation which belongs to the life of spirit in general. Tragedy is thus not only a special form of the work of art in and through which spirit expresses itself; it is something like a template for the general situation, and the logic, which is proper to spirit. The great service, the special merit of its contribution to our understanding of the life of spirit, is that tragedy is especially adept at illuminating the ethical dimensions of the conflicts and crises which spirit must endure. That is why tragedy serves as perhaps Hegel's favorite model for his efforts to present and clarify the dialectic of spirit in general, and that is why its presence in Hegel's texts inevitably signals an attempt to heighten our awareness of the real ethical stakes of that dialectic.

But Hegel's understanding of the tragic work of art is not without its special complications and even, at times, confusions, since it is such a central notion for his thought generally and since he presses it into service in so many instances and to so many ends.[118] Nonetheless, it remains clear that the role of tragedy in Hegel's thought is unsurpassed in its importance for his understanding of how it is that speculative thought retains the richness and diversity worthy of the name of the Absolute. Hegel finds in the idea of the tragic a way of preserving the vital, the inextinguishable, life of negation proper to spirit; it thus becomes one of the principal notions which he enlists in order to avoid the great danger of speculative thought, namely, an absolute which is like a night in which all the cows are black. The presence of the idea of the tragic, of this conflicted dynamic which enacts itself up all the way to the point of the death of natural life, is Hegel's most enduring and reliable way of articulating a conception of the Absolute which is truly *hen kai pan,* truly differentiated within itself. Although Hegel does acknowledge the role of pathos in the tragedy, although he does not regard it simply as an abstract logic, it also seems clear that, for Hegel, the tragedy is at its best when it becomes an idea. The suffering, agony, the heartbreak, the torment, and the ruin which the tragedy displays, which is at the root of what Aristotle found so significant in our responses of fear and pity, become for Hegel lessons which spirit must learn if it is to know itself better. A line that Hegel wrote in another context, but which bears very much upon the force of the tragic in his thought, leads one to pose the question about how much the force of the tragic has been felt here: "The wounds of spirit heal and leave no scars behind."[119]

Nonetheless, one can never doubt that the question of tragedy, and the force of the idea of the tragic, remains one of the central concerns for

Hegel throughout his life. And even if his systematic appropriation of this question blunts its force by the very fact that it is absorbed in a system, that it is a speculative treatment of tragedy, when one reads Hegel writing about tragedy one sees and senses a mind which made an honest effort to pay tribute to conflict so deep that it always threatened to overwhelm the very life of the mind.

4 Hölderlin

In love with language, which he experiences most deeply in the twin languages of love and of sorrow, Hölderlin's fascination with Greek tragedy—in which he finds the summit of the possibilities of language and the most profound experiences it can bear—borders on what seems like an obsession. It is Schelling who points the way to the question of tragedy at this time, and it is Hegel who absorbs this question into the systematic possibilities of thinking, and together they explore the question of tragedy from a speculative point of view. But it is Hölderlin whose work is most thoroughly absorbed into the question of tragedy. One might say that he does not simply "take up" the question of tragedy into his work, as if it were one among many, even the preeminent question among many; rather, the question of tragedy frames his work as a whole, and so is that into which all other questions are themselves taken up. Hölderlin is taken over by this topic to such an extent, and so creatively, that in him the problematic of tragedy will be born anew. While it is true that Hegel will be the one who calls attention to the role of performance in the accomplishments of Greek tragedy, it also needs to be said that it will be Hölderlin who will most directly seek to enact, to perform, the truth of tragedy as he understands it. Consequently, one quickly comes to understand that for Hölderlin tragedy is not simply a theoretical issue, it is most of all a matter of the practice of thinking and so could never be touched as a question apart from this practice. His fidelity to this practice, the rigor and concentration with which he seeks to enact what he experiences in the language of tragedy, cannot be overestimated. For Hölderlin, the tragic could never be captured by an idea, nor could it ever serve as an interpretive model for any other topic, since it would always exceed any possible capture in an idea and it would always already saturate every other topic.

Finally, as one approaches this topic of tragedy for Hölderlin, one needs to begin by understanding that like his erstwhile friends, Hegel and Schelling, he will initially approach the topic of Greek tragedy from a speculative point of view. Initially, at least, tragedy places us before the supreme speculative moment; it is the "metaphor of an intellectual intuition."[1] However, it will also always be, but with increasing intensity, the most compressed site of the "caesura . . . the counter-rhythmic rupture" of the speculative.[2] In short, the topic of tragedy for Hölderlin will itself repeat, and so perform, the highest conflict: it presents us simultaneously with the speculative unity of life and the caesura of the speculative. Here the very same gesture which will resolve the divisions of life will rend life. Understanding how this can be the case, why it must be the case, and understanding how it is that the human relation to the word is at the center of this powerful event is requisite for any understanding of Hölderlin's remarkable contributions to the topic of tragedy. All that needs to be explored. But what most needs to be said even at the outset is that it is not difficult to see that in Hölderlin the topic of tragedy will find a compression, a force, and a creative expression that is simply unsurpassed. Hölderlin will let the path opened up by the question of tragedy define the course of his life and work, and what he experiences as the heliotropic pull of ancient Greece[3] will give his life and work its distinctive character. In the end, then, to take up this theme is to take up the whole of Hölderlin's work. It is even needed to try to understand the story of his life, which conversely is helpful in understanding his work since he, more than most, has managed to take the stuff of his life and find a way to make it the stuff of his work. But there are some ways in which this topic can be narrowed and thus made manageable—at least to some extent—and indications of how this might be accomplished are needed.

There are a variety of formats—all of which need to be understood as performative—in which Hölderlin takes up his concern with tragedy. Six different forms, each giving a special context and shape to the issues, frame the question of tragedy for Hölderlin: letters, translations, theoretical works, plays, poems, a novel. Although the form in which he addresses the question of tragedy does play a significant role in how the question is shaped and the issues around which it unfolds (for instance, his translations of Sophocles obviously make the question of language the axis around which the issues develop), there is one overarching theme, one quality, which seems to unite all of Hölderlin's texts on tragedy: there is a profound and enduring sense that the tragic confronts us with the experience of the foreign and the question whether or not this can be brought into what is one's own without, by this action, assimilating and thus destroying, the foreign as itself.[4] Like the task of translation, the task of thinking which confronts the question of tragedy as Hölderlin understands it is to repeat anew what that experience discloses, to bring it to life in the word in such a way that it is not blunted, but rather wins a new life. Although he will struggle to give a name to this elemental experience of the tragic, and although he will give it many names over the years, one might reasonably suggest that, for Hölderlin, this experience is the experience of finitude. One of the more pristine expressions of this is found in an early version of Hölderlin's *Hyperion*, the so-called Metric Version, in which he writes

> Permit me to speak humanly. When our original, infinite, being first began to suffer and experienced the free and full power of the first barriers, when poverty appeared coupled with abundance, love was there. You ask, when was that? Plato said: on the day on which Aphrodite was born. So then, when the beautiful world began for us, then we became conscious, then we were finite. Now we feel profoundly the limitation of our being, and there is something in us which gladly holds onto these chains—for if the divine in us was not limited by any resistance, we would know nothing outside of ourselves, and so also nothing of ourselves, and to know nothing of one's self, not to feel oneself, and to be annihilated, is for us the same thing.[5]

Here one finds virtually every significant key word in the Hölderlinian vocabulary, and a simple list of these words makes clear that this passage eloquently compacts into one thought so many conflicted themes. Here, in this brief passage, one finds the following being invoked: infinite, suffer, free, barrier, poverty, abundance, love, beauty, world, conscious, finite, limitation, resistance, self. Here, then, one begins to see the relay of experiences, all of which belong together as expressions of human finitude. All of these words become names for the intimacy with which we sense our finitude.

Since the topic of tragedy is such a sweeping and all-encompassing theme for Hölderlin, it is necessary to focus the investigation of this topic somewhat arbitrarily. To that end, in this chapter three of the above mentioned formats in which Hölderlin addresses this topic will be taken up: the notion of tragedy in his novel, *Hyperion;* the presentation and analysis of the tragic in his theoretical, his poetological, works; and in *The Death of Empedocles,* which is Hölderlin's own, original effort to write a tragic drama. This selection has the merit of addressing works from each stage of Hölderlin's productive life,[6] works that have also had the greatest influence in the years since Hölderlin's death.[7] Throughout these three discussions, references will be made to the other arenas within which the question of the tragic is addressed by Hölderlin; in other words, when it is helpful, references will be made to the letters, his translations of Sophocles (from which he gained his first fame), and several of his poems.

Before doing this, one final preliminary point should be noted. As already indicated, Hölderlin's life and the circumstances of his personal life—here one thinks most of all of his relation to Susette Gontard (whom he called "Diotima"), his love for her and her early death—are drawn directly into his work in such a way that his biography becomes important for understanding his work. But the same situation is also the case with the historical events of Hölderlin's day. In particular, the French Revolution plays a powerful role in the Hölderlinian sensibility.[8] Revolutionary hopes, the dream of equality, and the deep sense of newness all run deep in Hölderlin's world, and they are fueled by an awareness that such situations, such times, are in need of fresh ideals and clarity of aims. Acutely aware of the insufficiency of the cultural ideals which were so failed that they could produce only the need for revolution, Hölderlin's effort to rejuvenate the political and cultural life of his times is the motive driving his fascination with ancient Greece. It was in the Greek world that he saw something which could provide a clue to how those ideals might be understood in the modern world. The turn to Greece, which relentlessly indexes every moment of Hölderlin's work, is imbued with the flavor of this political dream. But to understand this fixation upon the Greek world, especially as it is realized in the language and art of Greece (above all the art of tragedy), as a simple form of nostalgia is to fundamentally misunderstand its nature and the impulses which nourish it.[9] In this regard Hölderlin's relation to Greece is to be distinguished from that which is found in Winckelmann, for example, since Winckelmann, like many others of this time, was chiefly interested in a sort of restoration of the Greek world and art; Hölderlin, on the other hand, is interested in a creative discovery of a Greek world that might never have been. If one tries to characterize Hölderlin's relation to Greece by speaking of it as a longing for home, then one needs the qualification that home is a place we have not yet been. In the background of this turn to Greece, then, one finds the dreams let loose by the political transformations symbolized in the French and American Revolutions. The turn to Greece thus needs to be understood not as the recovery of a bygone time, but as the opening to a new future only hitherto found in the form of the promise of Greece—a promise never yet realized.

But, of course, the matter is not so easily resolved, and so in the end Hölderlin's relation to Greece will present itself, along with the themes opened by tragedy, as one of the central puzzles one needs to confront as one takes up his work. One simply needs to approach his work with an understanding that the image of Greece here is not one that is easily understood. Hölderlin's Greece possesses what he will call an "oriental vitality"[10] and so, from the outset, is thrown outside of the empire of the West.

In the end, though, Hölderlin's concern, however politically inspired, remains an intimate one. It would be thoroughly inappropriate to suggest that it is on this account something personal or existential, that somehow in Hölderlin we find a figure like Kierkegaard, for instance. Such is very far from being the case. As one reads Hölderlin, one needs to be alert to the radicality of his search for new forms of speaking and thinking which would measure up to the needs of the day and were, at last, commensurate with the deepest possibilities of language, which Hölderlin knew fundamentally define human being. If Kant needs to be acknowledged as the one who first gave a voice to the "categorical imperative," then it is fair to suggest that Hölderlin should be acknowledged as the one who brought into view what we might call the "poetic imperative." It is no less ethically important, no less politically meaningful, than Kant's great insight. It is nonetheless only able to be formulated in the intimacy of the poetic word. And the effort to speak from out of that experience of the word will be what guides Hölderlin through his relation to the question of tragedy, and it will be this that drives him deep into the heart of the ancient Greek world.

*   *   *

Hölderlin's first major work is the epistolary novel *Hyperion*, which he began in March of 1792 shortly after he read Kant's Third Critique. His reaction to the Third Critique was, like that of his friends Hegel and Schelling, one of almost unbridled enthusiasm and excitement. He says as much in a letter to Hegel when he writes that "Kant and the Greeks almost exclusively occupy my readings."[11] It was an enthusiasm that would never fade, but would only grow and run deeper in Hölderlin's view of the world and his political hopes for the future (since he, as most everyone else, knew that the Third Critique needed to be read as a book very directly concerned with the future possibilities of political and ethical life). Some years later in a lengthy letter that he would write to his brother on New Year's Eve of 1798 and the first day of 1799, Hölderlin would again express this extreme admiration for Kant by saying that "Kant is the Moses of our nation, the one who led us out of the Egyptian torpor rooted in the open and solitary desert of its speculation, and who brought the energetic law from the holy mountain."[12] In Kant, Hölderlin saw one who provided the philosophical justification for the great speculative experiment that

Hölderlin himself would undertake in the name of beauty, and for the sake of ideals which might breathe new life into the world.

Hyperion is the story of a "hermit" living on a Greek island during the Greek war for independence from Turkey.[13] It is a story told completely in the form of letters, all but one of them composed by Hyperion. The one exception is a letter from his lover, Diotima, to Hyperion, which he encloses in a letter to Bellarmin, who is the recipient of the bulk of the letters (a few are addressed to or from Diotima and Notara). Because the novel is presented in the form of these letters, all of the main characters explain or present themselves only in relation to someone else. Even though Hyperion's sense of isolation is often profound, his loneliness nigh on unbearable at times, his entire existence, at least as we come to know it, is through his relation to Bellarmin and Diotima. One sees as well in these letters a sort of *Bildungsroman,* a story of the evolution and education of a consciousness carried out in the reflective process of letters.[14] One sees also how these letters themselves become not simply the vehicle whereby events are communicated, but also, maybe more so, themselves the form in which Hyperion is affected and changed. The process of writing itself, of the reflections it demands, clearly alters Hyperion's self-understanding. Strangely, one learns precious little about the recipient of these letters, of the one who posed the question which set this chain of reflections in motion,[15] of Bellarmin himself, and nothing of him from himself. All we learn about the details of his life is that he is a German who, like Hyperion, is severely critical of Germany and Germans. Despite lacking the particulars of Bellarmin's life, one ultimately comes away with a sense of the profound intimacy which Hyperion must feel for him, since these letters have a confessional and honest tone that could only be used with a close friend; one always suspects that Bellarmin somehow connects with these letters and their appeal.[16] And this sense of the connection between friends—or at least the protracted attempt to establish such a connection—runs through this book, which is very much concerned with the notion and possibility of belonging to another.

The setting for the story that is eventually told is an island in Greece, somewhere on Corinth, and the ruins which populate the island, the residue of another time, are very much part of its geography.[17] Nature and the details of the features of the island are very present here; at times it seems as if the geography of the place figures as a living character in the story that is told here. The island and its ruins together combine to present a powerful image of fragmentation, of a sort of disunion and separation—the setting of the letters intensifies the mood that will saturate them. Two more points should be remarked upon before turning to the letters themselves: first, both the temporal sequence and the time which is addressed in the letters are important to watch as the letters unfold and tell Hyperion's story; second, one should not overlook the epigrams which introduce each of the two volumes of the novel as a whole. Regarding the first point, one should note that though the time in which the story of the letters is set is the present age, it is the Greece of antiquity that lives everywhere in these letters. The past sometimes seems more present than the present itself. The strong image of ancient Greece found here haunts these letters and, together with another image of loss, namely, the loss of Diotima,[18] the woman Hyperion loves, gives these letters their special character and distinctive mood. But one should also note that the letters do not always address times in the same sequence in which the letters themselves are composed. In others words, the content of the letters is not linear, but present the temporal structure of the development of Hyperion's self-understanding as entangled and as possessing what one might call a self-rewriting character. Regarding the second point, the epigrams here, one should bear in mind that they are the only passages of the novel which are not part of the letters. They are the only element which is added from outside of the letters proper. Interestingly, both epigrams are quotations. The first is from a Latin text by the founder of the Jesuit order which reads "Not to be contained by the largest, to be surrounded by the smallest, is divine."[19] The second is, significantly, a passage from the celebrated choral ode in Sophocles' *Oedipus at Colonus,* which reads "Not to be born is best of all; the second best however (after one has seen the light), is, by far, to go as quickly as possible to where one came from."[20] The mood of the two volumes is reflected in the epigram which introduces each: the first volume is much more directly centered on the possibility of belonging and the divinity that emerges out of the union of things. In this regard its speculative aspect is quite pronounced. The second volume, as the epigram indicates, is somewhat more attentive to the failures, the struggles, and the agonies of his experiences. But the second volume, which ends with the enigmatic words "Next, more,"[21] also ends with a hint that the future is still an open matter, and a riddle.

The story that Hyperion narrates begins after a period in which he had traveled abroad, eventually going to Germany, after the death of Diotima and the collapse of his dreams. He has finally returned home to Greece and from there begins the process of reflections which constitute the stuff of the letters. The story he tells opens with Hyperion in great despair, and this despair is continually deepened by the thoughts which are awakened in him by the character of the island on which he lives. Indeed, the very idea of an island, of a land set apart, becomes emblematic of his situation. In particular, he finds himself overwhelmed by the feeling of separation which he senses so totally. He suffers greatly from this sense of being pulled away from something to which he naturally belongs, and this sense of an absence, of a longing for a union with what has been lost, is the central concern of his opening letters. One reads early on how this separation is experienced by him: "I have nothing of which I can say it is my own. Far and dead are my loved ones."[22] A powerful sense of loss, of separation and of mourning, wafts over the text of these letters from the outset. One detects early on that Hyperion is suffering greatly from this perceived lack, and the tone that is struck, a tone that is one of lament, only ever becomes milder from time to time, but never fully recedes.[23] Commensurate with this suffering, the letters take on a lyrical and elegiac tone; the style of the prose here ranges from lilting passages in which the memory of happy times flows through the words, to the wistful passages in which the longing for another time is present but not an agony, to the tormented passages in which one can almost palpably sense the pain of the suffering which Hyperion is expressing. That is why one must say that the emotions here are performed, they are displayed in the language and not simply recounted dispassionately. The language of these letters is frequently pierced by a sadness that, in the end, one might best describe as the sadness of time. This sorrow is the central experience out of which Hyperion thinks and reflects upon his life.

One of the chief questions which will plague Hyperion as he struggles to come to grips with this experience is just why this separation has happened. That he experiences it so deeply that it almost needs to be understood as a form of death is clear. But the precise character of this separation, the roots which hold it in place, remains to be understood. What is clear is that it is the other of this experience of separation, namely the desire to belong, that is the deep desire holding Hyperion in his struggles: "To be one with everything, that is the life of the divinity, that is the heaven of human being."[24] What is desired, then, in the language of philosophy, is a speculative experience. Hölderlin is here already describing something akin to the experience that is described in the document to which his name is attached—along with the names of Hegel and Schelling—namely, the "Earliest System-Program of German Idealism" but which would only be composed three years later. Furthermore, as Hyperion struggles to speak of this speculative experience of belonging to the whole, he finally arrives at a point from which he can give it a name: "The name of that which is one and all? Its name is beauty."[25] In a later letter, when the effort is to ask how beauty appears in the world and how it might be summoned, Hyperion says that "The first child of the human, of the divine beauty is art. In it, the divine human being rejuvenates herself. . . .That is how it was for the Athenians."[26] And with this he announces to himself how this separation from the one and the all (the *hen kai pan* of which he would speak along with Hegel and Schelling) is to be overcome: beauty is the glimmer of the highest speculative experience for a human being, and we beckon beauty, we call it into being, in art.

But this discovery of the importance of the beautiful—both in nature, where it comes unbidden as a gift, and in art, where we summon it as best we can—is a double-edged discovery. On the one hand, with the realization that beauty is the name of the one and all, the *hen kai pan,* Hyperion knows how this speculative experience will be found for a human being. On the other hand, because he senses all too powerfully the lack of this experience, the "lack of holy names,"[27] he also now comes to realize just what is lacking. Life is bereft of beauty, yet without the beautiful life is pointless. The task before him, then, is to find beauty, to summon it wherever possible, and to find it wherever it is given. This becomes the task of making art and of cultivating a living relation to nature, and this dual task gives purpose to Hyperion's suffering. In each is a moment of liberation. He knows, however, that this search is not entirely subject to what he is able to control: "We speak of our heart, our plans, as if they were our own, and yet there is a power outside of us which tosses us about as it pleases until it lays us in the grave, and of this power we know nothing, neither where it came from nor where it is going."[28] In other words, the struggle to cope with this suffering is itself a reminder of the vulnerability to which Hyperion is constantly exposed. This vulnerability, coupled with this suffering, become the keynotes of Hyperion's self-understanding, and so confronting them becomes a means of confronting himself.

As Hyperion reflects on his present situation and on the suffering upon which he is impaled, he finds himself increasingly drawn to the past, both his own past and the past of the art in which he finds some hope for grasping this suffering speculatively. The understanding of the nature of his suffering yields some clues as to how art needs to be thought if it is to answer to the task at hand. The first clue that he takes from his reflections is that this art must not shrink from facing this suffering; quite the contrary, the greatest possibilities in the realm of art are those that directly confront suffering as such. Bearing witness to this pain, art can redeem it. Such an art, an art which speculatively transfigures suffering into a unity with the all and one—the separation from which is at the root of this suffering—is tragedy. Tragedy is the art which takes this pain of separation upon itself as the reason for its being, and it celebrates it, even up to the greatest separation we suffer in the death of others. Paradoxically, it is this art, which does not kill the separation and the pain, which holds the promise of our relation to the unity of life. The task of art requires that Hyperion increase his awareness of his separation from the whole of life, of nature, of the divine. In the end, the ruins of his life, lived among the ruins of the island, find the possibility of some sort of intelligibility in the achievements of tragedy, the art dedicated to presenting the force of ruin in life. The second clue he finds which will guide him as he searches for this art is that such an art was the excellence of ancient Greece: "But the Athenians! I said that I was very close to them. The great saying, the *hen diapheron eauto* (the one which is differentiated in itself) of Heraclitus,[29] could only have been discovered by a Greek, for it is the essence of beauty,

and until that was discovered there was no philosophy."[30] Greek art, tragedy above all, becomes the magnetic north of Hyperion's hopes. It is no
surprise, then, that the second volume of the letters, which begins just
after the point that the centrality of Greek tragedy has become evident
to Hyperion, opens with the epigram from Sophocles, an epigram that
speaks of the reunion with the one and all that death promises: "Not to be
born is best of all; the second best however (after one has seen the light),
is, by far, to go as quickly as possible to where one came from."[31]

But the discovery that Greek tragedy is a key to the overcoming of his
suffering is a paradoxical solution since it has the effect of intensifying
that very same suffering which it is trying to overcome. Nonetheless, it
also has the effect of giving a new clarity to the nature of that suffering
and so begins to open a way to thinking that suffering from a new understanding. Hyperion speaks of his relation to the art of ancient Greece in a
passage that echoes one of the most poignant passages in Homer: "It is
something beautiful that it is so difficult for us to convince ourselves of
the death of that which one loves, and there is perhaps no one who goes
to the grave of a friend without the quiet hope that the friend will really
be found there. I am gripped by the beautiful phantom of ancient Athens, like the form of a mother who has returned from the realm of the
dead."[32] There is in this passage, this confession of how the Greek world
lives in its absence for him, a gentle and yet powerful allusion to book 11,
"The Gathering of the Shades," of the *Odyssey* in which Odysseus meets
the shade of his dead mother when he travels to the underworld of the
dead. What Odysseus learns there is what Hyperion learns about the art of
Homer in which that death is presented for us: it is, in the end, absent,
and its absence is permanent.[33] But with this realization of the permanent
absence of what is so deeply loved, Hölderlin begins to specify the nature
of this separation, namely, that it is a separation in time.

One needs to distinguish the forms of separation between that which
is a separation in time and that which is in space. The latter can be overcome: if one is separated from a loved one by such a distance, one can
travel across it and be reunited with the absent one. However, a separation in time cannot be overcome in this way, since such a separation is the
province only of the past (although, in some sense, we are separated from
the future, it is clearly of a different nature since time itself will overcome
it). Separation in time can only be suffered, and, as Hyperion knows, but
learns again with the death of his beloved Diotima, the final form of every
separation is death and the finality of separation that it inserts into every
life. Here Hyperion's opening remarks come back to haunt the reader:
"Far and dead are my loved ones."[34] But one must ask how that which is
separated in time is presented. How is that which is absent, and felt profoundly precisely *as* absent, preserved? The easy answer, but an answer
which is more of an enigma than a solution, is in memory. But how does

memory do its work? Here the answer must be that memory resides in language itself. *Language, then, is the site in which this pain of our separation from the unity of life is felt.* Words bear witness to our being and are, at the same time, the source of the torment that we feel; they remain for us an indication of our tormented relation to life. That, in part at least, is what Hyperion means when he says, "Believe me . . . when I speak to you from the depths of my soul: language is a great surplus. What is best always remains for itself and rests in its own depths, as a pearl at the bottom of the sea."[35] Words, with which Hyperion has a great love affair, are, in the end, what break his heart. The language of these letters does not simply speak about this sorrow, it self-consciously enacts it. Ultimately, it is this special form of the self-consciousness of the language here that gives these letters a sense that what they enact is not simply a complaint, but a promise: "True pain inspires. One who stands upon his anguish, stands taller. And that is what lifts us up, that in suffering the soul first truly feels its freedom."[36]

With this series of realizations Hyperion gradually comes to understand more of himself and of what the future might hold (it should never be forgotten how very concerned with the future Hyperion is even at the moments he is most single-mindedly indexing his attentions to the past). A number of themes have emerged as central to how he will eventually come to think of himself and his situation. There are obviously those themes which are clearly announced, even thematized in the letters— Greece, tragedy, love, death, and nature—all of which are mementos of our finitude. But other themes, which remain more or less on the level of subtexts, have shown themselves to be equally crucial for the issues which Hyperion confronts in these letters—time, language, and memory above all—and it is these themes which will eventually become the central concerns for Hölderlin's own reflections, especially his reflections on tragedy.[37]

Hyperion concludes his letters without a clear resolution, but nonetheless with some indications of a changed consciousness. He chooses to lead the life of a hermit from this point. In some regard this is a defeat, in other respects an affirmation of the struggle that he knows he must wage. Two realizations temper the end of these letters and introduce a new tone into them: the first is about the role of change in life, the second about the dissonance that is the companion of such change. About change, Hyperion concludes that "The stars have chosen constancy, they flow constantly in a still fullness and do not know age. We present the fullness of ourselves in change."[38] In other words, change is the form in which the completion of human life is exhibited. Nothing constant, nothing still, characterizes those who age and are destined to die. But this means as well that mortal life is a life full of the dissonance and friction which such constant change brings in its wake. But it is not the petty dissonances which are in need of understanding and which fracture the sense of belonging for which one aches. Death is the dissonance above all others, and it ultimately needs to be reconciled with life if one is to belong to life. This is perhaps the final riddle which Hyperion confronts, and he begins to come to terms with it insofar as he finds a place in nature where death most clearly is able to be seen as belonging to the rhythm, the movement of change, of human life. The question of nature thus takes on an even more potent role in the questioning which drives Hyperion to write these wonderful letters.

The letters end with a new understanding of this dissonance and of its hidden kinship with love and the unity which love signals: "The dissonances of the world are like the quarrel of lovers. Reconciliation is in the midst of struggle and everything that is separated finds itself again."[39] It is a conspicuously Heraclitean sensibility expressed here and quickly brings to mind the fragment which reads "They do not apprehend how being at variance it agrees with itself: there is a back-stretched connection, as in the bow and the lyre."[40] What reconciliation is found is like love, which is the highest form in which the human being can experience a speculative unity. Love unites the two tendencies which define mortal desire: to be everything and a something at once. With these words about love, dissonance, and reconciliation, Hyperion begins to draw his reflections to a close. These final words are words that Hyperion writes in the final letter to Bellarmin, but he tells Bellarmin that they were originally words which he spoke to himself in the cold night of human life, a night on which he wept with joy that he was so blessed and on which he spoke words to himself as they occurred to him. He describes the words that remain, and that he now writes to Bellarmin, as but "ashes" of the fire of rapture in which they were born; these words are only a residue of the experience from which he speaks. But these ashes, these final words, point to something to come, something which will remain fundamentally indeterminate. And so the last words of the text, the final word which Hyperion speaks to himself and now writes to his friend Bellarmin, who has been his absent companion on this route of self-reflection, are perplexing (and almost untranslatable): "Next, more."[41]

Hyperion is an early work of Hölderlin's, and it is his only novel. From this point on he will devote himself only to poems, theoretical texts, translations, and the effort to write a tragic drama (the letters which are now so important to our understanding of Hölderlin were never intended for publication). But *Hyperion* would set the tone for the work to come, and it would define the themes which would preoccupy Hölderlin for the rest of his life. Henceforth, the topic of tragedy, especially the achievement of Greek tragic art and its language, would form the center of Hölderlin's attentions. As he explores the trajectory of the human relation to art, it will seem, at times, that Hölderlin might agree with Joseph Bueys's fascinating remark that "Art is the greatest enigma of all. The human being is but one answer to it." But whereas *Hyperion* speaks *about* tragedy in the structure of the novel, his future works will be more clearly intent upon *reenacting* the truth of tragedy. Throughout, the self-apprehension of mortal life will manifest itself both in and as the struggle with the word. Consequently, the force of the poetics of finitude announced in these letters, this struggle of mortal life with the word, will only deepen over the course of Hölderlin's life.

Likewise, over the course of Hölderlin's life the question of nature will marry ever more deeply with this theme of tragedy and its distinctive poetics of finite life. In the end this wedding of the experience of nature and tragedy will reach its highest point in Hölderlin's own efforts to compose a tragedy for these times, in *The Death of Empedocles,* where nature itself will appear as one, if not the chief, hero of the tragedy. Hyperion learned early on that one who is not in harmony with nature cannot be in a harmony with oneself. Hyperion's itinerary, his often paradoxical struggle to give expression to his struggles, is from a despair without direction to the point at which his despair and suffering themselves become indicators of the direction he must head. It is an itinerary that deepens the role that Greece and tragedy will play in the future, but it is equally one in which the experience of nature, which announces its importance in Hyperion's first letters, is ever anew reconfirmed in its elementality for human life. What is new at the conclusion of these letters is that the experience of nature is no longer able to be found independently of the work of tragedy. That is the destiny of the modern world which Hyperion comes to learn.

Although Hölderlin begins *Hyperion* in 1792, the second and final volume will not be published until 1799. Near the end of the writing of *Hyperion* Hölderlin formulates the first clear outline of his own effort to write a tragedy (with nature and the philosopher of nature, Empedocles, as its chief characters).[42] The years immediately prior to 1799, and that year especially, would prove to be pivotal years in Hölderlin's life. That is the period in which he meets and falls in love with Susette Gontard (who Hölderlin would call "Diotima"), the woman who was mother and wife in the house where he was employed as a private tutor in Frankfurt. During that period both he and Hegel lived for a while in Frankfurt.[43] By 1799 Hölderlin was working intensively on his own plans for the tragedy about Empedocles, and he was seriously translating Sophocles. In short, by 1799 the topic of tragedy had become something of a preoccupation for Hölderlin. However, his translations of Sophocles and the "Remarks" which accompany both translations would not be finished and published until 1804, while his own tragedy, *The Death of Empedocles,* would undergo three thorough revisions and never be published in his lifetime. Only two years after the publication of his translations of *Antigone* and *Oedipus the Tyrant,*

Hölderlin would be hospitalized because of his "madness." That will mark the final period of his life, since he would remain in the care of others for the next thirty-six years, until his death in 1843. But in the years between 1799 and 1804, we find both an intense concentration upon tragedy in a variety of forms, and we find as well a life in which Hölderlin's personal sufferings are acute.

Before taking up the products of these years—the "Remarks" accompanying Hölderlin's Sophocles translations and *The Death of Empedocles* —which form Hölderlin's most direct contributions to the question of tragedy, there is one other document of this period which needs some consideration, namely, Hölderlin's celebrated letter to his friend Böhlendorff. The letter was written on December 4, 1801[44] (he will also write a letter to his brother, Karl, on the same day),[45] just before Hölderlin leaves Germany for almost seven months (he leaves on December 10th, setting off for France on foot). There are two reasons this letter needs some special attention. First, it seems to be the occasion for Hölderlin to formulate with great precision his relation to the question posed to him by tragedy and to ancient Greece; second, it proves to be a remarkably influential document in twentieth-century interpretations of both themes. It is a pivotal moment in Hölderlin's understanding of the place of the questions of Greece and of tragedy in his life's work. This is the point at which he crystallizes much that was expressed over the whole of *Hyperion,* and in this more compressed expression Hölderlin also introduces new elements in the way he will take up these themes in the years to come. This letter has an added significance: Hölderlin will return from France in June or July of the next year; during the intervening period we have only scant information about his life (only three letters, all to his mother, exist from his time in France). When Hölderlin returns to Germany his life will be profoundly different: he will return in extremely bad health (and signs of his madness will first be evident), and the woman he loved, Susette ("Diotima"), will die just at the point of his return to Germany. This letter, then, marks the end of much for Hölderlin, and, though he could not know the full extent of what that would mean in his life, the letter is very attuned to a mood of loss and ending. The poignancy of its tone is very much an element of its substance.

*　　*　　*

The letter begins with Hölderlin praising Böhlendorff's play *Fernando or the Baptizing of Art: A Dramatic Idyll,* which Hölderlin calls an "authentic modern tragedy" (though, except for Hölderlin's own comments about it, the play has sunk into oblivion). The few remarks he makes about Böhlendorff's play sound like generous, but ultimately rather empty, praise for the work of a close friend with whom he says he shares a common destiny. In the letter that follows these opening words of praise it is not Böhlendorff's play, but rather the nature of closeness such as that between friends, and the direction of the destiny he believes he shares with his friend, that capture Hölderlin's attention. Intimacy and destiny are thus the first notions which form the initial focus of his letter in which Hölderlin struggles to speak both of how we belong to what is closest to us and of the dilemma of living in a time that seems to be without any destiny. It is out of his reflections on these themes that Hölderlin will eventually open up the question put to us by tragedy in the modern age.

The letter—which at times reads like a confession, at times like a manifesto—is very complex and dense, and following the matrix of its themes can be daunting. After the opening remarks of congratulations and expression of a sense of connection, Hölderlin introduces the notion of the national and uses this notion as a means of raising the question about the nature of what can rightly be said to be one's own. This is the point at which he takes up the question that most clearly holds his attention on the eve of his departure: to what does one most belong? The passage in which this is said most pointedly has become one of the more celebrated and analyzed sentences in all of Hölderlin's work; it is also the sentence which will ultimately serve to clarify the peculiar paradox for one who would raise the question of tragedy at the present historical juncture: "We learn nothing with greater difficulty than the free use of the national. . . . It sounds paradoxical. But I contend that the truly national always receives less preference in the progress of culture."[46] A few lines later he repeats this point, but amplifies it as well insofar as he substitutes the words "the ownmost" for "the national": "The *free* use of *what is most one's own* is the most difficult."[47] According to Hölderlin, what is most one's own arises out of the practice of a freedom; nonetheless, it is precisely this practice and this freedom that is most in need of being learned today. Strangely, against expectation, he implies that what is one's own is "most difficult" to express. In this letter, as frequently elsewhere, Hölderlin suggests that "the sole and unique human flaw" is the failure to know the direction in which this freedom of our nature finds its formative expression. We suffer from no other failing as greatly as we suffer from the failure to find a destiny, to find the direction in which that for which we are born—the freedom which art brings into the world—finds expression. The failure to understand that which is most one's own is the lack from which we most deeply suffer: "To know nothing of one's self . . . and to be annihilated is for us the same thing."[48] But it is important to understand why this annihilation is not rooted in any individual lapse or failing; rather, it is the failure of our age, it is the failing, the flaw, into which we are born today.[49] We suffer this as the destiny of our times. This is the sad destiny that he shares with his friend Böhlendorff.[50] Beginning with this letter, the question of having a destiny—only peripherally a question proper to the way tragedy is taken up in *Hyperion*—moves much more directly into the center of Hölderlin's concerns, and it will link up above all with the question of the possibility of tragedy. While Hyperion wrestled with his sorrows and came finally to understand them as bound up in his relation to the past, he did not so directly come to understand his sufferings as themselves an element of history, as somehow his own destiny. But that is the new sense that Hölderlin himself expresses in this letter. This, then, is the point at which the topic of tragedy begins to wed itself to the riddle of history in a new manner. Of course, to make such a claim—that the peculiar flaw of modernity is the lack of destiny, a lack of what is requisite for tragedy, and to do so in a letter about an "authentic modern tragedy"—needs to be heard as ironizing and so problematizing the relation of tragedy and modernity: how can a tragedy be written in an era in which the historical requisites for a tragedy are lacking? While *Hyperion* might have been the point at which Hölderlin discovered the full import of tragedy for life, this letter is the point at which he announces, however quietly, what seems to be the cause for despair about the possibility of writing a tragedy today. Of course, at this time he is still struggling to write *The Death of Empedocles*, which was to be his modern tragedy.

But the quiet and remarkably gentle despair which haunts this letter is not only rooted in Hölderlin's growing conviction that this is a time in which tragedy cannot be written, however much it is needed; it is also rooted in Hölderlin's own personal sense of failure and leave-taking. He writes this letter just before his departure for France, suggesting that he is leaving Germany because "they have no use for me."[51] The tone of the letter makes clear that these travels in a foreign land mark for Hölderlin the attempt to uncover the grounds of the homeland in which he might root himself as a poet, much like Hyperion's travels in Germany after his failures had led him to wander for a time. Most of all, Hölderlin is asking about that to which he can understand himself as belonging freely. And yet, as he unfolds his question, it is Greece, a place where Hölderlin had never been, and would never go, that dominates his reflections. Here, then, Hölderlin begins to speak in his own voice and of his own experiences, in much the same way he had Hyperion speak. It now seems as if he has assumed the role of his earlier alter ego, and when he does this he gives some added clarity to the claims one reads in Hyperion's letters. Much of what he says in this letter to Böhlendorff amplifies and augments points found in *Hyperion*, but there is one point where this letter marks a clear advance over the understanding of the issues which are addressed both in this letter and in *Hyperion*. In the letter to Böhlendorff, Hölderlin gives a new reason for suggesting that Greece poses an imperative for the present age, namely, for those who lack destiny: "But what is ownmost must be learned as well as the foreign. That is why the Greeks are unavoidable for us."[52]

One knows already from *Hyperion* that this comment should not be understood as it might be from the viewpoint of classicism, namely, as suggesting that the Greeks stand for what is most our own or that they represent a youthful mirror into which we might look in order to freshen our worn-out truths. There is absolutely no canonization of the Greek world or Greek art at work here. Quite the contrary: though Hölderlin acknowledges that "the highest" is the same for us and the Greeks, namely, to have a "living relation and destiny,"[53] what is more important, more in need of being experienced at this historical juncture, is that which is found in the Greek world and its art, but that is denied and foreclosed to us. By now it should be clear: the canonical conception of the ancient world—a view which has it as the stable foundation of late Western culture—is the greatest obstacle which Hegel, Hölderlin, and others faced in trying to uncover something alive in the Greek world. In Greece, Hölderlin experiences what is most absent in the possibilities which shape his own experience. Greece, then, is the name of the experience, an absence, even, one might say, of a sorrow. But it is a complicated absence which is named here, since the sense of what is missing which is conveyed is itself somehow once removed: even what is felt as absent is not immediately known, but is discovered only through the mediation of Greece. So Hölderlin's self-reflections in this letter, the way he speaks here of his search for what is most his own, is guided by the strange sorrow of exile from a foreign land. And it is precisely this exile and this sorrow that illuminate for Hölderlin the experience of what is most his own, namely, a lack of destiny.

The heliotropism that characterizes Hölderlin's relation to Greece is in full force in this letter. Late in his life when he speaks of flowers that are led to face the sun always by the charms of its rays,[54] it is clear that he is speaking of his own relation to ancient Greece that even now is defining him. By now it should be clear that the pull that the question of Greece exerts upon Hölderlin at this point, a pull already expressed in *Hyperion*, is not one that is best understood as drawing him into the already well-formulated terms of the *querelle des anciens et modernes*, nor can this pull of the ancient world be understood if it is taken as the ordinary experience of a nostalgia holding Hölderlin in its ever-tightening melancholic grip.[55] Rather, it seems better to say that "Greece" (the scare quotes are necessary because the word here is not employed in the customary geopolitical sense to which one is accustomed) names what Hölderlin describes in the first preface to *Hyperion* as one of the "essential orientations" of the "eccentric path"[56] on which we learn about ourselves. Greece is not being mythologized, nor is it being canonized, here. Precisely the opposite: it is becoming strange. And yet it is also acknowledged as the name of one of the paths down which the sufferings of our age—the sense of fragmentation and ruin and lack of purpose that initially held Hyperion in its grip—

might be grasped speculatively. But why Greece? Why does this eccentric path to human self-understanding orient itself to an experience of the foreign that is found so essentially in Greece? What is found in Greece that is needed for an overcoming of the specific weakness of this historical present?

One of the most distinctive features of the Böhlendorff letter is that there the question of Greece is coupled with the notion of the national, and understanding what he means when he introduces this notion is important for understanding how this letter brings a new clarity to Hölderlin's understanding of what Greece means today and why we need to index ourselves to what is accomplished in Greek art. With the word "national" Hölderlin should not be understood as asking about "nationhood" or "nationality" in the common sense of those words, but as speaking again about the nature of belonging and about that to which one rightly and freely belongs. It is out of this that something like a nation can come to be a home. In this regard it should be noted that Hölderlin uses the word "nationelle" rather than "national," which is the word that came into usage after the French Revolution and took on a more purely political sense. Hölderlin's sense of this word draws upon its roots in the Latin *nasci*, to be born, and as designating "the collective of peoples born under the same sky and thus sharing the same destiny."[57] Once one acknowledges this, namely, that it is belonging, birth, and nativity, more than nationhood that is the basic issue here, then one is in a position to understand the real meaning of the realm of Greece as Hölderlin puts it forward: Greece is more the name of an experience and a knowledge than it is a geo-political designation in the ordinary sense. When Hölderlin speaks of Greece in this sense it is the preeminence of poetic practices in Greece, it is something about the Greek relation to the work of art as he understands it, that guides him. Greece is the name of an experience that can provide a home for one such as himself—for one "born for art."[58]

Here one should recall that, like his friend Schelling, Hölderlin suggests that human nature and practices are to be understood by reference to a formative drive which expresses itself as a constant need for art. This drive forms the root and motor of human production. As the impulse of all production, as, in other words, lodged at the source of human history, it needs to be recognized that the destination, the *telos,* of this formative drive is porous and mobile and so never immune to the history that it generates. The roots of the human impulse to make art and the vitality and openness which characterize human history are found at the same point. Both are productions of human freedom, which expresses itself most of all in art. In the Böhlendorff letter Hölderlin claims that the outcome of the work of this formative drive, the history of the art in which freedom has sought to objectify itself, has led to a reversal of the original direction in which it expressed itself, so that in our time this drive needs to express itself otherwise than in Greece. Put in other words: the modern experience out of which art arises, and that to which it is directed and which it thus seeks to express, is the reverse of that which one finds in ancient Greece. Thus one must say that what is natural to Greece is foreign to us, and consequently our struggles to represent ourselves to ourselves are the photographic negative of the struggles that animate Greek art. This means that Greek art is not to be understood according to a model that takes antiquity as the childhood of our present where we find a sort of naive and innocent form of the art of the present; rather, it is to be understood as the realm in which what is most our own appears in the guise of something foreign, almost according to a model which regards Greek art as having transposed what for us is conscious and unconscious.[59] The encounter with Greek art which Hölderlin is trying to inaugurate therefore sets us into a quite intimate conversation, but one that is carried on in a language the code for which we have lost—much as we do not possess the code for understanding our own dreams. The attempt to take up the Greek work of art thus constantly calls for inventiveness, because, as we approach it, we approach something profoundly foreign to our own natures. Furthermore, this loss is not accidental, but constructive of our relation to such works at all. Greek art, then, becomes something like a dream we dream, intimate and most our own, but one in which we are nonetheless foreign to ourselves as an almost hallucinatory presence in which we dream the dream of a stranger.

The logic and form of our relation to Greek art is developed by Hölderlin rather schematically in the Böhlendorff letter according to the respective directions of the formative drives in antiquity and today. He emphasizes the contradictory directions in which these drives are headed in ancient Greece and modern Europe: "With us it is the reverse [of Greece]."[60] In the letter he says that Greek art, the formative drive of which is precisely the opposite of that which characterizes modernity (in Greek art the movement is from "sacred pathos" to "Junoian sobriety"), is unavoidable for us since its drive is to excessively form that which is most our own. But it is precisely for this reason that Greek art, tragedy above all, is unbearable for us since in it what is most our own appears as fundamentally foreign, as emerging according to a law of appearance not our own. For us, Greek art brings into the open what the law of the formative drive must hide, but which it nonetheless contains within itself as most our own. Consequently, our relation to Greek art is one in which we are "most exposed"[61] to ourselves. Taking up the Greek work of art—tragedy, the work par excellence above all—is something like the struggle to take up one's unconscious life. Just as one cannot understand unconscious desires according to the logic of one's conscious life, so too one cannot understand the achievement of the Greek work of art according to the

logic and assumptions of the modern world and the shape of consciousness it has achieved. Likewise, we cannot understand the full possibilities
of art in our times only in a relation to Greece: "It is also dangerous to
abstract the rules of art exclusively from the excellence of Greece."[62] But
even if the form of our relation to Greece is complex and in need of discussion, what is more problematic and still in need of an answer is the
question of the specific nature of the spell that Greece casts upon thinking today. What is it that comes into the open in Greece as Hölderlin understands it? To what experience does this orientation to Greece draw us?

The Böhlendorff letter does not give a clear answer to these questions, though it clearly presumes a specific answer. Hölderlin seems to be
assuming that his reader, his friend, shares an understanding of the special excellence of ancient Greece that is at the root of the achievement of
its art. Although this letter does not give any answer to this question, one
does find a clue to an answer in the final lines of "In lovely blueness . . . ,"
where Hölderlin writes the enigmatic line which says that "Myrtles are
found in Greece."[63] What needs to be remembered here is that myrtle,
the leaves of which are freckled just like the human being whom Hölderlin describes as suffering from the freckles drawn out by the sun, is,
according to legend, the plant of both eros and mourning.[64] Bearing this
in mind, that in Greece one finds myrtles, one can see that, for Hölderlin,
Greece is the name for the realm in which we experience the contradictory sameness of eros and mourning, joy and sorrow, life and death. Because Greek art emerges out of and is animated by an abiding experience
of such contradiction, tragedy, the art form that consummates such contradiction, necessarily becomes the summit of art in antiquity. Bearing the
stamp of this realm of impossible conjunctions, that is, as presenting the
unity of the most monstrous contradictions, Greek art, for Hölderlin, is
thus "the metaphor of an intellectual intuition."[65] But with us the matter
is different. For us, for those whose destiny is to lack a destiny, this realm
of Greek tragedy presents us with both what is most our own and what is
most foreign to us: it is thus indispensable and impossible at once. As
such, the art of Greece poses a riddle for us which we must confront, just
as Oedipus was confronted by the riddle of the Sphinx. Greek tragedy is
the question which history puts to our times.

Yet Hölderlin contends that in the present age we confront this riddle
inadequately because we lack an appreciation of the speculative truth of
what is confronted in the tragedy. The claim is that we will not begin to
take up the question before us, the question of tragedy, until we have
understood how it is the "metaphor of an intellectual intuition," but this,
most of all, is what we lack today. That, in part at least, is what Hölderlin
means in the letter to Böhlendorff when he says that "the tragic for us is
that we are packed up in any container [and] taken away from the realm
of the living; not that—consumed in flames—we make amends to the

flames we cannot subdue."[66] Such a relation to death, in which one is isolated in the coffin, "packed up in a container," and put in the ground (where the body is nevertheless separated from the earth), is indicative of the difference between our understanding of life and death and the Greek sensibility in which one is consumed by flames and in that way united with the whole of nature.[67] To be "consumed in flames" is, one might say, a speculative form of death. Whether one confronts death "according to our destiny or according to the destiny of antiquity,"[68] it is the duty of the poet to be present at that dying. In other words, it is the duty of the poet to find the speculative path whereby the sufferings of separation, of being apart from that to which one most belongs, are overcome.

After this remark about the obligation of the poet to present this dying, Hölderlin suggests that he will read Böhlendorff's play more closely. There is no indication from other letters that he did in fact do this. The conclusion of this letter alternates between quite personal remarks, even about other acquaintances, and Hölderlin's own plans for the next phase of his life which he is about to enter. One remark stands out above all in this final section of the letter. In it Hölderlin seems to speak not just of his immediate future, but also of the prospects of history, which is the theme he had just addressed. He says simply, "O friend! The world lies before me brighter than usual, and more serious!"[69] Here the tone of the letter reaches its clearest moment. Here the search that he has announced as the search for what is most one's own, for the home proper to those who are "born for art," seems to have a direction. And it is clear that this direction is found in that discovery of a new, and speculative, relation to the possibility of tragedy in the modern world.

*   *   *

The Böhlendorff letter was written at the end of 1801, just before Hölderlin departed for a trip to France. When he returned from that trip seven months after writing this letter, Hölderlin turned to his own poetry, to the revision of his translations of Pindar and Sophocles, and to work on his own efforts to write a tragedy. His translations of Sophocles would be published in April 1804, some twenty months after his return from Bordeaux.[70] Hölderlin would use that time to radicalize the language of his translations and to write the remarks which would accompany their publication. The result, both in the form of the remarks and in the striking translations, is a series of texts which engage Sophocles' tragedies in their very capillaries. Hölderlin's relation to the texts in these translations is as intimate as possible; in them he struggles with the stuff of the difference between Greece and Germany insofar as it is preserved in language. In the translations one sees Hölderlin wrestling with the language of Greek

tragedy, and that means, for him, wrestling with the locus of its real action, with the site in which the suffering is most properly found.

His translations of Sophocles stand as one of the most creative works
in the German language, perhaps on the order of the power of Luther's
translation of the Bible.[71] In the end, those translations might stand as
Hölderlin's ultimate testimony on the matter of Greek tragedy, but it is a
testimony one cannot translate beyond its own performance. One cannot
translate these translations without thereby destroying them since it is
precisely in their translation-character that they accomplish an engagement with the language of the tragedy.[72] In these translations, language
reaches an impasse, an end point, at which it cannot help but call attention to itself *as* language, moreover, as language that is strained and inherently strange to itself, as foreign in itself. These translations present such
a sharp and powerful instance of this general situation of translation that
Benjamin praises them by saying:

> In [Hölderlin's translations of Sophocles] . . . the harmony of the lan-
> guage is so profound that sense is touched by language only the way an
> aeolian harp is touched by the wind. Hölderlin's translations are proto-
> types of their kind; they are to even the most perfect renderings of their
> texts as a prototype is to a model. . . . For this very reason they are subject
> to the monstrous danger inherent in all translations: the gates of a lan-
> guage thus expanded and modified may slam shut and enclose the trans-
> lator with silence.[73]

Although it might be necessary to look at Hölderlin's translations to understand the full force of the language of tragedy as he thinks it, such cannot be done in any language outside of German.[74] The translations are
very much about the resistance of languages to one another, and about
the way in which languages harbor resistance within themselves. In them
language arrives at the point of perhaps its greatest density and intran-
sitivity, and in this respect the language of these texts comes to resemble
the language of the sign and symbol in which the intransitive element
preserves an insurmountable ambiguity (see chapter 2) which is normally
effaced or canceled by the Midas touch of the concept which converts
language to its own logic and the laws of intelligibility. Here, though, in
these translations, the Greek is not compressed into the syntax and sensibility of German. Rather, the converse is true: the German is challenged
to enlarge itself to speak with the syntax, word order, and sensibility of the
Greek. In the end, the German here becomes curiously foreign. So the
goal is not transparency and immediate intelligibility, but the repetition
of an experience of language proper to Greek. More precisely, what is
sought here is a repetition, a mimesis, of the way in which the tragedy is
an experience which resides in our relation to language. Here one finds

Hölderlin enacting his conviction that language itself is the site in which we experience the pain of our separation from the unity of life. One also finds him struggling to bring out the "oriental," the "eccentric," element of the experience here. His aim in these translations is not governed by any image of fidelity (he will even change names so that Zeus will sometimes be "Father of time" and sometimes "Father of the earth"). Hölderlin makes all of this clear in a letter to his publisher, Wilmans, when he writes that "I hope to make Greek art, which is foreign to us . . . more vital than the public usually experiences it, and so I have emphasized the oriental, which has been obscured [thus far]."[75] What he called the "sobriety" at which the Greeks aimed, and which he found in the clarity and poise of Sophocles' language, Hölderlin translates in such a manner that he brings out the fire and oriental passion of the language, which is native to the Greek spirit but which we today must struggle to present.

Accompanying these translations are two sets of "Remarks," one for each translation, each purported to serve as an introduction for the reader of the translations, but both of which are composed of prose similar in its density and strangeness to the translations which they are supposed to introduce. Rigorous and demanding to the extreme, these remarks probe the heart of the tragedies with the uncanny precision of an obsession guided by Hölderlin's deep commitment to the project of locating the tragic in the nature of language itself. The tragic difference, the conflict which is the seat of mortal suffering, is, in the final analysis, housed in the word. The "Remarks," each in its own way (they should not be collapsed since the differences between them are important), drive home this point. But that means that each seeks to come to the essential element of each tragedy. As one takes up these different efforts to lead the reader to this element, what one might most need to bear in mind is that while both tragedies are to be understood as in each case a "metaphor of an intellectual intuition," that is, speculatively, Hölderlin treats *Oedipus* as an example of what is "Hesperian"—that is, as "Western"[76]—while he presents *Antigone* as a supremely Greek drama and consequently as much more enigmatic to us than *Oedipus*. The way we detect this difference is striking in its strangeness: the different rhythms of the representation—more precisely, the direction in which these respective rhythms tend—illuminate the specific character of each of the dramas. Inclined in opposing directions, *Antigone* and *Oedipus* stand to one another as the ancient to the modern. Each arrives at the moment of the pure word, the caesura, the moment of rupture, in a different way. At the moment that the language of the tragedy turns upon itself, the "counter-rhythmic" moment, the result of the tragedies is the same: it is the point at which there is not a new representation which is presented, a new event, but what appears is *representation itself*. What appears is the nature of the event *as such*. Hölderlin puts this point as follows: "In the rhythmic sequence of representations, in which the tragic transport presents itself, that which one calls the *cae-sura* in poetic meter, the pure word, the counter-rhythmic interruption, is necessary; it is this namely in order to encounter the raging change of representations at its summit so that it is no longer the change of repre-sentations, but rather representation itself which appears."[77] The mean-ing of the caesura is the same in both *Antigone* and *Oedipus*, but the route, path, on which this summit of the tragic is met is different.[78] To begin to treat these two sets of "Remarks" it is helpful to note the points of their similarity, namely, to speak about the way in which the tragic in general is presented in them as the caesura.

While Hölderlin speaks of the tragic as the caesura in language, he does not let this stand without interpretation, but gives a variety of indica-tions of just how this summit of the tragic in language is felt. The com-mon feature of these indications is that in each case the monstrous is presented. One finds this said in one of the more pointed passages: "The presentation of the tragic rests preeminently upon this, that the mon-strous—how the god and man pair themselves, and the power of nature and what is innermost in man become one in wrath—grasps itself through the limitless becoming one through the limitless division that purifies."[79] The monstrous (the word is *das Ungeheure*, which is also Hölderlin's trans-lation of the word *to deinon* in the celebrated choral ode of *Antigone* and elsewhere), which is the pinnacle of the tragic presentation, is here de-scribed as the coupling of the divine and the mortal, the union of the most extreme opposites. That coupling can happen only as wrath, and it is limitless, it knows no end to itself. Hölderlin makes the same point in the "Remarks on *Antigone*" while taking it still further when he says that "The tragic presentation rests, as was indicated in the 'Remarks to *Oedi-pus*,' upon this: that the immediate god is completely one with man (for the god of an apostle is more mediated, is the higher intellect in the high-est spirit), [and] that the *infinite* enthusiasm conceives of itself *infinitely* (that means in oppositions) in the consciousness which elevates and de-stroys consciousness, separating itself in a sacred way, and that the god is present in the figure of death."[80] These difficult, yet crucial, passages make clear what happens in the moment the language of the tragedy turns upon itself, that is, what happens in the caesura. That is the moment the monstrous is visible. It is the moment in which the extreme oppo-sitions are united and in which the word itself becomes deadly, and at that moment, "The Greek tragic word is deadly factical, because the body which it seizes actually kills."[81] At that moment "man must sustain himself most of above all, that is why at this moment he is most open in his charac-ter."[82] What is perhaps most striking here is that the monstrous, the dead-liest moment and the moment in which the human being is most exposed for what one is, is a moment held open by a possibility of language. In line with this view, Hölderlin's presentations of both *Antigone* and *Oedipus* avoid virtually any mention of what one would normally deem an action or event. Against expectation, we are said to experience the monstrosity of the most powerfully tragic not when we focus attention upon Antigone's conflict with Creon or upon Oedipus's murder of his father or marriage to his mother. Such matters, such deeds in the customary sense of the word, almost pass by unnoticed when Hölderlin struggles to reach into the heart of the tragedy and hold fast to the point at which it pulses. What does come forward here as the pulse of the tragedy, the point at which we find its beat, is *how* we speak of such matters. Language itself harbors the experience proper to the tragic: "Everything is speech against speech, which mutually cancel each other."[83] The law of the tragic, the nature according to which it unfolds and holds us in its grip, is housed in (or, better, as) the law of the rhythm of the language itself. This is what Hölderlin means when he speaks of the "lawful calculus" out of which the tragedy arises. Speech presents this lawful calculus of the tragic, and the tragedy is thus to be understood as the presentation of "how the course of events and that which is to be established, the living meaning which cannot be calculated, are brought into a relation with the calculable law."[84] The tragedy is not simply the presentation of events; it is rather the clash between those events—and what they are to establish, which itself is incalculable—that is brought into speech and its lawful operations. The law of speech to which Hölderlin refers here is the law of succession, of sequence. It is a law, in other words, of time. *The caesura in language is thus to be understood as a crisis in time.*

This is perhaps the key point in the presentation of what is common to both *Antigone* and *Oedipus* for Hölderlin. It will also prove to be the central theme, and one might say even more pronounced than in Sophocles, of Hölderlin's own tragedy, *The Death of Empedocles*. But, despite its importance, Hölderlin does not expend much effort to clarify this point in these texts (though it will find more clarity in his "Ground to Empedocles," which is the text he composes to accompany *The Death of Empedocles;* there he will describe Empedocles as the "victim of time"). Nonetheless, some points can be gleaned about this provocative claim. The claim seems to be that the rhythm of the language of the tragedy is itself necessarily at odds with the living meaning that is to be presented, and, in this respect, the language of the tragedy presents us with a poetics of finitude not by virtue of what it conveys, by what is represented, but by virtue of its own rhythm, of the way speech cancels speech. The law of the tragic is found in the manner in which this rhythm, this calculable law of the poetic language, ruptures the sequence of representations, that is, in which language interrupts the course of events. Such a moment is the caesura, and in such a moment "there does not appear a change of representations, but rather [it is] representation itself which appears."[85] In such a moment, says Hölderlin,

Man forgets both himself and the god, and turns around, naturally in a sacred way, like a traitor—In the most extreme limits of suffering, namely, there consists nothing more than the conditions of time or of space. In this moment man forgets himself because he exists completely in the moment; the god, because he is nothing but time; and both are unfaithful, time because in such a moment it turns around categorically, so that the beginning and the end no longer rhyme with one another.[86]

In such a moment, the moment at which language halts its relation to the succession of representations, the moment in which the living meaning stands out, the moment of the caesura, what one confronts is nothing but the conditions of space and time. And this, above all, is the presentation of the monstrous.

While Hölderlin does not say so, one cannot read this passage without thinking of the analysis of the sublime one finds in Kant's Third Critique. There Kant distinguishes between the mathematical sublime and the dynamical sublime. The first can be understood as the pure experience of time; the second is the pure experience of space.[87] In other words, the sublime is the direct experience of the pure forms of intuition which form one element in the ground of human experience as Kant analyzes it in the First Critique. The abyssal quality of the sublime is that in it one confronts nothing but the pure form of possibility; one confronts oneself as nothing but space and time, and in such a confrontation one loses oneself. Such is the terror of the sublime for Kant. Hölderlin, who admittedly does not refer to the Kantian sublime here, seems to have something similar in mind. But here the emphasis is clearly on the experience of time which is opened in the caesura of the rhythm of the tragic work. One knows oneself as nothing but time, and in knowing oneself as time, one knows oneself as finite. The highest feeling, the boldest moment, is one in which

The spirit of time and nature, the heavenly which fastens upon man, and the object in which man is interested, oppose one another most wildly. . . . At this moment man must hold fast to himself most of all, and that is why he is open in his character then most of all. The flatness of time which is proper to the tragic, the object of which is of no interest to the heart, follows the rush of the spirit of time improperly. . . . it is unguarded, as the spirit of the eternally living, unwritten wilderness and of the world of the dead.[88]

Such passages, even in their diamond-like compression and density, point not only to the relation between language and time, the relation which is sustained by the poetic rhythm, but also to the relation between language and death, a relation which the word itself maintains. That is why Hölderlin speaks of "the actual murder with words"[89] in the Greek tragedy.

One sees here how much rides on the nature of the language in the tragedy. In particular, the manner in which language in the tragedy carries along the events, even the manner in which the rhythm of the language and the course of events contrast, is the heart of the Greek tragic work as Hölderlin understands it. The play becomes, in its deepest nature, the play of time itself. It is this that cannot be conceived, but can only be performed; furthermore, this life of the play as it is found in its rhythmic structure cannot be accounted for by the logic of what Hölderlin refers to as "categorical time," that is, a time understood as linear and successive. What is necessary here is to learn to think time differently, namely, as the time of destiny.

In the end, this will be the issue that comes to define Hölderlin's own tragedy, *The Death of Empedocles,* and it is there that the most extended treatment of the time of tragedy will be presented. But in the remarks, especially the "Remarks on *Antigone,*" there is one other point about this kinship of time and tragedy which is brought out, namely, that time is always measured best when it is measured in suffering. Calculated time, the conception of time that would reckon it according to some march of a sequence of nows, a sense of time that Hölderlin calls "categorical time," is derivative and so unable to grasp the original experience of time as it is unfolded in the tragedy.[90] There time is measured (if such can be the word in this regard) in how suffering progresses. Hölderlin explains that such is the case in the course of remarking upon the need to translate Zeus with the phrase "father of time; or father of the earth." There he says that "The golden stream of becoming refers to the rays of light which also belong to Zeus to the extent that the sense of time which is referred to there is calculable by means of such rays. But it is always this when time is counted in suffering, because then feelings can follow the changes of time much more feelingly, and thus the simple course of hours is grasped without the intellect enclosing the future in the present."[91] Suffered time is the ecstatic form of time in which we confront ourselves as nothing but time. It is the great merit of the tragic work, above all the relation of the language of the work to the events which it unfolds, to expose human being to this, its own, time. In this time which we suffer, we discover that we are nothing but time. At that moment the living meaning of the tragedy is present to us. Such is the moment of revelation: in it I learn that I am this time and, in the end, nothing but.[92] The crisis which the tragedy unfolds is a crisis of time and, as such, needs to be understood as opening me to the final meaning of time, namely, my death. Such is the time of destiny. This is what Hölderlin means when he says that

> The tragic presentation consists above all in the factical word which, more of a context and relation than a statement, moves from the beginning to end according to destiny; [the tragic presentation consists moreover] in the specific course of events, in the grouping of characters

against one another, and in the form of reason which cultivates itself in the terrible muse of a tragic time—as well as in the oppositions which are presented subsequently in their wild formation in human time—and is considered a fixed idea which is born of divine destiny."[93]

What we detect in the tragedy, in its poetic movement—and in the glare between the words and the events they unfold—is the force of destiny exposed as time. This poetics of time, this poetics of finite life, is what tragedy, in the end, is "about."

What is perhaps most difficult to grasp here is the extraordinary role granted to language. In the end, it is the human relation to the word alone that lets one see that and what one is, and that is why Hölderlin says elsewhere of language that it is "the most dangerous possession, which is given to man so that creating, destroying, and perishing . . . he might bear witness to what he has inherited, and that he has learnt from it its most divine trait, all-embracing love."[94] It is because we speak that we learn of ourselves, and poetic language, language which is folded back upon itself and brought to the point of its greatest density *as* language, is language in which the character of the word itself is most in evidence. Moreover, tragic language is this possibility of poetic language in the extreme. This extremity of language is what Hölderlin sought to repeat and even to heighten in his translations. The "Remarks" which accompany these translations call attention to this effort and emphasize the manner in which this extreme of language opens us to the experience of time as that which we can suffer, but never know. The argument here is a stunning one, and powerful. Taken to heart it tells us why it is that we can be greatly moved by rhythms, tones, and meter; here we can come to understand why the rhythm of language—as well as the movement of music, of time made loud—can stir us and touch us deeply, as deeply as possible.[95] In the time that is rhythm we sense something of ourselves; more precisely, rhythm mimes the course of life, and the rhythm that is specific to the tragic poem—a rhythm defined by its interior countermovements and by the moment of the caesura—is the rhythm which leads us to the point at which no content, no image or representation, is what we learn of ourselves. It leads us, rather, to the point at which we learn that we are nothing but time, and at this point we learn as well the nature of our destiny which ends in death.

Hölderlin's conviction, then, is that language is ultimately a reminder of death,[96] and that in the word we experience—simultaneously—the sweet pleasure of self-disclosure as well as the bitterness of the finality and finitude that is disclosed as our destiny. Such bittersweet language, the language which by virtue of its own poetic nature illuminates the sameness of life and death,[97] is the special province of the language proper to the tragic work of art. But it is in Greece, where "there are myrtles," that such a language has been spoken in a manner unsurpassed in beautiful suffering. The dream animating Hölderlin's translations of Sophocles is to rejuvenate the German language, which is itself unsurpassed in the clarity of presentation, in such a way that it too can summon this conflicted experience of bittersweet language. One might say that Hölderlin's ambitions in these translations is far more ambitious than simply providing translations of the tragedies into German; it is, rather, to teach the German language to speak Greek. But, of course, such a language would not simply be ancient Greek again. No restoration of an ancient, a dead, language or culture is intended here; rather, some new language, something hitherto unheard, unspoken, is to be the language of these translations. What the translation tries to reenact is not governed by an image of fidelity to any specific content of the language—as if the chief task of language in the poem were to repeat the representations of the language; rather, it is guided by the effort to repeat, to restore what Hölderlin calls elsewhere "the basic mood of the poet."[98] Such a mood is the conflicted mood attuned to the doubled truth that language in the poem exposes. It is the mood that Hölderlin will repeatedly refer to as sorrow, and it is this sorrow which, when properly felt, leads one who speaks such a language to a point beyond the capacity of thought to grasp its object, beyond the capacity of cognition. He speaks of Sophocles' language as conveying precisely such a mood and such an excessive knowing when he says of the language in *Antigone* that it is "charming, comprehensible in unhappiness and misfortune. The dreamy naive. The genuine language of Sophocles, since Aeschylus and Euripides knew how to objectify suffering and rage more, but less so the way that the human intellect wandered beneath the unthinkable."[99]

In the "Remarks" appended to the translations of *Antigone* and *Oedipus* Hölderlin makes clear that his chief concern is to highlight the role assumed by the language of the plays apart from the role which would be assigned to language by a view of language that finds its basic capacity in the possibilities of representation. But calling attention to the force of the language beyond its capacities for representation is not the only purpose of these remarks (though this concern with language does provide the largest context within which all the other matters will be understood). Hölderlin is also concerned with identifying and then with differentiating the specific natures of the structure and events of the two plays. Here what most needs to be said is that he finds *Oedipus* to be an illustration of the tendency of Greek tragedy to anticipate what would develop out of it, in other words, the Hesperian tendencies of Greek tragedy. *Antigone,* on the other hand, points back to the deepest, the most foreign to the Hesperian, roots of Greek tragedy. The way this is signaled is easily stated: Oedipus is defined by his incessant, insane, desire to know, whereas Antigone is defined rather by her relation to death and the dead.

The characterization of Oedipus is focused in the extreme on Oedipus's "foolishly wild search for a consciousness"[100] and as obsessed by the desire to know. Oedipus is who he is by virtue of his relation to this desire for a consciousness, not through any deed in particular. A number of passages serve to emphasize this trait and to find in it what is most distinctive about Oedipus and the roots of his tragic flaw. Thus he is described as interpreting the saying of the oracle "too *infinitely,* and thus ultimately seduced into *nefas* [impiety]"[101] and as driven by a furious curiosity which "wants to know more than it can bear or conceive."[102] This means that he knows no limits and so does not recognize himself for what he is; a finite being, he nonetheless interprets the oracle too infinitely, and because of this suffers the monstrous results. So instead of recognizing himself, he is driven ceaselessly forward by the limitless search for a knowledge beyond the limits he could bear, and this means that "In the end, there dominates in the speeches the deranged questioning for a consciousness."[103] Seeking to gain control of himself, Oedipus exposes himself to the real monstrosity, namely, that he "has an eye too many perhaps."[104] The only way to kill this monster is to blind himself; blinded, he can at last see, and he is revealed for what he has been. Significantly, the word that the chorus uses to describe Oedipus when he is first seen after his self-mutilation is *deinon.*[105] This flaw which defines Oedipus is, according to Hölderlin, the flaw that will define the course of the West, and it is in the growth and force of such a furious desire for knowledge that the modern world will set itself apart from ancient Greece. In Oedipus we find the most concise expression of the roots out of which the modern world will emerge from ancient Greece. The trajectory of Western culture is unfolded here since his flaw is the flaw which will define us: his eye too many is the very image of speculation that exceeds the speculative possibilities allotted to human being. In Oedipus the modern failure to have a destiny, the very notion that a destiny need be uncovered, finds itself expressed here in the form of an ancient Greek tragedy. In his passion, his mad obsession to know and to answer the riddle he has been assigned, one finds the need to destroy the mystery and the secret that limits preserve; the passion for sunlike clarity is the same passion that seeks, but always fails, to overcome the nature of what is hidden from knowledge. Oedipus is the one who saves the city by overcoming the riddle of the Sphinx, he is the one who solves riddles; however, it is this passion for answering riddles that defines him which will drive him mad in the end, when what he destroys is not the fact that knowing has its limits and that consciousness is shadowed by the unknown; rather, what he destroys is the one who would efface the hidden and not respect the limits of knowledge—he destroys himself. There is violence in Oedipus, and strangely the deepest form of this violence is not found in the fact that he kills the stranger, who is no stranger but rather his father, at a crossroads. The violence in Oedipus is rooted in the character of his consciousness: it is what destroys and what is ultimately destroyed by itself. The truth that Oedipus comes to learn, the knowledge that he wished he did not have to know about himself, is the source of the pain he most deeply feels. Thus, in the context of speaking about Antigone, for whom such an obsession to know is not an issue, but who is precisely one who respects the power of limits, Hölderlin writes that "It is a great resource of the secret working of the soul that at the highest moment of consciousness it avoids consciousness."[106] Not to respect this secret of the soul is to invite ruin into the life of the soul.

Oedipus does learn this secret, but at that point he is no longer the tyrant. Blinded and being led by the young Antigone as he wanders throughout Greece in search of a place to die, the Oedipus of *Oedipus at Colonus* presents an almost serene figure, certainly one who contrasts markedly with the driven Oedipus who is the king, still with an eye too many. This final, too often neglected, play of the Theban trilogy gives Sophocles' own answer to the situation of *Oedipus the Tyrant*. It is also the play that places Oedipus in a relation to the same question which possesses and defines Antigone: the question of death.[107] But Hölderlin never completed his plan to translate all three volumes of the Theban trilogy,[108] nor did he ever write a set of remarks which took up *Oedipus at Colonus,* and so one is left wondering if the full story of the destiny of Oedipus gets told by Hölderlin.

Be that as it may, Hölderlin does contrast the dynamics which drive *Oedipus the Tyrant* with those at work in *Antigone,* especially insofar as those dynamics emerge out of the differing natures of Oedipus and Antigone. Unlike Hegel, who finds gender to be one of the chief axes along which the operations of the tragedy spin, Hölderlin does not comment upon the gender differences at work in these two tragedies. While one might expect at least some acknowledgment that such a contrast is between a man and a woman, Hölderlin does not do this. Instead, he contrasts Oedipus's passion for knowledge with the manner in which Antigone is one who honors what is and must remain hidden. Two facets of Antigone's character can be understood as illustrating this point: her relation to the dead, and to the hiddenness that it represents, and her own death, which happens when she is concealed in the darkness of a cave. Antigone is the one who honors what is hidden and will be defined by her effort to maintain the honor of what one cannot know. The violence that stems from her actions, the manner of which "forces the god to appear," is found in her persistence in honoring the darkness in the full light of day (for instance, she does not keep for long the secret of her effort to bury her brother). As the champion of the idiom of the hidden, ultimately the idiom of death, Antigone represents formlessness and the daemonic agencies of the underworld, and in this regard—not first of all in her disobedience to Creon's edict—she needs to be understood as a rebel by nature. Hölderlin finds that in the language in *Antigone,* even more than the language in *Oedipus,* we find how it is that one "wanders beneath the unthinkable."[109] In the end, then, Antigone is driven forward by the need to honor what can never fully be accommodated. She is "lawless" and a "holy fool,"[110] and yet she is possessed by the god "in the figure of death." Death, the hiddenness which Antigone honors and which will claim her, is a destiny that cannot find a resolution, and so she represents a different sort of destiny, a different route to destruction, than does Oedipus. As one who honors death, even at the cost of her life, Antigone pays tribute to the final concealed repository of all human limits. In this honor paid to the deepest of limits, Antigone sets herself against the drive of Oedipus to transgress every limit. He suffers the monstrosity of his trespass; she suffers the sorrow of her honor. He must go blind to answer to his trespass; she must die to bear final witness to what she honors. Both suffer ruin.

Of course, more could be said about the particulars of both plays as Hölderlin understands them, and more could be said as well about the stresses that his translations put upon the tragedies.[111] For instance, one might give more due to the fact that Hölderlin reads *Antigone* as set in a time of "national revolution," and so Antigone's lawlessness needs to be understood as set in the dramatic context of a reevaluation of ethical and power relations. The conflict which is inevitable is made all the sharper in such a context. The crisis of the times exacerbates the crisis in time which the drama confronts. But in the final analysis what needs most to be borne in mind is that both Antigone and Oedipus, each in a distinctive way in conflict with the other way, expose what is "superlative in human spirit and thus rests upon a heroic virtuosity."[112] The strange beauty of the tragedies, each in its own way, rests upon this.

But it is also important to bear in mind, even when reading these magnificent translations, that they are not the last word on tragedy we find in Hölderlin. The period in which he is completing these translations and the "Remarks" is also one of the periods of his most intensive preoccupation with his efforts to compose an original modern tragedy of his own. His dreams of realizing such a new form are documented as early as October 1794, when he speaks of his plan for a drama about "the death of Socrates, following the ideals of Greek drama."[113] That was a plan conceived during the early stages of *Hyperion* and before the plan to translate Sophocles was concretized. Even then, before he formulated the plan which he would try three times to actualize, namely, the plan for *The Death of Empedocles* (1797), Hölderlin was convinced that his original modern tragedy would nonetheless follow the ideals of Greek drama and that an ancient Greek would need to serve as its hero. Not surprisingly, then, much of what still needs to be said about Hölderlin's contributions to the topic of tragedy can be clarified by looking at his own efforts to write a tragedy as well as his commentaries on the resulting drama.

*   *   *

There are three versions—significantly different from each other in a number of ways—of *The Death of Empedocles*. Here only the second version will be addressed directly, although the third version will be considered indirectly since Hölderlin's essay "The Ground to Empedocles" will be discussed. This essay, composed sometime between the second and third versions, not only serves to clarify Hölderlin's general intentions in his works, but also serves as a sort of means whereby Hölderlin advances his understanding of the needs of such a tragedy. This advance leads to the rewriting that produces the third version. But the second version not only remains the springboard for the themes that shape "The Ground to Empedocles," it is also the most sophisticated expression of the themes which all three versions would seek to display.[114] From Hölderlin's letters we know that he completed four acts of this version; however, only a portion of that version survives.[115]

Hölderlin's choice of the philosopher Empedocles as the human hero of his tragedy—the qualification "human" here is crucial and will be explained below—is deliberate and made with several considerations in mind. One of those considerations is found in the specifics of Empedocles' life (Hölderlin's source for this was Diogenes' *Lives of the Philosophers*); the other chief consideration is found in the specifics of the texts we have from Empedocles. The significant features of his life are easy to enumerate: Empedocles was said to be a pupil of Pythagoras, and he made public the secret Pythagorean doctrines in his own writings. He was a physician, and on the basis of his ability to heal he was said to be a miracle worker. He also wrote in verse form and was said to be an excellent orator.[116] He was also reportedly rather arrogant and full of pride. Finally, Diogenes suggests that Empedocles died by leaping into the crater of a volcano and that this was his final act of self-aggrandizement since he did it in order to confirm that he had become a god. All of these features find their way into Hölderlin's effort to dramatize the trajectory which ends with Empedocles' death.

But it is not simply the facts of his life that motivate the choice of Empedocles as a tragic hero. It is equally the key elements of his thought which make him so suitable. Empedocles is, along with Heraclitus, the thinker prior to Socrates who is most easily read as a speculative thinker. Two key notions run throughout his writings, *neikeos* (strife) and *piloteti* (love):[117] in the notion of strife we find conflict and differentiation, in love we find unity and harmony. Together one finds a powerful expression of the sense that all things belong together as one, yet are, in this very same oneness, perpetually in a struggle with everything. Here is another way of speaking of the *hen kai pan* that Hegel, Schelling, and Hölderlin had named as the speculative dream par excellence. In short, Hölderlin finds a kindred sensibility in the words of Empedocles, and in the life of Empedocles he finds one who unites in deed the opposing traits of both Antigone and Oedipus: he is obsessed by the desire to know all things and is willing to give honor to that knowledge, to testify on its behalf, even in the form of his own death.

When Hölderlin first conceived of *The Death of Empedocles,* he wrote an outline of what would become the first version of the play. The description of Empedocles fills the plan for the first act, and it remains perhaps the most precise formulation of the way Hölderlin was thinking of his tragic hero:

> Empedocles, who was destined to a hatred of culture and a contempt for any interest guided by distinct subject matters by his state of mind and his philosophy, was the deadly enemy of all one-sided existence, and for that reason dissatisfied, restless, suffering—even in truly beautiful rela- tionships—simply because they are relationships defined by particular- ity and . . . simply because he could not live and love them intimately with an omnipresent heart, like a god, because as soon as his heart and his thoughts embraced an existing reality, he is bound to the law of suc- cession.[118]

So Empedocles suffers from separation from the all—it is the suffering that the speculative soul must endure once it knows itself to be an indi- vidual—and this suffering is explained by saying that, no matter how he embraces the world, he is still bound to the law of succession, the law of linear time. Hölderlin's intention in *The Death of Empedocles* is to dramatize this predicament and to understand how it is that suicide is Empedocles' bid for a final union with the all that is the totality of nature.

There is, in a strict sense, no real action, no event, which takes place in the play. Again, as with Hölderlin's interpretations of Sophocles, lan- guage does the real work of the tragic drama; language is the heart of what happens. Once the conversation which opens the play begins, the transgression which will serve to define Empedocles has already occurred. Even before the beginning, the course of what will unfold in words is a fait accompli. The drama opens with a dialogue between two priests of the old and dying order, Hermocrates and Mecades. Empedocles is the sub- ject of that conversation, which he never knows about (Hermocrates and Mecades leave the scene as soon as they catch sight of him). It is a conver- sation in which Hermocrates especially accuses Empedocles of betraying sacred secrets and of spreading revolution to the people. He is described as possessing the potency of fire and as too brilliant for human eyes. Be- fore we see Empedocles, or hear his words as he would speak them, Mecades repeats a speech which he once heard Empedocles give. The words which are ascribed to Empedocles are telling, in particular when he is supposed to have said that

> My strength and my soul are fused into one,
> By mortals and by gods. . . . For I
> Companion the estranged,
> My word names the unknown,
> And the love of the living I carry
> Up and down; what one of them lacks
> I bring from another
> And, soul-inspiring, connect,
> Rejuvenating, transform
> This hesitant world
> And resemble no one and all.[119]

Even before we meet Empedocles we find him characterized as one who would unite all things in speech and love. This is a threat to the order that both Hermocrates and Mecades represent, and so they conspire to bring criminal charges against Empedocles even though they also believe that he will inevitably suffer from his own hubris independently of such charges. Nonetheless, they plot such charges, knowing full well that they would ultimately be only trumped-up charges, and they decide that even a charge of murder would not be taken as seriously by the people as would a charge of impiety and revealing holy secrets. So such will be the charge brought against Empedocles—more or less the same charges brought against Antigone, as well as against Socrates and Aristotle.

Empedocles finally appears in scene 2, which is entirely composed of what initially appears to be his soliloquy. But any possibility of understanding the play stands and falls with the recognition that in this scene in which only Empedocles speaks, the other hero, Empedocles' real counterpart, appears. Neither Hermocrates nor Mecades, bitter priests both, is a match for Empedocles. Neither one of them could serve as the other with whom Empedocles finds he must struggle. Here we learn of the real other of Empedocles' anguish when he opens his speech by addressing a "you" who is not given a proper name. This "you" is a riddle only for one who hears this speech; for Empedocles himself this unnamed "you" is his most intimate concern. But it is difficult to know who this "you" is since the scene itself is by and large without any context. Nonetheless, it clearly stands as the centerpiece of the entire play since in it Empedocles gives voice to his suffering in his own words, and in it we meet the one to whom he says he can trace this suffering. The words of this speech are deeply moving, almost searingly beautiful, and give an indication of Empedocles' inner turmoil since in this speech we find him expressing calm and sorrow, passion and anger, hurt and frustration, all in rapid succession. Here he articulates in words that enact the complex nature of his suffering. But however complex it might be, in the final analysis it is a suffering from too much love, too much of the dream of belonging to all and yet remaining unique. Empedocles' suffering is thus of the same nature as that suffering which defined and drove Hyperion; however, here it seems somehow rendered more acute, more extreme. It will be at this moment of the highest tension that the widest embrace of reconciliation will be found. But to understand how that is the case is to understand the heart of the drama here.

The speech begins with Empedocles' standing alone and speaking of his agony and loneliness. It is addressed to an unnamed "you," who we soon come to understand is nature. After saying

> In my stillness you came softly wandering,
> You found me deep in the hall of darkness,
> You kindly one! . . .
> And you, my trusted ones, you were working rapidly
> With your powers high above! . . .
> You happy, you flawless trees of my meadow!
> You rested and grew,
> And every day those who were contented drank
> From heaven's springs,
> Seeded with light and sparks of life

Empedocles names this you, saying, "O nature most intimate! You who are right / Before my eyes." Then he says that he suffers now because he feels abandoned by nature: "Do you still know your friend, / Who was most highly cherished, will you never recognize me again?" His words continue to speak of his relation to nature and of his sense that he has yet to find the way in which he can belong to nature as he knows he must, as he is destined by his nature, by love. And this desire, this love, is what now drives him mad. One striking element of this speech is that Empedocles describes himself as "the priest of the living song"—namely, as a poet—and as such as able to bring nature to life with song "like sacrificial blood gladly shed. . . . In me, you sources of life, you once flowed." Once a poet, and thus one who found a way to belong to the life of nature in the celebration of song, Empedocles now laments that his words no longer breathe life into the bond that held him to nature. And this he attributes to nature: "Why do you push away this heart, / Which lovingly divined you, / And lock it up in tight chains." Now his loneliness and sense of isolation is overwhelming and without remit. The ache of separation is unbearable; even his words no longer suffice to summon the sense of belonging to nature, and so he is reduced to uttering repeatedly the word "lonely," saying that the ultimate anguish is that he is left alone even to curse his loneliness: "Is there no avenger anywhere, must I myself alone /

157

Utter all the scorn and curses against my soul? / Must loneliness be even that?" Later in the play, Hölderlin will write that such loneliness is already a death: "To be alone / And without gods is death." Even before he commits suicide, Empedocles is dead.

These are the words of a crisis, a breaking point, rooted in an agony that strains the reach of words. Empedocles' pained state of mind is evident not only in the meaning of the words which he speaks, but equally, perhaps most of all, in the tone that the words convey. The next scene opens with Empedocles speaking with his friend and confidant, Pausanias, about his despair: "I feel the day declining now, my friend, / And all is growing dark for me, and cold." Pausanias expresses his deep concern about his friend and even repeats the lament which Empedocles had spoken to nature, now asking Empedocles, "Do you not know me now?" Empedocles is so blinded by his sorrow that he cannot fully recognize his friend. Nor does he know how he is loved by the people of the city. Nothing matters to him except the whole of nature. The madness which has gripped Empedocles is in full view now. His hubris switches easily to self-recrimination and self-mockery, and his tormented state of mind is evident not only in the words he speaks but also in the rapid shifts of mood. This scene ends without an ending since the manuscript that has survived breaks off in the middle of Empedocles' words (which are to be words at last spoken calmly). He does not speak again in the play. What remains is a dialogue between Panthea and Delia, who not only speak of Empedocles, but also lament the brevity of life and love. Then there remains an interchange between Pausanias, Panthea, and Delia, all of whom speak about Empedocles' whereabouts and the mystery of his fate, which we learn of only through intimations. The play, which remains only as a fragment of what Hölderlin wrote, breaks off with the final words spoken by Panthea, who opens by speaking to nature:

> Oh, those who fear death
> Do not love you, . . .
> Their heart no longer beats against your heart. . . .
> That is how it must happen to us,
> The spirit wants it that way
> And the ripening time,
> For once we who were blind
> Were in need of a miracle.

The riddle of the play, namely, the death of Empedocles, is the final topic of discussion. How is this death, this strange suicide, to be understood—if it can be understood at all? Is there any understanding at all that can be attached to this death?

It is important to remember that we are confronting a suicide and to note the difference between suicide and sacrifice.[120] Here one might contrast the deaths of Socrates or Antigone with Empedocles' death. Each of them suffers an elected death (since, after a fashion at least, both Socrates and Antigone could have avoided death). But both Antigone and Socrates elect the course that they know will result in their deaths out of a sense of *solidarity* (Antigone with her dead brother, Socrates with an idea), whereas Empedocles' death is clearly elected because he is swamped by a sense of *solitude*. But his suicide, though born of a sense of solitude, is his manner of overcoming that solitude. In death he understands himself to be united with the whole of nature. His fiery death, in which his body is transformed into smoke and ash, becomes the symbol of his union with nature. It is a death in which Empedocles can no longer be distinguished from nature, but neither can he be identified as himself. His identification with nature comes at the price of the loss of his own identity.

The play is puzzling in many respects (and its puzzles are only exacerbated by the fragmentary text that remains for us), but Hölderlin's comments in "The Ground to Empedocles" do provide some clues as to how this work is to be understood and why it is to be understood as a specifically modern tragedy. There we learn first that the tragedy is found in the story of the modern human (and for Hölderlin this means the modern poetic) relation to nature. We learn, in fact, that *this relation is one that could only be told as a tragedy*. The reason for this is clear: nature cannot appear in its fullness without art—"Art is the blossom, the perfection of nature: nature only becomes divine in conjunction with the diverse yet harmonious art"[121]—and yet it is the word, the human gift to nature, which will be the reason that the human relation to nature is one of separation. With the word, the human being is apart from this whole of nature since the word is the "product of a creative reflection"[122] in which the one who speaks is thrown outside of nature. One names the whole of nature, one finds the "holy names," but at the price of setting oneself apart from that very same divinity of nature. That is why Hölderlin could speak of Empedocles' vocation as a poet as "demanding a sacrifice."[123] One might put this complicated point in other words by saying that the unity and life of nature need the word, ultimately the poetic word, in order to appear since "nature is mute." The word is thus the self-reflection of nature, it is "the flower of the mouth,"[124] and, like the flower which unites heaven and earth, the word draws together that which in nature differentiates itself infinitely. However, while the word is this embracing power, the one who utters the word, the poet, suffers the same malady as Oedipus—namely, the poet has an eye too many. Perhaps. Significantly, Empedocles describes himself as a poet, and it is in his activity as a poet that he considers himself one of the priests of nature: "He seems in every respect a born poet."[125] But it is precisely in his self-understanding of the task of the poet that we find the roots of his decision to commit suicide, and it is this conception of the task of the poet which will be the real reason that his death will best be described as a tragedy. Of course, one cannot read these words without remembering that it is the poet Hölderlin who is writing them.

The overarching conviction driving Hölderlin here is that nature *needs* language, but that the gift of the word which the poet brings to nature comes only when the poet severs himself from the whole of nature. The paradox is that the divinity of nature which the word exposes must deny its ultimate foundation. The task of the poet requires the sacrifice of the subjectivity of the poet: "In the manner in which nature and art with Empedocles are united in the extreme of their opposition, what is active becomes excessively objective, and the lost subjectivity is replaced by the deep influence of the object."[126] The word is the site of the self-sacrifice of the poetic subject—his separation is unbearable, and there are no words which can overcome this condition brought on by the word—but it is a sacrifice on behalf of nature, which needs such words for its life to appear. That is why it is said of Empedocles that "he loves too much." What is left for the poet, then, is to rejoin nature in the only manner that remains, namely, to die and to do so in a manner—such as a fire—which does not disturb the unity, the life, of nature. In his death, Empedocles sheds all particularity, and not even a corpse—the locus of the tragedy that unfolds in *Antigone*—remains.

A deep paradox lies at the heart of such a conception of the tragedy of the relation between the tragic poet (remembering, of course, that the poet is simply supremely human) and nature.[127] The word is thought here as the divine in the human; it is the product of a creative and thoroughly synthetic act, and through the word nature is able to appear as a living totality. Yet precisely in this moment when the origin of the life of nature appears in its infinity, precisely then the antagonism with the poet appears. This paradox, which Hölderlin frequently casts as the paradox of pertaining to the relation of nature and art (or between the word and life), is the heart of the issue with which Hölderlin struggled in his efforts to write a modern tragedy. The differences between the three versions can be traced back to the changes in his conception of this paradox, and so in the third and final version Empedocles is seen in a new light, one which illuminates his suicide differently. Now it signals more of the reconciliation of art and nature; even more, it signals a genuine cultural transformation. In the third version of *The Death of Empedocles* the poet is a figure who ushers in a new age by bringing another epoch to a close.[128] The idea that there is a deep connection between the activity of the poet with respect to nature and the renewal of culture is expressed most clearly in "The Ground to Empedocles" (perhaps even more clearly than in any of the versions of the play itself). There Empedocles is presented as belonging to "his epoch [and] his fatherland [and thus as] a son of powerful oppositions,"[129] and there it is said that "the destiny of his time, the powerful extremes out of which he grew, did not demand song . . . it demanded a sacrifice."[130] In short, Empedocles' suicide takes on a different significance if it is no longer regarded with reference to the meaning of that sacrifice from the point of view of Empedocles himself, but rather is thought from the perspective of culture. The death of Empedocles in the second version of Hölderlin's effort to write of that death seems to be more an expression of the failure of words for the poet, whereas that same death in the third version is presented much more as the signal of a cultural renewal.[131]

But whatever interpretation one places upon this death of Empedocles, the alter ego of the speculative poet, it is clear that this death is owing precisely to Empedocles' relation to the poetic, the loving and thus unifying, word. The root of the tragic paradox which we suffer is found at the same point which lets the tragic appear as a work of art, that is, as a speculative work. It is found, namely, in language. It is almost as if the paradox is squared; in the word we find both danger and the saving,[132] and it is the province of the poet to be supremely aware of this double truth of the word. It is equally the province of the poet to seek to affirm this, and this struggle for an affirmation guides Hölderlin throughout the three versions of his *The Death of Empedocles*. He seemed to see in this death something of an acid test of such affirmation for a poet who would bestow "holy names" upon nature. To think that death, to understand the frame of mind that might render it somehow intelligible, became Hölderlin's deepest concern when he struggled to find a way to give tragedy a form appropriate to the modern world. Already in *Hyperion,* Hölderlin had found in Empedocles a figure of kinship. There, just after learning of the death of the woman he loved, Hyperion writes, "Where is there still a refuge?—Yesterday I went up to the summit of Aetna. There I recalled the great Sicilian who, fed up with counting the hours, intimate with the soul of the world, in his bold pleasure in life threw himself into the wonderful flames, for, according to someone who would later mock him, 'the cold poet needed to warm himself at the fire.'"[133] And just as Empedocles would be a figure with whom Hölderlin, as well as his other alter ego Hyperion, would identify, so too would his death remain a mystery, and it is this mystery which forms the heart of the tragedy Hölderlin struggles to write: "It is a terrible mystery that such a life must die, and I confess to you that since I looked into the heart of this I can find neither meaning nor faith."[134]

This, though, is the destiny of the poet for Hölderlin, and this destiny can be told only as a tragedy: it can be grasped only as suffered and it can be embraced only by that which is at the root of this suffering, namely, by the words by which one bears witness that one is. For the destiny of the poet (and it must be remembered that to be a poet is, for Hölderlin, the destiny of a human being, of one who speaks) is to suffer the fate of a self-laceration at the hand of that which defines one as a poet, and it is equally to celebrate the manner in which language unites as one what is otherwise infinitely differentiated. The word, the locus of the destiny of the human being, is thus equally the site of affirmation and anguish. Every word is thus a tragic word, for us at least.

Hölderlin struggles to understand his own destiny—which he once would say that he shared with his friend Böhlendorff, as well as the destiny of his times, which he understands as having lost any clear sense of the direction in which the free expression of what is one's own might develop—by wrestling with the death of his alter ego, Empedocles, someone who lived in another time and another place. He never seems to have found a satisfactory answer to the riddle of this destiny, at least in terms of his efforts to write a tragedy which might illuminate its nature. Instead he would rewrite the same tragedy three times, in three ways. But despite the differences between the three versions there is a clear continuity that one can see in these different versions.[135] That continuity is found in both a sensibility and a set of convictions common to these three plays which dramatize the plight of Empedocles and his state of mind. The common sensibility can be described as what Hölderlin would refer to frequently as the mood of the poet, namely, the sorrow; and the set of common convictions can be summed up by saying that time and language are simultaneously what define the destiny of human life, and what lacerate that life, thus handing it over to sorrow. All of the different versions of *The Death of Empedocles* can be understood as attempts to dramatize the life of these themes as they are played out in the effort of the human being to find a home in nature. In the end, the other key character of the tragedy is, in each case, nature itself understood both as that which exceeds any reach of the human and what it can either know or regulate, and as that which is in need of the word. The story of the relation of the human being and nature, though, is one that can be told only as a tragedy, as a story pinned to sorrow and to the crisis let loose in the world by the word. Such a tragedy of a life opposed to all particularity and yet bound to the law of succession in time has no resolution, it cannot be overcome, and it must result in the death of the poet. That is why Panthea says at the end of the second version of *The Death of Empedocles* in her address to nature, "Oh those who fear death do not love you." Hölderlin knew this, and so in the different versions of his play he sought to find a way to love and affirm that which he could not heal.

*   *   *

It is difficult to try to compress Hölderlin's understanding of the nature and meaning of tragedy into any neat formulation. It seems, rather, that one begins to understand Hölderlin once one acknowledges that his entire effort seems to compress his very being as a poet into the idea of the tragic. It is the notion which defines his own self-conception down to its very capillaries, and so it seems that everything emerges out of this fundamental notion of the tragic. Although he writes contemporaneously with his erstwhile friends Hegel and Schelling, and although they all begin quite literally on the same page regarding the role of art in ethical life and its achievement for the ends of philosophy, Hölderlin's relation to the question of the tragic somehow stands apart. Perhaps one might clarify the manner in which he distinguishes himself from his friends by remembering that for Hölderlin the enigma of tragic experience is not a conceptual issue. The tragic is not the name for a problem or a situation about which one might theorize. It is, rather, the name for the destiny proper to the full life of a human being, one who can speak and who can love, and as such it poses a question one can only endure. Paradoxically, the realm of any possible response to this destiny—namely, the realm which is opened by language—is itself the most original source of this fate: "Life itself drives us out of life."[136] Wrapped in such a destiny human life finds itself most alive, most itself, in the intimacy with that which "exists only in feeling and not for knowledge."[137] Rigorously adhering to this insight, Hölderlin *performs* the question of the tragic. One finds his relation to it in the tone, in the rhythm, and in the movement of his language. One finds it also in the translations which put on display the extreme to which one must take the experience of language if one is to be faithful to this destiny.

What is perhaps most remarkable about Hölderlin in regard to these questions is the persistence with which he addresses them and the passion which animates that drive. It is quite right, completely correct, to say that Hölderlin is somehow harnessed to the same speculative dream which held both Hegel and Schelling in its thrilling grip. But even though such a remark is true, it is not the best that one might say about what is distinctive in Hölderlin. It seems, rather, best to say that one sees in Hölderlin the deep expression of the human need to belong, to love and to be loved. One can speak of this need as a speculative need—in many ways that is precisely how Hegel thinks the speculative—but perhaps the need to belong that wells up so powerfully in Hölderlin is something other than the need for a unity of differences, for the *hen kai pan*. His letters—perhaps even more than any theoretical texts, translations, or plays—provide some of the most moving testimony in this regard. It is no accident that *Hyperion,* his only novel and a work in which he finds his first fictional alter ego, is a novel in the form of letters between close friends.[138] It is perhaps also no accident that, with one exception, the letters do not receive any evident reply.

It is always a temptation—though one to be avoided at all costs—to romanticize the image or the work of Hölderlin, to aestheticize the longing which is expressed in it. For a long time, at least until the work of Hellingrath, Beissner, Benjamin, and Heidegger overturned it, a sentimental-ized view of Hölderlin did prevail, and he was typically presented as a gentle and tormented beautiful soul. While it might be true to say that he was both gentle and tormented, what also needs to be said is that the passion and the rigor with which he persisted in confronting the sources of his own torments are unsurpassed. What makes this worthy of note is simply that it is language itself which defines this source, and that the passion to understand this destiny and this passion to connect manifest themselves in a deep and abiding love of language. This kinship of lan-guage and the need to belong are echoed perfectly in the opening words of the letter to his friend Böhlendorff: "Your good words and your pres-ence in them gave me great pleasure."

We find ourselves most present to others in the shape of a word. And so when one gives another one's word, and gives another one's time, one gives all that one has or is. Such is the deep conviction out of which Höl-derlin tries to answer the riddle of being human. But there is nothing sentimental in this conviction since it equally expresses the conviction that separation—by virtue of our belonging both to language and to the order of successive time—is our fate. To struggle with this fate and this riddle is, in the end, the task of the tragic work of art. This means, though, that the lack of such works, which Hölderlin finds is the special character of the present historical juncture, is the lack of a destiny, a direction in which the drive to form these struggles can find its free expression. But, and this above all haunts how it is that Hölderlin takes up the task of tragic art, such works were found in ancient Greece. It is not by accident that Greece produced such works, nor is it an accident that those very same works contributed to the foreclosure of the possibilities out of which they could be produced. The twofold task of the present age is to grasp this strange enigma of Greece and to find how it is that today the free expression of what is most one's own is to find its proper direction. Ulti-mately these twin tasks are the same, since in the final analysis the enigma of the foreign and the ordeal of one's own are both ways of speaking of what is at stake in the experience of the tragic.

APPENDIX C

Letter to Böhlendorff

Letter from Hölderlin to Casimir Böhlendorff
   Nürtingen near Stuttgart
   4 December 1801

   My dear Böhlendorff!

Your good words and your presence in them pleased me a great deal.

Your *Fernando* took a great weight off my chest. The progress of my friends is such a good sign for me. We have a destiny. If things move forward with one of us, then the other will not lag behind. My dear friend! You have achieved so much in matters of precision and suppleness and not lost anything of warmth; quite the contrary, like a good blade, the elasticity of your spirit has proven itself only more powerful in the discipline of submission. That is what I congratulate you for above all else. We learn nothing with greater difficulty than to freely use the national. And, I believe, that it is precisely the clarity of presentation which is so natural and original for us, as the fire from heaven is for the Greeks. That is why they will need to be surpassed in beautiful suffering, which you too have retained, rather than in that Homeric presence of spirit and gift of presentation.

It sounds paradoxical. But I will say it yet again, and submit it to your test and your free employment, that in the progress of culture, the truly national becomes of limited advantage. That is why the Greeks are less masters of sacred pathos, because it is innate to them, whereas they excel in the gift of presentation from Homer onward, because this extraordinary man was sufficiently soulful to conquer the Western Junoian sobriety for his Apollonian empire, and thereby to truly appropriate the foreign.

With us it is the reverse. That is why it is also so dangerous to abstract the rules of art exclusively from the excellence of Greece. I have labored on this long and now know that, with the exception of what for the Greeks and for us must be the highest, namely, to have a living relation and destiny, we must not bear any resemblance to them. But the ownmost must be learned as well as the foreign. That is why the Greeks are unavoidable for us. Only we will not follow them in our own, our national, since, as said, the *free* use of *one's own* is most difficult. It occurs to me that your good genius inspired that in you when you chose to deal with the drama in an epic manner. It is, on the whole, a *genuine* modern tragedy. Because the tragic for us is that we are silently packed up in a container and taken away from the realm of the living, not that consumed by flames, we pay the penalty to the flames we could not tame.

And yet it is true! the former moves the innermost soul as well as the latter. It might not be so imposing, but it is a deeper destiny, and it is a noble soul that guides such a mortal through fear and compassion and that keeps the spirit up in the midst of wrath. The wonderful Jupiter is after all the final thought of a mortal who is dying, whether he dies according to our destiny or according to the destiny of antiquity—that is, if the poet is to present this dying, as he should, and as you obviously intended, and, as you have, on the whole and in the details have achieved in some masterful gestures:

> "A narrow path leads into the dark valley,
> He was forced down there by treachery."

and in other passages. You are on a good path, stay with it. I want to study your *Fernando* properly and take it to heart, and then perhaps I will be able to say something interesting about it to you. In no case could I say enough!

There is little to say about myself and how I have been, how much I have remained worthy of you and my friends and what has become of me, what I do now and will bring out. I will write to you of those things next time from the neighborhood of your Spain, namely, from Bordeaux where I will travel next week and to take up a post as a private tutor and minister in a German Protestant household. I will have to keep my wits about me in France, in Paris; I also take pleasure in the sight of the sea and of the sun of the Provence.

O friend! The world lies before me brighter than usual, and more serious! It pleases me, how things come out, it pleases me as when in summer "the old holy father shakes blessed lightning flashes out of rosy hued clouds with a calm hand." For of everything that I can see of God, this sign has turned out to be the one that I have chosen. At other times I could have rejoiced about a new truth, a better outlook on things above us and on what surrounds us, but now I fear that, in the end, I will turn out like the old Tantalus who received more from the gods than he could endure.

But I do what I can, and when I see that I must go my way as others do, I think that it is godless and maddening to search for a path that would be safe from any assault, and on which no herb for death grew.

And now live well my cherished friend, until later. I am now full of parting. I have not wept for a long while. But it cost me bitter tears when I decided to leave my country, perhaps forever. For what do I have that is more precious in the world? But they cannot use me. I am and must remain German, and even if the needs of the heart and for nourishment drive me to Otaheiti.

My regards to our Morbeck. How is he? Surely he is doing well. He stays us. Forgive my ungraciousness. I did recognize you, I saw you, but only through yellow lenses. I had so much to say to you, you good people! Probably you to me as well. Where will you stay in the future, my Böhlendorff? But those are worries. If you write to me, address your letter to the merchant Landauer in Stuttgart. He will surely send it to me. Also, write to me of your address.

Your H.

APPENDIX D

Letter to Brother

Letter from Hölderlin to his brother
Nürtingen near Stuttgart
4 December 1801

My dear Karl!

I come to the time of departure. But let us not complain! in such cases I always prefer to hold onto the satisfied spirit which, in order to honor God, silences the mournful one, and looks to the good.

This much I must confess: that nothing in my life was more deeply rooted than that which was rooted in my country, and in life nothing was so highly prized as the company of my family, and I would dearly love to preserve those for myself!

But I feel that it is better for me to be outside of those things now, and you, my dear one, feel that too, and you know that, if we are to endure, God's protection belongs both to staying put and to moving along. In your own way being busy preserves you. Otherwise, you would feel too restricted. For me it is necessary, above all, to choose rightly with respect to what is most my own. Otherwise, I would be torn up and scattered.

Do not let the old brotherly love between us fade. It is a sacred happiness, when, through all the differences of life's course, people nonetheless will stay together by means of those bonds like ours. Such is the grand sense of things which ignites and saves everything. And human souls do not especially need that one be like another when there is love between them. But without that openness of the heart there is no happiness for them. Oh, my Karl! Forgive me that it might be pure between us.

And so live well! Things will go well for you in all that is between us, since you do so well in what is yours alone. Think of me from time to time!

Your Hölderlin

APPENDIX E

"In lovely blueness . . ."

In lovely blueness with its metal roof
The church tower blossoms. The cry of swallows
Surrounds it, the most touching blueness
Encircles it. The sun
Rises high above all this and colors the tin,
But in the wind above, silently,
The weathercock crows. If someone
Descends those steps, beneath the bell, then
It is a silent life, because,
When a figure is so set apart,
The plasticity of man emerges.
The windows through which the bells chime are
Like portals upon beauty. That is to say,
Because those portals still take after nature, they
Resemble the trees of the forest.
Purity however is also beauty.
A solemn spirit arises from within, out of diversity.
Yet these images are so very innocent, so saintly,
That one is actually often afraid to describe them.
But the heavenly ones,
Who are always good, in all ways,
Are rich in virtue and joy.
One may imitate that.
May, if life is only a fatigue, a man look up and say:
I want to be like that? Yes. So long as kindness
Remains in a pure heart,
Man may measure himself not unhappily with the divine.
Is God unknown? Is he revealed like the sky?
That is what I tend to believe. It is the measure of man.
Full of merit, yet poetically,
Man dwells on this earth.
But the shade of a starry night is not purer, if I may say so,
Than one, who is called an image of divinity.

Is there a measure on the earth? There is none.
Never have the worlds of the creator turned back the course of thunder.
A flower too is lovely, because it blossoms

Under the sun. Often, the eye
Finds in this life creatures
That would be much more beautiful to name than flowers.
Oh! I know that well!
To bleed in body and heart, and to cease being whole,
Does that please God?
But the soul, it is my belief,
Must stay pure,
Otherwise the eagle would wing its way as far as the almighty
With songs of praise and the voice of so many birds.
It is the essential, and it is the form.
You lovely little stream, you seem touching,
As you flow so clear,
Like the eye of God, through the Milky Way.
How well I know you, but tears well up in my eyes.
I see a serene life in the figures of creation blossoming around me,
Because, not unfittingly,
I compare that life to the solitary doves of the churchyard.
But the laughter of people afflicts me,
For I have a heart.
Do I want to be a comet? I believe I do.
For they have the swiftness of birds;
They blossom with fire,
And they are like children in purity.
To wish for a greater good
Is something that human nature cannot presume for itself.
The serenity of virtue also deserves to be praised by the solemn spirit,
Which flutters between the garden's three columns.
A beautiful virgin must wreathe her head with myrtle blossoms,
Because she is simple in her being and in her feeling.
Myrtles however are found in Greece.

If one looks into the mirror,
A man, and sees in it his image, as if painted;
It resembles the man.
The image of man has eyes,
Whereas light belongs to the moon.
King Oedipus had an eye too many perhaps.
The sufferings of this man,
They seem indescribable, unspeakable, inexpressible.
When a drama shows us such a sadness, it comes from that suffering.
But what comes over me now, when I think of you?
Like streams the end of something tears me away, and expands like Asia.
Oedipus, of course, suffered in the same way.

Of course, it was for a reason.
Did Hercules suffer as well?
Certainly.
Did not the Dioscuri also endure suffering
In their friendship?
Of course, to struggle with God, like Hercules, that is suffering.
And to share in the deathlessness which is the envy of this life,
That too is an agony.
But it is also an agony
When one is covered with freckles from the summer sun,
To be completely covered with stains!
The beautiful sun does that:
Namely it draws all things up to their end.
Youths are led on their way by the charms of its rays,
Which are like roses.
The sufferings that Oedipus bore seem like this,
Like the lament of a poor man
Who complains that something is missing.
Son of Laios, poor stranger in Greece!
Life is death, and death is also a life.

APPENDIX F
Empedocles *(1798)*

You search for life, search and it flares and shimmers,
  a divine fire comes to you deep from out of the earth,
   and you, aflutter with desires,
     throw yourself down, into the flames of Aetna.

Thus were pearls lost to wine for the vanity of the queen;
  and yet she wanted that! Oh poet, if you
   only did not sacrifice your treasures,
     throwing them in the boiling crater!

But you are sacred to me, as the earth's power
  that pulled you under, intrepid victim!
   and if love did not hold me back,
     I would follow the hero into the depths.

APPENDIX G

The Death of Empedocles *(Second Version)*

ACT ONE SCENE ONE

Chorus of Argigentines
MECADES AND HERMOCRATES

MECADES: Do you hear the drunken people?
HERMOCRATES: They're looking for him.
MECADES: The spirit of the man
    is potent among them.
HERMOCRATES: I know, like dried grass
    The people ignite themselves.
MECADES: That a single person should move
    The mob like that, is to me like Jove's lightning
    Seizing a forest, and more terrible.
HERMOCRATES: That is why we wrap that band
    Around men's eyes, so that they do not
    Feed upon the light too powerfully.
    What is divine
    Must never be present to them,
    Nor may their hearts
    Discover what's alive.
    Do you not know those ancients
    Named the favorites of Heaven?
    They nourished their breasts
    Upon the world's powers
    And gazing up into the bright light
    Deathless things were near.
    That's why the proud ones
    Never would bow their heads
    And, confronting the powerful ones,
    Could not leave
    Intact what was other;
    It was transformed right in front of their eyes.
MECADES: And he?
HERMOCRATES: That which made
    Him too powerful was
    That he won the trust

Of gods.
His word sounded to the people as if it
Rang out from Olympus.
They give him thanks
For stealing from Heaven
The flame of life, and for
Betraying it to mortals.

MECADES: They know nothing but him.
He is to become their god.
He is to become their king.
They say, Apollo built
The Trojans their city,
But better still to be helped
Through life by an exalted man.
They say much that is unintelligible about him, and that he respects
No law, no custom, no necessity.
Our people have turned
Into an errant star and
I fear this sign portends
Future events to come which
He is hatching in silence.

HERMOCRATES: Be calm, Mecades.
He will not.

MECADES: Are you more powerful then?

HERMOCRATES: One who understands is stronger
Than the strong
And this singular knowledge is known to me.
He grew up too happily;
From the outset
His mind was pampered, so
That little things lead him astray; he will pay
For having loved mortals too much.

MECADES: I too have felt
That he will not last long,
Yet it is long enough
If he only fails once he's succeeded.

HERMOCRATES: And he has already fallen.

MECADES: What are you saying?

HERMOCRATES: Oh, don't you see it? That noble spirit
Has been led astray by the poor in spirit.
The blind were his seducers.
He cast the soul before the people,
Good-naturedly betrayed the grace of gods
To the common people;

But the fool amply was repaid
With hollow echoes from their own dead hearts.
And for a time he endured it, and grieved,
Patiently, not knowing
Where the fault lay; meanwhile
The people's intoxication grew; and shuddering
They listened when his breast shook
With his own word, and said:
That is not how we listen to gods!
And, the slaves gave names, which I will not name for you,
To the proud mourners,
And in the end the thirsty one takes the poison,
That wretch who neither can contain his senses
Nor yet find other minds, akin to it,
And with their raving adoration
Consoles himself, goes blind, becomes like them,
That soulless, superstitious rabble;
His power has ebbed away,
He walks in a night and does not know how to help himself out of it
And so we help him.

MECADES: Are you so sure of that?

HERMOCRATES: I know him.

MECADES: An arrogant speech occurs to me,
    One that he made when last
    He came to the Agora. I do not know
    What the people had said to him beforehand;
    I had just arrived, and stood far from him:
    You honor me, and rightly so,
    For Nature is mute,
    Sun and Air and Earth and all her children
    Like strangers live around one another,
    The solitary, as they belonged to no one.
    True, ever strong, by virtue
    Of spirit that is divine,
    The free, immortal powers of the world
    Round about the other
    Ephemeral life,
    But wildflowers growing
    On wild soil,
    All the mortals have all been sown
    On the lap of the gods.
    But that ground would seem scantily nourished and dead
    If someone did not
    Attend to it, raising up life,

And mine is that field. My strength and
My soul are fused into one,
By mortals and by gods.
And more warmly immortal powers embrace
The aspiring heart and, infused with
The freedom of their spirit, feeling mortals more richly thrive,
And all's awake! For I
Companion the estranged,
My word names the unknown,
And the love of the living I carry
Up and down; what one of them lacks
I bring from another
And, soul-inspiring, connect,
Rejuvenating, transform
This hesitant world
And resemble no one and all.
Thus spoke the arrogant one.

HERMOCRATES: That is still very little. Worse sleeps in him.
I know him, know his kind, the excessively happy
Spoilt sons of heaven,
Who feel nothing other than their own souls.
If once the moment shakes them out of themselves—
And those too tender ones are easily shaken—
Then nothing calms or comforts them, they're driven
This way or that way by a burning wound,
Their hearts incurably seething. And he too!
Calm though he seems, disgusted with the people,
Deep down he glows now with tyrannical desire.
Him or us! There is no harm
In sacrificing him. He must go under
In any case.

MECADES: Do not provoke him, though. Do not give the pent-up flame
room,
But let it starve and choke!
Leave him! Give him no cause to act!
If he, the arrogant one, himself finds no one
For insolent deeds, and only in his words can sin,
He dies a fool and does not harm us much.
Day-dreaming let him walk on clouds, or fly!
A strong opponent makes him terrible,
And only then, you see, does he feel his power.

HERMOCRATES: You fear him and everything, poor man.

MECADES: I only want to spare myself remorse,
To spare whatever can be spared.

The priest who knows everything,
The holy one, who hallows everything, does not need that.
HERMOCRATES: First understand me, novice that you are,
Before insulting me. The man must fall,
I tell you. If he could be spared, be sure
I'd spare him more than you would. For he is closer
To me than to you. But learn this;
More ruinous than sword or fire
Is human spirit, which is godlike
If one cannot keep silent and preserve
One's secret unexposed. If in its depth
It lies at rest and proffers what is needed,
It is wholesome, a consuming fire,
When one breaks out of one's chains.
Away with that man who lays bare his soul
And, with it, his soul's god, recklessly seeks
To utter the unutterable, wasting
His dangerous wealth as if it were water lightly spilt.
That something is worse than murder, and you
Speak on his behalf? It is his fate,
He made it for himself, and like him
All those who betray the gods will live and perish in pain, and
        promiscuously
Delivers into human hands
Powers that are secret.
He must be taken up!
MECADES: Must he pay so dearly who of his soul's
Fullness entrusts the best to mortals?
HERMOCRATES: He might do that, but Nemesis will not be kept away.
Let him speak grand mighty words, let him
Dishonor life that should be chastely veiled,
Drag into daylight the gold of great depths,
Let him use that which was not given
To mortals for their use, but he will be
The first to perish. Has it not confused
His mind already?
How his entire soul has become will.
And how self-willed he has grown,
The one who communicated all,
The good man! How transformed he is
Into an insolent man who looks upon
Both gods and men as playthings for his hands.
MECADES: Of dreadful things you speak, Priest,
And your dark word sinks into me as true. So be it!

You have me for your bidding. Only I do not know how
To grasp him. However great
A man may be, to try him is not hard;
To overpower a man supremely powerful, though,
Who, like a magician leads the mob,
That strikes me as something else, Hermocrates.

HERMOCRATES: Fragile is his magic, child, and he has made
Matters easier than is necessary for us.
For at a moment opportune to us
His anger turned; his proud, indignant mood
Turns in upon itself, and though he had
The power, he would not heed it, he only mourns
And broods upon his downfall,
Looking back he searches for lost life,
The god whom
He's driven out of himself with his chatter.
Gather the people to me; I will charge him,
Pronounce the curse on him, they should recoil
In horror from their idol,
They should cast him out into the wilderness
And, never returning, there he shall pay
For making manifest to mortals more
Than they are fit to hear.

MECADES: But on what account will you accuse him?

HERMOCRATES: The words which you cited,
They are sufficient.

MECADES: With that feeble charge
You hope to draw him away from the soul of the people?

HERMOCRATES: At the right time, every charge possesses power,
And this one is not lacking.

MECADES: If you were to charge him with murder
In front of them, it would have no effect.

HERMOCRATES: That is just the point! The public deed they forgive,
Those superstitious ones! Invisible
The offence must be for them,
It must be mysterious! It must hit them in the eye,
That moves the stupid.

MECADES: Their hearts depend upon him, and these you will
Not easily tame or guide! They love him!

HERMOCRATES: They love him? Of course! So as long as he blossoms,
But what good will he do them
Once he is darkened and desolate? There's nothing
Here that could be used with which to shorten
The tedious hours; that field has been picked bare.

It lies forsaken now, and now
The gales and our paths pass over it at their whims.
MECADES: Provoke him, then, provoke him! But watch out!
HERMOCRATES: I hope, Mecades! He is patient.
MECADES: The patient one will win.
HERMOCRATES: Nevertheless!
MECADES: You've no respect for anything, and will
Ruin yourself and me and him and everything.
HERMOCRATES: The dreaming and the scheming
Of mortals—it's true, I never will respect it!
They want to be gods and
Do homage to themselves as gods, and to endure for a while!
Are you afraid the suffering man, the patient one, will sway them?
He will rouse the fools against him,
In his suffering they will recognize
The dearly paid deception; brutally
Exacting retribution from their idol
For being weak as they are; and it serves
Him right.
MECADES: I wish I were done with all this, Priest!
HERMOCRATES: Trust me, and do not shy away from what must be.
MECADES: Look, there he comes. Go on, then, seek yourself,
You poor crazed mind! And meanwhile you lose all.
HERMOCRATES: Leave him! Away!

SCENE TWO

EMPEDOCLES (ALONE)

In my stillness you came softly wandering,
You found me deep in the hall of darkness,
You kindly one! You came not unhoped for,
I took note of your return
From your activities above the earth.
It was a beautiful day,
And you, my trusted ones, you were working rapidly
With your powers high above!—and now you are near me once again,
As you once were,
You happy, you flawless trees of my meadow!
You rested and grew,
And every day those who were contented drank
From heaven's springs,
Seeded with light and sparks of life,
Flowering out of the aether.—

O nature most intimate! You who are right
Before my eyes, do you still know your friend,
Who was most highly cherished, will you never recognize me again?
The priest of the living song
Who brought song and life to you like sacrificial blood gladly shed?

Oh, by the holy wells
Where waters from the veins of the earth
Gather themselves and
On hot days
Satisfy those who are thirsty! In me,
In me, you sources of life, you once flowed
Out of the depths of the world and
Came together in me, and
The thirsty came to me—but how is it now?
Saddened? Am I completely alone?
And is it night out here even in the daytime?
One who saw higher than ever a mortal eye,
Is now struck by blindness, and gropes his way around—
Where are you, my gods?
Oh, will you now leave me here like a beggar,
And why do you push away this heart,
Which lovingly divined you,
And lock it up in tight chains,
A heart which was born free, which came
From itself and nothing else. And now
Shall he wander, this one who was pampered for so long,
Who, in those divinely blessed times, often felt
As though one with the life of all living things,
And who had a heart filled with a world,
And with its regal divine powers?
Shall he now go forward, an outcast? Friendless, who was
The friend of the gods? Always feeding upon his nothing
And his night,
To bear the unbearable like the weak, who
Are welded to daily work
In dreaded Tartarus. Reduced to that?
For no reason? Ha!
One thing you had to leave me! Fool! You are
The same person still and yet you dream that you are
Feeble. Once again! Once more everything will be alive for me,
That is what I want!
Curse or blessing! Humble one,
Do not underestimate the power you have!

I want space around me, a new day
Shall dawn from my own flame! You should
Be satisfied, poor spirit, prisoner! You should feel free
And great and wealthy in your own world—
And yet lonely again, oh! And again lonely?

Oh! lonely! lonely! lonely!
And never again will I find
You, my gods,
And never again will I return
To your life, nature!
Your outcast!—Oh! It is true that I did not
Respect you, but held myself above you, even though
You embraced me with warm wings, you precious one,
You saved me from my sleep.
Your compassion coaxed this fool, seeking nourishment,
To your nectar, so that he would drink of it
And grow, and flourish, and having grown strong and drunken
Would mock you to your face—oh, spirit,
Spirit, who raised me up, you have
Raised your lord, old Saturn,
You have raised a new Jupiter for yourself,
Only a weaker and insolent one.
This malicious tongue can only revile you,
Is there no avenger anywhere, must I myself alone
Utter all the scorn and curses against my soul?
Must loneliness be even that?

SCENE THREE

PAUSANIAS, EMPEDOCLES

EMPEDOCLES: I feel the day declining now, my friend,
    And all is growing dark for me, and cold.
    Backward I go, dear friend, but not to rest
    As when provided, satisfied with the booty,
    A bird will swathe his head for pleasant sleep
    And fresher wakening—different it is with me.
    But spare me the complaint. Ask no more questions.
PAUSANIAS: How very strange you have become to me,
    My Empedocles. Do you not know me now?
    Nor I know you, the glorious, as I did?
    Can you be so transformed, your noble face
    Become a riddle to me,

And so to earth may suffering bow down
Heaven's own favorite? Are you not he?
And yet! We thank you for it all.
And never, amid golden joy, a man
Wielded such power, as you, in his people.
EMPEDOCLES: They honor me? Go, quickly then, and tell them
They are to cease. That ornament
Does not fit me well now.
And does not the green foliage
Wilt, too, on trunks uprooted?
PAUSANIAS: But you still stand, and the cool little brooks play
About your roots, and mildly round your crest
The sweet air wafts, and that which is not transient
Sustains your core; the great immortal powers
Shape and watch over you.
EMPEDOCLES: You remind me of days of youth, dear friend.
PAUSANIAS: Life's middle strikes me as still more beautiful.
EMPEDOCLES: And gladly, now that noon declines,
Once more the eyes of those look back
Who still more swiftly, and forever, fade,
Look back, but to give thanks. O time of youth!
Delights of love, you ecstasies when my soul,
Awakened like Endymion by the gods,
Childish slumber opened wide,
Spirits of life in their magnificence,
The genii—beautiful *Sun*! No man had taught me
To name, to know them; it was my own heart
Immortally loving, driving me to immortals,
To you, to you, for nothing more divine
Is found than you, still light! And as you
Never stint life in your daily day's fullness
And lavishly, taking no care, expend
Your golden wealth, so I, being yours, was glad
To give away to mortals my best soul,
And, fearlessly candid, so
My heart to serious *Earth* I dedicated,
The many-destined; to her in youthful joy
As now, so lifelong, to devote my life
I promised her at many a solemn hour,
Pledging a firm, dear pact with her till death.
Then through the grove a different rustle ran,
And tenderly her mountain's wellsprings murmured—
Yes, all your pleasures, *Earth,* which true as she,
And warm and full, with love and labor ripen,

All these you gave me. Often when I sat
High up, on some calm peak, and marveling
Pondered the tangled, mutable ways of men,
Too deeply gripped by your vicissitudes,
And felt the nearness of my own decline,
Then the *Aether* would breathe on you,
Healing me of a breast full of the wounds of love,
And like the clouds of fire, my care and grief
Up in the blue heights lost themselves.

PAUSANIAS: O, son of Heaven!

EMPEDOCLES: Yes, that I was, and now will tell the story,
Wretch that I am, once more, and only once
Recall to my own soul
The working of those powers of genius
The glorious powers whose companion I was, O nature,
So that my mute, desolate heart may resound once more
With all your various music.
Am I myself, O life, and did they once
Ring out to me, all your winged melodies, and did
I hear your ancient harmony, great Nature?
O, did I not, lonely, live with her,
This holy Earth, and live with you, this light,
And you from whom no soul can bear to part,
You Father Aether, and with all that lives,
The friend of gods at home on real Olympus?
And now they've cast me out, and now they've left me
Utterly lonely, and now anguish is
My companion through the day and in sleep.
No, do not come to me for blessings my friend!
Ask me no questions. Do you think I'm dreaming?
Just look at me! Nor is there any need,
Kind as you are, to wonder how can it be
That I have come to this; for sons of Heaven,
When too much joy, too much good fortune has been theirs,
A downfall like no other is reserved.

PAUSANIAS: I'll not allow it!
Such words from you! From you? I'll not allow it.
You should not frighten your own soul and mine
With blasphemous talk. It seems an evil omen
To see the ever clear and radiant minds
Of mighty men beclouded.

EMPEDOCLES: You sense it, then? It means that soon
They must come down to earth in a thunderstorm.

PAUSANIAS: What has he done to you, you gods of death,

This pure one, to deserve the darkness fallen
Upon his soul? Is it that mortals have
Nothing that is their own, nowhere, and
The terrible reaches them in their hearts,
And even in the breast of those who are strong
Eternal fate governs? Tame your grief
And use your power, for still you are the one
Who can do more than others. Let my love
Remind you of the man you were and are,
Think of yourself, and live!

EMPEDOCLES: You do not know me, nor yourself, nor life, nor death.

PAUSANIAS: Death I know only little, true,
For I have given it little thought.

EMPEDOCLES: To be alone
And without gods is death.

PAUSANIAS: Leave it, in your deeds I recognize you,
In its power I experienced your spirit,
And its world, when often a word
From you, in a sacred moment
Made a life for me of many years,
So that at once a whole great age began
For your disciple; and like the hearts of stags
When far away the forest roars, recalling
Their homeland to them, my heart would beat
When you evoked primeval worlds of bliss,
Versed in those pure day's lore, and all Fate's ways
Lay open to you. Did you not trace for me,
With mighty strokes, the lines of the future,
Your hand, your eye as sure as any painter's
Who adds the missing detail to the whole?
Are you not intimate with the powers of Nature,
And like no other mortal
Do you not silently guide them as you please?

EMPEDOCLES: Quite true, I know all things, can master all.
Like my own handiwork thoroughly I control it,
And as I please, a lord of spirits, rule,
Manipulate, make use of all that lives.
Mine is the world, submissive and subservient,
To me are all its powers,
Nature herself,
Unfit, as well you know, to have her way,
Is now my servant girl; such honor
As men accord her still, she owes to me.

And what indeed would heaven be and the ocean
And islands and the stars, and all that meets
The eyes of men, what would
This dead stringed instrument be if I did not give it
A tone and language and soul?
What are the gods, and what their spirit, if I
Do not proclaim them? Now say, who am I?
PAUSANIAS: Out of mere bitterness mock yourself and all
That makes men glorious,
Their workings and their word; make me ashamed
Of my own courage, call me and drive me back
Into my childhood. Freely admit it: You hate
Yourself and those who love and follow you;
Your will is focused on what you are not, your fame,
Grown strange to you, to strangers will betray you.
Not to remain on earth
Is your desire, you long to perish. Oh, in
Your breast there is less peace than in me.
EMPEDOCLES: You innocent!
PAUSANIAS: And you accuse yourself?
What is it, then? O do make for me a riddle.
Of your affliction. You are tormenting me.
EMPEDOCLES (WITH CALM): Serenely, should men,
Who ponder, act upon
The life around them, to further and make bright
For full of lofty purpose,
Of silent power, unexpressed,
Great Nature surrounds their
Foreknowing minds, to fashion a world,
Deep-rooted
Within them a mighty longing leaps up
So that her spirit will come to light.
It enables him to do much, and glorious is
Man's word, it transforms the world,
And where his hands have [Text breaks off here.]

ACT TWO (CONCLUSION)

PANTHEA: Surely it was not you,
The human labyrinth,
That spoiled
His heart? What could you give him,
Poor as you are? Now that the man

Longs to be gone and join his gods
They wonder at it, as if it were they, the foolish,
Who had endowed him with a lofty soul.
Nature gave him all, not without reason.
Those you love best more briefly linger here!
Too well I know it.
They come and grow, and none of us can say
How they grew great, and so again they vanish,
Those happy ones. O leave them, let them go!
DELIA: Is it not good
　　To live among mortals? My heart
　　Knows of no other joy, it rests
　　Upon this one man, but sadly, darkly before
　　My eyes now threatens the end
　　Of the inconceivable, yet even you,
　　Panthea, bid him go?
PANTHEA: I must. For who wants to bind him,
　　To say to him, you are mine,
　　When to himself that living one belongs,
　　For him no law but his own mind is valid?
　　And should he stay here to save
　　The honor of mortals
　　Who have reviled him, when now
　　The Father himself,
　　Opens the arms of the Aether,
　　Opens his arms for him?
DELIA: Look! Glorious too
　　And kindly our Earth is.
PANTHEA: Glorious, true, and more glorious now.
　　Not without presents may
　　A bold man part from her.
　　Still he must be delaying
　　On one of your green heights, O Earth,
　　You changing one,
　　And gazes now across the billowing hills
　　Down to the open sea, and snatches
　　A joy from you, the last. Perhaps we will never
　　See him again. Good child,
　　Of course this affects me too, and gladly
　　Would, have it otherwise, but feel ashamed of the wish.
　　His choice it is! That, surely, hallows the deed?
DELIA: Who is that youth
　　Coming down the mountain?

PANTHEA: Pausanias; poor fatherless boy!
Must we meet again like this?

LAST SCENE ACT TWO

PAUSANIAS, PANTHEA, DELIA

PAUSANIAS: Where is he? O Panthea,
You honor him, look for him too,
And long to see him once more,
That frightening wanderer who alone is fated
With glory to walk that path
Which no other might tread without flight.
PANTHEA: Is it pious for him, and great,
This way that all men fear?
Where is he?
PAUSANIAS: He sent me away, and I have not seen
Him since. Up in the mountains
I called his name, but did not find him.
He will surely return, having kindly promised me
That he would stay until nightfall.
If only he'd come! More swiftly
Than arrows the loveliest hour goes by.
For we shall yet enjoy his presence,
You, Panthea, and she as well,
The noble stranger who only once
Will see him, bright and brief, a meteor.
But you are weeping. Of his death
You've heard, then?
You grieve for him. See him as he blossoms,
That exalted man.
And that which grieves you,
That which to mortals seems most terrible,
May well look milder to eyes that are blessed.
DELIA: How you love him! And yet in vain
Implored the earnest man? The plea
Is mightier than he is, and you deserved
To win him over.
PAUSANIAS: How could I, when
In answering he speaks his will
And touches my soul?
For his refusal even gladdens us.
What could I do? The more that marvelous man

187

Insists on his own way,
The deeper is the resonance in our hearts.
Nor is it vain persuasion, believe me,
When he gains such power
Over life itself.
Often when he was quiet
In his own world,
Supremely satisfied,
I watched him in his vague divining,
My own soul active, full of vigor, yet
I could not feel it, and I was almost awed
By his impalpable presence.
Yet when the decisive word came from his lips
A heaven of joy echoed in both him
And me, and without contradiction
I yielded to it, relieved and liberated.
If he could err, why, all the more deeply
By that I should know the inexhaustible truth of him.
And if he died, all the more brightly his genius
Would flame from his ashes before me.

DELIA: Being great, your soul is kindled
By a great man's death, but the hearts
Of mortals too like to bask
In milder light, and attach
Their eyes to that which is lasting. O tell us,
What now shall live and last? The most quiet
Fate uproots and sweeps away,
And if, prophetic, they ventured out,
Soon it repels those brave ones; the young
Die on their hopes.
Nothing that loves remains
In its flower and prime—and the best,
Even they seek out their destroyers,
The gods of death, and with pleasure
They perish, and make it our shame
To linger, to dwell among mortals.

PAUSANIAS: Damn you

DELIA: O Nature, why do you
Make it so easy
For your hero to die?
Too gladly, Empedocles, too gladly
You sacrifice yourself.
The weak are tossed about by destiny, and the others,
The strong, care little whether they fall or stand

And become like the frail.
You glorious man, you suffered what
No slave could suffer,
And poorer than the poorest beggar
You roam across the land.
Yes, indeed it's true,
Not those tossed away
Are wretched, as your loves, their gods,
Once disgrace has touched them.
He took it beautifully.

PANTHEA: Yes, he took it well
And how could he not?
When always and always nonetheless the genius
Must outlive
That which is stronger than he is—did you think
The thorn would stop him? The pain accelerates
His flight, and like the charioteer
When wheels begin to smoke on the track,
The one who is endangered, only rushes faster towards his garland.

DELIA: It's joy you feel, then, Panthea?

PANTHEA: Not only in the blossom and purple grape
Is holy energy, life nourishes
Itself on suffering too, sister!
And drink happily, like my hero, even from
The chalice of death!

DELIA: Dear child, is that
How you comfort yourself?

PANTHEA: By no means! Only it cheers me, that sacredly,
That when it must be, when it must happen
The dreaded thing, that it happens with glory.
Like him, in the past
Did not more than one of the heroes go to the gods?
Though shocked, weeping aloud,
The people came from the mountain,
Not one I saw who reproached him,
For not like despairing men
In secret he flees, but all of them heard it,
And in their sorrow their faces shimmered
With the words he spoke.

PAUSANIAS: Festively, then, the star
Goes down, and drunken
With its light the valleys shine?

PANTHEA: Festively, yes, he goes down—
The grave man, your favorite, Nature!

Oh, those who fear death
Do not love you,
Deluding them, care chains their eyes,
Their heart no longer beats against your heart
They wither, divorced from you—
Oh, holy all!
Living! Inward!
To thank you and to bear witness to you,
You deathless!
Laughingly he throws his pears
To the sea from which they came,
The bold one.
That is how it must happen to us,
The spirit wants it that way
And the ripening time,
For once we who were blind
Were in need of a miracle.

5 Nietzsche

The first enemy of the aesthetic was meaning.
—Roberto Calasso,
The Marriage of Cadmus and Harmony, p. 241

By the time Nietzsche begins writing *The Birth of Tragedy* (it would be published in 1872), the question of tragedy had already been firmly established in Germany. In less than a century from the appearance of Schelling's reference to Greek tragedy as the site of a solution to the enigmas of post-Kantian philosophizing, the topic of tragedy had taken root in German thought so deeply, so fundamentally, that the history of its presence in nineteenth-century German thought was almost as important as the original history of Greek tragedy that belongs to fifth century B.C.E. Athens (curiously, when Nietzsche first confronts it, the first life of this question—as it is found in ancient Athens and played out in the theater—is only as long as the second life of the question—which is found in Germany—and is played out in academic publications). By the time Nietzsche broaches the question of tragedy and its relation to the modern world, the history of the second life of this question is, by and large, for better or worse, owned by Hegel. When the young Nietzsche begins to take a serious interest in Greek art, especially Greek tragedy, Hegel's argument (or, better, the Hegelian argument as it was canonized by his epigones) that the structure of tragedy was ultimately a dialectical structure had become

191

something of a commonplace. In the middle decades of the nineteenth century, Hölderlin's work would alternate between lapsing into obscurity and being thoroughly misrepresented, while Schelling's fate was to be ignored and overlooked after his youthful success, and Kierkegaard had not yet been found sufficiently even to be lost. The effective history of the modern form of the philosophic question of tragedy—in Germany at least —was so powerfully defined by Hegel, that to take up the renewal of the issue of the tragic meant, in some measure, to engage Hegel. Such would remain the case until Nietzsche himself would redefine the parameters of the issue and open radically new dimensions of the question of the tragic.

So from Nietzsche forward the second history of the question of the tragic—the history that emerges in Germany—will intervene in almost every attempt to take up Greek tragedy. Access to the Greeks becomes ever more complicated as it becomes ever more important to gain such access. Nietzsche is the first to have to confront this hermeneutic problem, and though he will often, more often than not, write as if he were discovering Greek tragedy for the first time, nonetheless it is also clear that he does this fully aware that his efforts need to separate themselves sharply from those of Hegel.[1] Greece had been increasingly colonized as an idea in German thought over the years, and so at this point to take up the idea of Greece—itself still very much a German project—meant liberating it from the forms it had been assigned in German philosophy. "Greece" had become an ever more complicated idea, one not fully able to be separated from the idea of "Germany."

For Nietzsche, the means of this liberation and the first steps en route to what is not simply a reflection of German images, but is rather a struggle with the foreign, were taken by Jacob Burkhardt, who exposed Nietzsche to a different, a darker, image of Greece very much at odds with Hegel's view.[2] Burkhardt systematically debunked the romanticized and sanitized view of ancient Greece which presents Athens as the cradle of democracy and as the home of a proto-Enlightenment. It was counter to the image of Greece that characterized the view presented as Hegel's, namely, the view that in ancient Greece we find the innocent and still pure childhood of the mature spirit of Western culture.[3] Burkhardt's understanding of ancient Greece saw it as the locus of a play of forces— destructive and constructive, dark and light, tyrannical and liberating— and this play of powers was condensed in the making of the polis, which was the decisive experience of the ancient world. This was an understanding of Greece that saw the formation of the political culture there as deeply wedded to the conflicted play of forces which had free range in the life of culture. Above all, it was an understanding of Greece which found that "of all civilized peoples, it was the Greeks who inflicted the bitterest and most deeply felt suffering upon themselves."[4]

The influence of Burkhardt upon Nietzsche was significant: Nietzsche was smitten with this view of the Greek world from his first encounter with it, and Burkhardt in turn acknowledged Nietzsche by attending Nietzsche's lectures at one point.[5] Most of all it was the dark core of Greek culture that Burkhardt exposed which captured Nietzsche's imagination and appealed to his already sophisticated conception of the ancient world. The early years of Nietzsche's career, the period of his activities in Basel, where he was Burkhardt's colleague, are the time of his most intensive and single-minded involvement with the topic of Greek tragedy (although the topic of Greek tragedy would be one of the dominant axes of Nietzsche's thought throughout his productive life, and so it is a mistake to presume that the final word on the topic of tragedy would ever come for Nietzsche).[6] Much that is worthy of attention is to be found in the work of those early years where one finds the work of a brilliant and young mind, full of imagination, and unencumbered by the agendas which would later grip Nietzsche's interpretations of tragedy. But, in the end, *The Birth of Tragedy* remains the work that most represents Nietzsche's understanding of Greek tragedy. In it the work of the early years finds its most crystalline expression, and the impulses and concerns which would guide him in later years can be seen, even if sometimes only *in nuce*. In *The Birth of Tragedy* one finds the two strands in Nietzsche's thought at this time coming together systematically: on the one hand, one finds here an analysis of tragedy which is presented in the context of an understanding of both culture and the individual life; on the other hand, one finds a sharp critique of the contemporary forms of life and culture, a critique which is rendered ever sharper by virtue of the contrast with the cultural forms of the ancient world. Here one sees most clearly how it is that Nietzsche's analysis of Greek tragedy needs to be understood as part and parcel of the development of a political, even an ethical, sensibility.

The political and ethical element of Nietzsche's analysis of Greek tragedy should not be underestimated; indeed, it is paramount in this analysis. Although he was trained as a classicist, and even though he announces that he is interested in questions of the work of art, Nietzsche's interest in Greek tragedy carries in itself his concern with the historical present; his treatment of Greek tragedy will prove to harbor the proto-form of his later scathing criticisms of the forms of contemporary life, of nihilism, and of decadence. His intent, in part at least, is to demonstrate that since the passing away of Greek culture, most of all since the rise of Christian culture, cultures have lacked the courage to confront the deep wisdom of the tragic. Instead of regarding history as a matter of the progress of cultures, he thinks it as a progressive dilution and decline. Although this is the reverse of what one finds in Hegel, what needs to be recognized is that it is precisely in this respect that Nietzsche is to be situated as part of the tradition which Hegel eventually defines: like Hegel, he takes up the question of tragedy as a political and ethical question. And, like Hölderlin, he takes it up as a question about the difference between the possibilities of the ancient and modern worlds. The second life of the philosophical question of tragedy in which Nietzsche will participate is, like its first life, to be understood as a question of political and ethical life.

And yet it must also be said that the analysis of tragedy in *The Birth of Tragedy* is motivated most of all by a fascination with the place of the work of art in human experience. His clear intent—and here again he belongs to the tradition that is defined by Hegel, Schelling, and Hölderlin—is to show that the roots of tragedy, both in the Greek world and in its deficient forms in the modern world, are to be traced back to the deepest moments of human being. The notion of a *Bildungstrieb* (a formative drive) which is so central to Hegel and his friends, and which is said to explain the profound kinship of tragedy and human nature, will be repeated by Nietzsche, largely unmodified in its basic sensibility, in his notion of a *Kunsttrieb* (a drive to art). In short, *The Birth of Tragedy* is the site of Nietzsche's thoroughly problematic relation to the tradition of post-Kantian German philosophy; in it one finds the simultaneous effort to deepen and to repudiate that tradition. But, without attempting to disentangle this thicket of problems and relations, what needs to be stressed as one approaches *The Birth of Tragedy* is that when Nietzsche takes up the topic of tragedy, he does so by working out of a highly conflicted relation to the recent history of this question. But this hermeneutical complexity is so thoroughly submerged in the book itself that one easily overlooks it. Nonetheless, struggle as he does to open the question of tragedy more radically than hitherto, and with a fresher, more Greek, sensibility than previously known, Nietzsche knows himself to be in a contest with a recent history that has by this time sedimented into a form of Hegelianism. Among the many battles—and it is very much a book of battles[7]—he must wage in this book, the quiet struggle with Hegel's dialectical conception of tragedy should not be forgotten.

*　　*　　*

It should also be said that this book would become the site of many of Nietzsche's own battles with himself. This is nowhere more evident than in the "Attempt at a Self-critique," which Nietzsche composes as a preface to the second edition of the book which was published fourteen years (1886) after the original version. Much had changed for Nietzsche in the intervening years since the first publication of this book (most of all his relation to Wagner, the sole addressee of the initial conception of the book), and this new preface struggles to adjust itself to these changes. This preface is an astonishing work in which Nietzsche seems to lambaste the achievements, style, tone, and substance of the book itself. It is not, at least on first blush, the sort of preface bent upon winning new readers. Quite the contrary, on a casual reading it seems that Nietzsche speaks openly and sarcastically of what he takes to be the manifest failure of the project of *The Birth of Tragedy*. It seems that he is disowning the source of his own early fame. But it is a brilliant introduction, full of double entendres and of multiple layers of meaning. He calls the book that he is reintroducing "questionable," "strange," "inaccessible," "bold," and "impossible." While these words do refer to Nietzsche's later reservations about the book, it needs to be said that they also serve to describe the themes that the book itself will discuss; in other words, this is a book that takes up the questionable, strange, inaccessible, bold, and impossible in life. Such is one of the ways in which this "Attempt at a Self-critique" simultaneously owns and repudiates the work that follows.

Despite the differences in Nietzsche's thought that had opened up in the intervening fourteen years between the publication of the book and this new preface (and the differences are real and notable), in many ways this new preface serves to highlight and reaffirm in a new light the very same themes and strategies that the book had already disclosed. But there is one difference which this difference cannot plaster over, and when Nietzsche takes note of it in the new preface he does so fully aware that this is the point on which the self-announced goal of the book must fail. The passage which names this failure has a sadness and poignancy about it: "It should have *sung*, this new soul—and not spoken! How sad that I did not risk saying as a poet what I had to say then: perhaps I could have done it!"[8] There is perhaps no other comment that could damn the achievement of *The Birth of Tragedy* so succinctly, so hitting at the heart of what it sets out as its own task, as this remark. What makes this passage such a fundamental critique of *The Birth of Tragedy*, and what makes it important to bear in mind as one reads the text itself, is that one of the most pervasive arguments of *The Birth of Tragedy* is that the style of thinking needs to be appropriate to the content of thought. In other words, thinking must be understood as performed and not as able to be conveyed in simple propositional language. The argument, which will be considered in detail below, is that the language of metaphysics, conceptual and propositional language, is simply incapable of coming to terms with the depth of the abyssal truth that is disclosed in the work of art. Here there is a passionate plea on behalf of the language of the passions. But when in later years Nietzsche comes to write that "it should have sung, not spoken," the limitations of *The Birth of Tragedy* to enact its own truth were painfully apparent to him.[9] It was an insight that Nietzsche already had, but insufficiently realized, in *The Birth of Tragedy* when he wrote that "language can never adequately render the cosmic symbolism of music, because music stands in symbolic relation to the primordial contradiction and primordial pain in the heart of the primal unity, and therefore symbolizes a sphere which is beyond and prior to all phenomena. . . . Language, as the organ and symbol of appearance, can never and in no case disclose the deepest interiority of music."[10]

In light of this severe criticism of *The Birth of Tragedy*, and in light of later remarks such as the one found in *The Joyful Science* where Nietzsche writes, with reference to his own presentation of Zarathustra, "Incipit tragodia,"[11] one might suggest that *The Birth of Tragedy* is not the text one should turn to above all others in order to understand Nietzsche's contribution to the philosophical appraisal of tragedy. There are, of course, good arguments to be made to support such a view, and there are a number of reasons one might turn to *Thus Spoke Zarathustra* as the work in which the insight of the tragic is most powerfully *enacted* and not simply said. Nietzsche will even tacitly recommend such a turn to *Thus Spoke Zarathustra* when he concludes the "Attempt at a Self-critique" with the citation of a lengthy passage from that work (one that significantly refers to laughter rather than suffering). However, three reasons make *The Birth of Tragedy* an ineluctable work: first, it remained Nietzsche's most extensive and focused treatment of the question of tragedy; second, it was the work Nietzsche himself would continually take up and take as a touchstone for all other experiments with the experience of the tragic; third, it was (and one could argue continues to be) the text that wins Nietzsche the widest readership. It is true that the topic of Greek tragedy, and the notion of the wisdom of tragic experience, saturates Nietzsche's work at every stage. One could legitimately turn to almost any work of Nietzsche's and find something sufficient to take up the topic of tragedy. But, in the end, *The Birth of Tragedy* is the work which most needs to be confronted as the touchstone for Nietzsche's understanding of what he will call "tragic wisdom." All the other works in which he addresses this insight will, in the end, need to take *The Birth of Tragedy* as some form of a point of reference—even if only by virtue of its introduction of the twin sources of the tragic, the Apollonian and the Dionysian, that is announced on the very first page of this, Nietzsche's first major book.

* * *

"The Attempt at a Self-critique," which would serve as the new preface to the 1886 edition of *The Birth of Tragedy*, would not be the only time Nietzsche tinkered with the text when its reprinting gave him such a opportunity to do so. Sometimes it seems that Nietzsche would never find a way to free himself from the dreams of this text, and so he would continually seek to adjust it, criticize it, praise it. He changes it for the 1878 edition only slightly, but nonetheless significantly: the title is changed from *The Birth of Tragedy Out of the Spirit of Music* to *The Birth of Tragedy. Or: Greece and Pessimism.* The shift—only in the title—is significant in that it does not indicate any change in the content of the text, but it does indicate something of a change of heart for Nietzsche. The early dreams which would drive the text, inspired by Wagner, not by Sophocles or Homer, had begun to darken over the years, and Nietzsche's change in the title signals a change in the locus of the final issue in which the concerns of tragedy is condensed. One might put the point with reference to a proper name: the move is away from Wagner.

But Wagner was, and will always remain, the single intended reader of *The Birth of Tragedy.* The Preface to the book will be addressed only to Wagner. It never ceases to stun every other reader who opens this book only to find that the Preface is addressed to one person. Just as Aristotle would write his *Poetics* by treating "Sophocles and the Essence of Poetry"— to paraphrase Heidegger's text on "Hölderlin and the Essence of Poetry" —so would Nietzsche take up the task of writing a poetics by writing something like "Wagner and the Essence of the Tragic." Wagner will haunt the text and will provide a quiet, yet still curious, background note to the treatment of Greek tragedy that is unfolded here. And with Wagner, Germany will become a vital part of the question of tragedy: it is a "seriously German problem that we have to deal with here."[12] While the figure of Wagner would remain a positive presence only for the first six years of the life of this text, the question of "Germany" would never disappear. And just as his relationship to Wagner would shipwreck over the years, so too would his hopes in Germany die: "Meanwhile I have learned how to think this 'German nature' with a sufficient lack of hope and mercy."[13]

Nonetheless, the text begins in Greece—more precisely, with the Greek gods who inhabit every one of us: Apollo and Dionysus. The first sentence packs in much of what the book will need to present: "We will have won much for the science of aesthetics once we grasp not merely by logical insight, but by the immediate certainty of seeing that the progressive development of art is bound to the duplicity of the Apollonian and of the Dionysian: in a similar manner procreation is dependent upon the duality of the sexes, where there is perpetual struggle and only periodically intervening reconciliation."[14] It is a remarkable sentence which suggests that the achievement of the work of art cannot be grasped by "logical insight" or by any form of logical reasoning which follows the trajectory of the concept. Rather, the knowledge opened by the work of art—which he has already deemed the "highest task and the true metaphysical activity of life"[15]—can be won only by an immediate "intuition" or "seeing." Years later Nietzsche would make a similar point when he writes, "One who not only conceptualizes the word 'Dionysian,' but rather conceives of oneself in the word 'Dionysian,' has no need of any refutation of Plato or Christianity—such a person smells their decay."[16] In other words, what needs to be "known" if the work of art is to be "known" is a knowledge that can only be displayed and enacted. It cannot be told. Near the end of *The Birth of Tragedy* Nietzsche will come back to this point indirectly when he says that "Those who have never had the experience of having to see and at the same time of seeing beyond all seeing, will find it difficult to imagine how definitely and clearly these two processes belong together."[17] From the outset he warns the reader that something new is needed if this book is to live up to its own insights. One is warned from the outset that what Nietzsche himself needs to disclose must, in the end, possess the immediate certainty of an intuitive knowing. Nothing could be further from the dialectical mediation of the Hegelian conception of the tragic. Or so Nietzsche wants to claim at this point.

But this first sentence does not stop with such indications about its own self-imposed requirements. This requirement that an immediate certainty be won regarding the work of art, this highest task of life, is directed to a specific knowledge; namely, the knowledge that the development of art is bound to the duplicity of the traits of two Greek gods, Apollo and Dionysus. Everything begins to spin at this point because we have to deal not only with the traits of the two gods and the relationship that emerges out of those traits, but also, maybe more so, with their respective "duplicity." Nothing is straight any longer, nothing able to be only what it appears to be: two opposing divinities in a tense relation, each entering that relation full of duplicity.[18] Even before finishing this first sentence Nietzsche moves to clarify, provisionally at least, the specific character of this complexity which is said to be at the heart of the work of art. He does this by likening the *duplicity* of these divine traits, and the duplicity of their relationship as well (the sentence is ambiguous, one is tempted to say duplicitous), to the *duality* of the sexes. Needless to say, Nietzsche's view of the relation of woman and man—that it is a continuous battle marked only by periodic reconciliation—is striking, especially if one does not permit this relation to be reconfigured by the treatment of the Apollonian and the Dionysian which follows. In other words, Nietzsche sets up an analogy between sexual difference and the different roots which define the human being, and this analogy should not be treated statically. The book will treat the dual roots of human life, the Apollonian and the Dionysian, extensively, and that thorough analysis should, in the end, be read back into these opening remarks about sexual difference. But at this point Nietzsche wants only to liken the roots of the creativity of art, the Apollonian and the Dionysian, to the way procreation requires the duality of the sexes. In the process of setting up this analogy he *eroticizes* the relation of the Apollonian and the Dionysian. The roots of art and the erotic impulse will find themselves bound together.[19] In the end, the fact that the character of this relation is erotic will prove to be the reason that the Dionysian has a sort of privilege in this relation since it is the impulse that is most closely related to the erotic. Although they are equals in this relationship, the character of their relationship will have to be explained in terms that are more clearly drawn from the Dionysian. Nietzsche will eventually pick up on this point and grant this privilege to the Dionysian. But what Nietzsche will overlook in the analysis that follows is that this eroticization of the relation between the Apollonian and the Dionysian must be understood, in some measure at least, as a homoerotic relation: these are, after all, two male gods, and the analogy to the duality of the sexes might make this point a complicated one, but it must not obscure the homoerotic quality of the relation that is presented.

Nietzsche does not mention this. What he does do is drive home the differences between these two divinities, and to suggest that what one sees in them is a "monstrous opposition."[20] The Apollonian and Dionysian impulses, which stand in a necessary and erotic relation, will be the source of the first—and the foremost—of the many monsters which populate this text.[21] To understand their unstable and volatile relationship is the chief task of this book; it is this relationship which will provide the Ariadne's thread to an answer to the overarching question of the book: "Wozu—griechische Kunst? . . ."[22] But the presentation of the dynamic they define will be deferred for the first four sections of the text (it will begin only with section 5).[23] First, Nietzsche will undertake an analysis of each of these impulses, these drives which define the human being and the whole of nature, separately. He does this knowing, of course, that they are, for us at least, necessarily never able to be fully separated. Thus, alternating between the features of each, Nietzsche presents the trademarks of the Apollonian and the Dionysian. But it is worth bearing in mind as one takes up these notions separately not only that, in the end, they do not exist separately, but also that neither shows itself directly as itself. Each is known first by its effects: thus the Apollonian is known in *dreams,* while the Dionysian is felt in *rapture.*[24] And these, in turn, are conceived of as "separate art worlds."[25]

The Apollonian is unfolded with reference to the dreams of one asleep: "The beautiful world of the dream, in the production of which every person is an artist, is the presupposition of all plastic art, yes, even, as we will see, of an important half of poetry."[26] The point is simple and compelling. When the mind is alone and by itself, when the world other than that which the self itself defines is shut down—in other words, when one sleeps—the mind is free to turn to what is most native to itself, to its most intimate forms, and when it does this it dreams. At the moment we are most intimate with ourselves, most purely individuated, we make images of light in which we converse with ourselves. Dreams are the conversation of the soul with itself, and the language of this conversation is light and the images which this light forms. This is why Nietzsche refers to Apollo as the "divinity of light."[27] Everything beyond this realm of light is epiphenomenal; in the dream the real stuff of the self is most directly experienced. Indirectly, it is the experience of the Apollonian tendency that drives the self. But this intensification of the self in the dream, this intimacy of the self with itself in the dream world, is what leads Nietzsche to interpret the Apollonian tendency as expressing the principle of individuation. It is the tendency in which one of the deepest drives of life encloses the self upon itself and thereby individuates it to the hilt. My dreams are mine alone, and, if they are a riddle to me in my conscious life, they must be recognized as an insuperable barrier for the understanding of anyone else. My own relation to my dreams in my conscious life is tenuous at best, but my capacity to communicate my dreams to another is marked by an extreme failure. I am, in other words, individuated in and by my dream life.

But the Dionysian is the polar opposite to this tendency, and so it is with the collapse of this principle of individuation that we first begin to glimpse the character of the Dionysian. While the Apollonian is exposed in the analogy with the dream, the intimate experience of the Dionysian is found in the analogy of rapture. Initially Nietzsche gives two examples of what he means by such rapture, both relatively tame compared to the images of the Dionysian which will follow: the influence of intoxicating drinks and the powerful feeling of the coming of Spring that penetrates all of nature. Both are illustrations of experiences in which everything subjective eventually vanishes into complete self-forgetfulness. Whereas the dream is the manner in which the self comes to communicate with itself as itself, rapture is the experience in which the self vanishes for itself. In rapture, in ecstasy, we experience the capacity of all that lives to become other to itself. One is tempted to say that the experience of the Dionysian is akin to an experience in which one dreams the dream of another; in such an experience one is simultaneously intimate and utterly strange to oneself. The example of sexual ecstasy—in which flesh is no longer the name of the barrier dividing us, but is rather the way in which we are unified—is perhaps the most compelling of the many illustrations Nietzsche gives for the Dionysian. But the point to be made should not be confused with the way the point is illustrated. The point is that the Dionysian impulse—named for the god of wine—names the tendency of all that lives to lose itself, to become other to itself and to forget itself: Dionysus "blurs the frontiers between the divine and the human, the human and the animal, the here and the beyond. He sets up communion between things hitherto isolated, separate. His eruption into nature, the social group, and each individual human being, through trance and regulated possession, is a subversion of order."[28] And it is precisely in this respect that the Dionysian and the Apollonian are polar opposites. In the Dionysian boundaries are trespassed, excess is the rule; in the Apollonian boundaries are inscribed, order is the rule. Both, however, do not accomplish their aims simply, without duplicity, and the logics of both—of desire and rapture, of the image and the dream—operate far afield, each in its own way, of the logic of reason. That is why the opening sentence of the text suggests that what is to be known in these matters cannot be known by "logical inference" but only by the immediate certainty of vision.

Yet in Nietzsche's presentation both impulses, both drives are divinized: the god of the sun and of wine, of light and of the blood of the earth, steer life here. In other words, this polarity is of what is immense and beyond what we can conceive or control. The conflict of these impulses is not something that a human being could ever manage or contain; here we have to do with forces of nature, forces of life. Everything hinges on finding the manner in which this conflict can unfold itself as nature, as life, will have it. The task of this book is to come to an appreciation of this relation, one that will strangely be called "justice,"[29] and that will unfold itself most directly, most as itself, in the form of tragedy.

But, before that can be said, more must be known of the general nature of the conflict that drives this erotic and yet mutually destructive relationship between the Apollonian and the Dionysian. First, it needs to be understood that these energies "burst forth from nature herself"[30] without any mediation, any help, from the human being. They are, simply put, powers greater than that which we define or control. Outstripping human being, they are the "drives to art" which animate life as such. Because they define us and yet drive us in countervalent directions—to self-forgetfulness and to utmost individuation—they set us in conflict with ourselves, and we can only suffer their relation. They are forces of nature, the original and originating drives of life itself, and so the struggle to reconcile them—a struggle which we cannot evade since these impulses define us—is a struggle with the deepest forces of life.

This perpetual struggle, the drive toward self-forgetfulness and toward self-individuation, cannot be avoided. To step outside of this struggle would mean that one had ceased to dream and one was no longer capable of losing oneself in desire. It would be to be dead to the world. But it also needs to be said that these drives do not stand in direct and absolute contradiction to one another in every sense. In fact, there is a very real sense in which they reaffirm and reinforce one another. After all, it is the case that dreams and desires each carries the other within itself. So the relation between the divine impulse which is known in the illusory world of dreams and the divine impulse felt in the blur of desire is not even one of direct competition. It is, as Nietzsche writes early on, a "duplicitous" relationship that we have to confront as our own struggle. It is not a relationship that can ever resolve itself, be sublated, or be translated to another plane; rather, this is the most basic relation of all relations. It will unfold itself ceaselessly. The task for one who would do honor to this relation—the task of what Nietzsche understands himself as doing—is to see into the mutual neediness which holds them together. It is to understand how the Dionysian and the Apollonian, despite every opposition, actively need one another. To succeed at this is to see into the birth of tragedy.

Art is the true result of this ongoing struggle of these natural impulses. It is the manner in which the deepest drives of the will objectify themselves and repeat themselves as if in a "transfiguring mirror."[31] One might also say that works of art belong to this space of difference which defines the human being, and that they affect us so powerfully, speak to us so deeply, because they lead us to speak with ourselves precisely as this ongoing struggle of drives. Art accomplishes this, it brings us into a sort of self-conversation, not simply in the words or surfaces or images in which it is embodied; rather, it does this by opening the space in which a self-conversation can take place, and this space is the space of the struggle of the Apollonian and Dionysian impulses. As such, art presents with great clarity something of our own nature which is otherwise hidden, namely, the conflicted struggle which animates us and cannot be grasped according to the unconflicted linearity of logical reason. Tragedy is simply the perfection of this struggle, the art of struggle enacting the struggle that gives birth to art. For Nietzsche this means that the destination of art as such is tragedy. One might be tempted to suggest, with a bit of hyperbole, that he would argue that all art is striving to become tragic art. Such a remark might grossly oversimplify the richness of the field of art, but ultimately it would not be entirely incorrect. And the reason is rather easy to see: since art is born of conflicting impulses which by nature cannot be reconciled, the form of art which exhibits the greatest fidelity to its own source is the art which pays tribute to irreconcilable differences. The highest form of such art works is tragic art. Furthermore, Nietzsche notes that the consummation of tragic art presents itself in Attic tragedy, at the moment these impulses each come into being as themselves, the moment in which the struggle is most intense and still without a history.

When Nietzsche suggests that the origin of tragic art is found in Greece he is not relying upon any chronological sense of firstness. Greece is not an origin by virtue of some sort of chronology or history. Rather it deserves to be acknowledged as the origin, as the locus of the first birth, of tragedy because of proximity to the sources of art which one finds there. It first introduces tragedy as an art form not because it starts an innovation in the realm of art, but because it moves close to the natural sources, the original impulses, of life itself. Greece is the site of the birth of tragedy because one finds in Greece a culture which encourages rather than inhibits the drives proper to art; the origin is determined by the character of nature and aesthetics, not by chronology, and the perspective from which this is first visible is the perspective of life itself.[32] This is the point from which Nietzsche will come to the conclusion which he repeats three times in the text, namely, that "it is only as an *aesthetic phe-*

nomenon that existence is justified."[33] But Greece is the origin of the art which most directly accomplishes this—tragic art—because its culture resembles the original nature out of which such art emerges. More precisely, "Greece" is the name of a culture which is not afraid to confront the deep and unresolvable conflict of these drives, as well as the suffering which is the consequence of such conflicts: "In the Greeks the 'will' wished to see itself directly, in the transfiguration of genius and in the world of art; in order to glorify itself, its creations had to find themselves worthy of glorification, they had to see themselves repeated in a higher sphere. . . . This is the sphere of beauty, in which they saw their mirror images, the Olympians. With this beautiful mirroring the Hellenic 'will' combated its artistically correlative talent for suffering and for the wisdom of suffering."[34] The genius of Greece is found in the way in which a readiness for suffering transfigures itself. Of course, this means that the true root of the work of art is found in the capacity for great suffering. The revised title which Nietzsche gives the book when he republishes it with the new self-critical preface gives some indication of this point and a sign that he believes it is in need of greater emphasis: the new title refers to "Greece and Pessimism." In short, the despair which is the companion of this friction proper to the will is what Nietzsche wants to bring into sharper focus. And so he says as well in the new preface that the basic question of the book is "the relation of the Greeks to pain."[35] Referring to what he calls "Greek folk wisdom," Nietzsche cites Sophocles as a way of clarifying how deep this consciousness of the relation of pain and life runs in the Greek world. Speaking through the "wise Silenus, companion of Dionysus," he repeats a passage from *Oedipus at Colonus* as the most compact expression of this folk wisdom: "Oh wretched race of ephemeral people, children of chance and misery, why do you compel me to tell you what it would be most expedient for you never to hear? That which is best of all is utterly unattainable for you: not to be born, not to be, to be *nothing.* But the second best for you—to die soon."[36] The Greeks are the masters of tragic art because they are so singularly capable of suffering, and the genius of the Greeks is that they allowed themselves to suffer the struggle of the deepest impulses of life and thereby to give birth to tragic art.

The process of this development of art is a complex one that passes through both epic and lyric poetry. Tragedy is not born in one instant and without a struggle between the forms of art which are represented here by Homer and by Archilochus. The brief sections (5 and 6) in which Nietzsche takes up this process, which he describes as a "labyrinth," present a view that is startlingly similar to the history of Greek art one finds in Hegel. Despite every difference—and to be sure there are differences—Nietzsche sets up the arrival of the tragic form as something like a dialectical sublation of the disparate achievements of epic and lyric poetry. However, once tragic art does arrive as an art form everything becomes different: a leap in the forms of the consciousness of life and of suffering is made. Nietzsche is confident that the nature of this leap, the originality of tragedy, has yet to be grasped: "I do not think I am unreasonable in saying the problem of the origin [of tragedy] has as yet never been seriously posed."[37] The reason for this is simple: no one has yet understood the role that physiological phenomena—dreams and rapture—play in the formation of tragic art. Hegel, for instance, might have well understood the movement of the logic of the various poetic forms which lead up to tragedy, but he never grasped the abyssal depths which are the impulse driving this movement to tragedy. In Nietzsche's language, he never understood the Apollonian and the Dionysian drives of life which we suffer. But this point is fundamental, and without it misunderstandings abound. For instance, without an appreciation of the fundamentality of the dream world, of the Apollonian, one cannot understand the inversion of the classical schema of mimesis to which Nietzsche alludes when he speaks of the "veil of Maya." In the end, the dream world is what the waking world "imitates." "The sphere of poetry does not lie outside of the world, as a fantastic impossibility spawned by a poet's brain: it desires to be precisely the opposite, the unvarnished expression of truth."[38] The dream is the truth that the conscious life is struggling to comprehend.[39] *Conscious life is the fiction from which art struggles to wake us.* The tragic work of art is not imitative of life; rather, conscious life is what imitates the truth of the tragic work. Here, then, is the final inversion of the classical scheme of mimesis which sees the work of art as a copy of a real world.

When Nietzsche begins to elaborate upon the origin of tragic art he does so by remarking how it emerges out of this primal phenomenon of art which conscious life mimes. He begins to do this by noting a truth found in the otherwise misguided tradition of efforts to give an account of tragedy, namely, that "tragedy arose out of the tragic chorus."[40] While he will align himself with this view that the chorus was the site of the real proto-drama, he will not subscribe to the two concomitant traditional views which suggest that the chorus is either an "ideal spectator" or the "representative of the people."[41] Instead, he sees in the chorus "the self-mirroring of the Dionysian man,"[42] and more precisely it is "the only reality" out of which the so-called "action" of the tragedy is generated as the discharge of Apollonian images. The action and the dialogue of the tragedy, the drama, is the Apollonian dream world of the Dionysian chorus: "Thus the choral parts, which are woven throughout the tragedy, are, in a certain sense, the womb of the whole of the so-called dialogue, that is of the entire world of the stage, of the real drama."[43] Thus the chorus should not be taken as rendering a running commentary on the action or the dialogue of the drama; rather, the action and dialogue need to be understood as dream images of the chorus, which is the true heart of the tragic work. The tragedy is thus the Apollonian dream image of a Dionysian nature. But this means both that the "action" of the tragedy moves according to the nonlinear logic of dream, and, more importantly, that the erotic tension, the powerful conflict and struggle, between the Apollonian and the Dionysian is the heart which provides the beat of the tragic work as a whole. Furthermore, since this dynamic cannot be grasped according to the linear logic of the concept, metaphor is the natural form in which it is exhibited: "Metaphor, for the genuine poet, is not a rhetorical figure, but a vicarious image that he truly beholds in place of the concept."[44]

So the struggle of the Apollonian and Dionysian impulses which form the basic drives of life is not only the productive impulse which drives human being to make works of art; it is equally, perhaps more so, the struggle which is being played out in every tragic work no matter what the specifics of the dialogue or the action depict. This is the leap that must be taken for the tragedy to come to be: "The drama is the Apollonian embodiment of Dionysian insights and effects and is for this reason separated by a monstrous gap from the epic."[45] Everything becomes different with the formulation—which is really to be understood as a sort of liberation of the deepest drives of nature itself—of the tragedy. What is produced in the tragic work is a transfiguring mirror, a vision in which one sees life itself, above all one's own conflicted life, displayed. Seeing the tragedy is for us akin to the capacity to dream the dream of another: it is strange, displacing—one might even say that it is "othering"—and yet it is for these reasons very much a matter of seeing oneself. In short, tragedy is the sublime, the uncanny, experience of the self itself, and in this experience of the self—without ground, without fundament, or any glassy essence—the deepest impulses defining the self display themselves and their monstrous strangeness. In this way, the tragedy is the supreme form in which one may contemplate oneself. In the tragedy one "sees oneself transformed before one's own eyes and to begin to act as if one really were in another body, in another character. . . . Here we have a surrender of individuality. . . . And this phenomenon happens epidemically: a whole throng feels itself enchanted in this manner."[46] The performance of the tragedy—especially as it was performed in ancient Athens where it did not function as a bourgeois cultural escape, but as an event of the city involving all its citizens—is a sort of mass Dionysian event since it is an event in which "excess reveals itself as truth [and] contradiction, the bliss born of pain, speaks from out of the very heart of nature."[47]

Nietzsche introduces a brief discussion of Sophocles' *Oedipus at Colonus* by describing what happens in the tragedy with powerful words: "The language of the Sophoclean heroes so surprises us with their Apollonian precision and lucidity that we have the sense that we are looking into the innermost ground of their being, with some astonishment that the path to this ground is so short."[48] But this image of the hero is but a mask, a "bright image projected on a dark wall," which is there to protect us from the deeper, the abyssal, truth which the tragedy discloses. The character of the hero is not yet the heart of the tragedy, not yet the depth which it can reveal, and if we linger too much, too long, on a concern for the character, then we will never see into the dark truth of the tragedy: "When after a mighty effort to look directly at the sun we turn away blinded, we see dark colored spots in our eyes which are there as a sort of cure: conversely, the luminous images of the Sophoclean hero—in short, the Apollonian aspect of the mask—are necessary products of a glimpse into the interior and the terror of nature; they are illuminating spots which cure eyes which have been damaged by gruesome night."[49] With this said, with the understanding that the trials of the hero are not, in the end, the true focal point of the tragedy, Nietzsche turns to *Oedipus at Colonus* in order to speak of the "monstrous suffering" of Oedipus, who is the "most sorrowful figure" of the Greek stage. Of course, as we turn to the figure of Oedipus we do so with the understanding that, in a curious way, the image of the blind Oedipus "protects" us from what we really are seeing in the tragedy.

The choice of *Oedipus at Colonus* as the tragedy which will provide the model for Nietzsche's reflections up to this point is significant. Most interesting is that he zeroes in upon the image of Oedipus there as, in the end, possessing a magical power, one that remains effective even after his death, that is somehow wedded to the manner in which he has endured his suffering: "In *Oedipus at Colonus* we encounter the same clarity, but one that is raised up in an infinite transfiguration; this old man, facing an excess of misery, abandoned purely to *suffer* what befalls him, is confronted by the otherworldly clarity that descends from the divine sphere and this suggests to us that the hero attains his highest activity, which extends far beyond his life, in his purely passive behavior."[50] Nietzsche tries to understand how this magical calm and clarity has descended upon Oedipus by noting that "There is an ancient popular belief, found especially in Persia, that a wise magus can only be born from incest; with respect to the riddle-solving and mother-marrying Oedipus we must immediately interpret this to mean that where prophetic and magical powers have broken the spell of present and future—the rigid law of individuation—and in general the real magic of nature, some monstrous unnaturalness—such as incest—must be presupposed as a cause."[51] Oedipus has so radically removed himself from nature ("the man who solves the riddle of nature—that Sphinx of two species—must, as the murderer of his father and the spouse of his mother, break the most sacred of natural orders")[52] that he is in a position to know the Dionysian wisdom, the wisdom that cannot be imparted except through the most radical experience of becoming "other." "Wisdom is a crime against nature,"[53] and this crime is Dionysian in character since it is a crime of excess and self-forgetfulness, a crime of desire. That is why Nietzsche is able to say that "The tradition is undisputed that Greek tragedy in its earliest form had for its sole theme the sufferings of Dionysus."[54] Once this privilege of the Dionysian in the birth and nature of the tragic work of art is established the general features of the birth of tragedy are completed. At this point the character of its coming to be and the basic elements which define its nature have been exposed. Above all, the upper hand of the Dionysian in the work of tragic art needed to be made clear before it could be said that the birth of tragedy had been prepared.

But immediately on the heels of this birth the death of tragedy is announced. This means that the tragic work lives a very short life in this text about its "birth" since the beginning of section 11 begins to try to fathom the nature of the death of tragedy (the birth begins in section 7, so only four of the twenty-five sections of this book are devoted to the birth and life of tragedy). In fact, the question of the death of tragedy and of the possibility of the rebirth of tragedy in the modern world will hold Nietzsche's attention far longer than the analysis of its first birth and life. Nietzsche, like all others who take the question of tragedy to heart, cannot help but be struck by the brevity of the active life it had in Greece. If one thinks of the history of this art as moving largely from Aeschylus to Euripides, then its history is only about a century long.[55] Nietzsche will tacitly allude to this brevity later when he writes that "it is true in all things that the favorites of the gods die early, but it is equally true that then they live eternally with the gods. One ought not demand of what is noblest of all that it have the durable toughness of leather."[56] But it is not simply the brevity of the life of the tragic form which so strikes Nietzsche, it is rather that tragedy died at the hands of a tragedian. When this death is announced as happening in the form of death appropriate to tragedy, it dies as a form of art by suicide, "as the result of an unresolvable conflict."[57] Tragedy "died tragically, while all the other arts passed away calmly and beautifully at a ripe old age."[58]

Euripides will be the author of tragedy's suicide; his manner of presenting the tragic form will script the moves according to which the Apollonian and Dionysian struggle is displaced—and eventually replaced—and, as a consequence, the life blood of tragedy is drained away. He will do this by means of a simple, yet fateful, gesture: he will place the spectator on the stage of the drama. Euripides will attempt to give the stuff of tragedy the veneer of "reality"; in other words, he will try conscientiously to depict "everyone" as the possible hero of his tragedies by taming the passion of his language and by rendering the strangeness of the tragedy—its deepest Dionysian element—ordinary: "Through Euripides, the human being of everyday life forced his way from the spectator's seats to the stage, the mirror in which previously only great and bold traits found expression, now showed with embarrassing fidelity even the misfired contours of nature."[59] What happens is that the strangeness, the otherness, which is proper to the fully developed tragic work is muted, and the spectator, the one who should experience the tragedy as a radically disturbing work, now sits in judgment of the "accuracy" of the work. Now the spectator, rather than being moved by the work, sits in judgment of it. No longer a form in which the deeper drives and desires of life are displayed and set free, the tragic work now becomes a form in which the conscious life, the intellect rather than the dark drives of the Dionysian, finds its validation. When this happens, the life of the tragic work, the life that depended upon the hidden reservoirs of life being let loose, is over. The shell of tragic art, the corpse of the erotic tension between the Dionysian and the Apollonian, is all that remains, and this becomes fodder for the comedic poets. When he says this, Nietzsche seems to have Aristophanes' *The Frogs* in mind, a fascinating work in which Dionysus must travel to the realm of the dead (and in this the resemblance to the "Myth of Er" in Plato and book 11 of Homer's *Odyssey* should not be overlooked) in order to bring back good tragic writing to Athens. The choice is between Euripides and Aeschylus: Aeschylus is chosen while Euripides plays the role of the popularizer who does not grasp the depth of the possibilities of the tragic, and so in the end Dionysus brings Aeschylus back to life. It is a very nontragic comment on the state of tragedy after Euripides.

But Nietzsche is clear that while Euripides might be the immediate figure effecting the suicide of tragic art, he is not the greatest force which leads to its death: "Even Euripides was, in a certain sense, only a mask; the divinity which spoke through him was not Dionysus, not even Apollo, but rather a completely new born daemon named *Socrates*. This is the new opposition: the Dionysian and the Socratic, and the art work of Greek tragedy fell to pieces on it."[60] The duplicitous and erotic relation of the Dionysian and Apollonian impulses, displaced by Euripides, is now replaced by the new relation—one defined by simple opposition and lacking all passion—between Socrates and Dionysus. The dreaming element of the tragedy, its Apollonian impulse, is now occupied by the conscious intellect which is the chief characteristic of the Socratic. But it was this dream element which gave the tragedy its life as the dream of the Dionysian chorus. Now the Apollonian is suppressed by conscious life; gone is the unconscious freedom of the dream, and with this the Dionysian is rendered impotent and unable to express itself, to free itself in the projections of its dreams. Even more, the relationship between the Socratic and the Dionysian lacks all passion, it lacks the eros which was the character of the Dionysian and Apollonian relation, and this means that the fundamentally Dionysian nature of the source, the site of the birth, of tragedy is removed. Socrates becomes the opponent of the Dionysian. Philosophy wages war with all that the Dionysian sets free: ecstasy, rapture, otherness, strangeness, and the forgetting of the self. This is how the death of tragedy, which begins with Euripides but ends with Socrates, is played out. When Socrates moves to exile the tragic poets in the *Republic* and *Laws* he is simply making a gesture that completes a process begun by Euripides. The link between Socrates and Euripides is a strong one for Nietzsche, so much so that he recounts what he takes to be an ancient rumor that "Socrates used to help Euripides write his plays."[61] But whatever the specifics of its death are, whatever role is to be accorded to Euripides and to Socrates, what most needs to be understood is that the death of tragedy belongs to its own truth and destiny.

Nietzsche suggests that "With the death of Greek tragedy a monstrous sense of deep emptiness was felt everywhere."[62] But this void did not remain for long since it is precisely this sense of vacancy that becomes the locus of the new opposition between the Socratic and Dionysian. It is out of this void left by the death of tragedy that philosophy will grow, and it will grow lacking the life blood of the drives of nature that characterize the tragic work of art. What happens with this growth of philosophy in the place once occupied by the Apollonian is that now the force of dream life is taken over by the force of conscious life; the claims of the logic of the dream are supplanted by the claims of the logic of the concept. Now "to be beautiful, everything must be intelligible."[63] What Euripides begins, Socrates perfects, namely, the substitution of conscious intelligence for the unconscious power of the dream. Now the rational mind and logical inference govern, and with this new legislation of the logical the tragic work of art is no longer able to be seen since, as the very first sentence of *The Birth of Tragedy* has argued, the tragic cannot be perceived by logical inference. The death of tragedy is rendered forgotten, invisible as it were, by virtue of the way in which Socrates has dislodged the possibilities of even registering the force of the tragedy. Now it will need to be reborn, reanimated, if even its original, Greek, forms are to be set free. But that, of course, is what Nietzsche understands himself to be doing in this book and, one might argue, in every book he will ever write.

One prong of what will prove to be the multipronged task of the overcoming of philosophy and the displacement of tragic art that it perfects in the wake of tragedy's own suicide is to call the force behind this displacement by its real name, to show the "truth" of Socratism. Nietzsche does this when he writes

A key to the essence of Socrates is offered to us in that wonderful appearance which is designated as the "daimonion of Socrates." In exceptional circumstances, when his monstrous intellect faltered, he found a firm support in the divine voice which expressed itself in such moments. When it comes, this voice *dissuades*. The instinctive wisdom only shows itself in this thoroughly abnormal nature in order to *hinder* conscious knowledge here and there. While in all productive people it is the instinct that is the creative-affirmative power, and it is consciousness that operates critically and dissuasively, in Socrates it is instinct that becomes the critic, and consciousness that becomes the creator—a true monstrosity per defectum![64]

The monsters do not disappear with the arrival of Socratism; rather, a new form of monstrosity appears—it appears in the form of "the monstrous driving force of logical Socratism which is set in motion *behind* Socrates and which must be intuited through Socrates as through a shadow."[65] Now instead of the blinded Oedipus, we are confronted with "the Cyclops eye"[66] of Socrates which is focused above all else on the tragic form, which must be dislodged if Socratism is to live and thrive. Everything natural, all the passions of life, are drained away. Now "the Apollonian tendency has withdrawn into the cocoon of logical schematism . . . the Dionysian has been translated into naturalistic affects."[67] Reason triumphs and with it comes an optimism, a faith rooted in the progress of reason which knows its own dialectical nature, that becomes the final signal of the death of tragedy: "Optimistic dialectic drives *music* out of tragedy with the scourge of its syllogism; that is, it destroys the essence of tragedy, which can be interpreted only as a manifestation and projection into images of Dionysian states, as the visible symbolizing of music, as the dreamworld of a Dionysian rapture."[68]

. Here, then, in the analysis of the death of tragedy, we find the first substantive reference to what the subtitle of the first printing of this book named as that out of which tragedy grows: *music*. Here too is a reference to the end station of the form of philosophizing which begins with Socrates: *dialectic*, which is the final other of music, the ultimate form of the death of tragedy, and thus what most of all needs to be overcome. Now a new type of existence is formed, one modeled after the life, and, even more, after the death of Socrates—the life of the *theoretical man*, the life of one who no longer lives, but seeks only to know life in order to try to "observe" and ultimately to "correct" it. Socrates' position at the outset of the *Republic*—sitting apart from the festival and the celebrations that were being held, not participating, only observing and judging—is emblematic of the detachment of the theoretical person from the celebration of life. Likewise, later, when Socrates exiles the tragic poets from the city which he concocts in speech, that exile of poetry needs to be understood as the exile of the final form in which the body and its desires are preserved. Governed by the unshakeable faith that reason can know the abyssal depth of nature, of life, and guided by a suppression of all that has to do with the Dionysian impulses of desire, such an existence is the sign of the extreme repression of the flow of life in the human being. That is why Nietzsche suggests that Socrates is the chief turning point, the "vortex," of what is called "world history."

But there is a necessary chink even in this brittle and arid form of existence which defines the theoretical life. The more rigorous the fidelity to the dialectic of reason, the more reason is spurred on by the illusion of its inexorable perfection, the more surely it will—of necessity—speed relentlessly toward its own limits, to the point at which "its optimism, concealed in the essence of logic, fails . . . [and one] gazes into that which cannot be illuminated. When one sees to one's horror, how logic coils up upon itself at these limits and finally bites its own tail—then a new form of knowing breaks through, *the tragic knowledge,* which, in order to be endured, needs art as a protection and a remedy."[69] The trajectory of Socratism, the destiny of the theoretical life which commits itself to the illusion of infinite clarity, is to recoil upon itself, to consume itself when, true to the dispassionate obsession of its drive for completeness, it meets its limits. At that point it must begin to discover again the depth of the tragic—but only on the condition that it no longer subscribes to its own illusions. One suspects that Nietzsche might have Kant's discovery of the limits of pure reason in mind here; in other words, he might be granting that, against his own delusions, Kant does indeed begin to widen the fissures in the illusion of completeness which governs the theoretical life. Nietzsche never traces how it is that these limits are eventually exposed. He does suggest, however, that this ideal of the theoretical life never really deluded itself as completely as it might have pretended: "For with respect to art, that despotic logician occasionally had the feeling of a gap, a void, of half a reproach, a possibly neglected duty. Often, as he tells his friends in prison, there came to him the same apparition in a dream which always said the same thing: 'Socrates, make music!'"[70] Just as the seeds of the death of tragedy belonged to its origins and evolution, so too do the seeds of the collapse of the theoretical life belong to its own origins. But this collapse is still in need of the forces which would accelerate it; for life to return to culture, for the deep, abyssal impulses of nature to be freed, Socratism and the ideal of the theoretical life must be cleared away. The final rubble of this world historical event, this death of the sources which give birth to tragedy and so liberate life to be suffered, is what Nietzsche finds in his present. Now the task is to marshal the forces which would give a new birth to tragedy. For that to happen, and happen it must, philosophy must give way to art. This is the same move that Nietzsche will find so crucial years later when he writes in the collection which will be published after his death under the title *The Will to Power* that "we have art, lest we perish of the truth."[71]

And so Nietzsche finds it necessary to speak of the *rebirth of tragedy*. In fact, one could fairly argue that such a phrase would be equally justified as a title for this entire book, so basic is his concern with its possibility here.

Like Hegel, with whom he sets himself in the most intense of quarrels, Nietzsche regards the present age as a time of exhaustion and consequently as a time of transformation. Later he will make this quite explicit: "What does this monstrous historical need—the collecting of numberless other cultures, the consuming desire for knowledge—of dissatisfied modern culture point to if not the loss of myth, to the loss of the mythical home, of the mythical maternal womb?"[72] Living at a moment of rapid technological progress and astonishing transformations in the material conditions of life—by and large thanks to the very theoretical tendencies of the West which Nietzsche finds anathema to all he hopes to restore and liberate—he nonetheless finds that what "blessed hope" there might be for "Germany" will come not from any so-called "progress," but from the possibility of a rebirth of tragedy. Understanding why this is the case, and understanding how it might come to pass, is the task of the final sections of the text. Doing that will require gaining an appreciation of the hitherto hidden roles of what is most lacking in the modern world: music and myth.

*　　*　　*

The recovery of music, out of the spirit of which tragedy will be shown to have been born, is the highest task. Now it is requisite that music win its preeminent place among the arts, showing itself to be the supreme form of the tragic possibilities of art. Here, at least until Nietzsche writes the self-critical preface of 1886, Wagner plays the leading role. It is a role in German culture which needs to be understood as analogous to the role that Sophocles played in Greek culture. Citing Wagner, Nietzsche opens this final section of *The Birth of Tragedy* by suggesting that it is only once art is shorn of its relation to the category of beauty that the insight of music—indeed, any form of art—can begin to be intuited: "When the essence of art is conceived (as it commonly is) according to the sole category of appearance and of beauty the tragic cannot in truth be derived; only out of the spirit of music do we understand the pleasure in the annihilation of the individual."[73] First, then, one must dispense with the very notion of beauty if the achievement of the work of art is to be set free. The death of the beautiful in art is the first step in the recovery of the work of art. Of course, this does not imply that the other of the beautiful is what is now required. It means simply that the category of the beautiful—the sole signature of the work of art for Kant, Hegel, and Schelling—must be shown to be thoroughly inappropriate to the force of the work of art. The notion of the beautiful, of the work of art as somehow soothing, is at best irrelevant to what is presented in the work of art. At the worst, it is an active distortion and distraction from the work.

What is needed, says Nietzsche, is the capacity to grasp the "joy in the annihilation of the individual." But that, of course, is nothing other than the capacity for the Dionysian. Now, however, he does not elaborate upon the character of the Dionysian by reference to rapture, but by reference to a ceaseless annihilation, and this annihilation is said to be the secret and special excellence of music. This is the distinction of music: "That it is not a copy of appearance, or more accurately, of the adequate objectivity of the will, but is rather an immediate repetition of the will itself."[74] Music is not a copy, but is the force of life itself made loud. But this force of life, this Dionysian annihilation of the individual, is time, which brings all things to nothing. Music, which is nothing but time made loud, is the true "language" of the abyssal drives of life itself. Out of its Dionysian spirit, tragedy is born. And if tragedy is to find a rebirth in the modern age, it will once again be from out of the spirit of music.

At this point Nietzsche regarded Wagner's music to be exemplary of precisely the music which can expose that art's true spirit.[75] The reason Wagner stands out so clearly among those who make music is twofold: he is distinctive by virtue of the specific character of his music, especially the role of *dissonance* in his music; and he is distinctive because he has recovered the relation to *myth* which is requisite for art to live once again. In the gesture toward Wagner, the political and national character of the issues Nietzsche is raising first becomes evident.[76] This element of the issues under discussion will become ever clearer as the text advances its argument.

For now, though, the point Nietzsche is most keen on establishing and unfolding is the nature of music itself. Initially he speaks of it as a sort of "language," saying that music "is in the highest degree a universal language, which is even related to the universality of concepts much like concepts are related to individual things."[77] Looked at in this way, music appears to be a sort of super-language, language in the extreme form of its possibilities, a superior language which is more universal even than the universality which belongs to concepts. And yet, because it is universality in the utmost, it must be said that music works on a more elemental plane and is more all encompassing than the word can ever claim to be. Even concepts, the mother tongue of philosophizing, with their claim to universality are but disparate and distinct atoms when compared with the primordial embrace and sway of music. However, even with the clear caveats it places upon itself, it is obvious that this analogy with language and its special kinship with the concept is problematic if for no other reason than as Nietzsche has already indicated—in the very first sentence of the text— because the concept and the form of thinking proper to it cannot grasp the depths of the work of art. It is so problematic, in fact, that it represents only a dead end for one who would pursue the paradox of trying to think, to fathom in words, the true nature of the musical. In the end, what needs to be said is that words cannot reach the dark dissolution that is exposed in musical dissonance. Likewise, music will always need to be understood as outstripping the potential of the word; music always debases language, even the language of poetry, to the level of reflection. So, rather than pursuing the conception of music which would liken it to a language, even a superior language, Nietzsche moves to underscore the unique character of music by referring to the special temporality which drives the possibility of music. True music for Nietzsche—music which, like the tragic work of art to which it gives birth, opens up the experience of suffering—is the music of passage. And true music, which does not give comfort to such suffering, does not plaster over the irreconcilability at work in time, is the music of dissonance. This music of dissonance suffered, this music which is able to be fused with the magic of a Dionysian rapture and which is wedded to the symbolic potential of myth, is what Nietzsche finds in Wagner's music. Clearly everything comes down to this spirit of music which Nietzsche believes—at least at this time—that one finds set free in Wagner. But before the full force of this new music, this "music of the future," can be felt, the final residues of Socratism need to be confronted and exorcized from contemporary culture.

*   *   *

Before one can be freed to the experience which music unleashes—before one can "really, for a brief moment be primordial being itself and feel the raging desire for existence and joy in existence; the struggle, the agony, the annihilation of appearances"[78]—one needs to free oneself from the delusion of being able to heal the eternal wound of existence by virtue of the Socratic passion for knowledge. Implicit in this claim is the view that thinking is not immune to its cultural conditions and the force of history. There is the tacit assumption of a hermeneutic force that needs to be confronted and destroyed, namely, that the language and presumptions with which one begins are not neutral matters. This sense that the force of history is effective and potent is a point that Nietzsche would make in several forms throughout his life. It would lead him to write one of the most quietly desperate sentences to be found in his work: "I fear we shall believe in God so long as we possess grammar."[79] In *The Birth of Tragedy*, however, the concern is simple and clear: for the spirit of music to be heard, for the grounds for the rebirth of tragic art to appear, the legacy of that which supplanted Greek tragedy, namely, Socratism, must be destroyed. The name of the cultural form which is the institutionalized form of Socratism—the residue of the force which hastened and consolidated the death of Greek tragedy—is Alexandrian culture: "Our whole modern world is entangled in the net of Alexandrian culture and it holds as its highest ideal the *theoretical man* who labors in the service of science and is armed with the highest forms of the power of knowledge—the archetype and progenitor of this ideal is Socrates."[80] One might suggest that we are not yet in a position to fully hear this music of the future, and as its prelude we need to shed the final delusions born of the culture grown out of the death of tragedy.

The supreme delusion concerns knowledge, and it is expressed by a "faith in the explicability of nature and the universal panacea of knowledge."[81] In Nietzsche's eyes no one embodies this faith more exactly than Hegel, who at one point goes so far as to promise "the thought of God before creation."[82] Socrates might be the inventor, the exemplary first figure, of the ideal life in Alexandrian culture, but Hegel is its end station, its perfection. Not surprisingly, one finds in Hegel the expression of what Nietzsche takes to be the obstacle which such a faith in the explicability of nature poses for the disclosure of the deepest life of nature: in Hegel we find the conviction that ultimately "the wounds of spirit heal and leave no scars behind."[83] Yet it is precisely this soteriological conviction, this view that in the end reconciliation is possible and suffering—in whatever form it might take—comes to an end, which stands as the greatest obstacle to the capacity to hear the music of suffering and dissonance, the music out of which tragic art might be reborn. Nietzsche puts this point eloquently when he writes, "It is an eternal phenomenon: by means of an illusion spread over things, the insatiable will always find a way to detain its creatures in life and to compel them to continue to live. One is held prisoner by the Socratic passion for knowledge and the mad delusion that with knowledge one can *heal the eternal wound of existence*."[84] Later in his life Nietzsche will let this thought play a key role in the story of how his own hero, Zarathustra, will speak when he says, "Pain speaks: go away! But all pleasure wants eternity—wants deep, deep eternity."[85] The dream of healing the wound of existence, of putting an end to suffering, amounts to the dream of arresting time. Since it is out of the readiness to suffer that the full force of the lacerating experience of time in music is heard, this dream of ending suffering, which is simply the final delusion of the Socratism, stops up the ears which would hear the Siren's song of music. It was the Greek readiness for pain, their capacity to permit themselves to suffer, which let them be the culture in which tragedy was born. It was a failure of courage that gave rise to the optimistic dialectic of philosophizing. Born of weakness and passivity, the cultural forms which the ideal of the theoretical man produced stand as the props which block music. The overcoming of these forms, above all the overcoming of philosophy, is the prerequisite for any grasp of the deeper truth that music exposes. This project of the critique of culture will become ever more important for

Nietzsche as the years progress, and will reach an even more feverish pitch in the last works. While that later critique will focus on the passive nihilism of contemporary cultural life, and the language of Alexandrian culture will by and large fade away, the structure, intent, and shape of the later critiques of nihilism will be very much indebted to the critique of Alexandrian culture that is developed in conjunction with this project of paving the way for the rebirth of tragedy.

The signs of Alexandrian culture are everywhere and, of course, are even, perhaps above all, felt in the art works proper to such a culture; after all, this monstrous metamorphosis is, at bottom, a dislocation of the elemental artistic impulses at the root of life: "Is it not to be supposed that the highest and most truly serious task of art . . . must degenerate to an empty and distracting tendency toward diversion under the influence of Alexandrian flatteries?"[86] But in the final analysis it is Christianity that needs to be understood as the final perfection of this dislocation of the instinct of life, and thus it represents the form in which the possibility of the tragic is effaced in a fundamental manner. So the emblems and signals of this dislodging of life, of the decadence of Alexandrian culture, show themselves in various forms, all of which must be overcome for tragic art to reappear and redirect the possibilities of life in culture. For instance, Nietzsche suggests that with regard to drama one finds such symptoms in the deus ex machina and the dénouements of new dramatic forms; and with regard to the real lives of those who submit themselves to its delusions, one finds in it the reflection of life and desire, in the mortification of the body and in a basic fear of life: "It is certainly a sign of the 'rupture' which everyone is now accustomed to speak of as the primal malady of modern culture that the theoretical man, terrified of and dissatisfied with his own consequences, no longer dares to trust himself to enter the icy current of existence: he runs timidly up and down the bank . . . he no longer wants to have anything whole."[87] Throughout his life much of Nietzsche's energies would be devoted to criticizing these symptoms of the decline of Alexandrian culture and the weak nihilism, the resentment toward life it props up. He engages in this critique in order to destroy these symptoms and to make way for new cultural forms. Yet this project of the destruction of the symptoms of decline that mark modern life, this project of philosophizing with a hammer, is ultimately not complete until there is a restoration of the possibilities of tragic art. Then and only then is the "cause," the real root of this nihilistic and life-denying culture addressed, since it is the lack of the possibility of a properly tragic art that first lets this Alexandrian culture take root and develop.[88]

But the cracks in the Alexandrian culture have begun to appear, and the first steps toward overcoming its optimistic facade and calling it by its real name have already been taken. Kant and Schopenhauer, who have placed before us the darker elements of the finitude of life and demonstrated its ineradicability, are singled out for their "monstrous courage and wisdom."[89] They have unmasked the dark riddle which lies concealed in the essence of logical reason, and they have done so from within the operations of that very same reason. Guerrilla warriors in their own, unexpected way, Kant and Schopenhauer mark the front line of the struggle to unseat the dominance of Socratism in Western culture, and they have accomplished this by using the tools of that very same Socratism. But precisely because they have begun the destruction of the pillars of Alexandrian culture from within the presumptions of that culture, they mark only the initiation of a new beginning, not its first consolidated moment. That moment will come only with the arrival of a new form of music: "Out of the Dionysian root of the German spirit a power has arisen which has nothing in common with the basic conditions of Socratic culture and can neither be explained nor excused by that culture; rather, it is felt by this culture as that which is terrible and inexplicable, as the overwhelming hostility—*German music,* which we chiefly understand in its powerful solar orbit from Bach to Beethoven, from Beethoven to Wagner."[90] This is the moment when the possibilities of tragic culture are fully prepared. It is the moment which Nietzsche's own work will announce, consolidate, and advance in one fell swoop.

Two new themes now appear with this rebirth of tragic art that follows in the wake of the overthrow of Alexandrian culture: the topic of nationality, specifically of the "German," and the topic of time. Both themes—neither of which was an issue in the first discussion of tragedy—dominate the conclusion of *The Birth of Tragedy* and saturate its most elaborated vision of tragic art. What is difficult, but nonetheless necessary, is to see how they collaborate in the new conception of the possibilities of tragedy which Nietzsche offers.

*   *   *

Nietzsche begins his effort to illuminate the prospects for a recovery of tragic art by speaking first of the significance of such a moment for Germany: "We have the feeling that the birth of a tragic era only has the significance of the return to itself of the German spirit, a blessed self-rediscovery after a long period in which monstrous powers had penetrated into it from outside and compelled it to live in a helpless barbarism enslaved to its own form."[91] Released from the servitude to the Christian and Roman influence, such a renewal of the German spirit, precisely at the point of its apogee, will lead to the recognition of the "Hellenic genius" and thereby prepare the way for the establishment of "an enduring love affair between German and Greek culture."[92] How this new German spirit will be felt and what its shape will be remain open questions for Nietzsche, and yet this question is epochal in its significance. Only one parallel gives any indication of the enormity of the event signaled here: "We can only learn from the Greeks what such a miraculously sudden awakening of tragedy means for the innermost life ground of a people."[93] Only this much is clear: that this "monstrous power" is in truth a "healing power."[94] The monstrosity here is not only the magnitude of the event; it is equally what is released in the event of this renewal of tragic art. The healing element is found in the way in which the deepest forces of life are released and with them the possibility of community is established.

Nietzsche is not very clear about why it is that this element of what seems to be simply nationalism is introduced at this point. Two general reasons for this move are discernable, however: first, but perhaps least important, is the fact that all of those who are responsible for preparing the way for this rebirth of tragic art are Germans (but this is no accident for Nietzsche), and so it is the German language and mythology which will animate this new art; second, as became apparent in ancient Athens, the immediate effect of tragic art is to galvanize a "people" and to lend it an identity. Together these two points give a hint as to why Nietzsche had early on designated the question of tragedy as a "seriously German problem."[95]

While there is an obvious family resemblance between this invocation of the "German"—especially as situated in some sort of love affair with "Greece"—and the kindred claims one finds in Hegel and Hölderlin, it is also the case that something new is at work in Nietzsche's references to "the German." This new element of the concern with Germany does not, however, become clear in the first significant moment of its appearance, that is, in *The Birth of Tragedy;* it only becomes evident subsequently when Nietzsche speaks of "breeding."[96] What becomes clear in this concern with breeding is that—even if only implicitly—Nietzsche is enlisting himself in a discussion of race. This, by and large, is what separates Nietzsche's reference to "the German" from what one finds in Hegel and Hölderlin, and it is this which will profoundly complicate the question of tragedy for those who take some cues from Nietzsche, for Heidegger above all.

The history of the discussion of race in philosophy is only now beginning to be told,[97] but when it quietly leaks into Nietzsche's concerns with tragedy and the manner in which the work of art forms a community, a "people," the debate about the meaning of race is still largely unformed and lacking the most horrifying and unthinkable of its consequences. And yet it is difficult (and perhaps not even advisable) to take up the shadowy presence of the question of race in Nietzsche except from the perspective opened up by the consequences of how this topic would be answered in Germany only a few decades after the publication of *The Birth of Tragedy.* Kant and Fichte frame the discussion of race as Nietzsche will inherit it: Kant by virtue of having first elevated the notion of "race" to the level of a theoretical concept, and Fichte by joining this notion to the political concerns he announces in his *Addresses to the German Nation*.[98] Of course, Herder sits in the background of every such discussion in Germany. Although Nietzsche's remarks on these issues do not explicitly make reference to either Kant or Fichte—Darwin is rather the point of his entry into a wider debate about race and nationality—it is important to bear in mind that Kant and especially Fichte have moved the question of German identity to the point at which it is necessary to ask about the specific grounds of this identity and whether those grounds are cultural or biological. In later years it will be difficult to sort out Nietzsche's own views on this matter, but in *The Birth of Tragedy* it seems rather clear that the sense of "Germanness" attached to the rebirth of tragic art refers to a cultural, not biological, identity which is crystallized in this historical event. In the final analysis "any people—just as, incidentally, any individual—is worth only as much as it is able to press upon its experiences the stamp of the eternal."[99] The formation of a "people," as well as the decision about its achievements, is a cultural matter, not a biological one. But though this does seem to be rather clear, at bottom, Nietzsche's remarks about the "German" stand as one of the—perhaps unanswerable—puzzles of *The Birth of Tragedy*. But what can be said with some confidence about this matter is that these remarks are one more indication that the achievement of the work of art cannot be understood either logically or even solely as a matter of aesthetics; rather, the work of art saturates the whole of life, in the end it even sets into being the way life in time is shared—it defines the possibilities of "a people." The rebirth of tragic art must therefore be acknowledged as an event that is originally a political event.

While Nietzsche seems to take for granted that a national sensibility will be rejuvenated with the rebirth of tragedy, he does not speculate much about its details. The topic of the national here juts into the discussion powerfully but never coalesces into any clearly determined conclusion. It remains as vague as it is important. What does, however, come forward in the conclusion and get unpacked as the final word on the topic of tragedy in Nietzsche's first and most decisive engagement with this topic is the role which *time* plays in it. This is the genuinely new element in the understanding of tragedy which fully appears only with the second birth of tragic art. Now it can be told how it is that tragedy is born, as the subtitle of the first edition of the book says, "out of the spirit of music." If the rebirth of tragedy can be said to mark an advance in its possibilities, a sense in which something new happens with this renewal, then it is with regard to the manner in which we are now self-conscious about the vital force of time in tragic art.

Music makes this evident. Yet, somewhat to the contrary of what one might expect that its role in the rebirth of tragedy would be, music is initially explained with reference to the restoration of the Apollonian impulses of life: "Where the Apollonian received wings and was elevated

through the spirit of music, we had to recognize the most extreme intensification of its powers and thereby we had to recognize in that brotherly
bond of Apollo and Dionysus the apex of the Apollonian as well as the
Dionysian aims of art."[100] To be sure, the Apollonian impulse was the element which was replaced with the death of tragedy (whereas the Dionysian drive survived this calamity and remained in the displacement of the
dyad it formed as the counterpart to the Socratic impulse), and so it is
above all the Apollonian impulse which is most urgently in need of a re-
animation. Nonetheless, since Nietzsche initially described it with reference to the dream and to the mute image which is proper to the dream as
he understands it, one would not expect that here, from the side of the
Apollonian, music would first reawaken the erotic relation between the
Apollonian and the Dionysian. Yet such is the case. And understanding
why this is so is crucial for an appreciation of the real role of music in the
future of tragic art.

What music accomplishes is to open us to the "experience of having
to see and at the same time longing to transcend all seeing."[101] In short,
music teaches the pleasure of seeing, of images. At the same time it ne-
gates this pleasure and opens up the higher pleasure of the destruction of
the world of appearance, and in this way it sets the Apollonian in its proper
relation with the Dionysian. Nietzsche does not address this almost magical power of music in any direct fashion, though a remark he made earlier might be helpful in coming to terms with this key point. When setting
up the initial relation of the Apollonian and Dionysian Nietzsche spoke
of "sparks of images" that fly out of the Dionysian music of one who is
asleep.[102] It is a strange and yet telling phrase that serves to remind us that
not everything that goes by the name of music serves to open this realm of
the "brotherhood" of the Apollonian and Dionysian. The music that succeeds in this is capable of generating images just as the chorus of Greek
tragedy is capable of generating the image of action in the tragic drama. This "inner illumination"[103] which music is able to project—in other
words, the tendency of music to drive the listener to the point of a remarkably interior visual experience—drives the images which we produce
to the point at which we deeply feel the need to go beyond every such
image, no matter how bright and intense. At this moment one takes delight in the destruction of the world of mere appearance, and one gives
oneself over to the pure passage, the destruction, which is music. Above
all, though, in order to grasp the deepest dynamics of this musical spirit
that has the magical power to reanimate the possibility of tragic art, one
needs to seek "the peculiar pleasure one takes in the purely aesthetic
sphere, without reaching over this into the realm of pity, of fear, of the
ethically-sublime."[104] In other words, one needs to avoid any recourse to
the view that such spirit, such art, could ever be understood by being
traced back to "moral sources." Instead, what one needs to grasp in order

to accelerate the liberating forces which are ready to be released in music is that such new music presents the experiences of suffering, strangeness, dissolution, birth, desire, and the inexorability of time all at once. The spirit of the music from which tragedy is able to be reborn is thus, like Greek tragedy, beyond the grasp of logical insight and its linear operations, beyond even the reach of words; it is, rather, an event, full of complexity and contradictions, one that in the end, like tragedy, can only be called "monstrous," perhaps even "unthinkable." In short, music has the Dionysian power of opening up an experience of excess, an experience of becoming other. That it accomplishes this in the production and the destruction of the realm of appearance—that it produces sparks of images—is what lets Nietzsche suggest that this Dionysian art form breathes new life into the relation between the Apollonian and the Dionysian.

The depth of what is musical is most clearly evidenced in the original trademark of the Wagnerian music which Nietzsche finds such an inspiration in this matter:

> This primordial phenomenon of Dionysian art which is so difficult to grasp is only intelligible and conceivable in a direct manner in the wonderful significance of *musical dissonance:* generally, only music which is placed next to the world can give an idea of what is to be understood by the justification of the world as an aesthetic phenomenon. The pleasure which the tragic myth produces has the same native ground as the pleasurable sensation of dissonance in music. The Dionysian, with its primordial pleasure belonging even to pain, is the common womb of music and of tragic myth.[105]

The capacity of music for dissonance, that is, the possibility of a multiplicity of differences, even incompatible differences, to appear simultaneously, is what renders music Dionysian. In this strange lapse in the logical order of reasoning, this experience of time—that is, of life—made loud in all of its contradictions, music gives birth anew to tragic art.[106] That is why "music and tragic myth are in equal measure expressions of the Dionysian capacity of a people, and that is why they are inseparable from one another. Both derive from a realm of art which lies beyond the Apollonian; both transfigure a region in which the pleasurable chords of dissonance as well as the terrifying image of the world fade away charmingly; both play with the thorn of primal pleasure, trusting in their thoroughly powerful magical art; both justify the existence even of the 'worst world.'"[107]

Music, which is pure passage, gives this truth of tragic art to be understood even more directly, that is, wordlessly, than the first appearance of tragedy in ancient Greece was able to make evident. Music, a "Heraclitean power,"[108] is pure passage, and through it we discover the joy in the destruction of appearance and of the individual. In it there is no "revenge against time and its 'it was,'"[109] and so it stands as our most immediate mode of communication with time which is not ossified into an image of an infinite and omnipresent image of God in which there is no becoming, no life. Infinitely playful and equally the model of erotic life—for what is music but notes in ever-shifting amorous relation?—music is an expression of love and affirmation. And yet, as ceaselessly passing away, living only as the annihilation of the individual notes, music is at the same time an image of death and of mourning. That is why music—which lives by virtue of the amorous relation of the notes which themselves continually die and are born and reborn—has an essential relation both to celebration as well as to mourning. When Wagner writes the *Liebestod,* the song of the sameness of love and death, he is writing the essence of the musical as Nietzsche understands it. In the end, then, music as Nietzsche thinks it stands as a powerful reminder not that time is about the so-called "moments" of time, about the calcification of the course of time into past/present/future, but that it is about dissonance. It is the same dissonance which pertains between the Apollonian and Dionysian.

This point of dissonance is the high point of the analysis of tragic art in *The Birth of Tragedy,* and because of this it is important to conclude with the realization that this dissonance is not a cognitive notion, it is not a thought, not translatable into a word. It is the name of life for us as Nietzsche finds it revealed in tragic art. Nietzsche makes precisely this point in one of the most moving and unambiguous passages he would ever write:

> If we could think a transformation into human life of dissonance—and what else is a human being?—then, if this dissonance were to be able to live it would have need of a splendid illusion which would throw a veil of beauty over its own nature. This is the true Apollonian aim of art: in the name of Apollo we comprehend all those countless illusions of beautiful appearance, which in every moment of existence make life worth living and prompt the desire to live on in order to experience the next moment.[110]

The dissonant nature that each of us is is too shattering to bear unadorned. But, we find this same dissonance to be the source of our capacity to make art, to create that which widens the realm of the bearable by means of a splendid illusion. The plasticity of such a dissonant nature, its capacity to see itself in a transfiguring mirror, is owing to the same lively dissonance which makes art necessary if life is to be justified: "It is only as an aesthetic phenomenon that existence and the world appears as justified."[111] But this abyssal truth—this truth without stable foundation, without a secure ground—would destroy us if it were not for the Apollonian power of transfiguration which enables this elemental Dionysian ground of the world to enter consciousness in measures that can, almost, be grasped. Rilke set this point as the opening for the first of his *Duino Ele-*

gies: "For the beautiful is nothing other than the beginning of the terror which we just barely bear, and which we marvel at so because it serenely threatens to destroy us." Art achieves this, it rescues us from our own natures, and it does so in a manner far closer to this "truth" than logical reason could ever hope to even approach. That is why it is "the supreme task of life."[112]

But the significance of this dissonance—and its expression in the duplicity of the relation of the Apollonian and Dionysian, which simultaneously reveal and conceal one another in the form of art—goes even further. These two dissonant drives necessarily unfold their respective drives to art, their distinct powers, "according to the law of eternal justice."[113] This strange law, which is self-ironizing insofar as it is a law that is meted out according to the *temporality* of dissonance, is the law of reciprocity between the Apollonian and the Dionysian. It is the law proper to the human being who can bear only so much truth, who "possesses art, lest we perish of the truth,"[114] and for whom "without music life would be an error."[115] This law is the justice which is proper to mortal life, to the life of those who must create if the truth is to be both visible and bearable. In this law of reciprocities we find both an image of justice and the justification of such a mortal life. And it is this double truth, above all, which the ancient Greeks learned from their tragedies, and that is why "this people had to suffer so much in order to be able to become so beautiful."[116]

*   *   *

Populated by monsters and leaping from one abyssal experience to another, Nietzsche's conception of tragic art nonetheless sets up tragedy as a healing power. It is a transfiguring mirror in which human life reflects its own deepest, its dissonant, nature in a manner which permits the truth of that nature to appear and not simply to destroy one who would bear witness to it. What must be remembered if the true originality of such works of art is to be appreciated is that the possibility of art is itself rooted in the very same dissonant human nature. It is that nature which expresses itself most immediately in the work of art, and it is the dissonance of that nature which tragic art is supremely able to express. Because such dissonance, such ineradicable contradiction, cannot be conceived within the orbit of logical reason, such art can only be directly intuited; it cannot be known otherwise. All of Nietzsche's efforts to pay tribute to the original truth of tragic art are shadowed by this severe and unliftable impasse which reason encounters in the true work of art. His own struggle to analyze and to bear witness to the wisdom of tragic art drives him to the acrobatics of style and strategy which are the hallmarks of his writing. But, according to his own estimation, in *The Birth of Tragedy* at least, this drive to avoid the trap of logical reason is one he never fully accomplished since by his own admission "it should have *sung*, this new soul—not spoken!"[117]

Thus Spoke Zarathustra is perhaps Nietzsche's most extended answer to what he perceives as the failure of *The Birth of Tragedy*. There one finds the full performance and linguistic enactment of the Dionysian character which Nietzsche first unfolds in the context of the treatment of Greek tragedy. There, after the profound disappointment which Wagner eventually became in Nietzsche's eyes, one finds what he takes to be the form that the rebirth of tragedy would take in its second life.[118] One needs to read *Thus Spoke Zarathustra* as Nietzsche's answer to the call which he issues in *The Birth of Tragedy*, for the new tragic art initially was an art which his hopes had led him to believe would be forthcoming from Wagner.

But questions abound about the shape of this new art as Nietzsche foresees it; *Thus Spoke Zarathustra* is not the sole form it might take. Most of all the question of the word, the image, and the tone still lingers despite—or perhaps even thanks to—Nietzsche's own remarks about their respective reach. The original shape of tragic art, namely, ancient Greek tragedy, will no longer suffice as the form which such an art needs to take at the present historical juncture. And so one asks how this dissonant art will take shape in the future. Nietzsche gives some indications of how he envisions the shape of such music, but one wonders about the possibilities of language in this regard, and in the end one finally comes to ask a question which Nietzsche himself seemed to avoid, namely, if tragic art could be painted. Such question takes one back to the opening sections of *The Birth of Tragedy*, where Nietzsche makes an extended reference to Raphael's painting "Transfiguration" and gives it all the qualities which he will later describe as requisite for the deepest forms of tragic art.[119]

One ends this treatment of tragedy, then, with a renewed understanding of the radicality and originality of the achievement of Greek art. One learns as well how it has tapped into an elemental force of life, and yet, at the same time, one learns how those very same forces permitted their own displacement. And so one finds as well just how necessary it is to recover the temperament, the courage to face life, and the transfiguring power which animated such Greek art. But, of course, one discovers that such a rebirth of tragic art—which is the real aim of this book—will have a shape which, as yet, is still unknown.

6 Heidegger

The Homeric heroes knew nothing of that
cumbersome word *responsibility,* nor would they
have believed in it if they had. For them, it was
as if every crime were committed in a state of
mental infirmity. But such infirmity meant that a
god was present and at work.
——Roberto Calasso,
The Marriage of Cadmus and Harmony, p. 94

"Nietzsche hat mich kaputt gemacht"—Nietzsche did me in. Those are
words that Heidegger never wrote, at least in any of the texts which have
been published up to this point, but they are words that friends report he
uttered frequently in the years after the Second World War. Often said
without context, said enough to be a sort of litany over an extended period of time, those words would remain thoroughly enigmatic and a thorn
in the side of one who would try to take up Heidegger's thought. While it
seems clear that no one single issue could be contained in that phrase, a
good case can be made to suggest that it is above all on the topic of tragedy that Nietzsche will do Heidegger in—though it will never be entirely
clear just what it could mean to be "done in."

Heidegger's most extensive engagement with Nietzsche took place
during the period of Nazi rule in Germany. It was also the period in which
Heidegger would most directly take up the topic of tragedy (though one
could argue that it will haunt works in which it is never directly mentioned as a topic). Not insignificantly, certainly not without deliberation,
his treatment of tragedy is inevitably mediated by his readings—often
explicitly—of both Nietzsche and Hölderlin. One figure, Hölderlin, will

225

eventually come to represent the prospects of a new form of thinking; the other figure, Nietzsche, will eventually come to be seen as the final form of the metaphysical tradition which Heidegger would spend his life trying to overcome. Both, however, are preoccupations, the compatriots haunting everything Heidegger will come to say on the topic of tragedy. While Heidegger's reflections on tragedy will signal a massive expansion of the realm within which it is seen to operate, and while his understanding of tragedy will be far from confined within the orbit opened up by Hölderlin and Nietzsche, each of his efforts to come to terms with the force of tragedy will index itself in some measure to either or both of them. But Heidegger will not always take up the question of tragedy in the same terms that Hölderlin and Nietzsche addressed it. He seldom, if ever, addressed it as a literary genre, and though he will take up tragedy under the rubric of a concern with the achievement of the work of art, it is obvious that art is not the most basic frame of reference within which he thinks the question of tragedy. Although Hegel is mentioned only infrequently at best, it remains the case that Heidegger will address the topic of tragedy most of all in the context of those concerns which Hegel first articulated, namely, within the context of *history*. Tragedy will become the paradigm for thinking history; it will be set up as the model of all appearance. The coincidence of the themes of history and tragedy, first outlined by Hegel, become the overarching axis along which Heidegger's interpretation of tragedy will unfold. The assumption behind this wedding of themes is clear: the present age is understood as the time of a fated ending, the destiny of Western metaphysics has reached its necessary conclusion, and the present epoch now shows itself to be the time of the emergence of impossible conjunctions which are rooted in the conflicted, yet hidden, foundations of metaphysics. The emergence of these contradictions is the arrival of a monstrous time, a time of extremity, in which the past exposes its untenability for any possible future. Indeed, the present age needs to be understood as the time of such a far-reaching crisis that it can be understood only according to the model for thinking such monstrous contradictions and catastrophic events that is found in tragedy. Shifted to the context of the effort to think the movement of history and to come to terms with the present historical juncture, while being at the same time an ongoing dialogue with both Hölderlin and Nietzsche, Heidegger's remarks on tragedy stand as the first effort to engage not only the phenomenon of Greek tragedy and what it presents for thinking; it is also a rather explicit effort to engage the German history of the appropriation of that phenomenon. While the genuine originality of Heidegger's conception of tragedy is not confined to this creative marriage of themes and points of view, his fullest contribution to the topic of tragedy needs to be seen against the backdrop of this synthetic effort to grasp the philosophic history of the question of tragedy.

This coupling of tragedy with the question of history will find its first significant formulation in the 1930 lecture course entitled "On the Essence of Human Freedom," a course which takes Kant and Aristotle as the centerpieces for the treatment of its theme. Early in that lecture course, in the middle of trying to unfold the problematic of freedom anew and yet alert to its legacy in the Western tradition, Heidegger makes a remark which will prove to be the first quiet indication of how a few years later the question of tragedy will marry the topic of history almost explosively: "In the history of everything essential, it is the right—but also the responsibility—of all who come later to necessarily become the murderers of their predecessors, and even to stand under the destiny of a necessary murder themselves!"[1] It is a stunning remark, which is difficult to place in a context (in largest terms one might say that the context here is in general the notion of tradition and the special problem posed by reading Plato and Aristotle). While there is no overt reference to tragedy here, the schema is clear (and rather clearly Oedipal), and the sense of destiny invoked will prove to be decisive when Heidegger does finally take up the topic of tragedy explicitly. The year that this remark is made is 1930. It will be just a few years later that the thematic of tragedy will move to the center stage of Heidegger's effort to address history—and most of all his own times[2]—and when that happens the question of tragedy will turn out to be one of the most fateful questions which Heidegger will try to pose. It will also turn out to be at the heart of his struggle to understand the character of life in a community. It is not by accident that Heidegger's concern with the question of tragedy will be most active in the years 1933–46, from "The Self-Assertion of the German University" to "The Saying of Anaximander," from a period in which Heidegger suffered from the delusion that he could educate a tyrant to a period in which he finds himself recovering from a nervous breakdown. To say that this was a period of a thousand years, a time of terrible tragedy the magnitude of which Heidegger could never seem even to begin to comprehend, might not be able to do justice to what those times would set as a task for thinking. But, however blind he himself might remain to the depths to which this question would point, it is precisely this question about the reach of tragedy, its capacity to shed some light on the dark moments of history, which drives Heidegger to bring the question of tragedy forward in union with his concern with the riddles of history.

*   *   *

It would seem that Heidegger's thought was ready-made for the appropriation of tragedy and tragic themes. Early in his career he develops notions such as "the hermeneutics of facticity" (that is already found in 1922) and of the inevitability of "ruin." He says pointedly and repeatedly to his classes in those early years that "Das Leben ist diesig, es nebelt sich immer ein" [life is misty, it always shrouds itself in fog] and by this wants to refer to the inherent capacity of life to throw itself ever anew into darkness. His sense of the struggles at the heart of human existence and of truth and his strong sense of the force of history in human life—one might even say of destiny—all work together in a manner which resonates in remarkable harmony with the sensibility which animates Greek tragedy. Furthermore, the conceptions of temporality and historicity which he develops in the early works, and which culminate in the formulation they receive in *Being and Time*, are expressive of what one might designate as a tragic view of life.[3] One could even say that Heidegger's critique of the metaphysical conception of time needs to be understood as a loss of the tragic sense of time which was replaced by a Christian-metaphysical image of eternity. Couple this with a lifelong admiration for Greek language and temperament, as well as with an appreciation of the way in which truth is not confined to the forms of conceptual reason and so actively works in art, and one sees why Heidegger's thought seems ripe for the topic of tragedy. And while such would be the case above all in the middle period of his life, tragedy would not appear as a theme, even remotely so, until some years after Heidegger had solidified his reputation with the publication of *Being and Time* (1927).[4] In short, although Heidegger's work is saturated with themes and sensibilities which are readily compatible with the image of life one finds in tragedy, references to tragedy are not to be found as extensively as one might expect.

In this regard, the role of the question of tragedy in Heidegger is to be distinguished from the role it plays in Hegel, Schelling, Hölderlin, and Nietzsche, all of whom turn to tragedy in their first works. Heidegger's turn to tragedy would happen rather rapidly, just as its seeming disappearance from his work would happen equally abruptly. There are only three brief indicators of the arrival of tragedy as a theme for Heidegger. The first reference to a Greek tragedy is found in the "Kriegsnotsemester of 1919," which was a lecture course entitled "The Idea of Philosophy and the Worldview Problematic." There Heidegger contrasts the modern astronomical conception of the sunrise with the image of the sunrise found in a choral ode from *Antigone*. The translation he cites is by Hölderlin, but in the end no sense that this citation is taken from a tragedy is forthcoming, no allusion to Hölderlin's struggles to come to terms with the language of this text is made. It is simply a citation from a poetic text, one stripped of any sense of its tragic element. The second moment in which an image of tragedy is found in Heidegger's work (1930), which was mentioned above, is the cryptic reference to what one might call the logic of parental murder which governs the operations of tradition. It does not make direct reference to a tragedy and only tacitly invokes something of a tragic work. The third reference (1932) would be found one year later near the end of a lengthy lecture course on Plato. There we find the second citation from a Greek tragedy, one which refers to a passage that would be the leitmotiv of so many of the references to tragedy which would preoccupy Heidegger over the years. While offering a reading of Plato's *Theatetus,* Heidegger would make the first of many references to the first line of the choral ode of Sophocles' *Antigone,* which says that "There is much that is strange, but nothing that is stranger than human being."[5] So while one finds tangential remarks and allusions to tragedy in Heidegger's work up to and somewhat past the publication of *Being and Time,* none of these references qualify as much more than asides, none of them seeks to take up the work of tragedy on its own terms, or as a question to be unfolded. But all will refer to elements of the tragic work that eventually come to be the focus of Heidegger's concerns, namely, the poetic dimension of language, the relation of tragedy to history, and the image of human life as strange. And all of these references will prove to be typical of most of Heidegger's references to tragedy: such references are made almost invariably with a motivation which enlists the tragedy under consideration in the service of some other questions. Tragedy will always be an illustration, an example, a model for thinking (it should be said that for Heidegger every tragedy will be a Greek tragedy; unlike those who turn to tragedy before him, he will not even problematize the difference between ancient and modern tragedy). The tragedy itself will go uninterrogated. This is so clearly the case that one must hesitate before suggesting that there is something like a theory of tragedy to be found in Heidegger. There is no book on the topic of tragedy; all the references to it will be embedded in works devoted ostensibly to other topics. At most one finds a reliance upon an understanding of tragedy that is itself, by and large, unformulated. But this reliance upon an understanding of tragedy is powerful and runs deep in Heidegger's thought, perhaps all the deeper for remaining so reticent. The lack of an extended and separate consideration of the topic of tragedy—something which Heidegger shares with Hegel—does not in the least diminish the force of the idea of the tragic in Heidegger's thought. Indeed, like Hegel, one might say of Heidegger that in him one finds a truly tragic thinker. But Heidegger himself will not turn tragedy into a serious concern until 1933, and at the same moment his hitherto quiet passion for Hölderlin and Nietzsche will burst into the forefront of his concerns. And, of course, one cannot separate this development in Heidegger's thought from the historical developments which were fomenting in Germany at this time.

When Heidegger makes his next citation of a Greek tragedy, the citation which will announce the beginning of a period in which the topic of tragedy will be quietly, but nonetheless constantly, present, it will be in the context of one of the most charged events of his life. It will also be one of the greatest blunders he would ever make, one that would turn out to be an error for which he would never find an answer—either for himself or for others. In other words, the next (and the first truly substantive) reference to a Greek tragedy would appear in a text that would open up the tragedy of his life and set it against the massive and unthinkable catastrophe of history that was beginning to unfold at that moment.

The text to which I am referring is, of course, the celebrated Rector's Address, which is entitled "The Self-Assertion of the German University." It was given first (it was also given several other times outside of Freiburg) on the occasion of Heidegger's assumption of the post of Rector of the University of Freiburg. The circumstances surrounding this decision, which would prove to be a fateful one both for Heidegger and for the university, have been amply documented.[6]

The politics of this appointment—both internal to the university and external within Germany as well as the wider philosophic community—are themselves rather complicated affairs. But, details aside, it remains the case that this is an address in which Heidegger exhorts his student listeners to find their task as members of the university in the context of the essence of an understanding of intellectual life which is no longer remote from service, defense, and labor. It is a text in which, whatever he would subsequently say to the contrary, Heidegger would lend a veneer of credibility to the newly secured movement of National Socialism. It is a subtle and often complicated speech (even the title of his talk needs to be taken as an issue),[7] but it is also a speech that clearly was heard in an uncomplicated and unambiguous tone by his audience. Much needs to be said on this speech, and one day—perhaps—we will find a way to read it as a philosophical work and not simply as a political speech which permanently nourishes itself on a movement which had an agenda that by this time anyone with eyes should have seen for what it was.[8] But for the moment it seems that readings of this pivotal text still must work to struggle to free themselves from the complicity of this work in the upheavals of a history which one could argue that Heidegger's work was, on the whole, dedicated to overcoming, not furthering.

Once we do begin to find a way in which we can seriously pose the question of what it means that a philosopher of Heidegger's caliber, a thinker of the first order who had already gone far to define the course of intellectual life in the twentieth century, could not only enlist his person in the cause of National Socialism but could also seek to enlist his thought in the service of that movement, I believe that we will find that we face a similar situation with Plato.[9] Plato too thought that he could educate a tyrant and turn the tide of power in the direction of reflection and, like Heidegger, he would learn the lesson of power as the great mistake of his life.[10] In the Rector's Address Heidegger, like Plato, would try not to be a king, but to educate the tyrant. Both overestimated their power to shape the events and people who wielded power. This is a point at which the propensity of philosophizing to tyranny might need to be addressed. It might not only be a matter of individual philosophers who have committed private errors in public life. It might be much more of a question about the very character of philosophizing itself that is at stake.

Here my intention is not to try to provide a thorough reading of the Rector's Address. Nor do I intend to make any protracted effort to understand how it is that Heidegger could err so greatly. Nor do I intend to try to situate this work in the larger context of its own times in order to understand how it is that this text might have been heard and to guess what Heidegger's intentions in this speech could possibly have been. Admittedly, then, large and important questions remain to be broached with respect to this text, but for the present purposes my intent is simply to confine my remarks to the manner in which tragedy is enlisted in the service of the general themes of this text and to look at how it is that, from this point forward, tragedy will become a serious concern for Heidegger as he tries to come to terms with the human condition in the first half of the twentieth century. I do this not to evade the thorny and endlessly disturbing questions which surround this text, but to begin to open the door to how it is that one might try to read it as a philosophical document. I also do this to try to secure the general claim that I would like to make about Heidegger's turn to the topic of tragedy in these years, namely, that it is motivated by an effort to address political and ethical life. It is no accident that the text in which tragedy first wins a significant place in Heidegger's work is an overtly political address to a wider audience.

*   *   *

By the time he had assumed the post of Rector of the University and was preparing the text of "The Self-Assertion of the German University," Heidegger had already come to two conclusions that would be advanced with great force in that text: first, that the present age is best described as a time of "decision"; it is a time for which, he says, the Greeks had the apt designation *acme*.[11] Second, he had made the discovery that "the more I find my way in my own work, the more certainly I am returned to the grand beginning which is to be found in the Greeks."[12] In other words, Heidegger had come to the clear conclusion—one which had been brewing for a long time—that thinking needed to confront the depths of the crisis of the present age and that the ancient Greeks offered the best resources for precisely this task.[13] What is not yet apparent to him, but will prove to be definitive in two unbearably long years, is just how profoundly he would find Hölderlin and Nietzsche mediating his own conception of these matters.

When Heidegger assumes the Rectorship, he sets a task for himself and for members of the university. It is a task that he understands to be situated within a larger arena of concerns; ultimately it is the task which he believes is assigned to Germany at this point in history. As is the case with Plato, one finds Heidegger operating under the conviction that education does have a role in the life of a people and that the auto-plasticity of human life is best guided by a form of reflection which self-consciously struggles to free itself from uninterrogated assumptions; in short, the conviction is that "science" should have the guiding hand in the formation of the spiritual life of a people. But the larger question of science here is taken up explicitly within the context of the proximate issue of the university which is Heidegger's concern here; consequently, the question at hand concerns the place of knowing, rigorous and systematic reflection, within the realm of history, especially at a time of revolutionary transformation.[14] The immediate task is to find the proper manner in which the university can insert itself into the transformations of the present age and to affirm its own place as carrying on the spiritual mission of a people. But after clarifying this task Heidegger immediately adds that such a self-assertion presupposes a self-examination. And so Heidegger moves to the substance of his lecture by asking how it is that the university can secure itself as the site of a fundamental questioning in the present age. What is science—here, of course, the reference does not signify the natural sciences, but rigorous inquiry and knowing—supposed to be in the modern age? What is the mission of the university at the time of a distress and crisis such as the present age? Heidegger suggests that the present is a time of an essential distress, an age in which the deepest contradictions of Western culture have begun to emerge and to expose the limits of that culture, and so a countermovement to this distress is required if the spiritual life of Germany is to be recovered, if it is to rejuvenate itself as a culture. Significantly, this will happen chiefly with reference to ancient Greece and the fruits of its culture, not by means of any devotion to German works and authors.[15]

So Heidegger argues that there is a bond between the project of the university—namely, to be the locus of fundamental questioning and thus the site of such a countermovement to the failures of Western culture—and the determination of a people as a people. Whatever else it is, this text sets itself the task of speaking in rather large and sweeping terms about the nature of education and the social mission of such education (and in this it resembles Plato's *Republic* and *Laws*); it is a text which argues against the professionalization and academization of thinking that have come to dominate the university in Heidegger's time—and, of course, in ours as well. It is an argument against the force of canonical thinking and of any form of reason which lets itself be ossified by the force of tradition. And whatever else it is, this text marks the beginning[16] of Heidegger's confrontation with a new image of Greek thought, one that is markedly different than the conception of the Greeks which he seemed to articu-

late up to this point. And so this text sets itself the task of calling for a re-
form; it is a manifesto for the self-assertion and self-affirmation of the true
task of the university, a task which goes beyond the issues found in the
technical and administrative organization of an institution.[17] But at bottom it is a text which is based upon the proposition that a philosophical
and spiritual effort can still triumph over sheer political power. It is a work
which expresses great faith in the power of knowledge to lead. Even if the
philosopher cannot become the king, the king can still be educated by
the philosopher. The political will readily subordinate itself to the force
of the philosophical. Such was Plato's delusion. It would be Heidegger's
as well.[18]

In the course of trying to lay out this project which would link education, history, a people, and science in a time of distress, Heidegger somewhat abruptly makes reference to the power of original moments, and he
suggests that among the most durable of such original moments is what
we find at the moment of the eruption of Greek philosophy. This moment
of eruption, of radical innovation, is precisely what is needed in the present age, and so it is to the Greeks that Germany must turn as an answer to
the distress of the present age. There, in the moment of the emergence,
the purely original moment, of philosophy, Heidegger claims that we find
two of the most salient features of the essence of science which must be
won back, must be repeated, if the present age is to overcome its own
distress. He introduces these decisive points by making reference to the
figure of Aeschylus's Prometheus, whom Heidegger calls "the first philosopher."[19] Such a remark comes as quite a surprise. Heidegger suggests
that such a view is a "long-standing claim of the Greeks," but that suggestion too comes as a surprise; it does not help much to justify the claim.
And so one is pressed to ask how it is that Prometheus, this figure of myth
and of a tragedy, needs to be recognized as "the first philosopher"?

The answer to this question comes in understanding the citation from
Aeschylus's *Prometheus* (line 514) which Heidegger immediately introduces: "*Techne* is weaker than necessity." It is a line cited without any context. Heidegger does not remind his listeners that Prometheus—whose
name means "forethought"[20] and who had a brother with the contrasting name of "afterthought" (Epimetheus)—is the remarkable figure who
brought *techne* to mortals. Prometheus, the protector of humankind, is
the god who gave the arts—for instance, of healing and of fabrication—to
human beings so that they might protect themselves, and for this he was
punished. Aeschylus's play depicts the sufferings of Prometheus for giving this gift of *techne* to humankind. He utters the line while bound and
being tormented. It occurs in the context of an exchange with the chorus,
which has just said that though Prometheus helped alleviate the sufferings of human beings, he cannot find a remedy to minister to his own
agony. Then, after Prometheus says that "Every *techne* possessed by human

beings comes from Prometheus," the chorus replies, "Do not benefit mortals beyond due measure," to which Prometheus replies with a comment that includes the line that Heidegger cites in the Rector's Address: "Not thus, nor yet, is fulfilling fate destined to bring this end to pass. When I have been bent by infinite pangs and tortures, thus only am I to escape my bondage. *Techne* is far weaker than necessity."[21] It is an exchange that one might characterize as colored by a tone of resignation. But why is it that in light of this exchange Prometheus merits the claim to be the "first philosopher"? What does it mean that the first philosopher appears in the context of this exchange in a Greek tragedy in which the force of necessity, the claims of destiny, is acknowledged?

What qualifies Prometheus as a philosopher is that despite his essential kinship with the power of *techne* (which Heidegger translates here simply as "knowing," thereby stripping it of any privileged link with technicity and technology as he will later interpret it), despite this commitment to the potency of the knowing proper to *techne*, Prometheus knows most of all the weakness of such knowledge, he knows its ineradicable limit, and this knowledge of limits is what qualifies him as a philosopher. Likewise, this knowledge of limits is what enables him to pay tribute to the greater power of historical necessity. This power of history, which Heidegger finds alive and posing a question in the present age, is what Prometheus brings into view, and it is this necessity, this work of destiny, which Greek tragedy explores and unfolds. In other words, the insight of Greek tragedy is seen as fully compatible with the first truth of philosophy. But recognizing the failure of *techne* is the condition for the recognition of the elemental power of history. Philosophy is in this sense a condition for grasping the truth of the tragedy.

Heidegger has a twofold purpose in making this complicated gesture to the figure of Prometheus, understood as a philosopher, and to Greek tragedy with its image of the workings of fate. First, he is opening up the topic of history by posing the question of how we can take measure of its depths and force (and tacitly he is asking thereby what it might mean to seize the possibilities of history in the present age). Second, he is opening up the lines for a radical critique of the power of *techne*. Both points must be heard in conjunction with the context provided by his concern with establishing the task of the university in the present age of distress. However, it is the second of these points opened here—the concern with delimiting the sway of *techne*—which is perhaps the most significant one to be explored. It is also the most distinctively Heideggerian element and one that he will continue to emphasize in his subsequent treatments of Greek tragedy.

But two points need to be established and thought together if the fuller significance of this gesture to the limits of *techne* is to be exposed. First, immediately after citing this passage from Aeschylus, Heidegger raises the question of the status of *theoria,* of the claims of "pure observation" which is so fundamental to the project of philosophy conceived of as metaphysics. He then makes the claim that "theory is itself the highest realization of genuine praxis."[22] Second, one needs to read this entire discussion in the light of the role of *techne* that is developed in Plato's *Republic* and *Apology.* This point is crucial, but not as evident from Heidegger's address as one might expect given its importance. Only the final sentence of the Rector's Address cites Plato. It is a line from the *Republic* and reads, in Heidegger's translation, "All great things stand in the storm."[23] But this line too needs to be set back into its full context to be understood. It occurs when Socrates gives an answer to his own obviously rhetorical question, "How can a city take philosophy in hand without being destroyed?" to which Socrates provides his own preemptive reply: "For surely all great things carry with them the risk of a fall, and really as the saying goes 'fine things are hard' [or, as Heidegger will translate, 'all great things stand in the storm']." The question which Socrates is posing and answering is the same one that Heidegger is putting to his audience: how can the city take into itself the project of philosophy, namely, the opening up of the force of history?

What needs to be recalled to see the contrast between how it is that Heidegger wants to answer this question and the answer it receives from Socrates is that for Socrates *techne* is the characteristic of *all* forms of knowing, even the knowing that would address itself to the place of justice in the city. As he indicates in the *Apology,* everything that human beings do is governed by the knowledge we call *techne,* and so it seems fair to suppose that the knowledge of political life, even the knowledge requisite for the education of just citizens, could be looked for as a *techne.* This is the point at which the metaphysical determination of the nature of the *polis* and of the role of education in the *polis* is framed and determined by a specific understanding of the overwhelming power of *techne.* But it is precisely this metaphysical determination of the nature of *techne,* this conception of knowledge as guided by a special foreknowledge, that is, a metaphysical conception of *techne,* that Heidegger wants to challenge in this address. He is opposing himself to the organization of knowledge within the university as well as the conception of the role of the university within the life of a culture, which understands it as a species of technical knowledge. Against this technic of knowing, this division of forms of knowledge into canons and disciplines, Heidegger poses what he takes to be the originary sense of *theoria,* which he contends is a relation to being that is radically open to the limits of the claims of *techne* and thus to the full force of history and its overwhelming necessity. The residual Platonic element of his critique of Plato, though, is the fact that he presents the original *theoria* as itself the highest form of praxis. In saying this, Heidegger manages to preserve one of the key traits of what one might call a Platonic metaphysics at the same moment that he calls into question the technologization of knowledge and of the *polis* that is inaugurated by Plato.

Heidegger's chief concern here is to counter the tradition which frames both the state and nature of education within the context of *techne*, of a form of knowing which is transmissible in an unproblematized manner and which regards itself as somehow immune to and above the claims of history.[24] The call for a spiritual renewal which Heidegger issues in this address is a call to overcome the domination of technique in the modern university and to radically pry open the field of history in an original questioning. In the end, Heidegger's concern is to reset the framework of the modern university and dethrone the dominance of the sciences and the scientization of the humanities, while replacing this situation with one that confirms philosophy as the highest form of science and as the unifying center of the university. That Heidegger sees this as something that might happen in conjunction with National Socialism simply makes no sense and has no warrant in the arguments of this address. It can only be explained as an instance of the alchemy of an astonishing blindness and hubris on Heidegger's part. He is clearly blind to the realities of National Socialism, even in that early period, and it is a mark of his hubris to believe that the force of his own theory could lead culture out of its spiritual distress. Nonetheless, it remains the case that Heidegger's purpose here is to dislodge inherited, metaphysical assumptions about the nature of education, of knowledge and the university, as well as about the place of these matters in the wider realm of culture. His effort is to dislodge the dominance of a conception of such issues that is rooted in a pride in human knowing and above all in that species of knowing that goes by the name of *techne,* and he wants to replace this with a relation to thinking, a theory, which is radically open to the force of history and which resolutely faces the task of a self-assertion of this thinking which knows itself obligated to radical self-reflection.

It is admittedly a disturbing speech for a number of reasons, above all the ease with which it sees its task as colluding with the agenda of National Socialism and the manner in which it absorbs into its own issues the language of that agenda. But one can dissociate the genuinely philosophical points addressed in this speech from that agenda which Heidegger piggybacks here, and while one might never cease to condemn Heidegger for having given this speech and for never having given an adequate account of it subsequently (the "Tatsache und Gedanken" of 1945 and the "Spiegel Interview" of 1966 do not go far enough in this direction), one should not on that account overlook the manner in which genuine questions about the task of education and the university, the character of human technicity, the nature of nature and the forms of its preservation, and its role in culture are posed here. What might most of all need to be noted is the

236

fact that these genuine issues are raised here in the framework of a citation from a Greek tragedy.

This reference to Aeschylus would be the first substantive reference
to Greek tragedy in Heidegger's work since the references found hitherto
had much more of the flavor of an occasional and passing remark. Up to
this point no real conclusion was drawn on the basis of a turn to tragedy;
here, however, everything hinges upon the insight which is opened up by
the figure of the philosopher in a Greek tragedy.[25] But after this turn to
Aeschylus in the Rector's Address, Heidegger would find the topic of tragedy claiming his attention with rapidly accelerating frequency. And, whatever else it might be, it would always be a gesture that signaled an attempt
to move to a new appreciation of history and an attempt to mark the limits of human technicity. Always the agenda would be a large one, one that
ultimately took a bearing upon the widest concerns of culture and political life.

The "Self-Assertion of the German University" remains a problematic
text at best. Its collusion with one of the worst imaginable movements of
the twentieth century, no matter how much one might seek to understand or qualify that collusion, will forever mark it as a text that needs to
be read against its times if the issues it does seek to raise are ever to be
addressed. It would prove to be a text that inaugurated a colossal error of
judgment on Heidegger's part, and self-important dreams of that moment would quickly show themselves to be delusions. Heidegger would
step down from the Rector's post in less than a year after this speech—an
unprecedented removal—and the error of this effort to align Heidegger's
views with the agenda of National Socialism would be evident to all involved. While it does seem sadly true that he never even began to grasp
the magnitude of the events of the Shoah even well after the war had
ended, it also seems clear that with the end of his role as Rector a period
of personal crisis and confusion began. Following his departure as Rector,
Heidegger would try to understand and come to terms with this event by
turning to a more focused reflection upon the themes which he had failed
to set forth in the Rector's Address. Consequently, to understand his own
situation, and to try to understand anew the crisis of the historical present,
Heidegger deepens his involvement with the question of tragedy which
had been the key to what he took to be the great insight of his greatest
blunder. So in the years immediately following the end of his Rectorship
the topic of tragedy, and the question of the work of art, will move very
close to the center of Heidegger's attentions. He gradually knows that he
has made a great error, the error of a lifetime, and though he does not
understand its specific nature he does seek to understand how the significance of an elemental error is to be understood. His involvement with
this question would gain in intensity over the decade of the 1930s, reach-

ing its most intense point in his *Contributions to Philosophy: On the Event.* Although a new tone would enter the treatment of tragedy (above all attention will be given now to both the roles of mourning and of strangeness), always—strangely even when Heidegger is most dedicated to comprehending his own personal confusions—the question of tragedy would signal not first of all a concern with human suffering, but with the crisis of history. Even to the degree that he seeks to understand himself as a figure in this tragedy it will be as figure in the play of history.

*   *   *

After relinquishing the post of Rector, after the debacle of the address for which he had the high hope of being heard in the highest of places, Heidegger returns to teaching with a full-blown passion for Hölderlin—a passion that is by no means new, only newly thematized—and, in part through Hölderlin, a renewed and deepened fascination for what is to be found in Greek tragedy. In the semester (1934–35) after his foray into the realm of politics Heidegger taught a seminar with the jurist E. Wolf entitled "Hegel: On the State." As tantalizing as the theme is, no record of the course remains, at least that is available at present. Nonetheless, given the topic, one might legitimately expect that Hegel's reading of *Antigone* would show up in such a seminar, since that reading plays a role in the foundation of the state as it is discussed in the *Phenomenology of Spirit, Natural Law,* and *Philosophy of Right.* During the same semester, Heidegger taught a lecture course entitled *Hölderlin's Hymns: "Germanien" and "The Rhine."* The topic of that course is the relation of poetic work and a people, and once again, as in the Rector's Address, the question is posed about the possibility of renewing culture by means of a repetition of the creative possibilities of a poetic language which opens itself to the force of history. The effort of the lecture is to think the being of a people and the nature of a nation independently of the claims of nationalism. It is a project which struggles mightily, and quite abstractly, with the issues of its time. The range of concerns is great, and it is Hölderlin who sets the agenda in motion (this would be the first of many such occasions on which Hölderlin would provide the creative inspiration for Heidegger's own concerns). In the course of those lectures we find a few, largely passing, references to Greek tragic figures and to Sophocles;[26] we also find a remark about Hölderlin's "Ground to Empedocles" as well as references to both "tragic poetry" and "tragic being."[27] More importantly, we find a sensibility that, even if not called by the name of the tragic, shares an obvious kinship with Greek tragedy. In short, tragedy is, however slightly, an increased presence for Heidegger in this lecture. But these still rather abbreviated references to Greek tragedy give no hint of the serious role which it will play in the lecture course of the next semester (1935), which would even-

tually be published (to some controversy because of a parenthetical remark about National Socialism at the conclusion, which may or may not
have been a part of the original lecture course) [28] under the title *Introduction to Metaphysics*. Here we find Heidegger's most extensive engagement
with tragedy (which he understands as without question a Greek matter
only), and here we find many of the same themes announced in the "Self-
Assertion of the German University" at last thoroughly developed.

The *Introduction to Metaphysics* is one of Heidegger's most dynamic
and wide-ranging works, and when it is taken seriously it actively resists
description since it constantly rewrites the assumptions from which it begins and radically calls into question so many of the terms with which it
must of necessity operate. It announces itself as a work that seeks to address its times in a manner which is proper and not merely as the positing
of yet another opinion or perspective on the stage of events. Rather, it is
an attempt to trouble and disturb the assumptions which animate notions
such as the relevance of philosophy, the constitution of a 'we', and the
most elemental assumptions which inhere in the very language we use.
The course is described as an "introduction" to metaphysics, but it is anything but that. It is rather a fundamental interrogation and challenge to
the very idea of metaphysics, of a point of view which is modeled on the
image of an infinite and omnipresent mind which suffers no death and
knows no limits. In other words, it is a challenge to the claims of ontology
that conceives of itself along the lines of a theology. Rather than providing what one might expect of an introduction to the tradition of metaphysics, this course stands as a protracted summons to get over the idea of
metaphysics and to break through the calcifications of thinking that characterize metaphysics. To that end, Greek tragedy will play an essential
role. The rehabilitation of the tragic poets, whom Plato sent into exile for
their political activities, is undertaken here, and it is done precisely for
the sake of the contribution that they make to the very possibility of a
community. One sees here the deepening of the lines of thinking which
were opened up by the lecture course on Hölderlin during the preceding
semester: the work of the poet, far more than the persuasion of the politi-
cian, is what is most needed for the foundation of a genuine community.[29]
Hölderlin will always be the preeminent figure of that poet for Heidegger,
but here, in *Introduction to Metaphysics*, he will share that title with Sophocles.[30] One sees immediately that a certain understanding of Nietzsche
has given this lecture course its final shape: here the destruction of metaphysics and the Christian tradition is coupled with a renewed sense of the
depth of the experience which is opened by the tragic work of art.

What is issued here, then, is the call for a new beginning of thinking,
one which takes its start in the realization that the tradition of metaphysics has exhausted itself, has played itself out and finally shown its truths to
be untenable (in this regard this book resonates deeply with the preface

to Hegel's *Phenomenology of Spirit,* which likewise opens by referring to the impoverishment of the present forms of thinking). Part and parcel to this call for a new beginning, for an overthrow of the presumptions of metaphysics, is the sharp critique which is leveled against the final forms which metaphysics has taken: the reign of values and the ascendance of technology, both of which are shown to be the fruits of a sense of congealed subjectivity, namely, of the signature of the ancient tradition of metaphysics. Greek tragedy will provide the counterforce to this metaphysical sense of the elemental character of human being since, against the conception of human being as a subject, it will present a view of human being as fundamentally strange, as the opening to an abyssal and inconceivable freedom. Also key to understanding the tradition of metaphysics is the manner in which the law of noncontradiction governs its operations. And again, Greek tragedy, which is the presentation of an unresolvable contradiction, the double bind which thinking can never surmount, is decisive in debunking this presumption of metaphysics. Although the discussion of tragedy will come only in the later portion of the course, it will take a central role in the project which is laid out here.

Heidegger is acutely aware of the difficulty of carrying out such a project. The hermeneutical problem is severe: he operates with the language of metaphysics and is so yoked to its categories. He knows that he cannot begin like a shot out of a pistol and pretend either that words were not already loaded with meanings or that he could simply invent a different language. Consequently, what he must do first of all is to win the possibility of making his point, and to do this he must rehabilitate the language he will use and the frameworks within which questions are to be posed. And, to be sure, that is the task of the greater portion of the course. So it is only after he has unfolded what he takes to be the basic questions of metaphysics and after he has analyzed the grammar and etymology of the word "being" that Heidegger begins to move to open the realm of a different style of thinking. That move to a form of thinking which does not harness itself to the prejudices of metaphysics is made by means of several extended and provocative references to early Greek texts. Heraclitus and Parmenides are Heidegger's first companions in the project; one might even say that he regards them as his true contemporaries at this point.[31] But in the end it will be Sophocles who takes center stage in this project and who provides the impulse for some of the most dramatic turns in this text.

All three of the Theban tragedies are mentioned in the *Introduction to Metaphysics.* Homer is mentioned and cited as well. Whereas all the references to Homer concern elements of language and the effort to retrieve the elemental force of words, the references to Sophocles make a sincere effort to appropriate something of the substance of the tragedies. Strangely, none of these references gives even the slightest indication of the plot or dramatic character of the works. Although Heidegger announces that what is disclosed here is specific to the character of the work as a work of *art,* nothing that he says in any of these instances gives any clue as to what would qualify as a matter of art. Every reference is ripped out of context and taken as an instance of thinking; here tragedy presents itself as the highest form of philosophizing.

Although all three tragedies in the Theban trilogy are mentioned, the only specific character mentioned is Oedipus. The real focus of the interpretations of tragedy here is human being in general, understood now as the figure of a grand tragedy. The first reference is to *King Oedipus,* which is enlisted to explain the most profound insights of the early Greek thinkers regarding the simultaneity of unity and contradiction. This double bind of being which repeats the aletheic movement of truth and which Heidegger is attempting to retrieve—and which is at least superficially akin to the *hen kai pan* which was the desiratum for Hegel, Schelling, and Hölderlin—is presented "in the highest and the purest manner in the poetry of Greek tragedy."[32] What makes this the case in Oedipus is the way in which he struggles, passionately and infinitely, to reveal the secret of his own appearance which is hidden from him. The trajectory of Oedipus's life is found in the move from the glory and divine favor of his first appearance in the play to his gruesome end. Heidegger describes this trajectory of a life as the singular struggle between appearance and unconcealment: "Step by step he must put himself into unconcealment, which in the end he can only endure by putting out his own eyes, i.e. by removing himself from all light, and letting the protective cloak of night fall around him, and, by crying out, as a blind man, for all the doors to be opened so that such a one could be manifest to the people as that which he *is*."[33]

Heidegger does not address the language which the chorus uses to describe the newly blinded Oedipus in this passage of the drama. But the language of the text is quite telling and would seem appropriate for Heidegger's concerns: *"ho deinon idein pathos anthropois, o deinotaton panton hos ego prosekyrs' ede"* (monstrous sight—the suffering, for all the world to see, the worst terror that ever met my eyes).[34] Those words of the chorus blend blindness, suffering, witnessing, and human life in one of the most compact sentences one can imagine. This is the moment in the tragedy when we discover that in the poetic imagination such blindness does not refer to a physical condition, but to a moral condition. Blinded, Oedipus now sees, and because he sees he knows he must make this sight public to the people. Now, as Heidegger citing Hölderlin will say, "King Oedipus has an eye too many perhaps."[35] This moment in the tragedy is what Aristotle described as the moment of both reversal and of recognition; both are compressed in the image of the blind Oedipus.

Heidegger does not discuss the character of this blindness, nor does he detail the significance of blindness in the ancient world. He does, however, make mention a number of times to the strange blindness of metaphysics, and, in one of the almost surreal images of this *Introduction to Metaphysics,* Heidegger even invokes the image of a "blind mirror that no longer reflects, that casts nothing back."[36] Without explicitly noting it, in doing this Heidegger is playing with a kinship between blindness, justice, and the poetic imagination which is deeply embedded in ancient Greek culture. Some basic points about this kinship should be noted.

*   *   *

This kinship between blindness, justice, and the poetic imagination is so basic to the Greek sensibility that such a relationship is essential that it was necessary for the Greeks to represent their preeminent poet, Homer, as blind. It is unclear whether there was in fact "a" Homer, but what is clear is that all the ancient legends that surround him find his blindness to be an element of his knowledge. That is even the case with his name: *homeros* means "hostage," which was a synonym for the blind who needed to be led by a guide (legend has it that there was a poet who was known as Melesigenes, but was given the name Homer because he was blind). In the final analysis, it is irrelevant whether or not there was a blind Homer. What is relevant is that the Greek imagination required blindness of such a poet of ethical life. The relation of the blind to the *logos* was more acute. We, for instance, do not find the blindness of a Milton or a Borges essential to their poetic character, even though both of them have written powerfully about it.

In Greece, a culture of light, blindness was the ultimate form of human suffering. Consequently, but nonetheless ironically, blindness came to stand as the most visible image for the human condition as suffered. In a culture that equated light and life, blindness bore a resemblance to death, and so it is no accident that blind Teiresias is the only one who can see in the underworld of the dead: that has always been his element, and in one respect it is this symbolic relation with death that is the source of his insight about the destiny of the living. (As an aside let me simply say that the experiences of Teiresias are especially important for a fuller treatment of this thematic, most of all because the stories of the way he became blind—no matter which story one tells—introduce the crucial dimension of desire into the issue of the poetic.)[37] But what is necessary is merely to indicate the extent to which blindness attaches itself to the Greek poetic imagination that thinks the riddle of *dike,* and to indicate further the centrality of blind figures in Greek tragedy specifically. To that end, one could refer to the blind poet Demodokeos, who was given the gift of song by the muse who took his eyes. One could refer to Thamyris, the blind poet who is the hero of the lost tragedy by Sophocles. Or one

242

could refer to Stesichorus, to whom Plato refers in the *Phaedrus,* suggesting that he was cleverer than Homer since Stesichorus knew how to recover the loss of his eyes: he simply wrote the lines—decisive in the *Phaedrus*—"This story is not true"[38] (that is a remark Socrates makes while he has a veil on his head, covering his eyes, a veil he removes upon uttering those words). What is important to note is that in those instances where the origin of a blindness is explained, it is typically a punishment for trespassing the limits of human knowledge. One goes blind because one knows too much, and it is the province of the tragic poet to chart the territory of this peculiar knowledge. Tragedy traces the path from one blindness to another, a different, one—one that nonetheless shows, even if it does not see. More could be said about the significance of the image of blindness in ancient Greece, but such is beyond the needs of reading Heidegger on this point.[39]

*   *   *

As I suggested, Heidegger quietly enlists the image of blindness and the contrasting image of seeing throughout the analysis of metaphysics in *Introduction to Metaphysics.*[40] Here, however, in his discussion of *King Oedipus,* he is more concerned with developing the line opened by Hölderlin's insight that "Perhaps King Oedipus had an eye too many." In other words, the effort here is to address an excessive capacity for seeing that nonetheless is at the root of a quite peculiar form of blindness. It is a remark made in the poetic text entitled "In lovely blueness . . ." (see the translation in the appendix to chapter 4), a remark that Hölderlin makes following the phrase "If one looks into the mirror, A man, and sees in it his image, as if painted; it resembles the man. The image of a man has eyes, whereas light belongs to the moon," and he follows it with the phrase "The sufferings of this man, they seem indescribable, unspeakable, inexpressible." The excessive sight of Oedipus, the excess of speculative power—not any specific deed such as the murder of his father or the marriage to his mother—is named as the key to his inexpressible sufferings. His suffering is linked with the passion to know which defines him (he is, after all, the solver of riddles), and it is precisely this passion to know which inserts Oedipus into the crossroads of two, conflicted, laws. Oedipus's agony and the source of his suffering do not simply happen to happen, they do not simply befall him from circumstance; rather, it is constitutive of his ownmost nature insofar as he is defined as longing for knowledge. Not blind chance, then, but destiny is at work here, and this destiny belongs to the nature of mortal being, of a singular, finite being, who relentlessly wills knowledge in order to assume a place in the realm of knowledge, the realm, in other words, of the universal. Later, in his analysis of the choral ode from *Antigone,* Heidegger will amplify this point by saying that this passion, this drive to know and so to place oneself in the peculiar relation to the world that defines knowledge, is what sets human being against another power, one that Heidegger will say is defined by Sophocles as *physis,* and it is *necessary* that the knower be violently torn open by this power which cannot be mastered. At this stage Heidegger clarifies the point at issue by invoking a phrase from Karl Reinhardt's interpretation of Sophocles in order to crystallize his own interpretation here. He says that what one sees in this exhibition of mortal destiny is evidence of the "the tragedy of appearance."[41] The destiny of mortal life, of a life that sets itself in a willing relation to knowledge, reveals the double bind which governs the law of all appearance: the singularity of all that appears struggles to take its place in the realm of the universal, and the end of that struggle, insofar as it succeeds, is that what appears is destroyed.[42] This law of appearance is equally the law of the destruction of what appears: all appearance is fated to an original transgression, all appearance is, in this sense, a crime. Characterizing the space of appearance, Heidegger writes, "The space which opens itself up in the interwovenness of being, unconcealment and appearance is what I understand as *errancy.*"[43] Errancy, which should be understood in a manner which brings to mind Aristotle's notion of *hamartia,* is the place and the fate of mortal life. Tragedy is the work of opening our eyes to the truth of such errancy. Metaphysics is the blindness, the tragic denial, to such truth.

But Heidegger's purpose in addressing this passage from Sophocles, in taking up Hölderlin's spin on it, and in referring to Reinhardt in order to characterize its largest significance is not yet to unpack this kinship between the will to know and the fate of mortal life. It is rather to draw a line which links the image and the passion of Oedipus and metaphysics. Oedipus is linked with metaphysics and its fate, and ultimately the figure of Oedipus serves as a model for the fate of Western culture, which has defined itself in terms of the possibility of the foundational knowledge of science conceived in a metaphysical manner. Here Heidegger goes beyond his own earlier crypto-reference to Oedipus in his remark about the murderous logic of history (in the 1930–31 lecture course) by suggesting that the basic drive of the metaphysical tradition, the drive to metaphysics itself, is founded in the same passion that is the hallmark of Oedipus's tragic flaw.[44] It does not take a great leap to see that Heidegger is setting up metaphysics as the outcome of a blindness, one rooted in the speculative excess of an "eye too many perhaps," and thus as the production of errancy. At the outset of the lecture course, Heidegger announced that he would take up the problem of "the destiny of Europe" and show how it was wrapped up in "the question of being."[45] This is the point at which we come to see how that destiny is bound with the problem of metaphysics, of errancy, and of the possibility of coming to see anew. The question that is posed is whether or not the West (and it should be said that for Heidegger neither America nor Russia belongs to his conception of "the West") will prove itself capable of opening itself up to something new from within itself and so seize the possibility of something new, something more radical than metaphysics, or whether it will complete itself in the reign of the final signatures of metaphysics, namely, technology and values. This theme, especially the concern with the form of knowing that configures itself according to the modern, subjectivist conception of *techne*, will be at the core of the next interpretation of a passage from Greek tragedy in this book. When Heidegger turns to the choral ode from *Antigone* the enigma of human technicity and the limits of the human attempt to master the world will be at the center of his interpretation.

*   *   *

Heidegger takes up the celebrated first chorus from Sophocles' *Antigone* hard on the heels of having worked through Parmenides' maxim regarding the sameness of thinking and being, *"to gar auto noein estin te kai einai,"* in which he had argued that one finds in this saying a definition of the essence of human being thought from out of the essence of being itself. When he turns to the choral ode, it is in order to deepen this understanding of the essence of human being and its peculiar relation to being. Purportedly he turns to the poetic work because "the determination of the being of the human which Parmenides carries out is difficult to access in any direct fashion and is strange."[46] That the rich, but uncommon and quite strained, rendering of Sophocles' passage should be seen as somehow more accessible is a baffling suggestion, for what Heidegger presents in this reading is an unfolding of the essential and enigmatic strangeness that lies at the heart of human being. Part of the way Heidegger moves to bring a reading of this passage to life is by means of his own translation of the ode (see the appendix to this chapter, where I have retranslated his translation).[47] But the heart of his interpretation of this Sophoclean text is found in a close, textual, nuanced, and yet coercive reading of the passage. Close to the text and to its language, Heidegger nonetheless manages to offer a remarkably imaginative rendition of the sense it bears, and he does this in part at least by prescinding from any consideration of the plot of the tragedy. It is no mean feat that he accomplishes, and the result is that the choral ode comes to be understood as an ontological document. What we find, then, is an understanding of this famous passage that is quite singular, provocative, and creative, and at times quite frustrating for having ripped the ode out of the context of the play. It is thus noteworthy that Heidegger's translation and consideration of the choral ode does not include the final verse, which the chorus speaks after Antigone has entered on stage and will immediately be denounced as the one who committed the crime of burying Polynices.[48]

The ode presents at first what seems to be a hymn to human inventiveness and the story of its unproblematic progress. In telling a tale of human *techne* as the triumph over human helplessness before the powers of nature, this ode bears some resemblance to the text of Aeschylus's *Prometheus Bound* that Heidegger cites in "The Self-Assertion of the German University." Heidegger's commentary on the ode is presented in three stages, each of which considers the complete ode from a different angle. All three manners of probing this passage take as their leitmotiv the word *deinon,* which Heidegger translates as *unheimlich* (strange or uncanny). It is a word that only seven years later, in a lecture course on Hölderlin, Heidegger will identify as naming "the essence of Antigone."[49] He will also suggest that this word presents the highest challenge to the languages in which we think today, and that it remains perhaps the word for which we lack a word today. It is the word in which we find the surest measure of the gap which separates us from the Greek, the word which we must come to understand if we are to grasp the truth of tragedy. The goal of this interpretation, then, is to summon the Greek sensibility animating this word and to drive to the heart of the dynamic which is working through it. Doing this requires, in part at least, an effort to restore to key words senses that have been long forgotten. One must read the text against our present-day, metaphysically colored, assumptions—especially the assumptions we make in the form of translation—if one is to begin to appreciate the full force of this key word *deinon* and how it is that human being is the strangest of all that is strange. What emerges from this reading is a view of human life that stands in stark contrast with the metaphysical sense of the human being as a subject, an agency, standing over and against a world of substances that it seeks to master. Here human life is presented as strange, powerful, dangerous, violent, and engaged in multiple struggles, and this —one is tempted to say Dionysian—sense of human being is compressed into the single word *deinon.*

The first three stanzas of the ode present an image of human being as full of power and cunning, as capable of riding the waves of the sea, of turning the earth to the production of food, of putting animals to a use for human ends, and of being able to fend off the attacks even of the weather. These capacities are all matters of *techne,* of that knowledge which is able to put matters into service of ends. But there is also a recognition of three intimately related special forms in which this power gathers itself, namely, in the word, in understanding, and in the rule of cities. It is not clear whether or not these forms of human power come under the rubric of *techne,* but Heidegger treats them as if they do. And this capacity of such knowledge is, according to Heidegger, why it must be said that among its meanings the word *deinon* must be understood to refer to the violent and even terrible nature of human being. We possess an overwhelming power, and the exercise of this power, its sheer presence in the world (its being-there), is a violence which shatters the limits of nature. The human being is not called violent because of any specific act; rather, human being exists as a fundamental violence. Our nature is to turn nature to our service—whether benignly or maliciously that violence will be our truth.

But this is also why Heidegger suggests that another meaning of *deinon* is found in the sense of the "uncanny," or the "unhomeliness": human being always, of necessity, finds itself cast out of its "home," its "natural" abode as it were. Because we are beings who make things, and thereby remake the world, we depart, and always have departed, from the limits of the familiar. There is a sense of perpetual dissatisfaction, of unanswered desire, at work here:[50] we are propelled forward by our capacity to relate to the world in the mode of one who knows. Here the reading is in full accord with the earlier remarks about Oedipus and the passion for knowledge which drives him. However, this drive, this "journeying everywhere," is now set against another truth of human nature: that, despite every skill and knowledge, we cannot evade death. In the end, all these journeys, all this making and remaking of the world, "come to naught." There is, for us, "no exit."[51] And this, says Heidegger, is why Sophocles says of us that we are *"pantoporos aporos,"* the end for us is an impasse, an aporia, and it is through this end that we first feel the full force of what it means that we are *deinon*. As Heidegger had already argued in *Being and Time*, in death we suffer the uncanniness of existence as we live it: "Here the entire strangeness of this greatest strangeness is disclosed; not only . . . that *as* the violent one he drives himself beyond his familiar home, but he becomes the most strange first of all insofar as, on all paths he has no exit, is thrown out of every relation to the familiar, insofar as *ate*, ruin, unholiness, catastrophe, come over him."[52]

This unfolding of the sense of human being as strange, uncanny, violent, and powerful comes to its sharpest formulation in the description of human life as consequently *hypsipolis apolis*. It is a phrase that is difficult to translate, but Heidegger proposes the translation "Hochüberragend die Stätte, verlüstig der Stätte," which means something like "towering high above the place, forfeiting the place." Heidegger calls attention to the parallel between the construction of this phrase and the phrase *"pantoporos aporos"*; both are linguistically conflicted and are ways in which the double bind, the tragic law of human life, is spoken out. Here, however, the concern is with the *polis*, and it is on this that Heidegger will center his remarks, saying

One typically translates *polis* as state and city-state; this does not cover the full sense of the word. *Polis* means most of all the place, the there, wherein and as which Da-sein [being-there] as historical is. The *polis* is the historical place, the there, *in* which, *out of* which and *for* which history happens. To this place and scene of history belong the gods, the temple, the priests, the celebrations, the games, the poets, the thinkers, the ruler, the council of elders, the assembly of people, the military forces and the ships.[53]

Here we find Heidegger's conception of the *polis in nuce*. It is not a matter first off of the relations between people or peoples, nor is it a matter of the government and its laws. It is rather the site which renders possible and so enables such relations and institutions. Seven years hence Heidegger will make a similar point in a passage that speaks directly to the misappropriation of his own concerns with Greece for the agenda of National Socialism:

One absolutely does no service to the comprehension and the evaluation of the historical singularity of National Socialism if one now interprets Greece in such a manner that one could believe that the Greeks all had already been "National Socialists." What concerns us is not a matter of the "political," rather we are concerned with the essence of the *polis* and more precisely the essential realm out of which it defines itself, and that means out of which and according to which the Greeks must remain the most *worthy* of questions. That the poet Sophocles speaks of the relation of human beings to the *polis,* and indeed in the context of speaking of the *deinon,* already alludes to the decisive point from out of which the *polis* as the place and middle of beings is experienced.[54]

Already in *Introduction to Metaphysics* one sees that Heidegger is struggling to arrive at another, a nonmetaphysical, manner of thinking the relation of human beings to that out of which such things as government, law, institutions, and human relation can come to be. And the starting point of this project is the notion that the "essence" of human being is captured in the Greek word *deinon* and in all of the polyvalent senses it exposes. Out of this strangeness, this violence, and this power a space of appearance is forged, and this space is what Heidegger understands as named by the Greek word *polis*.

But the choral ode says that human beings "tower high above" this place, and for this reason we forfeit our place in this place. The "reason" we tower above the scene which is exposed is the same "reason" it is opened at all: we are creatures possessing *techne,* and it is by virtue of this that we simultaneously create and rise above the scene of appearance. We exile ourselves by the very act that founds what qualifies as the most human place of all, the city. Ambiguity, a strange and uncanny doubleness, haunts the relation of the human being to the city, and this ambiguity, in the guise of the tragic law of the double bind, is precisely what Greek tragedy is dedicated to presenting. This is why Heidegger could consider Sophocles a thinker of political life in an original sense, and this is why Heidegger's reading of Greek tragedy needs to be read as an effort to plumb the original possibility of political life. From this perspective, political realities—which were exploding violently and dramatically all around Heidegger—seemed like epiphenomenal events which would never be able to be understood until this deeper possibility rooted in the strange nature of human being was exposed. It is out of this nature, which presents a view of human life as strange and so unable to be substantivized or regarded as a subject, that the freeing of life to itself is to be accomplished. This would be Heidegger's most cherished conviction regarding human life and the possibility of coming to an understanding of what it means that we share our lives in time. After the war was over Heidegger would write a letter to Hannah Arendt in which he expresses this same point, this time at the other end of a thousand years: "'Saving' means and yet is not only: to evade a danger, but rather in advance to set free into what is essential. This *infinite intention* is the finitude of human being. Out of it mankind is able to get over the spirit of rage. For a long while I have meditated on this, because a moral behavior alone does not suffice."[55] This is the same claim that Heidegger will make in "The Letter on Humanism" when he speaks of the need—which he sees himself as having addressed throughout his life—for an "original ethics."[56] Until we are freed to our ownmost nature, until the strange and uncanny character of human being wins its place and is grasped as at the heart of the scene of our own appearance in the world, free relations will not be possible. Heidegger's sense of the futility of any action which does not move to the originary point is complete; there might be moments of liberation or mitigation of unfreedom, but it will be only a superficial solution. His conviction that the metaphysical view of human being locks us into an untenable self-understanding is so complete that no compromise, no momentary resolution of human inequity, no battle for "justice" makes any sense to him. And he is also convinced that Sophoclean tragedy presents us with a profound insight into the nature of human being, which articulates precisely such an alternative to the metaphysics which this lecture course is supposed to "introduce."

As Heidegger deepens his effort to unfold the sense of human being as *deinon,* three themes become increasing important: language, death, and *techne.* Language and *techne* get special attention as doubled events, as violent events that both build and destroy. The treatment of *techne* is particularly important for several reasons: it links most directly with other works Heidegger is writing at this time (besides the Rector's Address, one thinks most of all of "The Origin of the Work of Art," where the question of *techne* is the central concern), it will link with some of Heidegger's concerns that will continue throughout his life, it will be the key to the third phase of his interpretation of this choral ode, and it will be the issue around which he will suggest the historical crisis at the center of which we find National Socialism is to be understood. For all these reasons, special attention should be given to following the line that is developed around the conception of *techne* which Heidegger finds working in this passage.

When Heidegger unpacks this notion he begins by asking where the "power" of *techne* resides:

> *Techne* means neither art, nor skill, not something like technique in the modern sense. We translate *techne* as 'knowledge.' . . . Knowledge in the authentic sense of *techne* is the originary and constant looking beyond what is given at any moment. . . . Knowledge is the capacity to set into work the being of any particular being. The Greeks called art and the art work in the authentic sense *techne,* because art most immediately brings being to stand in something present (in the work).[57]

It is a difficult "explanation," to say the least, but this much can be said with some clarity: that Heidegger is presenting us with a conception of *techne* as a form of knowledge which somehow is capable (whether it does this or not) of investing itself in a thing, and this thing distinguishes itself from other things in the world precisely because it is invested with this knowledge; hence it is called a "work" to acknowledge this difference. *Techne* is not to be confused with the work, though; the work is only the result of this knowing, which does not have to invest itself in a work in order to still qualify as *techne* since it is this by virtue of its capacity for such investment. The work of art distinguishes itself by virtue of stabilizing and manifesting this knowledge. A work is art because it constantly calls attention to its own character of being a work, not a thing.[58] It is one of the manners in which nature is brought to light, and it is one of the ways in which the human passion to know, the passion which defined Oedipus, perfects itself. It is, says Heidegger, a knowledge which "wrests being which is previously concealed into appearance as the being [in the work]."[59]

But this struggle to bring being to appearance that goes on in the work that *techne* accomplishes and that describes its essential power is a confrontation with another power which Heidegger says is what the Greeks identified with the word *dike*. It is a word that is typically translated as "justice" but one that Heidegger translates with the almost untranslatable word *Fug*. It is the same enigmatic translation which Heidegger will offer as an answer to the riddle of the Greek conception of *dike* in "The Saying of Anaximander" of 1946. Although he places a great deal of weight upon this translation, he does not work to give it a corresponding clarity. The only even seemingly remote connection of this word in German with any possible link with the idea of justice is found in the German expression "mit Fug und Recht," which means something like "to be fully justified" or "to have full right." It is closely related to the word "Fuge," which is a word that Heidegger will also use in his text on Anaximander and which has several possible meanings, among them the musical word fugue and the word for "joint" or "seam." To say that something is *Unfug* is to say it is out of place (one translates "time is out of joint" as "die Zeit ist aus den Fugen"). Finally, the verbal form, *fügen,* means something like dispensation, and here it links with the notion of destiny ("fügung des Schicksal" means something like "act of destiny"). What is most important here and cannot be borne by the simple translation of the word *Fug* is that here *techne* is understood to be in a struggle with another power, one which belongs to the order of *physis* and as such is overpowering. Human knowledge, which has the form of *techne* and which is at the heart of the strange nature of human being, necessarily finds itself in a conflicted relation with the overwhelming power of nature which it can never master, and it is this confrontation that names the doubled situation of the human being: "He weaves his way between the laws of the earth and the oath enjoined [*beschworenen Fug*] by the gods." Again, this capacity for knowledge, this *techne,* locates human being at an unresolvable site of conflict. That is what Heidegger means when he says that the human being is "tossed back and forth between fitting and not fitting [*Fug und unfug*], between evil and nobility."[60] The struggle which is opened at this point, one always "menaced by disaster," is beyond good and evil. It is suspended over the abyss of freedom.

This countervalent relation of *dike* and *techne* is then the strangest of the strange, it is the struggle which lets the human being be the being it is: it is the struggle between the presence of a world and the violent possibilities of existence which always courts disaster and ruin as its possibility. But this disaster is not simply a possible outcome of a life: it is rather basic to the possibility of human life, it belongs to the very scene of the disclosure of a world, to the possibility of the very space of appearance whatsoever: "Historical existence, the being-there, of human being means: to be posited as the breach into which the preponderant power of being breaks in appearing, so that this breach itself should shatter against being."[61] Heidegger continues by saying that "the Greeks had a profound intuition of this suddenness and singularity of existence, forced on them by being itself, which disclosed itself to them as *physis*, and *logos* and *dike*."[62] This experience of the ever-present possibility of a sudden reversal and of the singularity of each existence is what Greek tragedy preeminently exposes. And this is what Aristotle called attention to in his notions of recognition and reversal.

One final point remains to be noted about Heidegger's reading of this choral ode. On more than one occasion he stresses that "this essence of human being which is experienced poetically in a manner which takes it back to its ground remains closed to any understanding as regards its character as a secret if we prematurely take recourse to any sort of value judgments."[63] The point that is to be underscored is that the possibility of an original ethics which is exposed in Greek tragedy, above all in the conception of human life which is unfolded in it, is beyond—one is tempted to say beneath—categories such as good and evil. Although the choral ode refers us to the site out of which something like an ethics is possible, such an ethics cannot be decided as the struggle of good and evil. It is rather the struggle of appearance, the struggle of each thing to find its possibility in the space of appearance. Here the proximity to Nietzsche is undeniable and strong. One might even suggest that Heidegger's commitment to avoiding the metaphysical language of morals, the categories of good and evil, is stronger still than Nietzsche's. What one finds in the place of any such categories is a radical sense of freedom, a sense that sets human being into a struggle which could never be either comprehended or mediated by notions such as good or evil. This is perhaps the most difficult element of Heidegger's reading of the tragedy to grasp, and yet it is not elaborated upon in any detail in this text. It will, however, be the focus of Heidegger's postwar reflections on tragedy and the effort to link those reflections to the project of getting beyond the metaphysics of humanism and the value judgments proper to it. The sense will grow that something more than, something freer than, value judgments is needed if human life is to find itself at home fittingly in the world, if it is to find its just place.

But while the beginnings of that project can be seen taking root in this text, that issue goes beyond the concerns Heidegger has at this point. And so, after this reading of Sophocles, Heidegger returns to his discussion of Parmenides' maxim regarding the identity of thinking and being. He does this by bringing into play the vocabulary that he developed in the interpretation of Sophocles, so now we are confronted with an interpretation of Parmenides as something of a tragic thinker. It is in the context of carrying out his further discussion that Heidegger's final reference to Sophocles will appear. This time the reference will be to *Oedipus at Colonus,* and it will be to the same line that both Hölderlin and Nietzsche cite at crucial junctures. The line is again from the chorus (lines 1224 ff.) and reads *"me phynai ton hapanta nikai logon."* Unlike both Hölderlin and Nietzsche, Heidegger does not cite the remainder of this passage: *"to d', estei phane benai keithen hothen per hekei, poly deuteron, hos tachista."* The selection he cites is usually translated as "Not to be born is best, when all is reckoned in" (and the remainder of the passage reads "but once a man has seen the light the next best thing, by far, is to go back, back where he came from, quickly as he can"). Heidegger's translation is quite surprising: "Never to have entered into existence triumphs over the gatheredness of beings in the whole."[64] It is a strained translation at best, but one that is enlisted to coerce one more point from the reading of Sophocles; namely, to make one final point clear about the violence, the power, which belongs to the nature of human being. According to Heidegger's interpretation, what is spoken of in this passage is the supreme form of this possibility of violence, violence turned upon itself. He does not mention that the passage speaks of not being born and instead gives it a reading which understands it to be referring to the possibility of suicide. This is the only possibility of "the supreme victory over being."[65] Heidegger points out that this is not a statement of pessimism—such a view would be foreign to the Greeks—it is rather a way of paying tribute to the depth of the struggle that defines human being. It is a struggle that runs to the point of being and nonbeing. This struggle, not the struggle of good and evil, is the deepest one in which we engage and out of which we must come to understand ourselves. Not surprisingly, this theme of the struggle of being and nothing is the one that Heidegger will pursue in his reading of Parmenides which resumes once again at this point, continuing to develop the themes that the reading of the tragedy has opened up.

The direct treatment of tragedy in the *Introduction to Metaphysics* will conclude after this remark; however, the impact of the notion of tragedy—most of all its conception of human life and the manner in which it identifies the locus of human struggles in the world—will be great in the remainder of the text. Most significantly the result of this engagement with Sophocles will surface, in an only slightly concealed form, in what would prove to be one of the more controversial remarks Heidegger would make in this provocative work. Since the text of this lecture course was published only after the war (in 1953), its commentary on National Socialism would have a strange anachronistic quality that would amplify both the insights and the blindness of those comments. The remark to which I refer here is the celebrated claim made at the end of the lecture that "What today is peddled about as the philosophy of National Socialism—but which does not have the slightest to do with the inner truth and magnitude of this movement (namely the encounter of technique which is defined on a planetary scale and modern human life)—has all been made by anglers in these muddy waters of 'values' and of 'totalities'."[66] In this remark, which one needs to understand in part against the backdrop of Heidegger's interpretation of Sophocles as well as his reading of Nietzsche, Heidegger suggests that the crises of the present historical juncture need to be understood from out of the evolution of this profound struggle of *techne* and *dike,* this struggle of appearance, which is named in Sophocles. It is a remark in which Heidegger gives an indication that he did, perhaps still does (one cannot decide about this), believe that National Socialism marked the historical event in which *the metaphysical modification* of this possibility of human being, this capacity for *techne* which has formed itself into technology, would turn into a confrontation with the more original being of human being. This is what he takes to be the "inner truth and magnitude" at issue in the movement.[67] What he criticizes here is the effort to link this confrontation with the view that situates this historical event in the context of a confrontation between good and evil, as if what was at stake in the revolutionary moment of 1935 when this text was written could be grasped in the framework of "values." Heidegger would remain resolute in the view that our age is a time of epochal transformation, even of revolution. He would also remain convinced that the roots of this revolution are to be understood out of an engagement with Greek texts: tragedy will always be the text in which the deepest form of this encounter, this struggle, is exposed; metaphysics will always be the signature of a text which conceals that struggle and shifts it, in its collaboration with Christianity, into the battle of good and evil. Heidegger will try to understand the struggle, the *Kampf*, of the present age by means of reference to Heraclitus's notion of *polemos*, which he will translate in the politically charged Rector's Address as *Kampf*, rather than with reference to Hitler and his use of that word. Heidegger sees the unfolding of metaphysics as a grand historical tragedy. The present is the time of its catastrophe, the moment of reversal. The question put is whether—or better, how—the moment of recognition will arrive. His efforts, whether timely or not, are directed at exposing what the deepest stakes of this moment are, and Greek tragedy—above all Sophocles—provides the clearest presentation of the dark heart of this struggle.

*   *   *

Once again, a modern war will be the scene for an interpretation of Greek tragedy: Heidegger will return to Sophocles in the 1942 lecture course on Hölderlin's poem "Der Ister," and just as in Hölderlin's *Hyperion* (where the announced background is the Greco-Turkish war of 1770) and as with Nietzsche's *The Birth of Tragedy* (where the explicit background is the Franco-Prussian war of 1870–71), Heidegger will write of tragedy and of conflict during the world war and the Holocaust (rumors of which were finally beginning to circulate more widely in Germany at this time).[68] Here the effort which is somewhat submerged in *Introduction to Metaphysics* will be quite explicit, namely, to configure the conflicts of the present age according to which they are illuminated by Greek tragedy. Sophocles appears here as the preeminent of political thinkers. The monstrous events of the present age find their roots in the strange possibilities of human life, which has yet to grasp its own nature.

The lecture course in which Heidegger will deepen and somewhat modify his understanding of Sophocles is devoted to reading and interpreting Hölderlin's poem "Der Ister," which is the Greek name for the Danube, a river which metaphorically moves between the Eastern and

Western worlds.[69] The geographic scheme of the poem, like so many of Hölderlin's river poems, provides the occasion for a meditation upon the shift of possibilities that flow between cultures and that pervade the nature of human life on the earth. It is a poem that raises the question of how one is to find oneself at home with the possibilities of life: the nature of a river becomes an image of the nature of human life, which is unsettled. The poem was composed when Hölderlin was completing work on his translations of Sophocles and his so-called "Pindar fragments," and the presence, both in meter and sensibility, of these other works is palpable. In the middle of his lectures on Hölderlin, Heidegger notes the resonance between the poetic sensibilities of Hölderlin and Sophocles, and this becomes the point at which he turns once again to a reading of *Antigone*, this time quite extensively (it will be the stuff of almost ninety pages in the printed lecture course). This time one notes immediately three points which set this reading of *Antigone* apart from the previous one: it is explicitly mediated by a reading of Hölderlin, the central axis defined by the struggle of *techne* and *dike* has been replaced by another struggle (defined by the polarities of *polis* and *pelein*), and there are discussions of the drama and plot itself. Here the interpretation does not remain a decontextualized reading of the choral ode, but sets itself against the dramatic struggles of the tragedy. Here too the engagement is with Hölderlin's translation of, his "conversation" with, "the Greeks."

The question put by the possibility of translation here is central. The question is simple and direct: do the words remain with which the depth of what was experienced in Greek tragedy can be said again today? Heidegger will acknowledge this in a stunning remark: "Tell me what you think about translation, and I will tell you who you are."[70] Not surprisingly in light of the lecture course of 1935, Heidegger singles out the word *deinon* as the key word and acid test of the possibility of such translation. What is very surprising is that with only a brief exception Heidegger persists in speaking of Sophocles through his own, rather than Hölderlin's, translation of the passage.[71] In fact, when Heidegger does speak of the crucial opening lines of Hölderlin's translation he refers it back to an earlier version (1801) in which Hölderlin translates the word *deinon* with the much more Heidegger-friendly word *gewaltige* (powerful) rather than the word that Hölderlin will use in the final version (1804), *ungeheuer* (monstrous). Indeed, when Heidegger does speak of this word *ungeheuer*, he will quickly bend it to his own purposes by thinking it as the *Nicht-geheuren* (the nonfamiliar).[72] But in the final analysis, this question of translation is itself important not only in terms of the details at stake in this particular text, but even more so in light of the role that it plays in the new axis according to which Heidegger thinks the dynamic of the tragedy, namely, homelessness. The strangeness of human being is now to be thought in terms of an essential not-being-at-home—*Unheimlichkeit* is thought in terms of *Unheimischkeit*—and this character of not being at home is itself grounded in the relation between being and human being.[73] Language, which Heidegger will eventually name as the "house of being,"[74] has everything to do with how it is that human beings come to find a home in the world. The thematic of home now complements the unfolding of strangeness, and together these notions give expression to the conception of human being that emerges out of this encounter between Hölderlin and Sophocles as Heidegger thinks it. Now the task of the poet is to open the realm of this original home—the *polis*—and this is what unites Sophocles and Hölderlin in Heidegger's reading of each. The struggle to find our place in the world is now understood as a struggle to come to language itself. This is what now qualifies poetry in Heidegger's view as an originally political act (something which Plato knew as well).

Heidegger now sees this drive to the site exposed in language explicitly at work in a phrase that he spins differently than in *Introduction to Metaphysics* (but, importantly, he does not change his translation to accentuate this shift). The passage is the one that he translates with the phrase "looms larger," and the verb here that he will unpack in a new manner (and which he will now elevate to the central issue of the ode itself) is *pelein*. Heidegger notes that this word, which is common in both Homer and Hesiod, is typically translated (as Hölderlin does) as "is," but that it is an old word and conveys the original sense of finding a place and holding fast in it. Now *pelein* is the name of the manner in which the strangeness of human being presents itself. Strangeness now includes the manner in which such strangeness resides, "looms large," in human life. This is the word in which we learn how *es gibt*—there is—strangeness. Heidegger's reading of the opening line of the choral ode now has that line recoiling back upon itself, and so the essential strangeness of human life is now amplified: human strangeness shows itself in this strange manner. But more importantly, this strangeness now shows itself as a drive to unfold its own nature. It is, Heidegger will say, the way in which human being breaks into the open, into presence. Understood in this manner, *pelein* is a word that points toward the place, the scene, of the appearance of the human being, and this place will soon be defined as the *polis*. With this Heidegger opens up the question of the grounds of community in terms quite different from those which think it as the coming together of discrete subjects; now it will need to be rethought in terms of the manner in which it preserves this strange law of appearance of the human being. To think the *polis* in any other way, for instance, to think it in terms of the modern form of the state, is, according to Heidegger, to translate the truth of political life away from what is essential to the realm which forgets the double bind of human appearance. But it also must be said that this "violence," this translation of the original site of appearance into the framework of the state, in which man sets himself into an "empty errancy," shows that "human being is, in its essence, itself a *katastrophe*—a reversal which turns it from its own essential nature."[75] Now Heidegger is able to interpret the uncanniness of human being as the capacity for this reversal, as this doubling within itself, and this is how he interprets the paradoxical phrase *pantoporos aporos* from out of which Heidegger will come to unpack an understanding of the nature of the place that is the *polis*. When Heidegger says that "The *polis* does not let itself be defined 'politically',"[76] he is reaffirming his fundamental contention that it is only by thinking the possibilities of the space of appearance—possibilities which are always catastrophic possibilities—that we can come to think the realm within which human being together is intelligible. This is what it means to say

> The gods and the temple, celebrations and games, rulers and the council of elders, the people's commission and the military forces, the ships and the field soldiers, the poets and the thinkers—all belong to the *polis*. . . . All these are not elements which are presented by a civil order which lays a value upon cultural achievements, rather they emerge out of the relation to the gods . . . and out of the possibility of celebration, out of the relation of master and slave, out of the relation to sacrifice and battle, out of the relation to honor and glory, out of the relation of these relations and out of the ground of their unity that which is called *polis* governs.[77]

All this emerges out of the peculiar space of appearance which owes itself to the unfolding of the *deinon* nature, the strangeness, of human being. And the tragic poem will excel at exposing this strangeness.

Antigone will stand as the essence and supreme form of this strangeness. This means that now the dynamics of her tragedy will be interpreted as an illustration of the conflict that emerges out of the catastrophic possibilities of such strangeness. That is why on this occasion Heidegger is able to turn to some (still highly truncated) discussion of the events and exchanges of the drama: those events serve as confirmation of the view of human being which the chorus lays out in its ode. Antigone is an exemplary figure in the utmost, and yet she is this not because she chooses well but because she does not deny the force of human destiny and the impossible situation it may unfold. That is how Heidegger interprets the first exchange between Antigone and Ismene in which Ismene is seen as trying to pull her back from this catastrophic destiny. The operative word in this exchange is *tamechana,* which Heidegger translates as "that against which nothing is to be done. . . . It is that which is sent, destiny and its essential ground,"[78] and he suggests that the proper understanding of this word—spoken by Ismene, who is urging Antigone not to put herself in the service of the impossible—leads us back to the most original roots of Antigone's tragedy. Her tragedy is not rooted in any willfulness or disobedience that could be ascribed either to her or to Creon; rather, the conflict between Antigone and the state (in the figure of Creon) is exemplary of a human situation. It is not conscience which leads all the characters of the drama to the catastrophic events which descend upon them; it is rather the law of the double bind governing the space of human appearance, a law which forms the *polis* and is first announced in the word *pelein*. It is simply her presence, her nature really, which summons into being the counter-presence of Creon. She made no mistake, committed no crime that could have been evaded. To understand Antigone is to understand her fidelity to the most elemental, the strange, possibilities which are properly human.

What one sees, then, in the figure of Antigone is the figure of destiny as such; fulfilling the nature of her appearance as this singular being— singular in several ways, but here electing to identify herself as this sister—she entered the space within which not only did the overturning of that being become possible, but it even became necessary. This tragedy will never be able to be thought within the framework of good and evil. No calculus could ever reckon the countervalent claims of Antigone and Creon; each has made the other necessary. But this tragedy is not simply, nor could it ever be, a matter between two individuals since it belongs to the realm of appearance on the original level of the *polis*. Now we see that the tragedy is a public event; it saturates the life of a people. It exceeds any capacity which is proper to the individual and so is not, as in earlier treatments, to be thought in the passion of a single individual (Oedipus) or the challenge to the world of a form of knowledge (which Prometheus embodies). The tragic character of appearance belongs to the entire space and very possibility of appearance. Now, making one more attempt to give an indication of the manner in which this space gathers itself into a unity, Heidegger suggests that this, the true place of appearance, is referred to in the choral ode in the remarks which refer to the hearth, to *hestia*.[79] This word, which appears in the final verse of the ode, is the final name which Heidegger finds given to the site in which the strangeness of human life is able to appear.

Heidegger's discussion of *hestia*, of the hearth which is the heart of the home, finds it to be one of the names for the open space of appearance of which he has been speaking. He deepens his discussion of the character of *hestia* by making reference to Plato's *Phaedrus*, where we find the connections between the goddess Hestia and the home and the earth are forged.[80] Although his reference here is to the earth and the home, the discussion of the meaning of *hestia* that follows refers it once again, not to social relations such as one might find in a home, nor to the symbolic communication between the mortal home and the home of the gods (the hearth is the place where flames from the home reach to the sky and so unite the earth and sky), but rather to the site of appearance. It is not entirely unexpected, then (though it is of course a startling claim), when

Heidegger announces that "the hearth . . . is being itself in the light and shimmer, and glow and warmth, of which all beings have always already gathered themselves."[81] Now Antigone's allegiance to the hearth, to home, as well as her identification with the earth, show themselves not as the expression of any solidarity to other human beings, but as manifestations of her fidelity to the conditions of human appearance. She is thus a political figure not by virtue of any deliberate act for or against other individuals, but by virtue of her proximity to the original site of human appearance which goes by the names of both *polis* and *hestia*.

What is striking about Heidegger's reading of *Antigone* is the absolute conviction which guides it, namely, that the truth of communal life, the manner in which we can come to understand the conditions under which human beings share life in time and so forge a history, is to be grasped only by reference to an understanding of the way in which human life comes to appearance. His reading of the drama rips it completely away from any interpretation which would see in it a struggle between good and evil—no matter how those notions are configured or in what figures they are located; rather, he argues that in the drama we find an exploration of the nature of human destiny and of the struggle into which that destiny sets us. Adorno's charge against Heidegger—that he ontologizes beyond the limits of ontology, and this most of all in matters of political life[82]—is perfectly appropriate to Heidegger's reading of *Antigone* during the war which raged while he sought to understand this Greek tragedy. But though this complaint is one we need to hear, and though one cannot help but be taken aback by the absence of any sense that this tragedy is the work of human doings and needs to be understood as such, one cannot help as well but be taken by this drive to grasp an essential errancy at work in human life. There is no sense that Heidegger does this in order to excuse human failings—he truly is thinking here beyond good and evil. He has taken up Nietzsche's task in this reading of the drama; it seems that he is simply trying to understand, so far as understanding itself can operate, the nature which drives us into catastrophe, and he does this apart from any sense of what Nietzsche referred to as the "bookkeeper's scales of justice" on which one weighed out praise and blame. Precisely in this regard Heidegger's reading of *Antigone* is exquisitely "Greek" and evades the moralizing conception of tragedy—indeed, of human life—that comes to dominate as the approach to tragedy coming out of metaphysics and Christianity. The result of his unswerving commitment to this project of thinking the character of our appearance in the world prior to the categories of good and evil is a vision of the figure of Antigone as profoundly solitary. Those categories, which freeze ethical and political life and thus become the death knell of the deepest forms of human experience, cannot serve the task of thinking life radically. Thought to the point of this singularity of life, to the idiom of the human idiom, others *seem*—but only seem—to slip away. What is difficult to come to see is how it is that precisely at this point of the most elemental human solitude one is not isolated, but at the site of what will become communal life. This site, the original meaning of *polis,* is, as Heidegger thinks it, the locus of the idiom, but an idiom that is not able to be thought in isolation since the conditions of its appearance are wedded to the forces which open themselves as history. It is a conflicted site, the place in which a reversal of everything is possible, and it is this site which the tragedy has exposed. Antigone is who she is by virtue of the fact that she, above all, is riveted to this strange site. She is also—and quite importantly—not to be understood as a figure of the Western world. She now signifies the quality which the West and its traditions of metaphysics and Christianity cannot grasp. Here, as everywhere, Heidegger's image of the Greeks and their world throws them out of the Western canon and shows them rather to possess what Hölderlin once called an "oriental vitality."

*   *   *

The next time Heidegger will turn in any significant manner to the topic of tragedy will be shortly after the end of the war. It is a time of confusion, Freiburg is in ruins, Heidegger is about to have a breakdown, and the truth of what Germany had done could no longer be evaded or denied. It is still two years until the "zero hour" would be reached in Germany. Heidegger will have to confront his own past in the denazification proceedings after the war. And two texts, two of the most far-reaching of Heidegger's texts, come from this period: the "Letter on Humanism" and "The Saying of Anaximander," both from 1946. Both of these works need to be read as efforts to comprehend the possibility of a future from the perspective of a shattered present. Both of them need to be read together since each is dedicated to trying to open a way of thinking human being and history in a manner which does not submit itself to the framework of "humanism" and to the moral calculus of good and evil. Together their attempt is to open up what Heidegger will famously, and cryptically, describe as an "original ethics." Reading these texts together one comes to the conclusion that while the "Letter on Humanism" provides a radical critique of the metaphysical forms in which we think our shared life in time, "The Saying of Anaximander" provides a glimpse of how it is that such an "original ethics" might be opened up outside of the orbit which such forms define.

But the starting point of both essays is clear: Heidegger is now more convinced than ever that Western culture has exhausted itself, that it no longer offers resources that are tenable for addressing the enigmas of a possible future, and consequently some genuinely different conception of the task of being in history must be disclosed. But even the name of

260

that which he finds as the task of thinking in the present age is problem-atic: words like "ethics" and "justice" no longer suffice as cues for what it is that the present historical juncture most needs. Such words are no longer serviceable because they belong to an order of understanding that does not grasp the original riddle of human being. In order to find the vocabu-lary out of which an original ethics—an ethics that addresses itself to the original site of the very appearance of the human being in history—might be found, Heidegger turns to "the 'oldest' saying of Western thought,"[83] namely, the saying of Anaximander which, according to the usual transla-tion, speaks of the relation of time and justice.

There are several reasons that one might be taken aback by this text right from its first sentences: the very thought of turning to an ancient and exceedingly difficult Greek text at this precise historical juncture is astonishing (and to add to this astonishment Heidegger insists upon the urgency of this work), and one is surprised by the claim that this is the "oldest" saying of Western thought; it leads one to wonder according to what measure this is the "oldest" text we possess. One is only mildly sur-prised by the role that Nietzsche, the "last philosopher of justice" (who provides the counterpoint which propels this text forward on several oc-casions), plays in the formulation of the task of this essay. Likewise with the remark that "Hegel is the sole thinker of the West who has thought-fully experienced the history of thought."[84] So from the outset one is chal-lenged by the way in which this text announces its own assumptions. But immediately one recognizes as well the lifelong concerns and hallmarks of Heidegger's thought: here history is presented as an essential riddle of human being, not as a background event against which a discrete subject is to be portrayed; here the possibilities of *techne* and human technicity and their place in nature are central themes; and here we find an ex-tended meditation on the question of destiny and necessity. It is a text that opens with the same reference to the time of crisis which opened the *Introduction to Metaphysics;* the only difference is a sense of the magnitude of this epochal moment: now Heidegger will use the word that he so re-luctantly brushed against in earlier years, now he will say, "Do we find ourselves even in the approaching time of the most *monstrous* transforma-tion of the entire earth and of the time of the space of history?"[85] And now he will try to answer his own question by making reference to how it is that history must be understood today. So Heidegger turns to this text of Anax-imander not in order to be the custodian of another time, but precisely in order to come to terms with the character of this time and to ask quite simply—apart from any economy of good and evil—What must be done?

"The Saying of Anaximander" is one of the most difficult and original of Heidegger's texts, and so it bears a careful reading even though I will not offer one simply because it exceeds the scope of my concerns here in so many significant respects.[86] However, some acknowledgment of the

261

role that the idea of the tragic plays is needed. It appears here in two forms: first, a citation from Homer, and, second, a reference to the essential kinship uniting history and tragedy. Neither of these brief references becomes the occasion for an extended reflection upon either a text or a topic drawn from tragedy; rather, both serve as linchpins in the argument of the text. But as such linchpins, they serve a key role in the text and show yet again how profoundly Heidegger has drawn upon an understanding of something he finds disclosed in the sensibility of Greek tragedy.

The reference to Homer is to the beginning of the *Iliad* (book 1, lines 79ff.). It occurs at the point the Achaeans had suffered nine days of losses from "the arrows of god" (a plague had been sent by Apollo), and in order to understand the cause of Apollo's rage, Achilles, whose own rage would set the whole of the tale told by Homer in motion, summons the prophet Calchas to tell what might be done to save the army from the plague. At this point we find the passage Heidegger cites: "Again Calchas, the Thestoride, the wisest of those who watch the birds, raised himself, who knew what is, what will be or once was, who had also led the Argive shifts to Troy by means of the wise speaking spirit with which the god Phoebus Apollo had honored him."[87] Heidegger is not interested in the context of this passage, and so nothing is said of the rage of Achilles or of the death and the war that raged at the time. Nor does Heidegger discuss the fact that Calchas, the seer, is blind (a theme which was so prominent in *Introduction to Metaphysics*). Rather, again, as in *Introduction to Metaphysics*, Heidegger turns to Homer in order to understand something of language. Here the question concerns the word (and of course the im/possibility of translation) *eon*, which is typically translated as "being" but which Heidegger will understand as "being present in unconcealment."[88] The manner in which Heidegger enlists Homer to the ends of his own linguistic argument is a bit strained, to say the least, and one need not try to retrace its steps since the argument could just as easily be made without this appeal to Homer's language. But what is worth noting about this citation is that here, as in the treatment of Sophocles, Heidegger finds us confronted with a word that speaks outside of the orbit of metaphysics, and it is to this that he most wants to call attention. The word *eon* as it is found in Homer opens up an experience of beings as presencing in unconcealment; in other words, here we find one way in which we can open ourselves up to an experience of the appearance of a world which has not, in advance, submitted itself to the law of appearance circumscribed by metaphysics and its presumptions. It is no accident that this language, the vocabulary which Heidegger so passionately seeks, is found in a work of tragic poetry. But that is not the point that Heidegger pursues, and the fact that here we have to do with the language of Homer is never fully problematized. Heidegger has another agenda here, and so this reference, though decisive in the text, remains largely only on the level of an illustration.

Heidegger's agenda here is to understand the kinship of justice and time, or, as he will morph the question, the kinship of history and injustice. It is a significant shift. When he comes to the point at which this kinship must be named he is clear:

> The experience of beings in their being, which is being brought to language here, is not pessimistic and not nihilistic; it is also not optimistic. It remains tragic. But that is a presumptuous remark. Presumably we arrive at a trace of the essence of the tragic when we do not explain it psychologically or aesthetically, but rather only when we reflect upon its essential form, being of beings, insofar as we think the *didonai diken . . . tes adikias.*[89]

Heidegger's gloss on this passage and his translation, which takes the passage almost to the point at which it strains simple comprehension, calls attention to the double logic of the presencing of what is present: "They let belong, the self-same, fitting (in overcoming) of un-fitting."[90] His point is to name the doubled truth of the appearance of beings, of what presences and lingers. The passage he draws upon to do this is taken from Anaximander's fragment, and this fragment of that fragment, which has been shattered almost beyond the point it can be understood, now bears the name of the essence of the tragic. What is clear is that here again the essence of the tragic is presented as a matter of the conflicted law of appearance. Furthermore, the same features which marked both the 1935 and 1942 interpretations of *Antigone* are evident here. One sees, for instance, that a linguistic doubling or a countervalent relation governs the passage (*hypsipolis-apolis; pantoporos-aporos; diken-adkias; techne-dike; polis-pelein*), and that this conflicted relation is not rooted in any human difference or antagonism but in the logic of being itself. One also sees that here, as well as in the earlier texts, the issue is the site of appearance *as such.* We do not come by the essence of the tragic insofar as we trace the conflict it displays back to anything "human," any act of the will or a subject, but only insofar as we see its origin, its original nature, in the very logic, the tragedy, of all appearance. The phrase that Heidegger adopted from Karl Reinhardt in 1935 to introduce his reading of the choral ode from *Antigone,* "the tragedy of appearance," will always remain the key to understanding how it is that Heidegger will think the truth of tragedy.

*   *   *

"The Saying of Anaximander" is one of the final texts in which the idea of the tragic plays a significant role in Heidegger's work. The virtual disappearance of the themes and problems of tragedy, especially of Sophoclean tragedy which plays such a crucial role in Heidegger's thought from 1933 until 1946, is difficult to explain but should not be ignored. Nor should one push aside the surprise at this fact: not only would the sudden but intense attention given to the topic of tragedy during the decade 1933–42 lead one to expect that it would not disappear, but also the central themes of Heidegger's postwar thought—language, destiny, technology, art, to name but a few—were key themes of the earlier treatment of tragedy. Likewise, Hölderlin and Nietzsche, the mediating figures of so much of Heidegger's own reading of tragedy, remain at the center of his concerns. Even the record of his trip to Greece, the very personal and highly re-flective text entitled *Aufenthalte,* does not serve as the occasion to revisit the question of tragedy. But while the word and the references to specific texts largely disappear, the issues which were opened up by this confron-tation with Greek tragedy remain prominent. In fact, they seem only to grow in prominence, so that one is tempted to say that the less the word "tragedy" is spoken, the fewer the citations from tragic literature, the more deeply the issue of tragedy penetrates to the heart of Heidegger's own concerns.

The timing of Heidegger's most intensive engagement with Greek tragedy should not go unnoticed. It is one signal that his turn to Greek tragedy is, in part, motivated by an effort to understand the crisis of his-tory and of community. What is conspicuous in the way this engagement with tragedy takes shape at this time is that it opens the path that he takes out of the metaphysical-Christian conception of history and human life which finds it to be intelligible only within the framework of good and evil, the framework of values. Nietzsche had exposed the failure of such a framework to grasp the deepest elements of life at work in human being; indeed, he had shown vividly how such a framework succeeds only in mor-tifying the real nature of such a being. Heidegger's turn to Greek tragedy is guided by his attempt to think the space of history, even the possibil-ity of community, that is, of a shared history, outside of the orbit of good and evil, yet with reference to the depth of freedom proper to the site of appearance. He is right when he suggests that the metaphysical concep-tion of values and its theological counterpart can never grasp this space in its fullest sense—right too when he argues that Greek tragedy can never be understood from the vantage point of such metaphysics. The complex-ity of human life, its conflicted roots, and the tragedy of all appearance emerge from Heidegger's reading of tragedy with unparalleled clarity and power. Why does he move away from any further consideration of Greek tragedy? Why not deepen what proves itself to be a productive avenue for thinking issues dear to Heidegger's heart?

It is unlikely that we will ever find clear answers to such questions, but it does seem that the move into Greek tragedy, which coincides with Hei-degger's assumption of the Rector's post at the University of Freiburg, helps to understand the move away from this same topic. Greek tragedy was a key to, ultimately the real focal point of, Heidegger's most explicit attempt to address the "realities" of historical and political life; it was also at the heart of his project of getting over metaphysics as well as the polarities of good and evil. After the war, when the realities of historical and political life seem to have overtaken Heidegger, I believe that he comes to the view that the distress of the present age is deeper still than he had been capable of imagining previously. Even tragedy is not sufficient to the task of thinking the epochal unfolding of history as he understands it. That does not mean that he beats a retreat from the question of history, nor does it mean that he abandons the theme of tragedy. What it does mean is that Heidegger will deepen his interest in that feature of tragedy which never received much attention from him in the early years, namely, the fact that here we have to do with a work of art in words. Whereas the first interpretations of Greek tragedy almost neglected their work character, and seldom spoke of the language of tragedy *as poetic language* (it would always be spoken of in order to ferret out the meaning of a word or to raise the question of translation), after "The Saying of Anaximander" Heidegger will find these concerns at the forefront of his own. But this ever deepening sense of language does not take him away from, but only ever closer to, the very same themes and enigmas that he first broaches in his discussion of Greek tragedy.

Adorno once famously commented that after Auschwitz poetry will no longer be possible. Likewise, George Steiner would write that after the Holocaust the German language would no longer be capable of speaking the idiom of freedom, which Heine had once dreamt as its greatest possibility,[91] because in the horrors it had learned to articulate and command it had forfeited its right to serve as the bearer of either civilization or freedom.[92] After the war Heidegger poses the question, tacitly, whether any language other than the language of poetry can be spoken. Can any manner of language other than poetic language measure up to the task of answering to the idiom of freedom in a time when the realities of history are so monstrous? Heidegger's conception of language which is capable of drawing close to the original point of human life—the point at which it suffers—will remain by and large the same after the war. But it will no longer be confined to the language of Greek tragedy. Sophocles no longer is the sole voice of such a language; now Trakl, George, Hölderlin, Lao Tzu, now Japanese and German as well as Greek will be some of the ways that Heidegger asks if language can still speak to the realities of human time. It should go without saying, but perhaps must be stressed nonetheless, that the limits of his list are not essential limits (and there is nothing to suggest that he would argue for such a claim); other languages, other poets, need to have the same question put to them. Just as Sophocles opens up a Greek understanding and Hölderlin a German one, so is English in need of the self-understanding which perhaps only language itself can offer. But, of course—as Heidegger early in his efforts to raise this question would insist upon reminding us—every such question is haunted by the question put to us of the possibility of translation.

One final haunting question remains as an element of the legacy of Heidegger's efforts to understand the insights of Greek tragedy. He turned to it as a literature, an achievement of language, which once, and perhaps once again, showed itself capable of disclosing the true nature of the distress of a shared life in time. Tragedy was called upon to shed light upon the crisis of history. Heidegger puts us before the question whether the insights of Greek tragedy—into errancy, destiny, blindness, and conflicted truths—remain helpful as we try to understand the distress of our monstrous and self-lacerating present. But after Heidegger one must ask as well whether insights are capable of explaining *our distress,* namely, that *we still do not understand.* We still have not found the words and understanding which might open the path to an answer to the same riddles that Heidegger once posed. And now we face another riddle, one very much about human errancy and blindness: how are we to understand how it is that one of the great minds of our times could be blind to something so decisive in his own times? Heidegger is not the first great mind to err so profoundly—Plato was only the first obvious case of the delusion of which such minds are capable—but Heidegger is the issue of our times. It does no good to tar Heidegger with the brush of his error. The stain of his collusion, and the puzzle of his subsequent reticence, are obvious enough, and the effort to shut the whole of Heidegger down—an effort far too widespread to simply ignore—must be seen as motivated by something other than a refusal of his undeniable political and human blunder. And yet the genuine question remains, and insists that it be posed until answered: how can one who thinks so penetratingly err so greatly? In the effort to understand what we still do not fully grasp about this matter, it might just be the case that tragedy, which offers some real insight into errancy and the reversal of natures, provides clues that should be taken to heart.

Plato argued that no one committed a wrong voluntarily, that knowledge was the final safeguard against our own monstrous capacities. Greek tragedy presents a different view of the matter, and, as Heidegger's own reading of the choral ode from *Antigone* shows, it stands as a powerful and persistent memento of the danger, the abyssal possibilities, which belongs to human life and which no knowledge can control.

APPENDIX H

Heidegger's Translation of the Choral Ode from Antigone *(1935)*

The uncanny is many-sided; nothing, however,
looms larger than the human in strangeness.
He travels on the effervescent tides
driven by the southern winds of winter,
crossing peaks of raging waves.
The gods, even the most sublime ones,
he wears down, and
the earth—indestructible and tireless—too
overturning her from year to year,
plowing back and forth with stallions.

Even the lightly moving race of birds he snares
and hunts the animals of the wilderness
and creatures native to the sea.
With cleverness he overwhelms the animal,
that wanders the mountains through the night,
he tames the shaggy neck of the stallion and the impetuous bull
placing them in a harness.

He has even found his way to the resonance of the word
and to an all encompassing intelligence, swift as the wind,
and even to the courage that rules cities.
He has learned how to flee
exposure to the arrows of weather, of unwelcome frost.

Everywhere moving forward, underway, lacking experience
having no exit,
he comes to naught.
The sole pressure that he cannot evade by means of any flight is death,
even if through some skill he has succeeded
in escaping some wasting illness.

Ingenious to be sure, mastering skills beyond dreams,
he falls sometimes to malice,
other times he happens again upon worthiness.
He weaves his way between the laws of the earth
and the oath enjoined by the gods.

Towering high above the city,
he forfeits the place who,
for the sake of risk,
always takes as existing the nonexisting.

Never will one who does such things
share my hearth,
neither shall my mind share the phantasms
of such a person.

APPENDIX I

Hölderlin's Translation of the Choral Ode from Antigone *(1804)*

Much is monstrous. But nothing
More monstrous than man.
For he, through the night
of the sea, when toward the winter
the south wind blows, he sets out
In winged and whispering houses.
And the heavenly sublime earth
The incorruptible, tireless earth
He erases; with the striving plough,
From year to year
He pursues his dealings, with the race of stallions,
And the lightly dreaming world of birds
He ensnares, and hunts them;
And the train of wild animals,
And of Pontos's nature animated by salt
With spun nets
This knowing man.
And with arts he catches game
That spends the night and roams on mountains.
And over the neck of the rough-maned stallion
He throws a yoke, and over the untamable steer that
Wanders the mountains.

And the honest and airy
Thoughts and the pride ruling over the city,
He has learned, and slopes of damp air where ill dwell,
And misfortune, the arrows,
He has learned to flee. Wandering everywhere
Unwandered. To naught he arrives.
Death, the future place, alone
He does not know how to flee,
And the flood of temporary plagues
He thinks through.

Possessing more of wisdom, and the skill of art,
Than he can hope for,
He arrives at disaster, on account of something else.

He complains of the law, of the earth, of the power of nature
With the oath of his conscience.
High cited, uncitied,
He arrives at nothing,
Where the beautiful
Is with him and audacity.
One who does this
Should never be with me at the hearth
Never be of similar mind.

Convictions
and Suspicions

What conclusions can we draw? To invite the
gods ruins our relationship with them but sets
history in motion. A life in which the gods are
not invited isn't worth living. It will be quieter,
but there won't be any stories. And you could
suppose that these dangerous invitations were in
fact contrived by the gods themselves, because
the gods get bored with men who have no
stories.
—Roberto Calasso,
The Marriage of Cadmus and Harmony, p. 387

Each of us is assigned a riddle. It belongs to the pure realm of the idiom
and is not translatable. I cannot answer the final questions which you must
put to yourself. And yet we are not on this account isolated from one
another; we do not forfeit our chance to trade stories simply by virtue of
this being in the singular. Quite the contrary. Paradoxically, human solidarity seems to find one of its deepest and sturdiest roots precisely in this
singular experience. Solitude and solidarity are not mutually exclusive
even if they move us in opposing directions. Torn by these twin impulses—
on the one hand a fidelity to singularity, on the other to a solidarity—we
find ourselves committed not simply to the idiom of a singular life, but
equally, even *by virtue of* this singularity, to the ideality of a genuine solidarity with what exceeds that life. We live then as this unsettled idiom of
the ideal. And so paradox compounds riddle. We confront a puzzle that
will not remain stable, no rules are given in advance, but what rules we
learn emerge as an element of the riddle itself. And this is just the beginning.

Oedipus was said to have stood before the Sphinx, riddle confronting riddle, and there he gave the answer to one riddle, in one word, "man," and with this answer he simultaneously saved the city and set himself on the path to his own destruction. The crossroads at which he confronted his father, Laius, only to kill him, was not the only, or even the decisive, crossroads at which he stood. The second crossroads came in the form of the riddle put to him. It was a riddle that he answered in general and in the abstract, but the other riddle, the riddle of his own identity, would be the one he would fail to understand until it was too late to bear its truth. Hölderlin charts the trajectory of this "deranged seeking for a consciousness" that defines Oedipus as precisely this failure to grasp the idiom of his own being which strangely we can see from the outset.

Antigone, Oedipus's daughter/sister, was wedded so completely to the ideal of the idiom that she herself dies on behalf of a corpse which is the emblem of the human idiom in its purest form. Appropriately, she will be the one who gently leads Oedipus to the place of his own death. Seemingly sure of herself, of who she is and of what she must do to honor that truth of herself, Antigone becomes the greater riddle for us. The reasons for her actions—her readiness to die to honor a corpse while at the same time conceding that she would not do this for any other love in her life, not even for her own children or husband if she had those—are opaque to us. She remains a mystery to us but becomes very much an ideal by virtue of her steadfast commitment to her own nature.

We find ourselves always between the abstract and the particular, the universal and the unique, the idiom and the ideal, solitude and solidarity, and somewhere in this conflicted identity the riddle which is posed unfolds as a life. It is a life that oscillates between being seen and understood and remaining very much in the dark, and it floats on a sea of reasons which do not always flow in the same direction and take us to places we might never have anticipated. Greek tragedy presents human life from out of this conflicted site, and one reason it speaks to us so powerfully of the experience of this site is that it finds a way to speak of it as the story of a destiny; in other words, it is an acknowledgment of the force with which these polarities pull and define us. Understood in this way, destiny is not the other to human freedom, it is not a denial of that freedom, but rather its price and even its supreme tribute. The Greeks had no word for freedom as we have come to conceptualize it in philosophy, but that is because it was such a clear, yet unspeakable given in the very idea of destiny.

And yet precisely in its sense of the force of destiny, Greek tragedy stands as a reminder of the role of chance in life. We realize that destiny is a reply to chance, to the simple fact that one day we find ourselves at a crossroads where we might find either a god or monster—or, as Oedipus found without ever knowing, even both in the same figure—who will alter the path of our choices and even retrodictively rewrite the story we have imagined for ourselves. That is why Aristotle could say that no one could be called happy while still alive.

In the end, though we "journey everywhere," we "arrive at nothing." Death—pure incomprehensibility, the ultimate compression of solitude and yet the only incontrovertible universal—is the sole fact, the only stability, in the turbulence of human life. The *Iliad* is about this fact perhaps even more than it is about a war between the citizens of different cities. There are seemingly endless numbers of individual deaths tallied in the *Iliad,* and most are noted by a proper name and are described in some detail (no two descriptions are alike). Throughout the *Iliad,* time is taken out of the story, and the tale of the war is repeatedly interrupted, so that the character of an individual death can be told. The finality of death does not, however, signal the finality of the story to be told.

Strangest of all in this mix of turmoil and suffering is the simple appearance and fact of language, of the *telling* itself. Everything finds its own nature in the possibilities of the word, and so it is in the telling itself that what little intelligibility we can eke out with respect to this riddle gets created.

Philosophy and art are the two chief forms dedicated to this struggle for some measure of intelligibility with regard to the riddle that we are. But they carry out this project with rather different—and *asymmetrical*—senses of the possibilities of language. Philosophy defines itself as a commitment to the idiom of the ideal; art is a commitment to the ideal of the idiom. In a curious way they resemble Oedipus and Antigone, and their relationship will be just as complicated and incestuous—at least as far as philosophy is concerned.

*   *   *

What is striking above all is that ancient Greece excelled at both philosophy and art. For a brief moment in the record of human history we find a culture and a language—a people—which gave rise to both forms. Of course, this took place at a moment prior to the division of forms of knowing and reflection into disciplines and canons, and so the difference between them was one that needed to be established. That effort to distinguish and adjudicate the differing claims of art and philosophy was a task that Greek philosophers took upon themselves, and for them it was a task of gravest significance. On the other hand, it must be said that we find no tragedian who takes up the question of this relation between art and philosophy such as we find in the works of Plato and Aristotle, who demonstrate a genuine interest in that relation. It was left to comedy to deal with the place of philosophy from the perspective of literary art. Aristophanes, not Homer, will be the one from whom we hear something of the nature of philosophy from outside of its own assumptions and laws. But what is important to note is that in Greece one finds both tragedy, this form of art in which it is said that human life is liquid contradiction confronting the weight of destiny, and, at the same time, this drive to philosophy which searches for a way to stabilize this liquidity of human life, thereby assimilating and taming the elemental claims of tragic art. The cohabitation of these two disparate forms is a contradiction which defines the highest productions of Greek culture. That subsequent cultures remain bent upon resolving this contradiction is one of the ways which set them apart from the sensibility animating Greek culture.

But in Greece philosophers and poets understood themselves as taking up the same issues—language, death, and affective life—and asking about the place of these issues in the formation of the community. It was also clear that these issues were of paramount importance for the development of the new form of political life which was still in the process of evolving, namely, democracy. What is most important to note, though, is that neither philosophy nor tragedy understood itself to be addressing these questions of political life within the framework of a conception of good and evil. Although these notions will have nascent forms in Plato and Aristotle, and although these will in large measure be formulated in their respective confrontations with tragedy, neither Plato nor Aristotle would understand tragedy as a morality play. That only fully emerges with the consolidation of the perspective of metaphysics and the insertion of Christianity and its concerns into that perspective.

Two points need to be noted and secured regarding the relation of philosophy and tragedy in ancient Greece. First, in Greece, *tragedy is not understood as a presentation of the conflict between good and evil, or right and wrong;* rather, it is one of the ways in which the horror that human beings can create for themselves is displayed and so reflected upon. Second, though we find Plato and Aristotle writing about tragedy, *we find no theory of the tragic in ancient Greece.* This simply means that what is to be found in tragedy is not yet taken up into the idea of the tragic.

*   *   *

But both of these decisive features of the relation of philosophy and tragedy that we find definitive in ancient Greece will be fundamentally transformed almost immediately upon the end of the classical period. Coinciding with the end of the creative age of Greek drama we find a basic alteration in the way in which philosophers take up the question of tragedy. The birth of Euripides might well signal the beginning of the end of tragedy as a living art form in Greek culture, but the death of Aristotle (323 B.C.E.) unquestionably marks the death of what is found in this art form as a matter for serious philosophical questioning. After Aristotle, the development of philosophy leads increasingly to the view that the truth of language is found in its conceptual possibilities, not in its capacity to present what we suffer. The result is a commitment in philosophizing to the ideality which is proper to the concept. And, in part as a consequence of this commitment, philosophizing after Aristotle tends to adopt the view that the work of art is simply a matter of "aesthetics." Now tragedy becomes the representation of an idea—the idea of the tragic—and, perhaps most importantly, even if it is not always announced as such, tragedy is now regarded as a morality play, as the struggle of right and wrong which is presented in the puerile form of art—that is, insofar as tragedy is taken up as a serious question at all. Indeed, what is most commonly the case is a fundamental *neglect* of the question posed by tragedy. After Plato and Aristotle we find no protracted effort to develop a theory of tragedy, or any significant engagement with tragic literature, of the same order of magnitude as we find in Plato and Aristotle. Until Schelling.

One might object that there are treatments of tragedy prior to Schelling that merit attention as something more than passing considerations. Here one might mention works by Lessing (1756) and Schiller (1792), but besides the obvious fact that they are largely contemporaneous with Schelling, it also needs to be pointed out that, until Hegel, there is no extended effort to systematically take up the question of tragedy as an essentially *philosophical* question. This almost total absence of any philosophical concern with the question of tragedy is striking. One reason for this fact is circumstantial: the texts of Greek tragedies were simply not widely available. The burning of the library at Alexandria (47 B.C.E.) saw the destruction of more literature than we know (this is one reason we only possess seven of Sophocles' 123 tragedies). Indeed, it was not until the mid–fifteenth century that Western countries would come into any significant possession of texts from the Greek world that could be copied and read (until then only excerpts were available; not only that, but these were in the original form of Greek, in which all the words were written in capital letters without word division, without accents and breathing marks, and with the change of speaker designated only by a dash; in other words, what was present had an almost unintelligible form). In short, until the Renaissance, *Greek* tragedy essentially disappeared from the horizon of known literature. But that still does not explain the absence of the question of tragedy *generally*. So, for instance, we tend to be taken aback when we realize that Descartes (1596–1650) lived almost contemporaneously with Shakespeare (1564–1616). What is surprising is that we do not expect that he would take up the question of the accomplishment of this literature (about which he surely heard, even though he could not read English), even though as a young man Descartes was quite interested in theater and wrote dramatic "ballets." Nothing in the conception of philosophy, namely *as metaphysics*, which guides Descartes and his age would leave room for the idea of asking about tragedy as a philosophical matter. That is why Alexander Pope's magnificent translation of Homer seemed to leave no mark upon English-language philosophizing whatsoever (whereas Hölderlin's translations of Sophocles, just short of a century later, would have a profound impact upon German philosophy). The conception of philosophy found in Descartes does not make the themes that tragedy represents necessary. Such would remain the case at least until Schelling opens the door for what will prove to be an escalation of the importance of the question posed by tragedy even beyond its place in Plato and Aristotle.

* * *

When it returns it does so specifically indexed to the *Greek* world, its people, and its language. And when it reappears it dominates *German* philosophy. Curiously, it does not seem to find nearly as much interest as a topic in any other language of philosophizing.

With regard to the interest in the ancient world, it must first be said that this does not mean that the question put by Greek tragedy is simply a matter of an antiquarian interest. Nothing could be further from the truth. It is no accident that the recovery of the question of Greek tragedy appears immediately on the heels of the French Revolution and that it was championed first by those who were inspired by the French Revolution (and to a lesser extent the American Revolution, which did not go unnoticed, but which was too remote to register with the same force as what was happening in France). It is also no accident that this recovery of the question follows in the wake of Kant and comes from those who took Kant's critique of metaphysics deeply to heart. The turn to the topic of tragedy, now in order to develop a *theory of the tragic,* has above all these dual motivations: the effort to think through the end of philosophy as metaphysics, which Kant first made a necessary concern, and the effort to think the radical transformation in history and the idea of freedom that is announced by the French Revolution. What Kant describes as "the peculiar fate of reason" will come to be seen as having a hidden resonance with the fate of freedom in human history: both will lend themselves to being illustrated and thought according to the model of Greek tragedy. Tragedy reappears as a theme for philosophic reflection at precisely this moment of *crisis,* a moment that understands itself as marking an epochal end and a new, still uncharted beginning.

A new constellation of possibilities for philosophizing begin to emerge from this point, and the idea of the tragic is very much at the center of the formation of those possibilities. To detail some of those possibilities has been the concern of this book, and so they need not be rehearsed again. What might not be so readily apparent from those details, though, is that the more seriously philosophers took up the topic of tragedy as a challenge, the more the attempt was made to assimilate its insights systematically into philosophizing, the more the character of philosophy was changed. One sees this most dramatically, or at least most self-consciously announced, in the case of Nietzsche, who raises powerfully, and in a manner we can no longer avoid, the question of the *performance* of thinking.

But however much the question of tragedy will evolve from the moment of its initial appearance in the work of Schelling, Hegel, and Hölderlin, it will not lose the two affiliations which define that first appearance: it will always be connected with the overcoming of metaphysics and Christianity, and it will always be linked with the idea of a historical crisis, ultimately with the possibility of a cultural revolution. Both of these links will only deepen over the course of the development of this theme, and they will come to play a decisive role in one of the most distressing philosophical developments of our century, namely, Heidegger's involvement with National Socialism. More must be said about this, but before that can be done two more points must be established. First, why is there this curious cultural kinship between post-Kantian German philosophy and ancient Athenian tragedy? Second, why is it necessary that tragedy be removed from the sphere of metaphysics of morals and simultaneously wedded to the realm of history?

It should be clear by now that "the Greeks" who are the object of such intense fascination and admiration for German philosophers are not the Greeks of philosophy or the moral dramatists of literature who have become canonized as at the foundation of Western culture. Hölderlin was the first to note it, but certainly not the last: "the Greeks" here possess a remarkably "oriental vitality." In fact, one might say that the turn to the Greeks does not seek to idealize the roots of Western culture so much as it seeks to demonstrate that the roots of Western culture are, in the end, nothing "Western." The image of the Greek world that is carved out in German philosophy is not a youthful form of the Enlightenment; rather, it is a world of essential strangeness, of a great sense of the power of life, nature, and destiny, and of an overpowering awareness of what exceeds what human beings can control. In sum, the image of the Greek world here is defined by virtue of its nonmetaphysical view of human life. The Greek world, as it comes to be discovered in this project of German philosophy, a world which is acutely attuned to the darker possibilities of life, does not stand as a confirmation of the most cherished project of the Enlightenment and Christian-metaphysical values; rather, it arrives as the greatest challenge to them. To regard the recovery of Greek thought, so essential to one facet of German philosophy, as the attempt to recover a static and pristine "origin" for philosophy is to mistake this relationship completely. Hölderlin would be the one who first and most decisively debunks such a view when he announces with great clarity and self-awareness that the turn to the Greeks is an engagement with the foreign. Moreover, this element of the foreign, of the strange in every sense of the word, is simultaneously profoundly intimate: it is not the wholly other (if such can ever be said to be a possibility at all); this strangeness of Greek thought, long presumed to be at the roots of Western culture, makes it clear that it is not what it was once thought to be. In this experience, this encounter with the Greek world, we turn out to be strangers to ourselves.

But one can rightly ask: if it is the case that Western cultural forms and frameworks of thinking are now coming to show themselves as exhausted, as no longer viable for the future, then why not simply look to other cultures? Why not turn to Asia, Africa, or wherever else one will? Why persist in looking to Greece? Is there something singular about Greece? Is it so unique that we will need to index ourselves to it eternally? These are serious questions which should not be evaded. And yet they are questions which, for the present at least, we might not be in a position to answer properly. But some remarks can and must be made at this stage.

Of course, it should be obvious that even if there is something truly singular to be found in the productions of Greek culture, that does not mean that other cultures are not equally the home of singularities of equal or greater significance. Greek culture is not a privileged singularity. There are a variety of fronts on which the critique of the present age needs to be carried out—a host of unthought and unassimilated elements of history. But what is—*though perhaps only for the present age*—singular about Greece is the effective history of its legacy. The role that the moment and language which is forged in Greek tragedy has played in the formation of Western culture is undeniable, and to expose the hidden and displaced dimensions of this moment and language is one of the ways in which Western culture begins to overcome itself from within. Nietzsche is the first to develop what must be called a sensitivity to this historical displacement of tragedy. He charts it as the conjunction of three epochal forces: the suicide of tragedy, the rise of the ideal of the theoretical life, and the triumph of the moral will and the image of the world as divided into values. The first two forces he traces back to the Greek world itself, showing that it is not an unambiguous resource for a thinking that would overcome metaphysics, which is the most general name of these forces of displacement.

Three general qualifications must be reinforced here regarding this project of return to Greek thought: first, this return is not without ambiguities, in other words, Greece is not simply an "ideal"; second (a point that follows directly from the first), what is being recovered here has perhaps never been grasped, it is not a reality that is being redeemed, but a possibility; and third, the qualification that the recovery of Greece is significant *"if only for the present age"* is necessary since Greek thought wins its place by virtue of history, and that means it is a place supported perhaps only for the moment. History, ever the region of surprise and reversal, will open new possibilities. What remains true and without qualification is simply this: Greece marks the last moment in which what has come to be the Western world has a contact with forms of thinking that are not defined by metaphysics or by the polarities of good and evil, and it is this above all else that lends to Greek tragedy a claim to distinction. For this reason, the return to Greece marks the effort of Western philosophizing to open itself to what metaphysics has subsequently closed off. It is an overture to a new relation to culture.

That might not have been the avowed intention of some of the initial drives to turn to the Greek world, and it is a confusion about this matter that permits a strange form of nationalism to enter the picture in this matter. This haunting presence of the national is a factor in the renewal of the question of tragedy one finds in Germany that is lacking in the Greek world—at least on these issues. Fichte, for instance, claims that the turn to Greece is one of the ways in which Germany can secure its place in the modern world as the inheritor of the place that Greece occupied in the ancient world. When he says this he is simply giving voice to the general tendency of the age. But then, as a reminder that this turn to Greece is a complicated matter and not without counterclaims, we must remember that Fichte's claim is made at almost the exact same time that Hölderlin is reminding his readers that the turn to Greece sets us into the ordeal of the foreign and the struggle to understand the other which hides in what seems intimate. But however the Greek and the German worlds are regarded, the heliotropism of German philosophy, which finds itself persistently pulled in the direction of some image of "the Greeks," will never be able to be an issue that frees itself fundamentally from the question of nationality. It will also never be able to be decided why this is the case. In part this strange and distressing shadow of the theme of the nation has to do with the circumstances of German culture and the struggles of German philosophers in the wake of the French Revolution to theorize the significance of that historical crisis (oddly, the chief impact of the French Revolution upon philosophy was found in Germany, where it was taken up as a systematic matter for the most general concerns of reflection, not in France itself). In part it is simply a question that fogs the issue of how tragedy is to be thought from the perspective opened up by philosophy.

However, once this question of the role of culture and of nationality begins to be posed, it needs to be extended beyond the question of Germany or Greece. It should, in a different manner, lead to a question which should be put to this book; namely, what are the stakes of this question for an American who writes in English? Why is it that this tendency of German philosophy to pose its deepest questions in terms of a presumed kinship with ancient Greece is significant for those of us who write in and out of a different cultural context? What is asked about in such questions goes far beyond the scope of what this book has addressed, but such are the new questions that open up in light of what is revealed in this tradition of German thought since Hegel. Somewhat unexpectedly, questions about the claims of nationality and the relation of the notion of the national to history begin to press forward. In the end, coming to terms with the case of Heidegger will require that these, among other questions, be addressed because it is perhaps precisely because Heidegger misunderstands the role of this notion of nationality that he makes the errors that he does.

*   *   *

Neither the question put to us by Greek tragedy, nor by the case of Heidegger, which is so thoroughly entangled in the question of Greek tragedy, can be answered, or even properly posed, by reference to this question of the national. Rather, one finds in the claims of tragedy something greater, something that might well draw the idea of the national in its wake, but only as a secondary matter. What is essential in Greek tragedy, what it poses as a question to philosophizing today, is that it awakens in us a renewed sense that we do indeed live in a world that is larger than we can either control or define and that we are held in the grip of that which we cannot comprehend. Understood in its most basic dimensions, it is a powerful testimony on behalf of human finitude. But it is a testimony that, by virtue of its form, of the manner in which it is exhibited and enacted, does not permit itself to be taken up by the language of the concept. It does not, in other words, let itself be assimilated into the systematic concerns of philosophizing, and so it stands as a persistent summons to reflection. I do not believe that Heidegger will represent the final figure in this history of efforts by philosophers to address the idea put to us by the tragic as exhibiting something unique for thinking. Quite the contrary. I believe that we are only now beginning to understand the force of what is put to us by this idea and the conflicted depths of the experience from which it emerges. The farther we move away from the assumptions governing metaphysics—ultimately the assumption of an infinite and omnipresent mind which suffers no death—and from the polarities of good and evil, the closer we come to the point from which we can begin to understand the real insights of Greek tragedy. But even more: it is perhaps all the more necessary for philosophy to take up this idea of the tragic since in the figure of Heidegger we have a philosopher who has shown himself—by virtue of his commitment to philosophical reflection—to be as blind as Oedipus. Heidegger's own efforts to link the history of philosophy to the figure of Oedipus do not exclude his own case; quite the contrary, it is most likely that at this point, when he links tragedy and history,

280

Heidegger begins to think of himself as just such a figure of tragedy. His error needs to be understood as intelligible only in the light of what tragedy reveals about the nature of the present age.

Heidegger knew better than most just how profoundly the world had altered from the time of the culture that produced such works of tragedy. Colonus, birthplace of Sophocles, which he would choose as the site of Oedipus's miraculous death, is now a bus stop surrounded by an industrial slum. One question which we cannot escape refers specifically to the force of this alteration: are we in a position to grasp the deepest insights into human nature unfolded by Greek tragedy, or have the alterations of time rendered such insights—which are so powerfully present at the inaugural stages of our culture—opaque to us? One of the most interesting and paradoxical elements of this situation is that it is precisely this force of history, this motor of alteration, that Heidegger, like Hegel, will try to understand according to the model opened by the idea of the tragic. The dynamic that has pushed the world of Greece into an ever more remote experience is best understood by taking reference to tragedy, which remains one of the greatest productions of that world. It often seems that the image of tragedy appropriate to our age is *Oedipus at Colonus,* which is the tragedy that depicts the figure of Oedipus after the catastrophe of self-knowledge has destroyed him, but before the destruction that followed from that self-knowledge has given way to a different future. Adorno lends credence to such a view with his celebrated remark that philosophy only remains alive because it has missed the moment of its truth.

Of course, we still try to tell the story of human life in terms of the tragic form: one would be foolish to suggest that the form itself ended with the end of ancient Greek culture. Shakespeare, Goethe, Brecht, Ibsen, O'Neill, Molière, Anouilh, to name only a few, certainly have advanced the form, as have filmmakers who are finding new possibilities in the realm of the stories that we tell in order to understand ourselves. Film might well open possibilities regarding that special form we still call tragic art. And, after Nietzsche, it should go without saying that opera always needs to be regarded as a form in which the questions of tragedy and the forces of destiny can be explored. But it does not in the least diminish the insights or achievements of modern and contemporary forms of art to suggest that there remains something hauntingly singular about the achievement of ancient Greek tragedy, and it is a lovely twist of fate that this singularity itself has everything to do with the character of being in the singular. Whatever else it addresses, Greek tragedy poses questions about the nature of the riddle that each of us is assigned by beginning with the simple fact of the singularity of our experience of that riddle. All else devolves from this fact of our strangeness, which is presented in Greek tragedy independently of structures and assumptions—subjectivity, the good, metaphysics—which history has shown to have been exhausted.

*　　*　　*

At the outset I suggested that three questions overarched the particular concerns of each of the studies that have been presented here. Those questions now need to be addressed directly, even if only very briefly.

The first question addressed the tendency to interpret the movement of history as the unfolding of a tragic destiny. It is clearly a tendency that one sees in Hegel, Hölderlin, Nietzsche, and Heidegger as equally powerfully present, but nonetheless leading to rather disparate conclusions. The common denominator of this turn to some image of tragedy as an interpretive model for thinking history is the view that the present historical moment needs to be thought as a *crisis of time* which cannot be reasonably comprehended unless it is regarded as somehow *destined*. Heidegger presents the case for this view with the greatest force. But this turn to a tragic model of history needs to be understood not as proposing that the destiny at work in history is a form of necessity that binds human freedom from something external to human being. Rather, the destiny guiding history owes itself precisely to the site of human freedom. Of course, it is paramount that human freedom not be understood as rooted in the doings of an agent, that is, that it be taken as the work of a subject over and against a world. Rather, freedom is rooted in the mystery of all appearance, in the simple fact of birth itself. It is this fact of freedom, this sudden appearance into the world of life, that binds itself to history in a singular manner. History is thus what we call upon ourselves, and its possibility emerges out of the tragic law of human appearance in the world. To think of history in this manner, as exposed in the view of human life that one finds in Greek tragedy, does seem to be an approach to the riddles of history that is genuinely insightful into its peculiar strangeness. Above all, it is one way in which we begin to see how it is that human beings are capable of inflicting upon themselves such sufferings. Schelling, who thought the essence of human freedom to be the abyssal point at which evil and good are indistinguishable, comes close to understanding both freedom and history precisely in this manner. Such a view of history does not set its workings into a moral framework. It cannot do that. Here we begin to understand as well that, while human inventiveness is capable of recoiling upon itself and bringing catastrophe in its wake, while evil is a real possibility for us, there is no safeguard, no guarantee against evil and disaster, to which we might appeal or turn. Here we see how it could be that notions of the good, even well-intended ones, provide no hedge against the risks that Aristotle long ago sought to name *hamartia*. Indeed, if we regard history from the point of view opened up in its kinship with tragedy, we are not surprised that the good has often been enlisted in the service of evil; the distinction between good and evil can no longer be maintained.

We are in some genuine respect defenseless against ourselves. But not entirely: the task of tragedy in ancient Greece was, so far as possible, to let us see without having first to go blind.

The second question posed follows from this last point. The question is whether or not the insights of tragedy permit themselves to be put into the language of philosophy, the language of the concept. The great struggle on the part of philosophy since Hegel has been to assimilate the insights of tragic art without destroying them. But, since Nietzsche made us acutely aware that the form of presentation belongs to the nature of the tragic itself, the untranslatability of what is disclosed in tragedy seems to make this struggle an impossible one. The problem is simple: no matter how it is flexed, no matter how agile it is made to be, conceptual language entails a commitment to synthesis and to linearity. It has, one might say, an allergy to contradiction and an intrinsic impulse to sublate conflict. However, the insight of the tragic work resides precisely in the double bind, the doubled truth, that is changed if it is conceptualized. It would be an oversimplification to suggest that philosophy is utterly incapable of addressing the insights of tragedy. The past two hundred years have proven very much otherwise. But, as this address is continued, it is important that it never be forgotten that the matter of language, that by which we bear witness to our presence, is at stake in this issue. And it should not be forgotten that the possibilities of language, metaphor and its stereoscopic possibilities perhaps most of all, are not exhausted in the language of the concept.

Here then the third question becomes apparent. It asked what it means that tragedy, which exhibits on stage great pain and suffering, death and grief, is nonetheless something that we call beautiful. Of course, it is this, above all, that holds the deepest riddle of the tragedy for us. But in this riddle is the secret that lets tragedy, which is about suffering, be something that, in the end, speaks of affirmation. The beauty of the tragic work in which conflict is displayed is, as Hegel, Schelling, and Hölderlin well knew, the true correlate of speculative unity; it is the glimmer of an affirmation that resides in the midst of what most terrifies us. Simply put, the beauty of the tragedy is the reminder that the conflicting possibilities of human life can delight rather than frighten us. Kant will put the point with exquisite clarity when he says that beautiful things indicate that we belong in the world.

Finally, there remains Hegel's promise that "the wounds of spirit heal and leave no scars behind." I suspect that from the perspective opened up by philosophy—from the idiom of the ideal—this promise is indeed reasonable. Philosophy, by virtue of the commitments of its own perspective, will always bear the signature of hope no matter how deeply etched its qualifications about this matter are. The fragility and reversibility of the realization of hope is, however, the commitment of the ideal of the idiom and its riddling character, and this is what governs the tragic work of art. In tragedy we find the memento of the very real capacity of human life to call catastrophe down upon itself suddenly, whether by accident, design, or simple blindness. We learn from it that, knowingly or not, we can bring disaster into the world, even monstrous evil. We learn too that there is no defense, no good, which might ward off this fate. To philosophize is to index one's thought to some hope of healing, no matter how many caveats one places upon its possible realization. Hegel's claim provides a very real insight into the character and commitments of philosophizing. The struggle of philosophers who address the great insight of tragedy is, in the end, to convert it into this hope and its language. But, in the end, the insight of tragedy will lodge itself in something other than hope. Perhaps one must say that it is an insight into something greater than hope. Tragedy presents an image of life that loves and affirms what is most difficult and strange in human being; the beauty of the work of art preserves this for one who understands it. And it does this even while reminding us forcefully of the limits of what we can understand and know; indeed, it is precisely at these limits that we first begin to grasp the need for an affirmation, even a love, of that which we cannot understand and which exceeds us. But, in the end, the truth of tragedy is that even the moments of happiness can suddenly be pierced by the sadness of time.

What we have then are the stories we can tell which, in their own way, retrieve those shattered moments in the name of another time. If only for a while.

NOTES

QUESTIONS

1. F. Nietzsche, *Der Wille zur Macht,* Aphorism 822.

2. *M.Heidegger–E. Blochmann Briefwechsel,* p. 91, letter of April 12, 1938.

3. G. W. F. Hegel, *Phänomenologie des Geistes,* p. 15.

4. M. Heidegger, *Gesamtausgabe,* vol. 31, p. 37. Henceforth volumes from Heidegger's *Gesamtausgabe* will be designated as *GA* followed by the volume number.

5. P. Lacoue-Labarthe, *La Fiction du politique,* p. 43.

6. M. Heidegger, *Einführung in die Metaphysik,* p. 81.

7. M. Nussbaum, *The Fragility of Goodness,* p. 5.

8. *EM,* p. 82. The phrase is taken from Karl Reinhardt's interpretation of Sophocles.

9. The reference is from Ruth Padel, *Whom Gods Destroy: Elements of Greek and Tragic Madness,* p. 246, but is itself a citation taken from a discussion of the phrase *pathei mathos* in *Agamemnon,* line 177.

10. F. Nietzsche, *Die Geburt der Tragödie,* p. x.

11. I. Kant, *Werke,* vol. V, Ak., 462. Henceforth indicated by the Akademie (Ak.) page number.

12. M. Heidegger, "Ursprung des Kunstwerkes," in *Holzwege,* p. 67.

13. On this point see Derrida's "The Force of Law," in *Deconstruction and Justice,* where the relation of the law to the idiom is powerfully elaborated. Derrida's reliance upon Kafka's work there and in "Before the Law" is especially suggestive: one could easily make the argument that Kafka's work stands as one of the more interesting alternatives to tragedy today.

14. *GT,* p. 15. See John Sallis's discussion of this passage in *Crossings: Nietzsche and the Space of Tragedy,* pp. 147–50.

15. W. Benjamin, "Aufgabe des Übersetzers," in *Gesammelte Werke,* vol. IV-1, p. 21.

16. *Briefwechsel,* p. 85, letter of December 21, 1934.

17. On the relation of language and pain see Elaine Scarry, *The Body in Pain.* Also see my "Black Milk and Blue."

18. It is interesting to note that Descartes—the most untragic—and Shakespeare—the greatest non-Greek tragedian—are almost contemporaries, and yet one cannot imagine Descartes driven by the same need that one finds in Plato or Aristotle, for instance, to take up the question of tragedy as it gets expressed in his own times.

19. I. Kant, *Kritik der Urteilskraft,* Ak., p. 104. By assuming that such a "place" is always available Kant is able to suggest that "war is sublime"—but such a remark is true only with the qualification: "but only for the generals."

20. Aristotle, *Poetics* 1452b9.

21. Kant uses an interesting phrase to speak to this point: *es belebt* (it quickens). Cf. Ak., 31. It is the word that was once used in medicine to name the moment life came into being.

22. This is what Kant means when he says, repeatedly and emphatically, that "beauty is what pleases us without a concept [being able to account for that pleasure]" (Ak., 32, 68).

23. *GT*, p. 104.

24. To say nothing of the withdrawal of the claims of beauty from our conception of nature. Today, it seems that to say of nature that it is beautiful is merely an adventitious claim and not, as for instance for Kant, a critical one. On this point, and on the connection between the claims of beauty in nature and art, see the discussions on technology in Benjamin, "Kunst im Zeitalter seiner technologischen Reproducierbarkeit," Heidegger, "Die Frage nach der Technik" (in *Die Technik und die Kehre* [Pfullingen: Neske Verlag, 1962]), and Adorno, *Ästhetische Theorie*. The coincidence between the renewal of the question of tragedy and the potent cultural transformations initiated with the acceleration and basic alteration of technological conceptions of the world is significant. In particular, one should not take up the question of the crisis of history without attention to the specific shape bestowed upon this crisis by technology.

25. R. M. Rilke, *Duinser Elegien*, p. 685. One sees this in a wide range of literatures today. Certainly Bataille's novels need to be read in this light, as do, for instance, Mishima's. Here one might also refer to Deleuze's *Masochism*. Early existentialist literature, such as Sartre's *La Nausée*, can be read as the prototypes of this literature.

26. G. Steiner, *Antigones*, p. 10.

27. Cf. *GA*, vol. 53, pp. 76ff., where the stress upon the question of translation is so strong that Heidegger is led to say, "Tell me what you think about translation, and I will tell you who you are." On this see my "Hermeneutics and the Poetic Motion" in *Hermeneutics and the Poetic Motion*.

28. Here one might note that it is the mistake of humanism to assume that the ethical and the human are co-terminus, and that it is the mistake of most theologies and faiths, especially Christian, to assume that the region of difference, the region of the ethical that is other than the human, could ever have a determination for us.

29. A similar strategy, with somewhat different results, can be found in Jacques Taminiaux's *Le Théâtre des philosophes*.

30. Cf. Plato, *Republic* 607b–c.

31. On the role of tragedy in Athenian culture and politics see Christian Meier, *Die politische Kunst der griechischen Tragödie*. For similar treatment of the role of the funeral oration see Nicole Loraux, *L'Invention d'Athènes*.

32. Cf. *GT*, p. 14.

33. Both Lacoue-Labarthe (*La Fiction du politique*) and Martin Bernal (*Black Athena*) pose serious questions about the politics of the German fascination with Greece. Both are also aware that in that fascination the self-production of an image of the present is at stake. See also Robert Bernasconi's "Heidegger and the Invention of the Western Philosophical Tradition."

34. The phrase is Reiner Schürmann's.

35. This is a sentiment that receives its supreme formulation in Hegel's remark that "The wounds of Spirit heal and leave no scars behind" (*PG*, p. 470). It is also this sense that Nietzsche criticizes as the illusion of being able "to heal the eternal wound of existence" (*GT*, p. 115).

36. Here one thinks, of course, of Aristophanes' *The Clouds*. Significantly, Aristophanes also saw fit to make tragedy itself the subject of a comedy in *The Frogs*.

37. Here, as an example of what I take to be one of the most creative efforts to write in a voice proper to the experiences at issue here, let me refer to Roberto Calasso's *The Marriage of Cadmus and Harmony*.

1. PLATO

1. Cf. 546a–547a. One might also suggest that the *Republic* ends with a kind of declaration of the mystery of birth since the one thing that Er could not remember about his sojourn in the afterworld was how he came back into his body. I owe these insights to John Sallis (letter of December 6, 1996).

2. For a fuller elaboration of this question of the relation of death and law see my "Can Law Survive?" Of course, as becomes clear in the *Phaedo*, Socrates' convictions about this relation are strong enough for him to give his own death as an answer. See also Katherine Verdery, *The Political Lives of Dead Bodies* (New York: Columbia University Press, 1999), pp. 185ff.

3. The questions posed by *Antigone* will be the focus of Hegel's interpretation of tragedy. There the significance of the dead body, the pure idiom with which we cannot communicate (since we can speak *of* the dead, but not *with* them), will be of central importance.

4. It would be interesting to compare ancient and modern tragedies with respect to this claim. Here the parallels and differences between *Antigone* and *Hamlet*, which confronts such questions as they are raised by a ghost rather than a corpse, would be worth pursuing.

5. A quick tally of the references to other writers in the *Republic* highlights this point. The count is as follows: Homer (31), Hesiod (7), Aeschylus (6), Simonedes (4), Pindar (3), Solon (2), Sophocles (1), Euripides (1), Stesichorus (1), Heraclitus (1), Protagoras (1), Pythagoras (1). That count does not include references to figures found in the works of those authors. Including such figures would make the number of references to Homer far greater still.

6. *Odyssey*, book 23, lines 252–53.

7. Cf. Allan Bloom's interpretive essay following his translation of the *Republic*, note 13, p. 471.

8. On this and the rather obvious parallels between the *Republic* and *Apology* see Bloom's interpretative essay; see also J. Sallis, *Being and Logos*.

9. The literary form of the *Republic*, a repetition of a dialogue, seems to confound the taxonomy of literary forms which the *Republic* itself provides in book 3.

10. See also the *Symposium*, where poetic creation is again likened to procreation.

11. For a presentation of a city without desire see Anne Carson, *Eros: The Bittersweet*, pp. 168–73.

12. The character of the speech belonging to this act of founding is important. When Socrates argues that "you and I, Adeimantus, are not poets at present, but the founders of a state" (379a), the implication is that making a state is not like making a poem. In saying this Socrates distinguishes the speech of the poet from that of one who would found a state, but he does not specify the character of the speech belonging to such a project. Clearly, though, the answer to this question is to be found in the nature of dialogue as it is enacted here. Some sense of the irony of this disavowal of the poetic here also needs to be taken into consideration (if only to acknowledge that the *Republic* is a book that seems to establish the need to censor books like itself). See *La Fiction du politique*, where Lacoue-

Labarthe takes up the question of the possible "fictioning" of the political. There the question is whether politics can be "made" (as a work of art is made) or whether a different principle must guide its coming into being. See also *Le Théâtre des philosophes*, pp. 7–68, where Taminiaux, following Arendt's analysis of the principles of political life, argues that the real distinction is between the *bios politikos* and the *bios theoretikos*.

13. Socrates will find it necessary to take up the question of medicine and the maintenance of the body (403c–412b). However, it is worth noting that the discussion of such matters is itself generated out of the discussion of the passions and the effect of the passions, which are excited by poetry, upon the body. The discussion of the body that follows is, by and large, notable for the neglect of the body which one notices in that set of exchanges.

14. A complete discussion of the capacities of the soul and the nourishments proper to its nature would, of course, need to refer to the tripartite nature of the soul (a discussion itself prompted in large measure by the question of the relation of language and the soul as it is posed in Book 3) and to the stages of its cultivation as they are described in Book 7.

15. The word is usually translated as "music" but refers to what today we call more generally the "arts" and not simply to music, which is to be numbered among the arts.

16. This is also the case in the *Phaedrus,* where Socrates says, "Writing, Phaedrus, has this strange power, quite like painting in fact" (275d–e).

17. On this point see H.-G. Gadamer, "Plato als Porträtist," in *Gesammelte Werke,* vol. 7, pp. 228–57, and J. Taminiaux, "The Thinker and the Painter," in *Poetics, Speculation and Judgment.*

18. Current debates about the impact of violence and pornography upon children generally rest upon the same assumption and the same general set of concerns that Plato has here.

19. Cf. *Phaedrus* 264. The corpse, as Maurice Blanchot has pointed out, is a curiously disturbing *mimesis* (as we prove when we say of a corpse "my how he looks like himself"); see Blanchot, *The Gaze of Orpheus.* This question of writing, of what sort of ethical act writing is, which belongs first of all to the *Phaedrus* and *Cratylus,* is of immense importance for everything that is said in Plato, since it is his concern with this question that leads him to write in the form of dialogues. It needs to be remembered that Plato was acutely aware that the techniques of writing were undergoing revolutionary changes. Much like today—with the alterations in forms of writing opened by computers (such as hypertext)—Plato lived at a moment when the tools of writing were having an impact upon the nature of writing itself (the Greeks devised the pen for use on papyrus and with this altered the nature of script; see *Phaedrus* 275). Just a few centuries before Plato the phenomenon of alphabetization and the increase in literacy contributed to the transformation of Greece from an oral to a literate culture. Plato is alert to the genuine shifts that such transformations produced in the linguistic imagination of his time.

On this topic see E. A. Havelock, *The Literate Revolution in Greece and Its Cultural Consequences;* E. G. Turner, *Athenian Books in the Fifth and Fourth Centuries B.C.;* J. Svenbro, *Phrasikleia;* H.-G. Gadamer, "Unterwegs zur Schrift," in *Gesammelte Werke,* vol. 7; A. Carson, *Eros: The Bittersweet,* pp. 42ff.; and my "Putting Oneself in Words . . ."

20. This is why Martha Nussbaum is right when she says that "Plato's repudiations of tragedy and of Athenian democracy are closely linked" (*Fragility of Goodness,* p. 127).

21. On this point compare the *Phaedrus,* especially the passage in which Soc-

rates, citing Stesichorus, invokes the phrase "This story is not true" (243b) as a remedy for the blindness suffered by speaking ill of Helen. See Nussbaum, *Fragility of Goodness*, pp. 200–233; see also my "What We Didn't See."

22. The argument laid out here that there should be such censorship of the representation of the gods is, by and large, guided by the same rationale that animates the Fatwah issued against Salman Rushdie. The difference here is that the apparent argument for censorship in the *Republic* is ironic; that means that it is self-consciously self-undermining. Were it taken without qualification, such an argument would ban books like the very book in which that argument was made.

23. The one exception is the passage which refers to Teiresias. The importance of Achilles in Socrates' own self-presentation needs to be borne in mind when discussing the individual passages which Socrates criticizes; see J. Sallis, *Being and Logos*, pp. 62ff.

24. For an interesting discussion of how this word is to be thought and how words themselves are mimetic in both writing and speech, see *Cratylus* 423c–425c.

25. This protean potential of language, its mimetic capacity that seems to liberate it without restraint, is, I believe, what Foucault refers to when he writes of the capacity of language "to unfold in the presence of nothing" and when Hölderlin writes of capacity of language to usher in "the simple advance of the unthinkable"; see my "Poetry and the Political."

26. See Padel, *Whom Gods Destroy*, pp. 128–29 on the meaning of *sophron* and the peculiar damage which threatens the mind in tragedy.

27. On this relation see, for instance, Ernst Bloch, *Zur Philosophie der Musik* (Frankfurt am Main: Suhrkamp, 1974).

28. This deep bond uniting language and music can be illustrated by reference to the experience of listening to someone speaking a foreign language. One can repeat words, even speak them well if one is sufficiently accomplished, but unless one understands the words, the rhythm of the speech is absent, and so it is evident that the words are not yet fully words that have been taken to heart.

29. In a similar manner, the power of language to shape the world is evident in the way language shapes the face. Speaking is clearly among the most continuous and vigorous ways in which the muscles of the face are exercised, and, just as the exercise of the body can tone and give shape to the body generally, so the language one speaks gives shape to the character of one's face.

30. See Nussbaum, *Fragility of Goodness*, pp. 122–35.

31. See A. Bloom, Introduction to the *Republic*, p. 426.

32. In a very different context Jean-Pierre Vernant suggests that this focus upon the idiom of the individual is precisely how tragic poetry engages the question of the law: "What tragedy depicts is one *dike* in conflict with another, a law that is not fixed, shifting and changing into its opposite. To be sure, tragedy is something quite different than a legal debate. It takes as its subject the man actually living out this debate, forced to make a decisive choice, to orient his activity in a universe of ambiguous values where nothing is ever stable or unequivocal"; see *Myth and Tragedy in Ancient Greece*, p. 26.

33. This is why Freud saw fit to name so many of the psychological complexes and torments after figures in tragic poetry. Hegel is especially aware of the relation of family, of the differences of gender and generation as well. That is why his most perceptive analyses of Greek tragedy, in both the *Phenomenology of Spirit* and the *Philosophy of Right*, are found in sections dedicated to the question of the role of the family in the life of Spirit.

34. In light of this, Nussbaum's suggestion that we should read the *Phaedrus* as the apology that Socrates calls for here in the *Republic* is an interesting one.

35. Here one should look to Carson, *Eros: The Bittersweet,* and the discussion of the relation of poetry, desire, contradiction, and dangerous love as it is played out in both Sappho and Plato. Carson points out that the Greek poetic conception of *eros* as *glukupikron,* as sweet then bitter, crystallizes the conflict that belongs to desire and the language of desires.

36. Nussbaum, *Fragility of Goodness,* p. 126.

37. Such a suggestion clearly needs a more elaborate defense than can be given here. Were such a defense to be made, it would perhaps best begin with a discussion of Socrates' concluding suggestion in the *Symposium* (223d), offered in the fog of encroaching sleep, that one who could write a tragedy could equally well write a comedy since the knowledge requisite for each is the same.

38. A. Bloom, Introduction to the *Republic,* p. 435.

39. See ibid., p. 471, n. 13, for more details about the allusions carried by the language which introduces this story.

40. *Odyssey,* book 11, line 625.

41. See chapter 6 on Heidegger for more about the relation of blindness and justice.

42. On this see Padel, *Whom Gods Destroy,* pp. 207–10, and W. Burkert, *Homo necans.*

43. This is the description of the third class of citizens given in book 8 (565a), namely, those "who do their own work, don't meddle in affairs, and don't possess very much." It would be interesting to compare Odysseus's choice here with the decision that Voltaire presents in *Candide* as worthy of admiration, namely, the decision "to cultivate one's garden."

44. On this see Hannah Arendt's *The Human Condition,* pp. 22–78, and *The Origins of Totalitarianism.*

45. Aristotle is never quite clear about how to classify these works; see *Poetics* 1447b9–11. Diogenes Laertius (3:48) is unequivocal about suggesting that in the dialogues Plato has invented a new literary form. See also Nussbaum, *Fragility of Goodness,* pp. 122–35.

46. See my "Kunst, Sprache und Kritik."

47. See *Phaedo* 99e.

48. This is what Hölderlin will refer to as "the simple advance of the unthinkable."

49. It is this power, which Nietzsche will call the "Dionysian," that will most attract him.

50. Here it is of utmost importance to separate Plato's arguments about art works and their censorship from the sort of "arguments" coming out of conservative political quarters in the United States today. One of the most pronounced differences is that Plato's elaboration of those arguments are self-reflexive and subtle, not self-righteous and reductive. Also, it is important to bear in mind that the political context within which each set of arguments is developed is significantly different. See W. Steiner, *The Scandal of Pleasure.*

51. J. Taminiaux, *Le Théâtre des philosophes,* pp. 24–33.

2. ARISTOTLE

1. In the end, this difference will prove to be of great significance: Plato defines the essence of poetry with reference to Homer, while Aristotle does so with reference to Sophocles. Were they to take up the same works, it is likely that their remarks about poetic practice would contrast less sharply.

2. For both Plato and Aristotle this fundamentality is, in part, evident in the

way in which each refers this topic to the experience of the child: both find children especially inclined to take the experience of art to heart and so to be especially vulnerable to its abuse and its advantages alike. In the *Nicomachean Ethics* I.iii.4–8, Aristotle suggest that the young and immature should not study ethics because they are guided by *pathos*, which, in the *Poetics,* he will identify as one of the essential traits of tragedy. There is a sense, then, in which some element of the work of the tragedy to cultivate a healthy sense of *pathos* is to prepare us for the work of philosophy. In taking childhood seriously as a stage in the life of a person and not simply as an undeveloped stage of reason, Plato and Aristotle again set themselves apart from the tradition that follows them. There are, of course, exceptions—Rousseau and Freud are obviously such—but they are rather rare. This question about the relation of the child to the force of images and the appeals of art which so deeply concerns Plato and Aristotle has an interesting contemporary form in the debates about the influence of television and film upon children.

3. For a discussion of the relation of the *Poetics* to Plato's works, and for some very interesting suggestions about the possibility that he and Aristotle are explicitly referring to one another in certain passages, see Gerald Else, *Plato and Aristotle on Poetry,* pp. 68ff.

4. This philosophic prejudice that judges art works that appear in the word as somehow "higher" forms is made explicit by Hegel, who traces the migration of art from mute stone (sculpture) up to the arrival of the word in the poem. However, neither Aristotle nor Hegel problematizes this assumption as such. Nietzsche, for whom wordless music outstrips the poetic power of the word, will be among the first to raise this question as such and in so doing challenge even the power of the language of philosophy to grasp the work of art at all. Others will make this challenge in other ways. Merleau-Ponty's analysis of images likewise challenges the tacit pan-linguisticality dominant in philosophic treatments of art.

Questions will need to be raised about the relation of the idea of the tragic and the word: can the experience of tragedy, of suffered knowledge, be found apart from language? For instance, can it be painted or sculpted or danced? Does the word, as Hölderlin will argue, have a privilege here? Is it the case that such knowledge belongs to us only as beings with language? For the present such questions are not yet adequately prepared and so will need to wait until the chapter on Nietzsche before they can be properly posed.

5. See *Physics* B.ii.199A12–14; see also my "Economies of Production."

6. Saying that we learn our first lessons "mimetically" helps to clarify the sense of the word *mimesis*; one need think only of how one learns a language, that is, by means of repetition. More precisely, Aristotle's remark specifies the nature of the "imitation" at work in *mimesis:* it is not a matter of producing a copy, a duplicate; rather, in the imitation that is *mimesis* we find a curious sort of repetition or reenactment. It is of utmost importance for understanding Aristotle that one not take *mimesis* to refer to a sort of "copy" or "reproduction." To say that the work of art is mimetic is not to say that it produces copies. When one has a proper sense of the Greek conception of *mimesis,* one is not puzzled by the fact that, for the Greeks, music is counted among the most clearly mimetic arts.

Contemporary conceptions of "imitation" tend to be shaped by technological conceptions of "reproduction" (this, for instance, is what Andy Warhol made such a theme for art), but Aristotle's sense of the mimetic is rather imitative by being performative. Indeed, the special mode in which the work of art "repeats" or "performs" an experience is what gives such works their charm.

7. On this see *Fragility of Goodness,* p. 412, where Nussbaum describes the

significance of the eyes of the friend with a marvelous reference to a scene from Euripides' *Hecuba*, saying that in the look "I come to be *in you*, I make my appearance inside your eyes."

8. See *Eros: The Bittersweet*, pp. 3–9, 116. Carson's book is among the best presentations of this paradox of the impossible knowing that belongs to poetic language proper. What she does not mention, though, is the way in which translation bears a kinship to metaphor in this regard. Moving between two languages one holds together resemblances that are not full identities. From this point of view, translation is a stereoscopic experience and a model for thinking *mimesis* in general.

9. *Rhetoric* 3.11.6. See A. Carson, "Just for the Thrill," p. 153; see also *Eros: The Bittersweet*, p. 116.

10. F. Hölderlin, *Sämtliche Werke*, vol. II, p. 62. Henceforth designated as *SW*.

11. Of course, the lost books on comedy form the secret that drives the plot of Umberto Eco's *The Name of the Rose*. From what evidence we have it is likely that Aristotle disapproved of the comedy of his day, finding its attacks upon individuals and foul language not to his liking. Curiously, it seems that Plato had a deeper appreciation of comedy (see the *Philebus* 48a–50a). Certainly many of the dialogues are comic masterpieces in their own right and exhibit a genius for lampooning those who make excessive claims to wisdom. On this question, see G. Else, *Plato and Aristotle on Poetry*, pp. 185–95.

12. Of course, as Hegel will note, this is where one finds a significant difference between ancient and modern tragedy. Although Freud chose to name psychological complexes after figures in ancient tragedies, it is clear that those figures themselves did not, as Aristotle notes, display their interior lives. One cannot imagine a character as haunted as Hamlet as a figure in an ancient tragedy. When Hamlet poses the question "To be or not to be," it is anxious and deeply personal. When the measure of life and death is taken in Greek tragedy, it is more the measure of a destiny. Kierkegaard perhaps comes closest to thematizing this difference as a difference; see *Either/Or*, "On the Tragic in Ancient and Modern Drama."

13. An important question for the concerns of this book is just how far the analysis of *praxis* in the *Poetics*, where it is examined through the optic of *poeisis*, and the treatment found in the *Ethics* simply confirm one another. The question is whether the "results" of those analyses are essentially the same, or whether there is an insight into the nature of *praxis* that is proper to the realm of art which is not covered by the insights offered by philosophy (and, of course, the reverse question needs to be posed as well). Plato would argue that the ethical "teachings" of art and of philosophy are not commensurate, but that there is a clear reason to favor the insights of philosophy over those of art.

14. There are, of course, two lengthier discussions of *katharsis* found in the *Politics* 1341a21 and 1341b32 ff. (where he suggests that *katharsis* is discussed in greater detail in the *Poetics*).

15. See D. W. Lucas's commentary in his Greek edition of the *Poetics*, p. 97.

16. See *Fragility of Goodness*, pp. 388–90, for Nussbaum's compelling arguments to this effect. See also Else, *Plato and Aristotle on Poetry*, pp. 158–60, for an interesting retranslation and rethinking of the entire passage in Aristotle.

17. In the *Rhetoric* (1390a23) Aristotle distinguishes the impulse to pity in the young and the old, saying that the young feel it because they identify with others while the elderly pity because they believe that suffering is always nearby. The first form of pity is the only one capable of effecting a *katharsis*.

18. Of course, it is a matter of judgment how one draws this line. One can

imagine, though, that Aristotle would find the tendency of some theater (and this is certainly the seduction of film as well) to spectacular visuals to be a detriment to its greatest possible achievement. Such exploitations impede rather than foster a mimetic identification of the audience with the events.

19. This seems to be a tacit reply to Plato's comment in the *Phaedrus* (264c) that any discourse, like a living thing, has a body that is best composed of proportionate parts. There seems little doubt that Aristotle is responding to the presentation of tragedy in the *Phaedrus* here in the *Poetics*.

20. J. P. Vernant and P. Vidal-Naquet, *Myth and Tragedy*, p. 139.

21. It should, however, be unmistakably clear that the ordinary way of speaking that refers to every death as "a tragedy" rather basically mistakes the specific nature of tragedy. Some echo of the insight of tragic art might indeed resonate in every death, but the full force of the tragic and its significance in our understanding of *praxis* is not confined to death. This becomes especially clear in the role played by *hamartia* in tragedy.

22. "Whom God wishes to destroy, He first makes mad." The source of this remark is unknown; see Padel, *Whom Gods Destroy*, pp. 3–8.

23. Nussbaum, *Fragility of Goodness*, p. 382.

24. On the word *hamartia* see Padel, *Whom Gods Destroy*, pp. 197–99, and J. P. Vernant and P. Vidal-Naquet, *Myth and Tragedy*, p. 62. See especially the *Nicomachean Ethics* (1135b11–25) where Aristotle distinguishes the various forms of involvement we might have in a wrongful deed. There *hamartia* is located between simple misfortune (*atuchema*) and an outright crime (*adikema*). It should also be noted that Socrates uses the word when he makes the celebrated claim that "No one willingly does wrong [*hamartanei*]." It would be interesting to think through this word in relation to the opening words of Dante's *Divine Comedy*, "In the middle of the course of life I found myself astray in a dark woods." There is a sense in which *hamartia* refers to a going astray, to a deviation from the proper path of action.

25. A full discussion of this point would need to draw upon the *Rhetoric* and would do well to counterpose the analysis of the elements of language in Aristotle to that found in Plato's *Cratylus*. On this, see my "Putting Oneself in Words . . ."

26. See both Nussbaum, *Fragility of Goodness*, p. 392, and G. Else, *Plato and Aristotle on Poetry*, pp. 67–73.

27. *Theatetus* 203b.

28. See E. A. Havelock and J. P. Hershbell, *Communication Arts in the Ancient World*, p. 31; see also Carson, *Eros: The Bittersweet*, pp. 53–55.

29. An interesting parallel is found in the symbolic nature of the Arabic system of numbering that we use today. It is a system of counting that involves an intellectual operation quite different, and far more complex, than that required of the Roman numeric system.

30. Cited in A. Carson, "Just for the Thrill," p. 153.

31. Here it would be interesting to bring into the discussion Kant's claim that there are two different forms of "logical" hypotyposis: the schematic (which he treats in the *Critique of Pure Reason*) and the symbolic (which he treats in the *Critique of Judgment*). The latter form is, from the perspective of the former, somewhat impertinent. See *Kritik der Urteilskraft*, par. 59.

32. *Rhetoric* 1412a17.

33. J. P. Vernant and P. Vidal-Naquet, *Myth and Tragedy*, p. 113.

34. See *Rhetoric* 1412a22.

35. J. P. Vernant and P. Vidal-Naquet, *Myth and Tragedy*, p. 120.

36. Nussbaum, *Fragility of Goodness*, p. 126.

37. *Oedipus Rex,* line 1298. It is a line that echoes the opening of the celebrated choral ode in *Antigone: "polla ta deina kouden anthropon deinoteron pelei"* (line 338).

38. There is an anonymous Byzantine work on comedy that bears some relationship to the *Poetics,* but just what that relationship is remains unclear. See G. Else, *Plato and Aristotle on Poetry,* pp. 185–95.

39. See J. Taminiaux, *Le Théâtre des philosophes,* pp. 33–47.

40. Such is also the description of the funeral oration given by N. Loraux in *The Invention of Athens,* pp. 13–14.

INTERLUDE: KANT AND SCHELLING

1. Of course, it is audacious to claim that between the fourth century B.C. and the nineteenth century tragic art does not find a central place in philosophic literature. But, even if there is something undeniably reductive in such a claim, it remains the case that until the early stages in the development of speculative idealism the question of tragedy does not fundamentally guide philosophic questioning even when it finds a place in such questioning. The episodic concerns with tragic art in philosophy up to Schelling remain largely episodes that do not fundamentally alter the course of philosophic questioning. Hegel suggests that this is, in large measure, due to the intervention of Christianity, which presents the death of Christ as the death of death and suffering, as the figure of sacrifice that ends the need for sacrifice. Henceforth it is sufficient that sacrifice live only in the form of ritualized repetition. It is no accident that the recovery of the topic of tragedy coincides with the advent of the death of God that begins with Kant and culminates with Nietzsche.

2. The choice of "letters" to a "friend"—either real or invented—is a common one in this period. It is a deliberate and important choice that bears much weight just as the dialogue form does for Plato. See Hölderlin's letter to Niethammer of February 24, 1796. One thinks also of Schiller's *Letters on the Aesthetic Education of Man* and the "Kallias Briefe," Hölderlin's *Hyperion,* and Bettine von Arnim's *Goethes Briefwechsel mit einem Kind,* to name only four works that are of special relevance to the concerns of this book. For Schelling the question of style and format is of utmost importance; most especially, one needs to understand the impulse to dialogue in Schelling. One sees this, of course, in the dialogue form of *Bruno* (which is admittedly quite unlike Platonic dialogues since there are lengthy monologues in it, and frequently it seems that the conversation partners are oblivious to one another), but one also sees this in Schelling's insistence that the true form of *On the Essence of Human Freedom* is a dialogue. See *Ausgewählte Werke, Schriften von 1806–1813,* p. 410 note. This is also a point that Walter Benjamin will address in his *Ursprung des deutschen Trauerspiels,* p. 208.

3. *ScW, Schriften von 1794–1798,* p. 260.

4. *ScW, Schriften von 1799–1801,* p. 629.

5. F. Nietzsche, *Wille zur Macht,* Aphorism no. 822.

6. Cf., for instance, Ak., 274: "Many people believe they are . . . improved by the performance of a tragedy when in fact they are merely glad at having succeeded in routing boredom."

7. This is of fundamental importance for the understanding of Kant. One sees this claim made repeatedly throughout the *Kritik der Urteilskraft;* nonetheless, the tendency to read the text as principally directed to the question of art is pervasive. That is perhaps the influence of Schiller's *Letters on the Aesthetic Education of Man,* which quite explicitly shifts the center of gravity of aesthetic experience away from the experience of nature to the work of art. Hegel reinforces this in his

Aesthetics when he says that spirit cannot satisfy itself nor find the enjoyment of its true freedom in nature, but does so only in art (see, for instance, vol. I, 152). In contrast to this see Adorno's *Ästhetische Theorie;* see also my "Was wir nicht sagen können . . ."

8. Ak., 246.

9. Ak., 319.

10. It should be noted as well that there is a reciprocal taming of Kant by those who follow him, specially regarding the force of the experience of nature.

11. *ScW, Schriften von 1794–1798,* p. 216. Here, see Appendix B.

12. P. Szondi, *Versuch über das Tragische,* in *Schriften I,* p. 157.

13. This topic needs to be distinguished from the celebrated *querelle des anciens et modernes,* which antedates the topic which emerges after Kant and which is centered on quite different issues.

14. S. Kierkegaard, "The Tragic in Ancient Drama Reflected in the Tragic in Modern Drama," in *Either/Or,* vol. I, p. 143.

15. Ibid., p. 149.

16. Quoted by C. Menke, *Tragödie im Sittlichen,* p. 9.

17. For Freud the matter is not so easily settled since there is a very interesting parallel in what belongs to the specifically Judaic character and tradition; see, for instance, R. Bernstein, *Freud and the Legacy of Moses.* For a fascinating glimpse into the immediacy of the images of ancient Greek art that Freud surrounded himself with in his home, see L. Gamwell and R. Wells, eds., *Sigmund Freud and Art.*

18. See Appendix A.

19. Ibid.

20. Ibid.

21. "The one and the all" was the motto that the young friends and schoolmates Hegel, Schelling, and Hölderlin took for their common concerns.

22. See Appendix A.

23. This is a view that Hegel himself could only ridicule. See the *History of Philosophy,* especially the remarks on Heraclitus, where Hegel speaks of the various forms of the appearance of the dialectic. The formulaic rendering of the dialectic as such a thesis, antithesis, and synthesis is merely a representation of the dialectic, one that ossifies what is otherwise agile and alive.

3. HEGEL

1. Here one thinks, for instance, of the analysis of family in the *Philosophy of Right,* and the treatment of crime and punishment, as well as the development of religious consciousness, in the *Phenomenology of Spirit.*

2. The *Aesthetics,* which was not published in Hegel's lifetime (though composed in the 1820s, it was not published until 1835, four years after Hegel's death), is a relatively late work and postdates by almost two decades some of the most decisive appropriations of an image of tragedy such as we find in the *Phenomenology of Spirit* and the *Philosophy of Right.*

3. So, for instance, one simply cannot understand those sections of the *Phenomenology of Spirit* devoted to ethicality and religious consciousness without seeing how a reading of *Antigone* is being enlisted to develop those themes. See P. Szondi, *Versuch über das Tragische,* p. 52, where he notes that though "the words 'tragic' and 'tragedy' do not occur in Hegel's essay on religion ["The Spirit of Christianity and Its Fate"], the definition of the Tragic found in the essay on natural law does derive from that early work."

4. On this, see my "Why I Am So Happy . . ."

5. *PG,* par. 807.

6. On this see my "Ruins and Roses."

7. These passages in both the *Phenomenology of Spirit* and the *Philosophy of Right* will serve as the focal point for two of the most innovative interpretations of Hegel of recent years: Irigaray's "The Eternal Irony of Community" and Derrida's *Glas.* Both of these works need more attention than they receive in this book. The only reason they have not been given all due care here is that both raise complicated issues that move far beyond the concerns of this book.

8. Just as one sees Homer alive in Plato's *Republic* and "Oedipus Rex" in Aristotle's *Poetics.* One finds such interiorization of another in several interesting instances: Mozart lives in Kierkegaard, Wagner in Nietzsche, Hölderlin in Heidegger.

9. *PG,* par. 446.

10. Interpreting family relations in terms of tragic figures, Hegel will anticipate some of Freud's greatest insights into the dynamics of family life.

11. This is also why there is a tendency to regard some historical conflicts through the optic of Greek tragedy.

12. But is it also important to recognize that Hegel's intention here is not to "interpret" woman, to tell the story of woman, whatever that might mean. The fuller sense of what belongs to the realm of woman as Hegel understands that realm is thought according to a variety of images and figures, not only with reference to Antigone. On this, see David Krell's "Lucinda's Shame," *Cardoza Law Review* 10, nos. 5–6 (1989): 1673–86. What is interesting to note, but not directly relevant to the issues at hand here, is the way the family relations defining the figure of Christ for Hegel are also significant for understanding what he represents for the development of consciousness: in this case we find Christ born of a father *without a body* and of a mother whose body remains "untouched." Here the body becomes an abstraction.

13. *PG,* par. 475.

14. Ibid., par. 246 ff.

15. Ibid., par. 457. In holding to this view Hegel takes to heart Antigone's otherwise puzzling remark that "Had I been a mother of children, and my husband been dead and rotten, I would not have taken this weary task upon me against the will of the city" (lines 961–63). On this see Herodotus's *Histories* and the story of Darius and Inaphrenes, and G. Steiner's *Antigones.*

16. This though the relationship of Antigone to Ismene is one of the most strained in the tragedy. Of course, it also needs to be noted that none of Antigone's family relationships is ever unambiguous (she is, for instance, the sister to her father).

17. Ibid., par. 457.

18. On this, see L. Irigaray, "The Eternal Irony of Community," p. 217: "This means that the brother is invested with a value for the sister that she cannot offer in return, except by devoting herself to his cult after death."

19. *PG,* par. 457.

20. Ibid.

21. Ibid., par. 463.

22. Ibid.

23. It is striking how few treatments of natality are found in the history of philosophy, especially in light of the number of discussions of mortality one finds. In this, H. Arendt is a powerful exception.

24. *PG,* par. 194.

25. Ibid., par. 451.

26. Ibid., par. 452.

27. Ibid. See also L. Irigaray, "The Eternal Irony of Community," pp. 214–15: "The purpose that moves blood relatives to action is the care of the bloodless. Their inherent duty is to ensure *burial for the dead,* thus changing a natural phenomenon into a spiritual act. . . . This supreme duty constitutes the divine law, or *positive* ethical action, as it relates to the individual."

28. Again, here one sees the roots of the passion which the representatives of the state express in seeking to control the woman's body by controlling abortion, or the body of its citizens by outlawing assisted suicide and reserving for itself the right of capital punishment.

29. *PG,* par. 455.

30. The final destination of this movement of the state reserving for itself the rights of the death of its citizens is found in Hegel's stunning analysis of the French Revolution and the Terror (pars. 590–595), where he finds that "The sole work and deed of universal freedom [in the Terror] is therefore *death,* a death too which has no inner significance or filling, for what is negated is the empty point of the absolutely free self. It is thus the coldest and meanest of all deaths, with no more significance than cutting off a head of cabbage or swallowing a mouthful of water." Here "Absolute freedom has equalized the antithesis between the universal and the individual will."

31. *PG,* par. 465.

32. L. Irigaray, "The Eternal Irony of Community," 220.

33. *PG,* par. 464.

34. One of the intriguing remarks Hegel makes at this point, but never really develops, is that this collision "is *comic* because it expresses a contradiction, namely the contradiction of an Absolute that is opposed to itself" (par. 465, emphasis added).

35. *PG,* par. 466.

36. The parallels with Dostoyevsky here are striking and would be interesting to develop.

37. *PG,* par. 469. On this see also paragraph 158, where Hegel explains the "inverted world" of crime and punishment and concludes with the stunning comment that "The punishment which under the law of the *first* world disgraces and destroys a man, is transformed in its *inverted* world into the pardon which preserves his essential being and brings him to honor." On the impossibility of innocence, compare Sartre's *Les Mains salle.*

38. *PG,* par. 468.

39. This analogy between a doubled relation and heterosexual relations will also form the basis for Nietzsche's presentation of the Apollonian and Dionysian relation.

40. *PG,* par. 469.

41. Ibid., par. 472.

42. Ibid., par. 470.

43. Ibid.

44. Ibid. (line 926 in *Antigone*). The word here for "erred" is *hamartanousi.* Two other citations of *Antigone* occur in the *Phenomenology of Spirit;* one is in paragraph 437 (lines 456–57), the other (same lines) is in paragraph 712.

45. Ibid., par. 472.

46. Ibid.

47. Ibid., par. 474. Hegel will take up the same theme of double-sided ruin later in paragraph 738, where the critique of ethical self-righteousness will be clearer.

48. Ibid., par. 662. Self-righteousness is found at most every stage in the education of spirit, and it is always worthy of ridicule, since even when it is in fact "right" from one point of view it is always "formally" an "error."

49. Ibid., par. 475.

50. Ibid., par. 477.

51. Ibid., par. 480.

52. Although there is no reading of the tragedy as such here, the implications for any possible understanding of tragedy, and the confirmation of its real achievement in our efforts to come to terms with ethical life, are clear.

53. He will also do this in the *Philosophy of Right,* where the issues at stake—for instance, family and its relation to the community—remain the same, but where the larger context is different (in the *Philosophy of Right* the issues unfold in the context of a concern with morality). One significant difference in the appropriations of *Antigone* in the *Phenomenology of Spirit* and the *Philosophy of Right* is found in the central role assigned love in the *Philosophy of Right,* where it is called "the most monstrous contradiction" (remark to par. 158).

54. The roots of the word "religion," *religare,* "to bind strongly," indicate something of this.

55. One even notes an increased frequency in the use of the word "reconciliation" from this point in the text forward.

56. *PG,* par. 671. One might argue that from this moment forward spirit knows something of love. Hegel's early text "Love," where he speaks of love as life "duplicating itself," resonates in significant ways with passages such as this one.

57. Here an interesting comparison is found with Kant's remark about finding a regular geometric shape in the sands of what one thought was a deserted island and coming to the conclusion that it could only be a product of art: "vestigium hominis video" (Ak., 370).

58. *PG,* par. 701.

59. These early rituals involve symbolic sacrifice and the consumption of nature. In other words, eating is presented as one of the ways in which the natural world is taken up into the life of spirit. On this see the remarkable passage (par. 109) in which Hegel speaks of "the secret meaning of the eating of bread and the drinking of wine . . . [in which] one brings about the nothingness of such things. . . . Even the animals are not shut out from this wisdom but, on the contrary, show themselves to be profoundly initiated into it; for they do not just stand idly in front of sensuous things as if these possessed intrinsic being, but, despairing of their reality fall to without ceremony and eat them up." See also paragraph 718, where Hegel discusses the relation of the cult to eating and animal sacrifice in the cult. Eating here is interpreted as the form in which humans produce a union with the gods.

60. Ibid., par. 710.

61. This crucial point is one that Hegel had made earlier (par. 508) when he said, "Language . . . alone . . . contains the 'I' in its purity, it alone expresses the 'I', the 'I' itself . . . in every other expression [of itself the 'I'] is immersed in a [different] reality."

62. *PG,* par. 713 (emphasis added).

63. Ibid., par. 726.

64. Ibid., par. 727.

65. He expresses this point eloquently in the *Aesthetics* (p. 236) when he writes that "man does not . . . carry in himself only *one* god as his 'pathos'; the human emotional life is great and wide; to a true man many gods belong; and he shuts up

in his heart all the powers which are dispersed in the circle of the gods; the whole of Olympus is assembled in his breast."

66. *PG,* par. 728.

67. Ibid., par. 732.

68. Ibid., par. 733.

69. Ibid., par. 734.

70. Ibid., par. 740.

71. Nietzsche will make much the same remark in *Birth of Tragedy* in speaking of Hamlet.

72. *PG,* pars. 740–41.

73. Ibid., par. 744.

74. Ibid., par. 747.

75. Ibid.

76. *Symposium* 223d.

77. *Aesthetics,* p. 11. On this see Heidegger's comments in the "Epilogue" to the "Origin of the Work of Art" in *Holzwege,* p. 66.

78. *Aesthetics,* p. 143. The question of nature is, however, a more complicated one than such a remark might indicate. See, for instance, Hegel's comment (p. 43) that "it must be said that, by mere imitation, art cannot stand in competition with nature, and, if it tries, looks like a worm trying to crawl after an elephant."

79. Ibid., p. 13.

80. Ibid., p. 31.

81. Ibid.

82. For an interesting discussion of the multiplicity of forms in which spirit becomes a work of art, see J.-L. Nancy, *The Muses.*

83. *Aesthetics,* p. 189. Compare Kierkegaard, *Either/Or,* vol. I, p. 149: "Our age has lost all the substantial categories of family, state, kindred; it must turn the single individual over to himself completely in such a way that, strictly speaking, he becomes his own creator. Consequently his guilt is sin, his pain repentance, but thereby the tragic is canceled."

84. On this relation of art to history and culture, see Hegel's *Aesthestics,* pp. 297–98: "A work of art cannot entirely free itself from the culture of its time."

85. Ibid., pp. 303–306. Much could also be said about the relation of the symbol and the sublime (see especially p. 303).

86. Ibid., p. 432.

87. Ibid., pp. 433–34. Hegel will also make the very interesting observation (p. 521) that "The supreme works of beautiful sculpture are sightless and their inner being does not look out of them as self-knowing inwardness in this spiritual concentration which the eye discloses. The light of the soul falls outside of them and belongs to the spectator alone."

88. There is an important discrepancy between the first two and the third manner in which Hegel treats the work of art. In the third part of the *Aesthetics,* Hegel considers all forms of poetry as romantic forms. This means he considers both epic and tragedy as romantic art forms. The reasons he gives for doing this primarily have to do with the fact that he considers all the arts having to do with language as examples of the final possible form of art. In the word the art finds its most spiritual "material": "Speech alone is the element worthy of the expression of spirit" (p. 1158). Nonetheless, even though Hegel takes up tragedy in this third part as an instance of the romantic form, there is no compelling reason to find in tragedy an illustration of the principle of subjectivity which he finds at the center of the romantic form: "The true content of romantic art is absolute inwardness" (p. 519). Moreover, Hegel tends to regard the romantic form as having a "Chris-

tian character," a trait which is thoroughly inappropriate as a way of characterizing Greek tragedy. Such a principle and such a character is however appropriate for the investigation of modern tragedy, and Hegel's remarks on it do emphasize its romantic character. However, the bulk of his treatment of tragedy in the third part centers on Greek tragedy, and when he takes up this topic he almost speaks as if he was treating a classical art form. In the end, tragedy disturbs Hegel's schema of artistic forms more than any other genre he considers. Since not much is at stake in this designation by itself, the question of the form proper to tragedy will not be addressed further here.

89. *Aesthetics,* p. 1051.

90. See ibid., p. 1052: "We must dismiss out of hand the idea that a truly epic action can take place on the ground of a political situation developed into an organized constitution with elaborate laws, effective courts of law, well-organized administration in the hands of ministers, civil servants, police, etc." This is why the closest approximation to the epic form found in the United States is life on the "frontier." Hegel himself seems to indicate something like this when he writes (p. 1062) of the possibility of epic in the future that one needs to "look beyond Europe . . . and turn our eyes to America." Here one might do well to compare Benjamin's conceptions of divine and mythic violence which he formulates in "Critique of Violence." Epic bears an interesting resemblance to Benjamin's sense of the founding violence that is "divine."

91. Ibid., p. 188.

92. On this compare Heidegger's frequent remarks about poetic "founding"; for instance, in the "Origin of the Work of Art," in *Holzwege,* p. 50.

93. He is aware of course that this makes Homer's *Odyssey* an interesting and important exception. As a sort of compensation for this exception, Hegel takes special note of book 11 of the *Odyssey* in which Odysseus descends into the underworld. There the sense of mourning and of destiny are most clearly in evidence.

94. An interesting qualification on this is that civil war is more suitable to tragedy; in it the nation is set against itself and is not struggling with an external power (see p. 1060).

95. *Aesthetics,* p. 1071.

96. Ibid., p. 1089.

97. Hegel notes (p. 1055) that in order to present us with a full sense of the life of a people, and not simply a people at war, Homer overcomes the restrictions of the setting of the *Iliad* in the scene depicting Achilles' shield (book 18) on which "Homer has brought together the whole sphere of the earth and human life, weddings, legal actions, agriculture, herds, etc., private wars between cites, and described all this . . . and not as an external paragon." See my "Like a Fire That Consumes All Before It . . . ," in *Lyrical and Ethical Subjects* (Albany: State University of New York Press, forthcoming).

98. *Aesthetics,* p. 1094.

99. Ibid., p. 1111.

100. Ibid., p. 1113.

101. Ibid., p. 1120.

102. Langston Hughes put it beautifully when he said that the lyric poem was the "human soul squeezed drop by drop, like a lemon, into atomic words."

103. *Aesthetics,* p. 1196.

104. See especially Plato's *Apology* and *Phaedrus.* See also J. Sallis, *Being and Logos.*

105. Plutarch, "Demosthenes," in *Lives,* cited by H. Arendt in *The Human Condition,* p. 26. A related feature of the Greek relation to language is the fact that silent reading was unknown in ancient Greece. One read and moved one's lips,

speaking the words. This too is an indication that words are not regarded as properly grasped in the interior and private space of the subject.

106. Hölderlin is one of the few who fully escapes this modern perspective and grasps the role of language in the tragic drama from the Greek point of view. This is the point of view from which one needs to understand Hölderlin's remark in his "Remarks on *Antigone*" that "The Greek-tragic word is deadly-factical, for the body which it seizes really kills."

107. It should be noted that death is seldom, if ever, witnessed on the stage. This is no accident, but is a form of acknowledging that death itself remains shrouded in darkness. In this regard epic, with its constant presentation of death (the deaths of 318 heroes are described in the *Iliad*, and 243 of those are named). Gender is also significant in both how a character dies and whether it is presented on stage or not; on this point see N. Loraux, *Tragic Ways of Killing a Woman*.

108. *Aesthetics*, p. 1210.

109. Ibid., p. 1211.

110. Ibid., p. 1220.

111. Ibid., p. 1222.

112. Ibid. Just as Sophocles, in Hegel's view, is the tragic author par excellence, so too is Aristophanes the best example of a comic author for Hegel. What should be noted here is that modern tragedy, which is governed by the principle of subjectivity and in this respect to be distinguished from ancient tragedy, is more akin to comedy.

113. Ibid., p. 11.

114. Ibid., p. 1236.

115. In this regard one is reminded of Kant's comment, "Die schöne Dinge zeigen an, das der Mensch in die Welt passe" (*Reflexionen*, Ak. 1820A).

116. *Aesthetics*, p. 2.

117. In this Hegel's conception of art is remarkably similar to Nietzsche's, which is propelled by the conflicting principles of the Apollonian and Dionysian impulses. Nietzsche's rationale for singling out tragedy as the highpoint of the possibilities belonging to the work of art is very similar to Hegel's at this point.

118. As just one illustration of this, one might consider Hegel's contention (*Aesthetics*, p. 522) that "We cannot say that the Greeks interpreted death in its essential meaning." In light of the role that death plays in the development of Greek art generally—as the destiny of the natural life of the individual which is the center of gravity of Greek art—one can only be surprised by a claim such as this one.

119. *PG*, par. 669.

4. HÖLDERLIN

1. *SW*, vol. II, p. 102. This phrase needs to be understood with reference to both Kant and Fichte. The idea of an intellectual intuition is perhaps most easily understood by the contrast between it and the notion of a finite, or derivative, intuition, which is a form of knowing defined by the difference between thought and sensation. Only such a finite form of knowing confronts the problem of the schematism and so requires the work of the imagination. Intellectual intuition, on the other hand, is a form of knowing in which the act of knowing (intellecting) and of sensing (intuiting) are the same. Such a form of knowing would be the speculative equivalent of a divine knowing, that is, a knowledge which had no need of mediation, but was simply immediate. This is why Hölderlin will say, "The tragic . . . is in its basic tone idealistic [i.e., indexed to the absolute]" (*SW*, vol. II, p. 104). But it should never be forgotten that Hölderlin qualifies the manner in

which the tragic presents us with an intellectual intuition; namely, it is the *metaphor* of an intellectual intuition, and that qualification removes his views completely from the orbit of any possible idealism. On this see chapter 2 above.

2. *SW,* vol. II, p. 310.

3. By this I am referring to the remark he makes in "In lovely blueness . . ." which likens our relation to ancient Greece to the relation of sunflowers to the sun. See the translation of this work in Appendix E.

4. Although Hölderlin does not comment on Hegel in this regard, one might expect that he would find Hegel's effort to appropriate the tragic for systematic purposes to be an illustration of how such an appropriation destroys what is proper to the foreign.

5. *SW,* vol. I, p. 513.

6. Born in 1770, Hölderlin lost his sanity sometime around 1806. Although he continued to write for many years until his death in 1843, Hölderlin's greatest achievements as a writer were made between the early 1790s and 1806. The first volume of *Hyperion* was published in 1797 (the second in 1799); the publication of his translations of Sophocles, perhaps the greatest success of which he was ever able to be conscious, was in 1804. To contextualize these events, one should recall that Schelling's *Letters on Dogmatism and Criticism* were published in 1795, and Hegel's *Phenomenology of Spirit* was published in 1807.

7. It is interesting to trace the course of the image which is projected both of Hölderlin's life and his work. What is especially notable is the difference between nineteenth- and twentieth-century images of him (the dividing line seems to have been drawn by Hellingrath and Dilthey). In the nineteenth century he is typically presented as a gentle, extremely sensitive, yet deeply disturbed poet of romance and longing; in the twentieth century it is much more common to regard him as a visionary, a radical and experimenter, and as a penetrating philosophical mind who was far ahead of his own times.

8. But the American Revolution is also not far from his mind. On this see his poem "An Hiller" (1793), which was written for his friend Hiller, who was planning to move to the newly founded United States and had hoped to settle in Philadelphia, which was the town most closely connected with the revolution and the sense of a new future. It was also associated with Athens. That is why Hölderlin speaks of "flying to the youthful, more blessed world of your Philadelphia" (*SW,* I, 145).

9. The word "nostalgia" was originally coined in 1678 by a Swiss physician who was translating the German word *Heimweh* (homesickness) to describe the medical condition of Swiss who were living abroad (especially mercenaries) and who suffered from their exile. See J. Taminiaux, *Poetics, Speculation, and Judgment,* pp. 73–74.

10. *SW,* vol. II, p. 925.

11. Ibid., vol. II, p. 540 (July 10, 1794).

12. Ibid., vol. II, p. 726 (January 1, 1799).

13. The characterization of Hyperion as a hermit is from the subtitle of the book, "or, the Hermit in Greece." Hölderlin was well aware that the life of isolation in ancient Greece, a culture in which freedom and meaning was found first in the public realm, was considered a life of burden. On this see H. Arendt's discussion of the public and private in ancient Greece in *The Human Condition,* especially pp. 22–39.

The setting of these letters is the years 1768–72. For important details regarding the setting, as well as some of Hölderlin's own resources for the presentation of the topography and the history of the region (like all the other Germans considered here, and most of the German Hellenists of his time, Hölderlin never visited Greece—the only exception among those considered here is Heidegger, who visited Greece only late in life), see David Constantine, *Hölderlin*, pp. 83–104.

14. In some respects it also qualifies as an autobiography. Just as one might characterize Hegel's *Phenomenology of Spirit* as the autobiography of spirit (and that means as well the autobiography of god), so too might one speak of *Hyperion* as the autobiography of one who is defined by an awareness of his separation from the divine.

15. Early in *Hyperion* Hyperion writes to Bellarmin (*SW*, vol. I, p. 616): "I thank you that you have asked me to tell you of myself and that you have recalled past times to my memory."

16. One also notes that the familiar *du* is used.

17. Although Hölderlin never visited Greece, he richly and vividly describes the landscape and the natural life of the region. Beissner gives the sources from which Hölderlin drew in the project of depicting the topography of the region. He also indicates that Hölderlin is remarkably acute in his descriptions. Of particular use to Hölderlin was Richard Chandler's *Travels in Greece,* which was translated into German in 1776.

18. It should be noted that *Hyperion* is dedicated to Susette Gontard who was Hölderlin's lover and whom he called "Diotima." The significance of some of the names of the characters here is worth calling attention to. Diotima is, of course, a reference to the woman who instructed Socrates about the nature of *eros* in Plato's *Symposium* (see esp. 201ff.). Hyperion is one of the thirteen Titans, the one most directly related to the sun.

Hölderlin's inscription to Gontard in the first volume (the two volumes of *Hyperion* were published separately) reads as follows: "The influence of noble nature is as necessary to the artist, as the daylight is to the plant; and as the daylight finds itself again in the plant, not as it is in itself, but only in the bright earthly play of colors, so too do all noble natures find not themselves, but dispersed traces of their excellence in the many forms and plays of the artist." The inscription in the second volume simply reads: "To whom besides you." It should also be noted that Gontard was very much involved in the completion of *Hyperion*. This we know from the letters she and Hölderlin wrote to one another at the time.

19. "Non coerceri maximo, contineri minimo, divinum est." It is from the collection *Imago primi saeculi Societatis Iesu* (1640). Hölderlin's source for this citation is unknown.

20. From lines 1224–27. These lines are also cited by Nietzsche in *The Birth of Tragedy* (see section 3).

21. "Nächstens mehr," in *SW,* vol. I, p. 760.

22. *SW,* vol. I, p. 614.

23. On the mood of mourning and its relation to melancholia, see Freud's essay "Mourning and Melancholia." For an interesting discussion of the intersection of mourning and melancholia, see Rebecca Comay, "Perverse History."

24. *SW,* vol. I, p. 614.

25. Ibid., p. 657.

26. Ibid., p. 683.

27. Ibid., vol. I, p. 322 ("Heimkunft. An die Verwandten"). The use of the word "holy" (*heilen*) needs some comment. Hölderlin is acutely aware of the etymological connections of this word to the words for health and healing and wholeness (this works both in German and in English), and he will emphasize that the holy refers to that which heals the rupture from which the life of a mortal suffers. It is not to be taken immediately as a word that will refer to a divine being.

28. Ibid., p. 643.

29. This is fragment B51 in the Diels/Kranz listing. See also Plato, *Symposium* 187a.

30. Ibid., p. 685. Of course, the intriguing suggestion here is that the Greeks inaugurated philosophy because they were the first to give expression to the essence of beauty—an interesting answer to the oft posed question of why philosophy had its beginnings in Greece.

31. *Oedipus at Colonus,* lines 1224–27. It is worth noting that near the end of the letters Hyperion will compare himself to Oedipus become homeless and wandering blindly, searching for a place to die (see *SW*, vol. I, p. 754: "Humbled I came [to Germany], like the homeless, blind Oedipus at the gates of Athens where the divine fields received him").

32. *SW*, vol. I, p. 688.

33. See the discussion of this passage in Homer above in chapter 2. See also my "What We Owe the Dead." The comparison of Hyperion and Odysseus works in other regards as well. Most of all one needs to understand both by the search for a home. That search is very much on Hyperion's mind, and it is a powerful issue for Hölderlin as he indicates in the preface to *Hyperion* and in the Böhlendorff letter of December 4, 1801 (see the next section of this chapter and Appendix C). A second reference to Homer is found near the end of the letters when Hyperion praises the poets and artists of Germany and concludes by saying, "They live in the world, as strangers in their own homes, they are like the suffering Odysseus when he sat at the gates of his own home wearing the garb of a beggar while the noise of a shameless celebration came from the halls and from whence he heard the question 'who brought us this poor country person?'" (*SW*, vol. I, p. 756).

34. *SW,* vol. I, p. 614.

35. Ibid., p. 721.

36. Ibid., p. 722.

37. This is perhaps nowhere more pronounced than in the "Remarks on *Antigone,*" where one reads, for instance, that "time is always measured in suffering" (ibid., vol. II, p. 372) and where he will later suggest that the word is deadly and that the God is present in the figure of the finality of death.

38. Ibid., I, p. 450.

39. Ibid., I, p. 760.

40. Diels/Kranz, Fragment 51.

41. *SW,* vol. I, p. 760.

42. However, he had earlier planned to write a tragedy on the death of Socrates. See the letter from October 1794.

43. A reference to this proximity between Hegel and Hölderlin and evidence of its familiarity are found in one of the most touching letters which is to be found in the collection of Hölderlin's correspondence. The letter was not written by Hölderlin, but by Henry Gontard, one of Hölderlin's charges and the son of Susette. Henry, who was ten years old at the time, wrote the following letter after discovering that Hölderlin had chosen to leave the household and no longer serve as the private tutor for the Gontard family (presumably problems with Susette's husband, Jakob, who frequently expressed displeasure with Hölderlin, were the reason for Hölderlin's rather abrupt departure). The letter is dated September 27, 1798:

> Dear Holder!
> I can hardly believe that you are gone. I was with Mr. Hegel today and
> he said that you had thought about leaving for a long time, when I re-

turned, I met Mr. Hänish, who came to visit us on the day of your departure, and who was looking for a book; he found it, at the time I was with
mother, he asked Jette [Henry's sister], where you were, Jette said that
you went away, he wanted to go right away to Mr. Hegel and ask more
about you, he walked with me, and asked why you had left, and said it
hurt him very much. At dinner father asked where you were, I said you
had left, and that you gave everyone your best wishes. Mother is healthy,
and sends you many regards, and says you should think of us often, she
had my bed moved to the balcony room and wants to make sure that she
goes through what you taught us with us one more time. Come again
soon my Holder; from whom besides you are we supposed to learn. I am
sending you tobacco and Mr. Hegel sends you the 6th issue of Posselt's
"Annals."

    Farewell, dear Holder.

        I am,

           Your Henri

44. A translation of the letter is found in Appendix C.

45. A translation of this letter is found in Appendix D.

46. *SW,* vol. II, p. 912.

47. Ibid. Of the many interesting treatments of this remark, see especially F.
Dastur, *Hölderlin: tragédie et modernité;* and C. Fynsk, *Heidegger: Thought and Historicity.*

48. *SW,* vol. I, p. 513.

49. It should be noted how much the tragic flaw always needs to be understood as that into which one is born, and not as a willful mistake or fault.

50. A few years later, in the "Remarks on *Antigone,*" he will make the same
point and say that it is exactly this flaw, namely "the lack of destiny, the *dysmoron,*
which is the specific weakness" of modernity (*SW,* vol. II, p. 374).

51. Ibid., p. 914.

52. Ibid., p. 912.

53. Ibid., p. 913.

54. See "In lovely blueness . . . ," which is translated in Appendix E.

55. See B. Allemann, "Hölderlin entre les anciens et les modernes," and J.
Taminiaux, *La Nostalgie de la Grèce à l'aube de l'idéalisme allemand.* Both Allemann
and Taminiaux argue, as I want to suggest, that Hölderlin's experience with
Greece opens up questions that cannot be thought in terms of a debate so defined
by classicism. Peter Szondi's influential article "Überwindung des Klassizismus"
does not go quite far enough in this regard. One important clue to the way in
which Hölderlin sets himself apart from the debates of his day over the relation of
modernity and antiquity is found in the fact that he prefers to speak of the relation of Greece to "Hesperia" rather than to modernity.

56. *SW,* vol. I, p. 489.

57. See F. Dastur, *Hölderlin: tragédie et modernité,* and F. Fédier, *Remarques sur
Oedipe/Remarques sur Antigone,* p. 169. Heidegger likewise tries to pull Hölderlin's
concerns away from the question of nationhood, but he moves them to a question of belonging to the destiny of the West. See especially "Brief über den Hu-
manismus," *Wegmarken* (Frankfurt, 1978), p. 335: "Hölderlin jedoch ist, wenn er
die 'Heimkunft' dichtet, darum besorgt, daß seine 'Landsleute' ihr Wesen finden.
Dieses sucht er keineswegs in einem Egoismus seines Volkes. Er sieht es vielmehr
aus der Zugehörigkeit in das Geschick des Abendlands."

58. *SW,* vol. II, p. 62.

59. Freud frequently referred to his own relation to Greek art as presenting us

with a master metaphor for the psychoanalytic process. See Gamwell and Wells, eds., *Sigmund Freud and Art,* especially pp. 15–19.

60. *SW,* vol. II, p. 912. For a clear presentation of this schema see Françoise Dastur, *Hölderlin: tragédie et modernité,* p. 22.

61. *SW,* vol. II, p. 912.

62. Ibid.

63. *SW,* vol. I, p. 909.

64. The legend is told by Roberto Calasso as follows: "Having gone down to the underworld to ransom his mother, Dionysus found himself face to face with Hades, as though looking in a mirror. The eyes staring at him were his own. Hades told him he would let Semele go, but only on condition that Dionysus gave up something very dear to him. Dionysus thought. Then he offered a twig of myrtle to the lord of the invisible. Hades accepted. How was it that such a humble plant could settle such a portentous deal? Myrtle was the plant young spouses were crowned with on earth. And Hades couldn't get enough of spouses and their nuptials. He wanted the kingdom of the dead to be mingled with the realm of eros. Not so as to conquer or subdue it. . . . No what he really wanted was to mix the two kingdoms together. The myrtle was Aphrodite's plant before it was Dionysus's and until this visit to the underworld it had been just the casual fleeting fragrance of lovemaking. But from now on it would spread the fragrance of another world as well, the unknown. Thus myrtle became the plant of both eros and mourning" (*The Marriage of Cadmus and Harmony,* pp. 215–16).

65. *SW,* vol. II, p. 102.

66. Ibid., p. 913. This comment, which seems to lament the practice of burying the dead in coffins as opposed to cremation, also needs to be read as commenting upon the meaning of death for an understanding of life in the modern world.

67. One wonders how Hölderlin understood his own remark here since the practice of cremation is not the sole form in which the Greeks dealt with the corpse. See E. Vermeule, *Aspects of Death in Early Greek Art and Poetry,* pp. 66ff., for a discussion of a variety of means in which the dead body was disposed of. Clearly, Hölderlin has Empedocles in mind, who, at least in the tragedy Hölderlin was writing at the time, died by leaping into a volcanic crater.

68. *SW,* I, p. 875.

69. Ibid., vol. II, p. 913.

70. This is the period in which Hegel is working intensely on the *Phenomenology of Spirit* as well. For some insight into the personal relation between Hölderlin and Hegel during this time, see D. Henrick, "Hegel und Hölderlin."

71. On Luther's translations, see Heine's comments in *Philosophy and Religion in Germany.* See also my introduction to that translation.

72. Although there is something that pertains only to the region of translation, to the between of languages in the plural (and here Bakhtin's notion of heteroglossia should not be overlooked when addressing this point), it is also the case that Hölderlin made an attempt to bring Greek language into German in much of his poetry. This is especially the case with "Wie wenn am Feiertage . . . ," which Hölderlin wrote with the metrics one finds in Pindar in mind.

73. W. Benjamin, "The Task of the Translator," p. 81. See also my "The Hermeneutic Dimension of Translation." The importance and scope of the question of translation needs to be acknowledged. One of the most dramatic statements of the stakes of the question of translation is made by Heidegger in his 1942 lecture course on Hölderlin's "Der Ister." In that course Heidegger takes up Hölderlin's translations of Sophocles, puzzling above all about the translation of the word *to*

deinon, and suggesting that the lack of a word for this word is today a signal of a basic difference between the Greek and the modern conceptions of the human being. In the middle of this discussion Heidegger interrupts his own analysis to say, "Tell me what you think of translation and I will tell you who you are" (*GA,* vol. 53, p. 76).

74. Of course, it is difficult to preserve the strangeness of the German even if one speaks of it in German. For a close and rather good analysis of the translation, see W. Binder, *Hölderlin und Sophokles.*

75. *SW,* vol. II, p. 925. Here it should be noted that the text Hölderlin used for his translations (the Juntina of 1555) is highly problematic and yet another indication that an orthodox view of scholarly fidelity is not guiding his relation to these texts. The translations were severely criticized after they were published. His friend Schelling even writes to Hegel that these translations "express his wasted state of mind" (cited by T. Pfau in the notes to his translations of the remarks in *Friedrich Hölderlin: Essays and Letters on Theory,* p. 174).

76. The equation "Hesperian" and "Western" is not fully justified. Hölderlin is deliberate and generally consistent in choosing not to use the word "Western," but he is not clear about his reasons for this insistence. "Hesperian" means not only "Western" but also "modern," which, one might argue, has spread beyond the boundaries of the West.

77. *SW,* vol. II, p. 310.

78. In both plays it is a speech by Teiresias which forms the caesura. The figure of Teiresias, the blind prophet, is an all-important one in Greek literature (for instance, he is the reason Odysseus must travel to the underworld in the *Odyssey*). Like Homer, or at least the legend of Homer, Teiresias was blind (it is no accident that the Greek image of the poet has the poet being blind; Homer's name is even related to the nickname given to the blind in Greece—*homeros* [hostage]). Teiresias came to be blind according to several legends—the most interesting of which involves his gender-switching past—but however he is said to have come to be blinded, what is always the case is that the arrival of that blindness is coupled with the arrival of his special relation to both the future and to justice. See my "What We Didn't See."

79. *SW,* vol. II, p. 315.

80. Ibid., p. 373.

81. Ibid.

82. Ibid., p. 370.

83. Ibid., p. 315.

84. Ibid., p. 309.

85. Ibid., p. 310.

86. Ibid., p. 316.

87. On this see Kant, *Kritik der Urteilskraft,* Ak., 248–66.

88. *SW,* vol. II, p. 370.

89. Ibid., p. 374.

90. Of course, one thinks here of the striking similarity of Hölderlin's conception of time here and Heidegger's analysis of time in *Being and Time.*

91. *SW,* vol. II, p. 372.

92. Again the similarities with Heidegger's *Being and Time* are striking. Here one is reminded of Heidegger's analysis of the *Augenblick.* See W. McNeill, *The Glance of the Eye.*

93. *SW,* vol. II, pp. 374–75.

94. Ibid., vol. I, p. 265 ("Im Walde").

95. It does not take much to see the kinship between poetry (and, of course,

music) and death, and understand the deep association that the two have. Plato understood this connection between rhythm and lamentation, and he feared it because of the force of death in the community. See my "Acoustics."

96. Once again one can see another point of kinship with Heidegger here in the notion that there is an essential relation between language and death. See "Das Wesen der Sprache," in *Unterweges zur Sprache* (Pfullingen: Neske Verlag, 1975), p. 215. See also my discussion of this passage in "Black Milk and Blue." One also can begin to appreciate the deep affinity between the concerns that drew Heidegger to engage the work of Hölderlin over such an extended period and finally to struggle to draw Hölderlin into his own orbit of concerns even when they exceeded or differed from Hölderlin's own. The result of this struggle, animated by this deep affinity, is a creative appropriation of Hölderlin's work that, though full of distortion from one point of view, remains an imaginative and exciting intellectual achievement precisely because it is born of an abiding sense of shared convictions such as this conviction regarding the relation of language and death.

97. See "In lovely blueness . . ." as well as Heraclitus, Diehls/Kranz Fragments 26, 62, 88.

98. *SW,* vol. II, p. 83.

99. Ibid., p. 370.

100. Ibid., p. 313.

101. Ibid., p. 311.

102. Ibid., p. 312.

103. Ibid., p. 314.

104. See "In lovely blueness . . ."

105. The passage in which this is uttered is one of the most powerful in *King Oedipus:* *"ho deinon idein pathos anthropois, o deinotation panton hos ego prosekurs ede"* (lines 1298–99). Curiously, Hölderlin here does not translate *deinon* as *ungeheuer* as he does most always. Here his translation reads: "O schröklick zu sehen ein Schmerz für Menschen, O schröklichster von allen, so viel Ich getroffen schon" (*SW,* vol. II, p. 301).

106. *SW,* vol. II, p. 371. This is a point at which one could make a fascinating comparison with modern tragedy, especially Shakespeare. One thinks in particular of the madness of needing to have knowledge, which is the chief characteristic of figures such as Hamlet or Lear. For some suggestive remarks in this regard (and an excellent study of madness in Greek tragedy generally), see R. Padel, *In and Out of Mind* and her *Whom Gods Destroy.*

107. It is also worth noting both that Colonus is Sophocles' birthplace and that the relation of Colonus to Athens (as well as the politics of Athens at the time of the composition of the play, the last years of Sophocles' life) is very much at the center of what plays out in the tragedy. Likewise, many of the enigmas of *Antigone* find their roots in this play. Above all one gains some clarity here about the reasons Antigone finds herself so wedded to the need to bury Polynices (see line 1625).

108. There is only a fragment of a translation of *Oedipus at Colonus* remaining. This fragment, a translation of a choral ode, probably dates from 1803 (though both Steiner and Constantine give the date as 1796; however, see the material in the collected critical edition edited by Knaupp, *SW,* vol. III, p. 440). What is at stake in the dating of this fragment is whether or not Hölderlin took up the possibility of translating *Oedipus at Colonus* early, perhaps first of all, and so let that influence some of the comments he will make about Oedipus in the "Remarks." I tend to believe that Hölderlin came to take a serious interest in the details of the

language and dynamics of *Oedipus at Colonus* only after completing the other translations. Taken up more extensively, I believe that Hölderlin might have found some challenges to his own understanding of Oedipus in this third play. Ultimately, however, the stakes of the dating of this fragment should not be overstated.

109. *SW,* vol. II, p. 370.

110. See Hölderlin's ode "Der Rhein."

111. One of the great merits of G. Steiner's reading of these translations in his *Antigones* is the way he pays close attention to the operations of the language in the translations as themselves revelatory of a special understanding of the plays.

112. *SW,* vol. II, p. 371.

113. See the letter to Neuffer on October 10, 1794, ibid., p. 550. There is some controversy regarding the possibility that Hölderlin wrote a plan for another tragedy entitled *Agis* about the Spartan king of the same name. Some of the early editors of his work believed that he had actually authored such a work. This is now disputed and likely to be denied. See *SW,* vol. III, p. 329.

114. Of course, such a claim is not without a measure of exaggeration and distortion. The first version, for instance, is the longest and, from that point of view at least, the most comprehensive of the three versions. The third is the final and, from that point of view at least, the most reflected upon of the three versions. But the second version is also unique insofar as its poetic meter is formal, whereas the other versions are composed in blank verse. Each version has its own special claim to distinction, and the three do not easily fit together into a single pattern of understanding. My reasons for the choice of the second version finally boil down to the simple fact that I find it the most exciting of the three. For summaries of the different versions, see David Constantine, *Hölderlin,* pp. 130–51. A translation of the second version is appended in Appendix G.

115. See the letters to Neuffer and his brother on June 4, 1799 (*SW,* vol. II, pp. 764–72). What remains of the four acts is only a portion of acts 1 and 2 (altogether 732 lines). Despite this inability to see the full execution of the plan in this version, some elements of that plan are remarkably clear in the light of Hölderlin's own commentary in "The Ground to Empedocles."

116. Interestingly, Aristotle singles Empedocles out in his *Poetics* as an illustration of the fact that simply writing verse does not constitute the writing of poetry. See *Poetics* 1447b10.

117. See especially Diehls/Kranz fragment 17: "A twofold tale I shall tell: at one time they grew to be one alone out of many, at another again they grew apart to be many out of one. Double is the birth of mortal things and double their failing; for the one is brought to birth and destroyed by the coming together of all things, the other is nurtured and flies apart as they grow apart again. And these things never cease their continual interchange, now through love all coming together into one, now again each carried apart by the hatred of strife. So insofar as they have learned to grow one from many, and again as the one grows apart grow many, thus far do they come into being and have no stable life; but insofar as they never cease their continual interchange, thus far they exist always changeless in the cycle."

118. *SW,* vol. I, p. 763.

119. All the translations from the second version will be found in my translation in Appendix G.

120. See my "Ruins and Roses."

121. *SW,* vol. I, p. 868.

122. Ibid., vol. II, p. 98.

123. Ibid., p. 872.

124. See "Brot und Wein," in ibid., vol. I, p. 376. The flower is a frequent image in Hölderlin, for whom it is an instance of the perfection of nature that can serve equally as a paradigm for human existence. See also the poem "Da ich ein Knabe war," in *SW*, vol. I, pp. 167–68; or *Hyperion*, where Diotima is frequently likened to a flower, and it is said that "her heart was at home among the flowers as if it were one of them." On the relation between language and the image of the flower, see A. Hornbacher, *Die Blume des Mundes*.

125. *SW*, vol. I, p. 871.

126. Ibid., p. 877.

127. On the specific nature of this paradox see the letter from Hölderlin to his brother dated June 4, 1799 (ibid., vol. II, p. 769).

128. This is why Pierre Bertaux suggests that at this point Hölderlin was interested in establishing a new form of democracy; see P. Bertaux, *Der andere Hölderlin,* pp. 78ff.

129. *SW*, vol. I, p. 870.

130. Ibid., p. 872.

131. This is why David Constantine suggests that in the third version Empedocles is something of a Christ-like figure inaugurating a new era. But that is also one of the reasons I have chosen to treat the second version as the most authentically tragic of the three. It is also certainly the most thoroughly enigmatic of the three. See Constantine, *Hölderlin*, pp. 149–51.

132. The allusion, of course, is to the celebrated line from "Wo aber Gefahr ist, wächst / Das rettende auch," in *SW*, vol. I, p. 447.

133. Ibid., p. 753.

134. Ibid., p. 751.

135. On this see David Krell's insightful comments in *Lunar Voices*, pp. 3–23.

136. *SW*, vol. I, p. 691.

137. Ibid., p. 868.

138. Here one would do well to look carefully at Krell's *The Recalcitrant Art,* in which he weaves the correspondence between Hölderlin and Diotima with a wonderfully original commentary.

5. NIETZSCHE

1. Despite the importance of Hegel, one also needs to be careful not to let his dominating presence obscure the role that others will play in the determination of the conception of the tragic. In the case of Nietzsche, Hölderlin is a very real influence. One also should not overlook the fact that Nietzsche, like Hölderlin, tried to write a tragedy based on Empedocles' life. On this, see especially David Krell, *Postponements.* There is a deep kinship between Hölderlin and Nietzsche. The point of their most evident difference comes in the tonality of their work, the mood out of which it is written (the language of suffering will sound different for each). However, on the whole their affinities will not be fully evident until Heidegger, who will do much to illuminate their similarities by virtue of his deep debt to both.

2. For a more detailed picture see Burckhardt's *Griechische Kulturgeschichte*. A selection from this work has been published in English as *The Greeks and Greek Civilization*. These lectures are fascinating for several reasons, including the manner in which they formulate notions such as race, culture, and political life.

3. Although, as I have argued in chapter 4, the image and reception of Hegel's conception of Greek tragedy are highly problematic and not as interesting as what one can find in Hegel's writings themselves.

4. J. Burckhardt, *The Greeks and Greek Civilization*, p. 36.

5. His lifelong relation with Burkhardt was ultimately a complicated matter. Burkhardt was twenty-six years older than Nietzsche, and so the relationship was one that struggled to find a point of equality between the two colleagues (both taught at Basel during the years Nietzsche was there). Their relationship initially flourished around their mutual interests in the ancient world, notions of history, and their shared love of Schopenhauer. From Nietzsche's side it remained always one of admiration, differences notwithstanding, but from the side of Burkhardt there was a clearer sense of the depth of their differences. One of Nietzsche's final missives, from Turin in late 1888, as he was descending into madness, is addressed to Burkhardt and calls him "our greatest teacher."

6. An interesting and illuminating discussion of this period is found in Michel Haar's introduction to the French translation of some of Nietzsche's early courses on Sophocles and on classical philology; see Nietzsche, *Introduction aux leçons sur l'Oedipe-Roi de Sophocle*, pp. 15–24.

7. It is quite significant that—like Hölderlin's *Hyperion*—Nietzsche's *The Birth of Tragedy* is self-conscious about its historical moment and the war which defines its own setting. Nietzsche comments upon this in the "Attempt at a Self-critique" when he writes that "Whatever may be at the bottom of this questionable book, it must have been a question of utmost significance and fascination, and a deeply personal question as well,—the proof of this is the time in which it came to be, *despite* which it came to be, the energizing time of the Franco-Prussian War of 1870/71. While the thunder of the battle of Wörth rolled over Europe, the muser and riddlefriend, who would be the father of this book, sat somewhere in the corner of the Alps, very bemused and confounded by riddles, hence simultaneously very concerned and unconcerned, and wrote down his thoughts about the *Greeks*" (*GT*, p. 11/*BT*, p. 17). The Kaufmann translation, *The Birth of Tragedy*, is henceforth designated as *BT*.

8. *GT*, p. 15/*BT*, p. 20. See John Sallis's wonderful discussion of this passage in *Crossings: Nietzsche and the Space of Tragedy*, especially pp. 147ff.

9. Nietzsche's relation to *The Birth of Tragedy* was a dominating concern throughout his life, and it was the text to which he most often returned in the context of other texts. One reason he simply could not let go of this book is that its topic, tragedy, was the single most enduring concern of his life and work. For an example of how this retrospective assessment of *The Birth of Tragedy* works see, for instance, the passages devoted to *The Birth of Tragedy* in *Ecce Homo*, where Nietzsche writes that it "smells offensively Hegelian" (*Ecce Homo* [Berlin: W. de Gruyter, 1988], p. 310).

10. *GT*, p. 51/*BT*, p. 55. On the relation of language and music, see my "Acoustics: Nietzsche and Heidegger on Words and Music."

11. *Die fröhliche Wissenschaft*, no. 342. See also the conclusion of no. 383.

12. *GT*, p. 24/*BT*, p. 31.

13. Ibid., p. 20/25.

14. Ibid., p. 25/33.

15. Ibid., p. 24/31.

16. *Ecce Homo*, no. 312.

17. *GT*, p. 150/*BT*, p. 140.

18. Here it should be noted that the Kaufmann translation obscures just how complex this opening sentence is by mistranslating *duplicität* as "duality" (which is the appropriate translation for *Zweiheit*, which appears later in this same sentence; Kaufmann translated this word as "duality" as well and thus conflates a difference that is crucial).

19. Here the kinship between Freud and Nietzsche perhaps finds its deepest expression. See especially Freud's "Der Dichter und das Phantasieren."

20. *GT,* p. 25/*BT,* p. 33.

21. The word *ungeheuer* will be used with astonishing frequency. Kaufmann often mistranslates it as "tremendous." See, for instance, p. 88 of his English translation, where the topic is the "monstrosity *per defectum*" one finds in the figure of Socrates, who is the anti-hero of Greece just as Hegel is this for Germany.

22. *GT,* p. 12/*BT,* p. 17.

23. The text can be outlined roughly as follows: sections 1–5 present the elements of art; sections 6–15 trace the birth and death of Greek tragedy; sections 16–25 treat the various forms of culture and their relation to tragedy, as well as the conditions requisite for the rebirth of tragedy and the relation of this rebirth to music.

24. Again, Kaufmann's translation of *Rausch* as "intoxication" is misleading.

25. *GT,* p. 26/*BT,* p. 33.

26. Ibid., p. 26/34. It is striking that the history of philosophy has so little to say of sleep. Heraclitus is an important exception to this (see, for instance, Diehls/Kranz fragments 22A16, 26, 63). Descartes, who begins the *Meditations* by worrying that he might be asleep, is more the rule.

27. Ibid., p. 27/35.

28. J. P. Vernant and P. Vidal-Naquet, *Myth and Tragedy,* p. 390.

29. *GT,* p. 155/*BT,* 143.

30. Ibid., p. 30/38.

31. Ibid., p. 36/43.

32. Cf. ibid., p. 17/22. It is this perspective which first enables one to see the repressive nature of moral reason.

33. Ibid., pp. 24/31, 47/52, 152/141.

34. Ibid., p. 38/44.

35. Ibid., p. 15/21.

36. Ibid., p. 35/42. The citation from *Oedipus at Colonus* is from the choral speech at line 1224. This is also the passage that Hölderlin cites as the epigram to the second volume of *Hyperion.*

37. Ibid., p. 52/56.

38. Ibid., p. 58/61.

39. A fascinating exploration of this inversion of dreaming and waking life, as well as a presentation of the strangeness of the dream image, is found in Wim Wenders's film *Until the End of the World,* which imagines the possibility of recording one's dreams in such a way that one could replay them for oneself and observe them in waking life.

40. *GT,* p. 52/*BT,* p. 56.

41. Here Aristotle, Schlegel, and Schiller are the chief targets of Nietzsche's criticisms.

42. Ibid., p. 60/63.

43. Ibid., p. 62/65.

44. Ibid., p. 60/63.

45. Ibid., p. 62/65. It should be noted that the Kaufmann translation makes a fundamental mistake here: the phrase "Apollonian embodiment" is translated in Kaufmann as "Dionysian embodiment." This simple error renders the entire point of this section unintelligible. This is also one of the examples of a passage in which Kaufmann translates *ungeheure* as "tremendous" and thereby downplays the force of the word which should be understood as much closer to "monstrous."

46. Ibid., p. 61/64.

47. Ibid., p. 41/47.

48. Ibid., p. 65/67.

49. Ibid. Of course, one cannot read this passage without hearing in it some form of a commentary on the role of the image of the sun and the allegory of the cave in Plato's *Republic*. See also the passage in the *Phaedo* where Socrates speaks of the manner in which words protect us in the same way that one needs to protect one's eyes when looking at the sun during an eclipse by looking at its reflection in water.

50. Ibid., p. 66/68. The word for "clarity" (*Heiterkeit*) Kaufmann translates as "cheerfulness." *Heiter* is a word used, for instance, to describe the condition of a clear or clearing sky. It does indicate something of an upbeat mood, but "cheerfulness" oversimplifies this condition. "Clarity" seems better but should also convey something of the upturn in mood that the word also names.

51. Ibid.

52. Ibid., p. 67/69.

53. Ibid.

54. Ibid., p. 71/73.

55. The time of Greek tragedy is, by and large, the fifth century B.C. It is also worth noting that precious few of the tragedies remain (of Sophocles' 123 only seven complete works survive intact). See A. Lesky, *Die griechische Tragödie,* and his *A History of Greek Literature,* especially pp. 241–321.

56. *GT,* p. 133/*BT,* p. 125. See Hegel's remarkably similar comment in the *Philosophy of History* that one should not confuse durability and truth, as if the rose which quickly exhales its life in fragrance were any less true than the long-enduring mountains.

57. *GT,* p. 75/*BT,* p. 76.

58. Ibid.

59. Ibid., p. 76/77.

60. Ibid., p. 83/82.

61. Ibid., p. 88/86.

62. Ibid., p. 75/76. Here again Kaufmann translates *ungeheure* as "immense" rather than "monstrous," and once again an appearance of the monstrous, so very much at stake in this book, is excised by the translation.

63. Ibid., p. 85/83–84.

64. Ibid., p. 90/88.

65. Ibid., p. 91/89.

66. Ibid., p. 92/89.

67. Ibid., p. 94/91.

68. Ibid., p. 96/92. The references to the optimistic dialectic are clearly directed at Hegel, who represents for Nietzsche the embodiment of Socratism in Germany.

69. Ibid., p. 101/98.

70. Ibid., p. 96/92.

71. *Der Wille zur Macht,* Aphorism no. 822.

72. *GT,* p. 146/*BT,* p. 136.

73. Ibid., p. 108/103–104.

74. Ibid., p. 106/102.

75. Strangely, Nietzsche will write the words and make this argument about music in precisely the years that the first recordings were being made and the phonograph was invented. It would prove to be perhaps the most significant transformation in the nature of music in history. It would also, perhaps, prove to signal the real death of the possibility of music as such. On this see Jacques Attali,

Noise: The Political Economy of Music. See also Theodor Adorno's scathing criticisms of recorded music in "Über den Fetischcharakter in der Musik und die Regression des Hörens" in *Dissonanzen: Musik in der verwalteten Welt,* pp. 9–45. Also interesting in this context is Adorno's "Musik, Sprache und ihr Verhältnis im gegenwärtigen Komponieren"; likewise, I. Stravinsky, *Poetics of Music.* Finally, see my "Acoustics."

76. Here it would be interesting to take up the treatment of music in Aristotle's *Politics,* book 8, where he discusses the kinship between music and moral character.

77. *GT,* p. 105/*BT,* p. 101. The effort to think the relationship between words and music was a lifelong concern for Nietzsche, and much is at stake in the answer to the question that he poses in words about the superiority of music. See especially his "Worte und Musik," in *Nachgelassene Fragmente,* 1871, 12(1). See also P. Lacoue-Labarthe, "The Echo of the Subject."

78. *GT,* p. 109/*BT,* p. 104.

79. *Götzendämmerung* (Berlin: W. de Gruyter, 1988), p. 78.

80. *GT,* p. 116/*BT,* p. 110.

81. Ibid., p. 110/106.

82. Hegel, *Wissenschaft der Logik,* p. 31.

83. Hegel, *PG,* par. 669.

84. *GT,* p. 115/*BT,* p. 109; emphasis added.

85. *Also Sprach Zarathrustra,* p. 286.

86. *GT,* p. 126/*BT,* p. 118.

87. Ibid., p. 119/113. The lack of longing for the whole which here is a sign of what is lost in modern culture is precisely the leading characteristic of Hölderlin's Empedocles.

88. It should be borne in mind as well that the overcoming of Alexandrian culture as Nietzsche conceives it is a liberation in several respects since "the Alexandrian culture requires a slave class in order to be able to exist permanently; but it denies, in its optimistic view of life, the necessity of such a class"; ibid., p. 117/111.

89. Ibid., p. 118/112. Note that Kaufmann again translates *ungeheuren* as "extraordinary," not as "monstrous."

90. Ibid., p. 127/119.

91. Ibid., p. 128/121. The external power here is the Roman and Christian world. Note that once again Kaufmann translated *ungeheure* not as monstrous, but here as "powerful." Here it should be noted that Nietzsche is not praising the current condition of German culture. Quite the contrary, he refers to it as "exhausted," and in this regard his assessment of its condition is quite well aligned to Hegel's diagnosis of the present state of culture in his historical juncture as "exhausted" (see *PG,* par. 7).

92. Ibid., p. 129/122.

93. Ibid., p. 132/124.

94. Ibid., p. 133/125.

95. Ibid., p. 24/31.

96. See, for instance, the remarks on "breeding" in *The Will to Power.*

97. See the ground-breaking work of Robert Bernasconi. Especially significant in this context is his "Who Invented the Concept of Race?" in *Race,* ed. R. Bernasconi (forthcoming).

98. See Fichte's "Reden an die deutsche Nation." See especially the fourth address, where the "spiritual bond" between Greece and Germany is most clearly formulated.

99. *GT,* p. 148/*BT,* p. 137.

100. Ibid., p. 150/139.
101. Ibid., p. 150/140.
102. Ibid., p. 44/50.
103. Ibid., p. 150/139.
104. Ibid., p. 152/141.
105. Ibid.
106. Here it should be noted how similar Nietzsche's conception of music as a sort of doubled event and the presentation of otherwise incompatible truths in dissonance is to Aristotle's conception of metaphor as a stereoscopic seeing, a seeing double.
107. *GT,* p. 154/*BT,* p. 143.
108. Ibid., p. 73/75.
109. *Also Sprach Zarathustra,* p. 179.
110. *GT,* p. 155/*BT,* p. 143.
111. Ibid., p. 152/141.
112. Ibid., p. 24/31.
113. Ibid., p. 155/143.
114. *Der Wille zur Macht,* Aphorism no. 822.
115. *Götzendämmerung,* p. 393.
116. *GT,* p. 156/*BT,* p. 144.
117. Ibid., p. 15/20.
118. Here it is worth noting that the original outlines for *Also Sprach Zarathustra* indicated that he was to have committed suicide. Such a death, like the death of tragedy in the ancient world at the hands of Greek tragedians, was to have put the final seal of the tragic on the figure of Zarathustra.
119. With regard to the possibility and idea of painting in this context see Homer's description of the shield of Achilles in book 18 of the *Iliad* and see especially the commentary which Alexander Pope provides to his translation. There Homer describes the shield which Hephaestus makes for Achilles by giving a detailed description of the image on the shield. It is, as Pope suggests, the image of the perfection of the possibilities of painting, but it is an image that could itself never be painted, only described in words. See also chapter 18 of Lessing's *Laocoön,* and Michel Haar's "Nietzsche and Van Gogh: Representing the Tragic."

6. HEIDEGGER

1. *GA,* 31, p. 37.
2. I should say at the outset here that unlike many I do not believe that Heidegger avoided addressing his times. Quite the contrary, many of the most penetrating of Heidegger's remarks need to be understood as efforts—however oblique—to come to grips with the present historical juncture and its special riddles.
3. Of special interest is section 74, "The Essential Constitution of Historicity," in which Heidegger takes up the logic of tradition and questions of generation, fate, and destiny. On this see T. Kisiel, *The Genesis of Heidegger's "Being and Time"*; see also J. van Buren, *The Young Heidegger.*
4. The only mention of any Greek literary figure in *Being and Time* is a reference to Homer found in a citation from the correspondence between Dilthey and Count Yorck, a fact which is surprising in light of the view of life which *Being and Time* formulates.
5. *GA,* 34, p. 198. It is worth noting that Heidegger translates as *unheimlich* (strange) the same word that Hölderlin and Nietzsche will translate as *ungeheuer* (monstrous).
6. On this see R. Safranski, *Ein Meister aus Deutschland: Heidegger und seine Zeit;*

G. Schneeberg, *Nachlese zu Heidegger;* H. Sluga, *Heidegger's Crisis;* H. Ott, *Martin Heidegger: Unterwegs zu einer Biographie;* V. Farias, *Heidegger et le Nazisme;* B. Martin, ed., *Martin Heidegger und der Nationalsozialismus.* Each of these works has sufficient bibliographical matter to point one in the direction of further details.

7. On this point see chapter 5 of Jacques Derrida's *De l'esprit.* While I will not be addressing Derrida's work in this context, I should say that I believe it stands as an essential landmark for anyone who would attempt to come to terms with the full significance of the Rector's Address.

8. I have taken some steps in this direction in "Changing the Subject." See also Charles Scott's "Heidegger's Rector's Address: A Loss of the Question of Ethics" in that same volume, as well as the excellent bibliography appended to the journal issue.

9. Gadamer's comment to Heidegger, "Back from Syracuse now?" is the question which must be answered. See Gadamer's "Back from Syracuse."

10. Here one needs to read Plato's "Seventh Letter" and the account he gives there of his effort to educate Dion of Syracuse in the ways of philosophy. Also significant in this regard is Plato's *Laws,* which stands as a massive, and always oblique, reply to the struggle of thinking to engage power. Interestingly, Heidegger recommends the Seventh Letter to Blochmann in a letter to her dated October 5, 1932.

11. See the letter to Blochmann dated April 10, 1932.

12. Letter to Blochmann dated December 19, 1932.

13. On this point see my "Heidegger and 'the' Greeks."

14. One should recognize here a certain resonance with Heidegger's inaugural lecture at the University of Freiburg in 1929 entitled "What Is Metaphysics?" where he poses similar questions regarding the project of science in the present.

15. There are four authors cited in the Rector's Address: Aeschylus, Nietzsche, von Clausewitz, and Plato. Heidegger is right when he suggest in "Tatsache und Gedanken" that one should also hear echoes of Heraclitus and Ernst Jünger in the speech. Jünger perhaps most of all stands as an unacknowledged, yet powerful, influence on Heidegger at this moment.

16. Even Jaspers could regard the Rector's Address in this way. See his letter (August 23, 1933) to Heidegger thanking Heidegger for sending a copy of the speech and praising the originality of his approach to the early Greeks.

17. The question of the university is not a marginal or incidental question for Western culture since, according to Heidegger at least—and in this I believe that he is on the mark—since its formation Western culture has defined itself in terms of its relation to its capacity for knowledge, above all its relation to its capacity for science. The organization of that knowledge, which is what the university accomplishes, is quite directly a reflection of the self-understanding of such a culture. On this see M. de Beistegui, *Heidegger and the Political* (London: Routledge, 1998), pp. 35–62.

18. In this regard see Heidegger's comment on the relation of the philosopher and the state in his remarks about this issue in Plato's *Republic* in *Nietzsche,* I.

19. "Selbstbehauptung der deutschen Universität," p. 11.

20. There is one legend about Prometheus's name of which I cannot discover whether or not Heidegger was aware. He does not mention it, and it is sufficiently obscure that even one well versed in ancient mythology might not discover it. It is not listed in the large edition of the Liddell and Scott Greek dictionary, nor is it listed in any of several of my sources, some German, regarding Greek mythology; for me the discovery was sheer accident: namely, that Prometheus's name derives from a Greek misunderstanding of the Sanskrit word *pramantha,* the swastika (or

fire-drill), which he was said to have invented. On this see Robert Graves, *The Greek Myths*, p. 148. It would be difficult, perhaps impossible, to learn if Heidegger was aware of this, and what is important to establish is simply whether he was aware of this when he gave this lecture. It is not, for instance, mentioned in Walter Otto's *Die götter Griechenlands* (Bonn: Verlag Friedrich Cohen, 1929). During this period Heidegger's chief reference work for such matters was Friedrich Kreuzer, *Symbolik und Mythologie der alten Völker, bei der Griechen* (Leipzig/Darmstadt, 1836–42), 4 vols. If he was aware of this, then of course its significance needs to be acknowledged.

21. Aeschylus, *Prometheus*, trans. H. Smyth (Cambridge, Mass.: Harvard University Press, 1988), lines 506–14.

22. "Selbstbehauptung der deutschen Universität," p. 12. On this move see Jacques Taminiaux, *The Thracian Maid and the Professional Thinker*, who presses the point that what is signaled here is an "allegiance to one text . . . Plato's *Republic*, i.e., a founding text for the entire tradition of metaphysics" (p. 41).

23. "Selbstbehauptung der deutschen Universität," p. 19. The line is from *Republic* 497d9.

24. This view is what Lacoue-Labarthe refers to as the "fictioning of beings and communities" (*La Fiction du politique*, p. 82). It is the view which regards "the city as a work of art" (p. 66) and thus conceives of both the state and of education as matters to be "produced."

25. It would be interesting to compare Heidegger's tragic figure of the philosopher, Prometheus, with Hölderlin's tragic figure of the poet, Empedocles. Each has found an alter ego in a Greek character that somehow is seen as speaking directly to the needs of the present age.

26. *GA*, 39, pp. 74, 216.

27. Ibid., p. 118. It is interesting that Heidegger never offers an extended interpretation of Hölderlin's "The Death of Empedocles." However, this might well be remedied by the publication (still only announced for next year) of volume 75 of his collected works entitled "On Hölderlin—Travels in Greece." An advance report on the contents of this volume makes the surprising remark that Heidegger admits that he "destroyed a manuscript of 92 pages" dealing with Hölderlin's "Empedocles." If that is true, it is a true loss—and a surprise.

28. See J. Habermas, "Mit Heidegger gegen Heidegger denken."

29. This is one of the key themes of the "Origin of the Work of Art," which was composed at the same time Heidegger was giving this lecture course and which should always be regarded as of a piece with the *Introduction to Metaphysics*. See the remarks about the manner in which art sets history in motion and is founding in an original sense; both of these points set the work of art in a distinctive relation with the notion of a "people." See especially *Holzwege*, pp. 61–65.

30. In the 1942 course on Hölderlin's "Der Ister," Heidegger will go even further and suggest that Sophocles is the true thinker of the possibility of the polis understood as the site of the possibility of the appearance of beings and the gathering together of human beings. See *GA*, 53, pp. 106–107.

31. This is a trademark of Heidegger's work, namely, that he does not make reference to other living authors. The exceptions are few and far between, and typically refer to literary authors rather than those one might typically call philosophers. This remarkable capacity to bring ancient authors to life—and can we read one of Heidegger's lecture courses on Heraclitus or Aristotle, for instance, and not acknowledge that he has genuinely animated the works of those thinkers?—is, I believe, the same capacity which led him to regard Hitler as the inheritor of Goethe, and Stalin as the representative of Dostoyevsky. His ability to en-

gage the past and to let it live came at the price of an inability to engage the proximate realities of the present.

32. *EM,* p. 81/*IM,* p. 106. The *Introduction to Metaphysics* henceforth designated as *IM.*

33. Ibid., p. 81/107.

34. *King Oedipus,* lines 1300ff.

35. *EM,* p. 81/*IM,* p. 107.

36. Ibid., p. 35/46. The sentence in which this image appears refers to the collapse of the age which was no longer able to measure up to the greatness of German idealism (here he speaks against the notion that German idealism has "collapsed").

37. The story of Teiresias's blinding that is most intriguing includes his change from a man to a woman and back to a man. See, for instance, Graves, *The Greek Myths,* chapters 25, 77, 85 105, 106.

38. Plato, *Phaedrus* 243A.

39. Were I to do that, though, were I to properly discuss the nature of poetic blindness, it would also be necessary to situate such characterizations of blind poets with respect to the enormous significance of the seeing eyes in Greek literature in general and Greek philosophy in particular. To provide such a context it would be necessary to range from philosophical presuppositions about the relation of sight to knowledge (examining the relationship between the word for "seeing" and "idea" would provide a rich beginning) to mythological images about eyes (ranging from the Cyclops Odysseus blinds, to the Gorgon, the sight of which means death, up to Argus, the all-seeing guard with a hundred eyes who, after his murder, was memorialized for his watchful service by having his eyes set in peacock tails). Here, of course, Plato, whose debate with the tragic ethical sensibility governs so much of what he writes, is decisive. One finds in Plato a number of passages about eyes, passages such as the one in the *Phaedrus* where he speaks of "the stream of beauty, entering the eyes that brings a warmth that nourishes the wings of the soul."

40. There are at least eight notable references to blindness in the text (see *EM,* pp. 34, 66, 81, 86, 88, 109, 114).

41. Ibid., p. 82/*IM,* p. 108.

42. Although Heidegger does not mention it here (and he would likely resist this point vehemently), the similarity with the dialectic of appearance that Hegel outlines in the *Phenomenology of Spirit* is strong. Also not mentioned, but equally resonate with Heidegger's point here, is the plot of *Antigone,* which pits the utter singularity of the corpse against the claims of the law to universality.

43. *EM,* p. 83/*IM,* p. 109. The notion of errancy should also be understood as bearing a strong kinship with what Heidegger means by the word *Holzwege,* which designates paths which lead nowhere, or paths that lead one astray.

44. Although he does not note it here, Hölderlin's characterization of Oedipus as one possessed of an "insane searching for consciousness and knowledge" takes the same approach.

45. *EM,* p. 32/*IM,* p. 42.

46. Ibid., p. 112/146.

47. Obviously a translation which is to serve the purpose of driving home the force of specific words in German and even the failure of such words cannot legitimately be translated. Nonetheless, I have translated his translation with an eye to highlighting some of the key elements which do not come across so clearly in the Mannheim translation. Heidegger's own relation to this passage constantly engages him in the project of translation. He would retranslate it in 1943 and

have that printed in a private edition which he would present to his wife on her fiftieth birthday.

48. In the Fagles translation that verse runs as follows:

Here is a dark sign from the gods—
what to make of this? I know her,
how can I deny it? The young girl's Antigone!
Wretched, child of a wretched father,
Oedipus. Look, is it possible?
They bring you in like a prisoner—
why? Did you break the king's laws?
Did they take you in some act of mad defiance?

49. *GA*, 53, pp. 127ff.

50. Here is yet another proximity to Hegel, and again it is one which Heidegger would likely dispute.

51. The resonance with Sartre's play *Huis clos* should not be overlooked.

52. *EM*, p. 116/*IM*, p. 152.

53. Ibid., p. 117/152.

54. *GA*, 53, p. 107.

55. Hannah Arendt and Martin Heidegger, *Briefe: 1925–1975*, letter of February 15, 1950.

56. There he also makes the remark that "The tragedies of Sophocles contain —if such a comparison is to be permitted—in their speech a more original sense of *ethos* than those found in Aristotle's lectures on 'Ethics'" (*Wegmarken*, p. 350).

57. *EM*, p. 122;/*IM*, p. 159.

58. See Heidegger's discussion of the relation of work and thing in "The Origin of the Work of Art," in *Holzwege*, pp. 10–28. This text is a very close companion to *Introduction to Metaphysics*, and the two texts become clearer when they are read as of a piece.

59. *EM*, p. 122/*IM*, p. 160.

60. Ibid., p. 123/161.

61. Ibid., p. 124/162.

62. Ibid., p. 125/164.

63. Ibid.

64. Ibid., p. 135/177.

65. Ibid., p. 136/178.

66. Ibid., p. 152/199.

67. Heidegger's reading of Ernst Jünger plays a special role in how the details of this remark are to be interpreted. In "Tatsache und Gedanken" (1945) Heidegger would say that his reading (in 1930) of Jünger's "Die totale Mobilmachung" and (in 1939/40) of *Der Arbeiter* were decisive events in the formulation of his confrontation with, and critique of, modernity. One sees this as well in the essay that Heidegger writes on the occasion of Jünger's sixtieth birthday, which is entitled "Zur Seinsfrage" (1955). Jünger's provocative and highly original work remains indispensable for understanding Heidegger's critique of modernity.

68. Here I should note that I am bypassing any effort to take up the question of tragedy in Heidegger's *Beiträge zur Philosophie* (1936–39). One could make an argument that the topic of tragedy plays a powerful, but not fully articulated, role in this massive and difficult work. For one key reference, see *GA*, 65, p. 374.

69. See Véronique Fóti's discussion of this point in her "Heidegger, Hölderlin, and Sophoclean Tragedy," in *Heidegger toward the Turn*, pp. 170ff.

70. *GA*, 53, p. 76. This is a sentence that has clear echoes with Fichte's claim

that one can say what sort of a person one is if one knows what sort of philosophy one has chosen, and with Jünger's claim to tell one who one is by knowing one's relation to pain.

71. To give some sense of the striking differences between these translations, I offer English translations of both in the appendices to this chapter. It should be clear that both are strained translations—Hölderlin's perhaps even more than Heidegger's—and that both, each in its own way, cleave closely to the Greek sense of the words and to an effort to stretch German to speak out of the same sensibility. In the English translations I have tried to give a rather close translation of each translation, one which highlights the mood of each.

72. Heidegger's complaint about the word *Ungeheuer* is that in the modern world its meaning invariably gets understood as a quantitative matter so that the word is heard as referring to something like "enormity" or "gigantic," and in this it loses its depth and becomes the final expression of metaphysics in the modern world. It becomes, he says, Americanism and Bolschivism (*GA*, 53, p. 86).

73. Ibid., p. 112.

74. *Wegmarken*, p. 311.

75. *GA*, 53, p. 94.

76. Ibid., p. 99.

77. Ibid., p. 101.

78. Ibid., p. 124.

79. On this point see M. de Beistegui, *Heidegger and the Political*, pp. 138–41.

80. The myth as Heidegger translates it is as follows: "Zeus, the great ruler of the heaven, driving his winged chariot is the first to set forth, governing everything and reflecting with care; but the host of gods follows him—ordered in eleven companies—even the fortunate-unfortunate spirits. There are only eleven, Hestia remains behind alone in the dwelling place of the gods" (246ff.). The context of the passage is not discussed by Heidegger, but it is the crucial point at which Socrates is discussing the properties of wings and so comes to speak of the difference that a wing makes—such as the wings which one finds when in love.

81. *GA*, 53, p. 143.

82. See especially his "Jargon der Eigentlichkeit," in *Gesammelte Schriften*, vol. 6, pp. 413–522.

83. *Holzwege*, p. 296.

84. Ibid., p. 298.

85. Ibid., p. 300, emphasis added.

86. For the contours of such a reading, only a beginning of what must be something quite extensive, see my "What We Didn't See."

87. *H*, 318.

88. Ibid., 320.

89. Ibid., 330.

90. Ibid., 329. The word translated here as "fitting" (*Fug*), which is Heidegger's translation of *dike*, was already an issue in his interpretation and translation of the choral ode from *Antigone*.

91. See H. Heine, *Religion and Philosophy in Germany*.

92. His claim is powerful and should be cited at some length: "The German language was not innocent of the horrors of Nazism. It is not merely that a Hitler, a Goebbels, and a Himmler happened to speak German. Nazism found in the language precisely what it needed to give voice to its savagery. . . . That is what happened under the Reich: Not silence or evasion, but an immense outpouring of precise, serviceable words. It was one of the peculiar horrors of the Nazi era that all that happened was recorded, catalogued, chronicled, set down; that words

were committed to saying things that no human mouth should ever have said and no paper made by man should ever have been inscribed with. . . . Languages have great reserves of life. . . . But there comes a breaking point" (G. Steiner, *Language and Silence*, pp. 121–24).

BIBLIOGRAPHY

Adorno, Theodor W. *Ästhetische Theorie.* Frankfurt am Main: Suhrkamp, 1970.
———. "Parataxis: Zur späten lyrik Hölderlin's." In *Über Hölderlin,* ed. Jochen Schmidt. Frankfurt am Main: Suhrkamp, 1970.
———. *Dissonanzen: Musik in der verwalteten Welt.* Göttingen: Vandenhoeck und Ruprecht, 1972.
———. "Musik, Sprache und ihr Verhältnis im gegenwärtigen Komponieren." In *Schriften,* Vol. 16. Frankfurt am Main: Suhrkamp, 1978.
Alleman, Beda. *Hölderlin und Heidegger.* Zurich: Atlantis, 1954.
———. "Hölderlin entre les anciens et les modernes." In *Cahiers de l'Herne: Hölderlin,* ed. J.-F. Courtine. Paris, 1989.
Anouilh, Jean. *Nouvelles pieces noires.* Paris: La Table Ronde, 1946, pp. 131–212.
Arendt, Hannah. *The Origins of Totalitarianism.* New York: Harcourt, Brace, World, 1966.
———. *The Human Condition.* Chicago: University of Chicago Press, 1998.
Ariès, Philippe. *Western Attitudes towards Death, from the Middle Ages to the Present.* Baltimore: Johns Hopkins University Press, 1974.
Attali, Jacques. *Noise: The Political Economy of Music.* Trans. Brian Massumi. Minneapolis: University of Minnesota Press, 1985.
Auerbach, Erich. *Mimesis.* Trans. Willard R. Trask. Princeton: Princeton University Press, 1968.
Bataille, Georges. "Hegel, la mort et le sacrifice." *Deucalion* 5 (1955): 21–43.
Beaufret, Jean. "Hölderlin et Sophocle." In *Hölderlin, Remarques sur Oedipe/Remarques sur Antigone,* pp. 7–42. Paris: Bibliothèque, 1965.
Beissner, Friedrich. *Hölderlins Übersetzungen aus dem Griechisch.* Stuttgart, 1961.
Benjamin, Walter. "The Task of the Translator." In *Illuminations,* trans H. Zohn. New York: Schocken, 1969.
———. *Ursprung des deutschen Trauerspiels.* Frankfurt am Main: Suhrkamp, 1978.
———. "Der Begriff der Kunstkritik in der deutschen Romantik." In *Gesammelte Schriften, vol. 1.* Frankfurt am Main: Suhrkamp, 1980.
———. "Kunst im Zeitalter seiner technologischen Reproducierbarkeit." In *Gesammelte Schriften,* Vol. 2. Frankfurt am Main: Suhrkamp, 1980.
———. *Gesammelte Briefe.* Frankfurt am Main: Suhrkamp, 1995.
Bernal, Martin. *Black Athena.* New Brunswick, N.J.: Rutgers University Press, 1991.
Bernasconi, Robert. *Heidegger in Question.* Atlantic Highlands, N.J.: Humanities Press, 1993.
———. "Heidegger and the Invention of the Western Philosophical Tradition." *Journal of the British Society for Phenomenology* 26, no. 3 (1995).
———. "'I Will Tell You Who You Are': Heidegger on Greco-German Destiny and *Amerikanismus.*" In *Phenomenology to Thought, Errancy, and Desire,* ed. Babette E. Babich. Dordrecht: Kluwer, 1995.

————. "Hegel at the Court of the Ashanti." In *Hegel after Derrida,* ed. Stuart Barnett. London: Routledge, 1998.

Bernstein, Richard. *Freud and the Legacy of Moses.* Cambridge: Cambridge University Press, 1998.

Bertaux, Pierre. *Der andere Hölderlin.* Frankfurt am Main: Suhrkamp, 1972.

Binder, Wolfgang. *Hölderlin und Sophokles.* Tübingen: Hölderlinturm, 1992.

Blanchot, Maurice. *The Gaze of Orpheus, and Other Literary Essays.* Barrytown, N.Y.: Station Hill Press, 1981.

Böhme, J. *Die Seele und das Ich im homerischen Epos.* Leipzig: Reclam, 1929.

Brainard, Marcus, et al., eds. *Heidegger and the Political.* Special issue of *Graduate Faculty Philosophy Journal* 14, no. 2–15, no. 1 (1991).

Brogan, Walter. "Is Plato's Drama the Death of Tragedy?" *International Studies in Philosophy* 23, no. 2 (1991): 75–82.

————. "The Tragic Figure of the Last Philosopher." *Research in Phenomenology* 24 (1994): 25–41.

————. "Socrates' Tragic Speech: Divine Madness and the Place of Rhetoric in Philosophy." In *Retracing the Platonic Text,* ed. Charles E. Scott and John Sallis. Evanston, Ill.: Northwestern University Press, 1999.

Burckhardt, Jacob. *The Greeks and Greek Civilization.* Trans. Sheila Stern. New York: St. Martin's Press, 1998.

Burkert, Walter. *Homo necans.* Berkeley: University of California Press, 1983.

Calasso, Roberto. *The Marriage of Cadmus and Harmony.* New York: Vintage, 1993.

Carson, Anne. *Eros: The Bittersweet.* Princeton: Princeton University Press, 1986.

————. "Just for the Thrill." *Arion* (1990): 142–54.

Célis, Raphaël. "Modernité et tragédie: à propos de *l'Empédocle* d'Hölderlin." *Cahier de l'Ecole des sciences philosophiques et religieuses* 1 (1987): 153–78.

Chandler, Richard. *Travels in Greece.* New York: Olms, 1976.

Chanter, Tina. "Antigone's Dilemma." In *Re-reading Levinas,* ed. Robert Bernasconi and Simon Critchley. Bloomington: Indiana University Press, 1991.

Comay, Rebecca. "Perverse History." *Research in Phenomenology* 29 (1999): 51–62.

Constantine, David. *Hölderlin.* Oxford: Clarendon, 1990.

Courtine, Jean-François. *Extase de la Raison,* pp. 15–72. Paris: Galilée, 1990.

Dallmayr, Fred. "Heidegger, Hölderlin and Politics." *Heidegger Studies* 2 (1986): 81–95.

Dastur, Françoise. *Hölderlin: tragédie et modernité.* La Versanne: Encre marine, 1992.

————. *Dire le temps.* La Versanne: Encre marine, 1994.

de Beistegui, Miguel. *Heidegger and the Political.* London: Routledge, 1998.

Deleuze, Gilles. *Nietzsche & Philosophy.* Trans. Hugh Tomlinson. New York: Columbia University Press, 1983.

————."Coldness and Cruelty." In *Masochism.* New York: Zone Books, 1989.

De Man, Paul. "Epistemology of Metaphor." *Critical Inquiry* 5 (1978): 123–38.

Derrida, Jacques. *Spurs: Nietzsche's Styles.* Trans. Barbara Harlow. Chicago: University of Chicago Press, 1979.

————. "White Mythology: Metaphor in the Text of Philosophy." In *Margins of Philosophy,* trans. Alan Bass. Chicago: University of Chicago Press, 1982.

————. *Glas.* Lincoln: University of Nebraska Press, 1986.

————. *De l'esprit.* Paris: Editions Galilée, 1987.

————. "Force of Law." *Cardoza Law Review* 11, nos. 5–6 (1990): 919–1045.

Descartes, René. *Meditations.* Indianapolis: Hackett Press, 1986.

Detienne, Marcel. *Les Maîtres de vérité dans la Grèce archaïque.* Paris: Maspero, 1967.

Donougho, Martin. "The Woman in White: On the Reception of Hegel's *Antigone.*" *The Owl of Minerva* 21 (1989): 65–89.

Dover, Kenneth. *Aristophanic Comedy.* London: Batsford, 1972.

———. *Greek Homosexuality.* Cambridge, Mass.: Harvard University Press, 1978.

Düsing, Klaus. "Die Theorie der Tragödie bei Hölderlin und Hegel." In *Jenseits des Idealismus: Hölderlins letzte Homburger Jahre,* ed. C. Jamme and O. Pöggeler, pp. 55–82. Bonn: Bouvier, 1985.

Edelstein, Ludwig. *The Idea of Progress in Classical Antiquity.* Baltimore: Johns Hopkins University Press, 1967.

Edmunds, Lowell. "The Cults and Legends of Oedipus." *HSCP,* 85 (1981): 221–38.

Else, Gerald Frank. *Plato and Aristotle on Poetry.* Chapel Hill: University of North Carolina Press, 1986.

Euripides. *Hecuba.* Cambridge: Harvard University Press, 1982.

Farias, Victor. *Heidegger et le Nazisme.* Lagrasse: Editions Verdier, 1987.

Fédier, François. *Remarques sur Oedipe/Remarques sur Antigone. [par] Hölderlin.* Paris: Union generale d'editions, 1965.

Fichte, Johann Gottlieb. *Werke.* Vol. VII. Berlin: de Gruyter, 1971.

Figal, Günter. *Martin Heidegger.* Frankfurt: Verlag Anton Hain, 1991.

———. *Socrates.* Munich: Beck, 1995.

Finley, M. I. *The World of Odysseus.* New York: Viking Press, 1978.

Fóti, Veronique. *Heidegger and the Poets.* Atlantic Highlands, N.J.: Humanities Press, 1992.

Foucault, Michel. *Histoire de la sexualité.* Vol. I. Paris: Gallimard, 1995.

Freud, Sigmund. "Der Dichter und das Phantasieren." In *Bildene Kunst und Literatur.* Frankfurt am Main: Fischer, 1969.

———. "Trauer und Melancholie." In *Psychologie des Unbewussten.* Frankfurt am Main: Fischer, 1975.

Fritz, Kurt von. "Tragische Schuld und poetische Gerechtigkeit in der griechischen Tragödie." In *Antike und moderne Tragödie,* pp. 1–112. Berlin: de Gruyter, 1962.

Fynsk, Christopher. *Heidegger, Thought and Historicity.* Ithaca: Cornell University Press, 1986.

Gadamer, Hans Georg. *Gesammelte Werke.* Tübingen: Mohr, 1995.

Gamwell, Lynn, and Richard Wells, eds. *Sigmund Freud and Art.* London: Freud Museum, 1989.

Graves, Robert. *The Greek Myths.* New York: Penguin Books, 1960.

Griswold, Charles. "The Ideas and Criticism of Poetry in Plato's *Republic,* Book 10." *Journal of the History of Philosophy* 19 (1981): 135–50.

Guthrie, W. K. C. *A History of Greek Philosophy.* Vols. III–IV. Cambridge: Cambridge University Press, 1969, 1975.

Habermas, Jürgen. "Mit Heidegger gegen Heidegger denken." In *Philosophisch-politische Profile.* Frankfurt am Main: Suhrkamp, 1984.

Havelock, Eric Alfred. *The Greek Concept of Justice.* Cambridge, Mass.: Harvard University Press, 1978.

———. *The Literate Revolution in Greece and Its Cultural Consequences.* Princeton: Princeton University Press, 1982.

Havelock, Eric Alfred, and Jackson P. Hershbell. *Communication Arts in the Ancient World.* New York: Hastings House, 1978.

Haverkamp, Anselm. *Laub voll Trauer: Hölderlins späte Allegorie.* Munich: Fink, 1991.

Heine, Heinrich. *Philosophy and Religion in Germany.* Albany: State University of New York Press, 1986.

Henrick, D. "Hegel und Hölderlin." In *Hegel im Kontext.* Frankfurt am Main: Suhrkamp, 1968.

Herodotus. *The Histories.* Oxford: Oxford University Press, 1998.

Holst-Warhaft, Gail. *Dangerous Voices*. London: Routledge, 1992.

Hornbacker, Annette. *Die Blume des Mundes*. Würzburg: Königschausen & Neumann, 1995.

Hösle, Vittorio, *Die Vollendung der Tragödie im Spätwerk Sophokles*. Stuttgart–Bad Cannstadt: Frommann-Holzboog, 1984.

Hyppolite, Jean. "Le Tragique et le rationnel dans la philosophie de Hegel." *Hegel-Jahrbuch* (1964): 9–15.

Irigaray, Luce. *Speculum of the Other Woman*. Ithaca: Cornell University Press, 1985.

Jones, John. *On Aristotle and Greek Tragedy*. New York: Oxford University Press, 1962.

Kahn, Charles. *The Art and Thought of Heraclitus*. Cambridge: Cambridge University Press, 1979.

Kant, Immanuel. *Werke*. Berlin: de Gruyter, 1968.

Kaufmann, Walter. *Nietzsche*. Princeton: Princeton University Press, 1974.

Keller, O. *Die antike Tierwelt*. Leipzig: Reclam, 1913.

Kierkegaard, Søren. *Either/Or*. Princeton: Princeton University Press, 1978.

Kirk, G. S. *The Iliad: A Commentary*. Vol. I, books 1–4. Cambridge: Cambridge University Press, 1985.

Kisiel, Theodore. *The Genesis of Heidegger's "Being and Time."* Berkeley: University of California Press, 1993.

Kitto, H. D. F. *Greek Tragedy*. London: Methuen, 1939.

Knox, Bernard. *The Heroic Temper*. Berkeley: University of California Press, 1964.

Kofman, Sarah. *Nietzsche and Metaphor*. Trans. Duncan Large. Stanford: Stanford University Press, 1993.

Kommerell, Max. *Lessing und Aristoteles: Untersuchung über die Theorie der Tragödie*. Frankfurt am Main: Klostermann, 1984.

Kondylis, Panojotis. *Die Entstehung der Dialektik*. Stuttgart: Klett-Cotta, 1979.

Krell, David Farrell. *Postponements: Woman, Sensuality, and Death in Nietzsche*. Bloomington: Indiana University Press, 1986.

———. "Lucinda's Shame." *Cardoza Law Review* 10, nos. 5–6 (1989): 1673–86.

———. *Lunar Voices*. Chicago: University of Chicago Press, 1995.

———. *The Recalcitrant Art*. Albany: State University of New York Press, 2000.

Lacan, Jacques. *Le Seminaire: Livre VII*. Paris: Éditions de Seuil, 1996.

Lacoue-Labarthe, Philippe. "La Césure spéculatif" and "Hölderlin et les Grecs." In *L'Imitation des modernes*, pp. 39–84. Paris: Galilée, 1986.

———. *La Fiction du politique*. Paris: C. Bourgois, 1987.

———. "The Echo of the Subject." In *Typography*. Cambridge: Harvard University Press, 1989.

Lang, Berel. *Heidegger's Silence*. Ithaca: Cornell University Press, 1996.

Lesky, Albin. *A History of Greek Literature*. Trans. Cornelis de Heer and James Willis. London: Duckworth, 1963.

———. *Die griechische Tragödie*. Stuttgart: Kroner Verlag, 1984.

Lessing, Gotthold. *Laocoön*. Trans. Edward McCormick. Baltimore: John Hopkins University Press, 1962.

Lilly, Reginald, ed. *The Ancients and the Moderns*. Bloomington: Indiana University Press, 1996.

Loraux, Nicole. *L'Invention d'Athènes: histoire de l'oraison funèbre dans la "cité classique."* Paris: Editions de l'École des hautes études en sciences sociales, 1981.

———. *The Invention of Athens*. Cambridge: Harvard University Press, 1986.

———. *Tragic Ways of Killing a Woman*. Trans. Anthony Forster. Cambridge: Harvard University Press, 1987.

———. *The Experiences of Tiresias*. Princeton: Princeton University Press, 1995.

———. *Mothers in Mourning*. Ithaca: Cornell University Press, 1998.

Löwith, Karl. *Von Hegel zu Nietzsche.* Stuttgart: Fischer Verlag, 1964.

Lucas, D. W. *The Poetics.* Oxford: Clarendon Press, 1968.

Lyotard, Jean-François. *Heidegger and "the Jews."* Trans. Andreas Michel. Minneapolis: University of Minnesota Press, 1990.

Marcuse, Ludwig. "Die marxistische Auslegung des Tragischen." *Monatshefte* 46 (1954): 241–48.

Martin, Bernd, ed. *Martin Heidegger und der Nationalsozialismus.* Darmstadt: Wissenschaftliche Buchgesellschaft, 1989.

McCumber, John. *Metaphysics and Oppression: Heidegger's Challenge to Western Philosophy.* Bloomington: Indiana University Press, 1999.

McNeill, William. *The Glance of the Eye.* Albany: State University of New York Press, 1999.

Meier, Christian. *Die politische Kunst der griechischen Tragödie.* Munich: Beck, 1988.

Menke, Christoph. *Tragödie im Sittlichen.* Frankfurt am Main: Suhrkamp, 1996.

Morris, S. *Daidalos and the Origins of Greek Art.* Princeton: Princeton University Press, 1992.

Murdoch, Iris. *The Fire and the Sun.* New York: Viking, 1990.

Naas, Michael. *Turning.* Atlantic Highlands, N.J.: Humanities Press, 1995.

Nagy, Gregory. *Pindar's Homer.* Baltimore: Johns Hopkins University Press, 1990.

Nancy, Jean-Luc. *La Communanté désoeuvrée.* Paris: Christian Bourgeois, 1986.

———. *The Muses.* Stanford: Stanford University Press, 1996.

Nehamas, Alexander. *Nietzsche: Life as Literature.* Cambridge: Harvard University Press, 1985.

Nussbaum, Martha Craven. *The Fragility of Goodness.* New York: Cambridge University Press, 1986.

———. *Love's Knowledge.* New York: Oxford University Press, 1990.

———. *Poetic Justice.* Boston: Beacon, 1995.

Ott, Hugo. *Martin Heidegger: Unterwegs zu einer Biographie.* Frankfurt am Main: Campus Verlag, 1988.

Padel, Ruth. *In and Out of Mind.* Princeton: Princeton University Press, 1992.

———. *Whom Gods Destroy.* Princeton: Princeton University Press, 1995.

Pfau, Thomas. *Friedrich Hölderlin: Essays and Letters on Theory.* Albany: State University of New York Press, 1988.

Plutarch. *Lives.* New York: Charles Scribner's Sons, 1910.

Redfield, James. *Nature and Culture in the Iliad.* Chicago: University of Chicago Press, 1975.

Reinhardt, Karl. *Sophokles.* Frankfurt am Main: Suhrkamp, 1947.

Risser, James, ed. *Heidegger toward the Turn.* Albany: State University of New York Press, 1999.

Roche, Mark William. *Tragedy and Comedy.* Albany: State University of New York Press, 1998.

Rorty, Amélie Oksenberg, ed. *Essays on Aristotle's Poetics.* Princeton: Princeton University Press, 1992.

Ryan, Lawrence. *Hölderlin's "Hyperion."* Stuttgart, 1965.

Safranski, Rüdiger. *Ein Meister aus Deutschland: Heidegger und seine Zeit.* Munich: Hanser Verlag, 1994.

Sallis, John. *Echoes: After Heidegger.* Bloomington: Indiana University Press, 1990.

———. *Crossings.* Chicago: University of Chicago Press, 1991.

———. *Being and Logos.* Bloomington: Indiana University Press, 1996.

Sartre, Jean-Paul. *La Nausée.* Paris: Gallimard, 1968.

Scarry, Elaine. *The Body in Pain.* New York: Oxford University Press, 1985.

Schadewaldt, Wolfgang. "Hölderlin und die Griechen." In *Hellas und Hesperian,* pp. 658–824. Zurich: Artemis, 1960.

Schiller, Friedrich. *Sämtliche Werke.* Vol. V. Munich: Hansen Verlag, 1993.

Schmidt, Dennis J. "Kunst, Sprache und Kritik." *Philosophie Rundschau* 34 (1987): 299–307.

———. "The Hermeneutic Dimension of Translation." *Translation Perspectives* 4 (1988), 5–17.

———. *The Ubiquity of the Finite.* Cambridge, Mass.: MIT Press, 1988.

———. "Economies of Production." In *Crises in Continental Philosophy,* ed. Arleen Dallery and Charles Scott, pp. 145–57. Albany: State University of New York Press, 1990.

———. "Hermeneutics and the Poetic Motion." In *Hermeneutics and the Poetic Motion,* pp. 1–10. Binghamton: TRIP, 1990.

———. "Poetry and the Political." In *Festivals of Interpretation,* pp. 209–28. Albany: State University of New York Press, 1990.

———. "Changing the Subject." *Graduate Philosophy Faculty Journal* 14, no. 2–15, no. 1 (1991): 441–64.

———. "Acoustics: Nietzsche and Heidegger on Words and Music." In *Dialectic and Narrative,* pp. 83–100. Albany: State University of New York Press, 1993.

———. "Black Milk and Blue: Heidegger and Celan on Pain and Language." In *Word Traces,* ed. Aris Fioretos, pp. 81–103. Baltimore: Johns Hopkins University Press, 1994.

———. "Can Law Survive? On Incommensurability and the Idea of Law." *University of Toledo Law Review* 26, no. 1 (1994): 147–58.

———. "Why I Am So Happy." *Research in Phenomenology* 24 (1994): 3–14.

———. "Putting Oneself in Words . . ." In *Library of Living Philosophers: The Philosophy of Hans-Georg Gadamer,* pp. 483–95. Chicago: Open Court, 1997.

———. "What We Owe the Dead." *Research in Phenomenology* 27 (1997): 190–98.

———. "Heidegger and 'the' Greeks: History, Catastrophe and Community." In *Heidegger toward the Turn,* ed. James Risser, pp. 75–92. Albany: State University of New York Press, 1999.

———. "Ruins and Roses." In *Endings,* ed. Rebecca Comay and John McCumber, pp. 97–113. Evanston, Ill.: Northwestern University Press, 1999.

———. "What We Didn't See." In *The Presocratics after Heidegger,* ed. David Jacobs. Albany: State University of New York Press, 1999.

———. "Was wir nicht sagen können . . ." In *Hermeneutische Wege,* ed. Günter Figal, Jean Grondin, and Dennis Schmidt, pp. 161–75. Tübingen: Mohr Siebeck, 2000.

Schneeberg, G. *Nachlese zu Heidegger.* Bern, 1962.

Schrift, Alan. *Nietzsche and the Question of Interpretation.* New York: Routledge, 1990.

Schürmann, Reiner. *Heidegger on Being and Acting.* Trans. Christine-Marie Gros with Reiner Schürmann. Bloomington: Indiana University Press, 1989.

———. *Hégémonies brisée.* Mauvezin: Trans-Europ-Repress, 1996.

Scott, Charles. "Heidegger's Rector's Address: A Loss of the Question of Ethics." *Graduate Philosophy Faculty Journal* 14, no. 2–15, no. 1 (1991): 237–64.

———. *On the Advantages and Disadvantages of Ethics.* Bloomington: Indiana University Press, 1996.

———. *The Time of Memory.* Albany: State University of New York Press, 1999.

Shapiro, Gary. *Nietzschean Narratives.* Bloomington: Indiana University Press, 1989.

———. *Alcyone.* Albany: State University of New York Press, 1991.

Silk, M. S., and J. P. Stern. *Nietzsche on Tragedy.* Cambridge: Cambridge University Press, 1981.

Sluga, Hans. *Heidegger's Crisis.* Cambridge, Mass: Harvard University Press, 1993.

Sourvinou-Inwood, Christiane. *"Reading" Greek Death to the End of the Classical Period.* Oxford: Clarendon Press, 1995.

Steiner, George. *The Death of Tragedy.* New York: Knopf, 1961.

———. *Antigones.* Oxford: Clarendon, 1984.

———. *Real Presences.* Chicago: University of Chicago Press, 1989.

Steiner, Wendy. *The Scandal of Pleasure.* Chicago: University of Chicago Press, 1995.

Strauss, Botho. *Ithaka.* Munich: Hanser Verlag, 1996.

Stravinsky, Igor. *Poetics of Music.* Trans. A. Knodel and I. Dahl. Cambridge, Mass: Harvard University Press, 1942.

Svenbro, Jesper. *Phrasikleia.* Trans. J. Lloyd. Ithaca: Cornell University Press, 1993.

Szondi, Peter. "Überwindung des Klassizismus." In *Hölderlin-Studien.* Frankfurt am Main: Suhrkamp, 1967.

———. *Poetik und Geschichtsphilosophie I.* Frankfurt am Main: Suhrkamp, 1973.

———. *Schriften I.* Frankfurt am Main: Suhrkamp, 1978.

Taminiaux, Jacques. *La Nostalgie de la Grèce à l'aube de l'idéalisme allemand.* La Haye: Nijhoff, 1967.

———. *Poetics, Speculation, and Judgment: The Shadow of the Work of Art from Kant to Phenomenology.* Albany: State University of New York Press, 1993.

———. *Le Théâtre des philosophes: la tragédie, l'être, l'action.* Grenoble: Millon, 1995.

———. *The Thracian Maid and the Professional Thinker.* Albany: State University of New York Press, 1997.

Turner, Eric Gardiner. *Athenian Books in the Fifth and Fourth Centuries B.C.* London: Lewis, 1952.

Van Buren, John. *The Young Heidegger: Rumor of the Hidden King.* Bloomington: Indiana University Press, 1994.

Vermeule, Emily. *Aspects of Death in Early Greek Art and Poetry.* Berkeley: University of California Press, 1979.

Vernant, Jean Pierre, and Pierre Vidal-Naquet. *Myth and Tragedy in Ancient Greece.* New York: Zone Books, 1990.

Warminski, Andrzej. *Readings in Interpretation.* Minneapolis: University of Minnesota Press, 1987.

Williams, Bernard. *Shame and Necessity.* Berkeley: University of California Press, 1993.

Winchester, James. *Nietzsche's Aesthetic Turn.* Albany: State University of New York Press, 1994.

Zeitlin, Froma, and John Winkler, eds. *Nothing to Do with Dionysos?* Princeton: Princeton University Press, 1990.

Zimmerman, Michael. *Heidegger's Confrontation with Modernity: Technology, Politics, and Art.* Bloomington: Indiana University Press, 1990.

INDEX

DENNIS J. SCHMIDT is Professor of Philosophy at Villanova University. He is author of *The Ubiquity of the Finite*, and translator of Ernst Bloch's *Natural Law and Human Dignity*.